THE ADOBE®
ILLUSTRATOR® CS
WOW!
BOOK

the red grape
menu · wine list
hours · location
reviews · red grape stuff
Visit The ArtGallery
Take a Virtual Tour
Upcoming Events

fresh basil

Book of Days

SHARON STEUER

The Adobe Illustrator CS Wow! Book

Sharon Steuer

Peachpit Press

1249 Eighth Street

Berkeley, CA 94710

510/524-2178

510/524-2221 (fax)

Find us on the World Wide Web at: http://www.peachpit.com

To report errors, please send a note to errata@peachpit.com

Peachpit Press is a division of Pearson Education

Copyright © 2004 by Sharon Steuer

Contributing writers: Victor von Salza, Steven H. Gordon, Dave Awl, Lisa Jackmore, Brad Hamann, Sandee Cohen
Wow! Series editor: Linnea Dayton
Copy editor: Mindi Englart
Tech editors: Julie Meridian, Brenda Sutherland, Teri Pettit
Book design: Barbara Sudick
Cover design: Mimi Heft, Lupe Edgar cover production
Cover Illustration: Brad Neal, Yukio Miyamoto, Brad Hamann, Lehner&Whyte, Zhiliang Ma, Marc LaMantia, Judy Stead, Ann Paidrick, Frank Jonen

Notice of Rights

Notice of Liability

Trademarks

ISBN 0-321-16892-5

9 8 7 6 5 4 3 2 1

Printed and bound in the United States of America.

The Illustrator CS Wow! Book Writers and Editors

Sharon Steuer is the originator of *The Illustrator Wow! Books*. When not working on *Wow!* books, Sharon is a painter, illustrator, columnist for creativepro.com, and the author of *Creative Thinking in Photoshop: A New Approach to Digital Art*. She lives in Connecticut with her cats, Puma and Bear, and radio star husband, Jeff Jacoby. She is extremely grateful to her co-authors, editors, testers, *Wow!* team members (past and present), Adobe, and Peachpit for making this book possible.

Victor von Salza returned to the *Wow!* team where he made sure that the many new features, enhancements, and changes to Illustrator CS were filtered into the hundreds of things they affected throughout the book. He and Mary Anne live in Portland, Oregon, where they enjoy working, gardening, walking, photography, and their bearded collie Spencer (www.vonsalza.com).

Steven H. Gordon is a returning co-author for Step-by-Steps and Galleries. He has too many boys to stay sane. If only they wouldn't fall off cliffs in Bryce—the National Park, not the software. Steven runs Cartagram, a custom mapmaking company located in Madison, Alabama. He thanks Monette and his mom for their encouragement, and the boys for their cessation of hostilities.

Dave Awl is a Chicago-based writer, editor, and Webmaster. Returning to the *Wow!* team, he revised and edited most of the chapter Introductions, as well as Chapter 1, and he authored the "What's New" section. Dave is also a poet, playwright, and performer whose work is collected in the book *What the Sea Means: Poems, Stories & Monologues 1987-2002*. You can find out more about his various creative projects at his Web site: Ocelot Factory (www.ocelotfactory.com).

Lisa Jackmore has returned as a contributing writer for Galleries, and the *Illustrator Wow!* course outline. She is a wonderful artist, both on and off the computer, creating miniatures to murals. By day, she wields a crayon and defends herself against shark-jets and galactic zappers with her son, Sam. By night, she picks up the digital pen and illustrates the adventures she lives during the day.

Additional contributing writers and editors: **Brad Hamann** (www.bradhamann.com) is a fabulous illustrator, and we're thrilled that he has joined us as a writer of Galleries and Step-by-Steps. **Mindi Englart** is back for the third time as our copy editor. Mindi is a ghost-writer, teacher, and author of children's books (m.englart@comcast.net). In the wee hours and during family vacations, Adobe's own **Julie Meridian**, **Brenda Sutherland**, and **Teri Pettit** collectively provided us with phenomenal help this edition. **Sandee Cohen,** a.k.a. vectorbabe.com, was our emergency technical consultant. Please see the Acknowledgments for a thorough listing of the *Wow!* team contributors.

Acknowledgments

As always, my most heartfelt gratitude goes to the more than 100 artists and Illustrator experts who generously allowed us to include their work and divulge their techniques.

First thanks must go to Mordy Golding, who, as an Adobe Illustrator product manager, continues to champion this book. He, along with Nancy Ruenzel, Kelly Ryer, and the Adobe Press folks at Peachpit, found a way to bring this book into the Adobe Press family. And thanks to all at Adobe who answered our zillions of questions, and came through with our special requests.

This revision required a major team effort, and would not have happened without an amazing group of people. Thank you Victor von Salza for becoming our stupendous *Wow!* taskmaster of all things great and small. Victor is quite brilliant at managing the zillions of details necessary to coordinate a team scattered across the country, and to produce this mammoth book. Oh, and that's in addition to his writing a bit, porting the book from QuarkXPress to InDesign, updating the style sheets to take advantage of InDesign features, *and* working on the *Wow! CD*. Thankfully, Steven Gordon agreed to return to the team to tackle a batch of new Step-by-Steps and Galleries— Steven always adds a dose of humor to his incredible resourcefulness, for which we're all exceedingly grateful. Dave Awl did a great job of reigning in his humor for this serious writing. Thank you, Dave for the meticulous revisions to *Chapter 1* and the other chapter introductions. Thank you Lisa Jackmore for doing such a great job with Galleries and the *IllustratorCS Wow! Course Outline* (from www.ssteuer.com/edu). Thanks to talented Laurie Grace for updating screenshots. Thank you Mindi Englart for returning as our *Wow!* copy editor—we couldn't have made it without you. Thank you to Peg Maskell Korn for being involved since the beginning, and biting the upgrade bullet so she could rejoin the team and get back to work! Thank you Julie Meridian, Brenda Sutherland, and Teri Pettit for the amazing technical feedback for this edition. As always, thanks also go to our stellar team of testers and consultants, especially Adam Z Lein, Jean-Claude Tremblay, Bob Geib, Vicki Loader, Gary Newman, Chuck Sholdt, Federico Platón, Eric Snowden, and Mike Schwabauer. Thank you to Sandee Cohen who continues as our official kibbitzer. And thanks to Emily Glossbrenner for the index! Thank you Mimi Heft and Lupe Edgar for the beautiful new cover design. Thank you Adam Z Lein for the fab online database that helps us to track each detail of the book. Thank you Kelly Anderson for your help updating and redesigning files for the *Wow! CD*. And thank you Suying Yang for the translation help, Thomas Phinney for the font help, and Thomas Hackett of AGT• Seven for the early proofs.

Thank you to all the folks at Commercial Document Services for the fabulous printing job. And thanks also to HotDoor, Virtual Mirror, Comnet, cValley, Barney's Mac Software, Artlandia, Avenza, Aridi, Dynamic Graphics, Image Club Graphics, Photosphere, and Ultimate Symbol for allowing us to include them on the *Wow! CD*. Last, but not least, thanks to Linnea Dayton for being the *Wow!* series editor, and to everyone at Peachpit Press (*especially* Nancy Davis, Connie Jeung-Mills, Jay Payne, Gary-Paul Prince, Hannah Onstad-Latham, Victor Gavenda, Lisa Brazieal, and Kim Lombardi) for all the things you do to make sure this book happens.

WOW! BOOK PRODUCTION NOTES:

Interior Book Design and Production

This book was produced in InDesign using primarily Minion Pro and Frutiger OpenType fonts. Barbara Sudick is the artist behind the original *Illustrator Wow!* design and typography; using Jill Davis's layout of *The Photoshop Wow! Book* as a jumping-off point, she designed the pages in QuarkXPress.

Hardware and Software

With the exception of some of the testers, all of the *Wow!* staff use Macintosh computers. We used InDesign 2, Photoshop CS, 6 and 7 (depending on the user), and Snapz Pro X for the screenshots. We used Adobe Acrobat 5 and 6 for distribution of the book pages to testers, the indexer, and the proofreaders. Adam Z Lein created an online *Wow!* database for us so the team could track the details of the book production.

How to contact the author

If you've created artwork using the newer features of Illustrator that you'd like to submit for consideration in future *Wow!* books, please send printed samples to: Sharon Steuer, c/o Peachpit Press, 1249 Eighth Street, Berkeley, CA 94710. Or email us a Web address that contains samples of your work (no files please!): **wowartist@ssteuer.com**

Contents

xvi   Important: **Read me first!**

xvii **How to use this book**

xx   **Preface: What's New in Illustrator CS?**

Illustrator Basics

2   Introduction
2   Computer & System Requirements
2   Setting Up Your Page
5   Making Your Moves Easier
6   Working with Objects
8   Watch Your Cursor!
9   Bézier-Editing Tools
11 Geometric Objects
12 Selecting & Grouping Objects
14 Joining & Averaging
15 Working with Palettes
17 Graphing & Charting
19 Transformations
22 Working Smart
24 Changing Your Views
25 Zooming In & Out
26 Show/Hide Choices
28 Color in Illustrator
31 Saving as PDF
32 Image Formats
33 PostScript Printing & Exporting
35 Actions
36 Scripting and Variables
37 Data-driven graphics

The Zen of Illustrator

40 Introduction
42 Building Houses: *Sequential Object Construction Exercises*
48 A Classic Icon: *Five Ways to Re-create Simple Shapes*
50 Zen Scaling
52 Zen Rotation
53 Creating a Simple Object Using the Basic Tools
54 A Finger Dance: *Turbo-charge with Illustrator's Power-keys*

3

Drawing & Coloring

64 Introduction

64 Basic Drawing & Coloring

69 Expanding Your Drawing & Coloring Toolset

72 Pathfinder Palette

78 Simple Realism:
Realism from Geometry and Observation

81 Gallery: Mark Fox

82 Cutting & Joining:
Basic Path Construction with Pathfinders

86 Add & Expand:
More Pathfinder Palette Basics

88 Divide & Color:
Applying Pathfinder Divide & Subtract

90 Cubist Constructs:
Creative Experimentation with Pathfinders

92 Isometric Systems:
Arrow Keys, Constrain Angles & Formulas

94–95 Galleries: Rick Henkel, Kurt Hess, Jared Schneidman

96 Objective Colors:
Custom Labels for Making Quick Changes

98–105 Galleries: Jean Tuttle, Clarke Tate,
Christopher Burke, Dorothy Remington,
Karen Barranco, Filip Yip, Gary Ferster

106 Distort Dynamics:
Adding Character Dynamics with Transform

108 Distort Filter Flora:
Applying Distort Filters to Create Flowers

111 Gallery: Laurie Grace

112 Vector Photos: *Pen and Eyedropper Technique*

115 Gallery: Brad Hamann

116 Advanced Technique: Intricate Patterns:
Designing Complex Repeating Patterns

118 Gallery: Tiffany Larsen

4

Brushes & Symbols

120 Introduction

120 Brushes

123 Symbols

124 Symbols vs. Scatter Brushes

125 Gallery: Chris Bucheit

126 Ink Brush Strokes:
Making Naturalistic Pen and Ink Drawings

128–131 Galleries: Sharon Steuer, Lisa Jackmore,
Jen Alspach, Ellen Papciak-Rose

132 Preparing Art:
Adding Brushes to Existing Artwork

134 Pattern Brushes:
Creating Details with the Pattern Brush

136–139 Galleries: Bert Monroy, Shayne Davidson,
Steve Spindler, Jacqueline Mahannah

140 Building Brushes:
Building Brushes for Lettering

142 Advanced Technique: Map Techniques:
Simplifying Complex Image Creation

145 Gallery: Joe Lertola

146 Symbol Basics:
Creating and Working with Symbols

149 Gallery: Sandee Cohen & Sharon Steuer

150 Advanced Technique: Organic Creation:
Painting with Brushes, Symbols, and Mesh

152 SPECIAL BRUSHES SUPPLEMENT
by Sandee Cohen

5

Layers

156 Introduction
160 Controlling the Stacking Order of Objects
162 Making Selections using the Layers Palette
163 Gallery: David Nelson
164 Digitizing a Logo:
Controlling Your Illustrator Template
166 Tracing Details:
Tracing Intricate Details with the Pencil
168 Colors with Layers:
Coloring Black & White Images with Layers
170 Organizing Layers:
Managing Custom Layers and Sublayers
173 Gallery: Nancy Stahl
174 Nested Layers:
Organizing with Layers and Sublayers
176 **Advanced Technique:** Varied Perspective:
Analyzing Different Views of Perspective

6

Type

180 Introduction
184 Working with Threaded Text
185 Wrapping Text Around Objects
185 Character and Paragraph Styles
186 Taking Advantage of OpenType
187 The Glyphs Palette
188 The Every-line Composer
188 More Type Functions (Type & Window menus)
189 Converting Type to Outlines
191 Using the Appearance Palette with Type
193 Exporting Illustrator Type
194 Custom Text Paths:
Trickling Type with Variations of Type Style
196 Stretching Type:
Fitting Type by Converting to Outline
198–199 Galleries: John Burns, Hornall Anderson
200 Masking Letters:
Masking Images with Letter Forms

201 Gallery: Gary Newman

202 Book Cover Design:
Illustrator as a Stand-alone Layout Tool

204 Brushed Type:
Applying Brushes to Letterforms

206–211 Galleries: Joachim Müller-Lancé, Tim Girvin,
Jennifer Bartlett, Louis Fishauf, Ellen Papciak-Rose,
Bjørn Akselsen, Pattie Belle Hastings, Frank Jonen

212 Crunching Type:
Transforming Type with Warps & Envelopes

214 Advanced Technique: Offset Fills:
Covering a Pattern with an Offset Fill

216 Advanced Technique: Antiquing Type:
Applying Scribble in an Opacity Mask

218 Gallery: Steven Gordon

Blends, Gradients & Mesh

7

220 Blends

223 Gradients

225 Gallery: Rick Barry

226 Examining Blends:
Learning When to Use Gradients or Blends

228 Shades of Blends:
Creating Architectural Linear Shading

229–233 Galleries: Janet Good, Gary Ferster, Linda Eckstein,
Peter Cassell, Steven Stankiewicz

234 Unlocking Realism:
Creating Metallic Reflections with Blends

236–237 Galleries: Jared Schneidman, Andrea Kelley

238 Unified Gradients:
Redirecting Fills with the Gradient Tool

239–243 Galleries: Filip Yip, Hugh Whyte, Caryl Gorska,
Tim Webb

244 Rolling Mesh:
Converting Gradients to Mesh and Editing

246 Advanced Technique: Mastering Mesh:
Painting with Areas of Color Using Mesh

249–252 Galleries: Ma Zhi Liang, Yukio Miyamoto

8

Transparency & Appearances

254 Introduction

254 Basic Transparency

263 Appearances

264 The Finer Points of Appearances

266 Transparency 101:
Assigning Opacity to Default Brushes

268 Advanced Technique: Transparent Color:
Customizing Transparent Brushes & Layers

272 Basic Transparency:
Blending Modes, Opacity & Isolate Blending

274 Basic Highlights:
Making Highlights with Transparent Blends

275–277 Galleries: Nancy Stahl, Tiffany Larsen, Louis Fishauf

278 Basic Appearances:
Making and Applying Appearances

280 Floating Type:
Type Objects with Transparency & Effects

282 Advanced Technique: Tinting a Scan:
Using Transparency Effects & Simplify Path

284 Advanced Technique: It's a Knockout!:
See-through Objects with a Knockout Group

286 Advanced Technique: Opacity Masks 101:
Applying Glows and Using Opacity Masks

288–290 Galleries: Peter Cassell, Adam Z Lein

9

Live Effects & Graphic Styles

292 Introduction

292 Effects vs. Filters

293 Raster effects

293 3D Effects

298 Scribble Effect

298 Warps and Enveloping

300 Effect Pathfinders

301 Effect > Pathfinder > Hard Mix and Soft Mix

302 Graphic Styles in Illustrator

303 Gallery: Steven Gordon

304 Scratchboard Art:
Using Multiple Strokes, Effects, and Styles

306 Embossing Effects: *Building 3D Appearances*

308 Blurring The Lines:
Photorealism with Blends and Effects

311 Gallery: Ted Alspach

312 Warps & Envelopes:
Using Warping and Enveloping Effects

316 Quick & Easy 3D: *Simple 3D techniques*

318 3D Effects:
Extruding, Revolving, and Rotating Paths

321–325 Galleries: Mike Schwabauer, Robert Sharif, Trina Wai,
Mordy Golding, Tom Patterson, Joe Lertola

326 Scribble Basics:
Applying Scribble Effects to Artwork

328 Gallery: Todd Macadangdang

Advanced Techniques

330 Introduction

330 Clipping Masks

333 Mask Problem-Solving Strategies

334 Advanced Technique: Colorful Masking:
Fitting Blends into Custom Shapes

336 Advanced Technique: Reflective Masks:
Super-Realistic Reflection

338–341 Galleries: Bradley Neal, David Cater, Gary Ferster,
Greg Maxson

342 Advanced Technique: Glowing Starshine:
Blending Custom Colors to Form a Glow

343–347 Galleries: Kenneth Batelman, Alan James Weimer,
Marc LaMantia

348 Advanced Technique: Masking Opacity:
Making Transparency Irregular

350 Advanced Technique: Modeling Mesh:
Shaping and Forming Mesh Objects

353–356 Galleries: Javier Romero, Ann Paidrick, Yukio Miyamoto

10

11

Web & Animation

358 Introduction

358 Working in RGB in Illustrator

358 A few thoughts on RGB and CMYK color

359 Assigning URL'S and Slicing

361 Release to Layers

362 Export File Formats

364 SVG

365 Data-Driven Graphics

367 Gallery: Ivan Torres

368 Off in a Flash: *Making Artwork for a Flash Animation*

371 Gallery: Kevan Atteberry

372 Layering Frames: *Turning Layered Artwork into Keyframes*

374 Webward Ho!: *Designing a Web Page in Illustrator*

377 Gallery: Steven Gordon

378 Advanced Technique (Illustrator with Photoshop): Making Waves: *Transforming and Blending for Animation*

12

Illustrator & Other Programs

382 Introduction

382 Placing Artwork in Illustrator

383 Illustrator & Other Programs

384 Illustrator & Adobe Photoshop

385 Illustrator & Adobe InDesign

385 Illustrator, PDF & Adobe Acrobat

386 Illustrator & Adobe Streamline

386 Illustrator & 3D programs

387 Gallery: Bert Monroy

388 **Illustrator with Photoshop:** Software Relay: *An Illustrator-Photoshop Workflow*

391 Gallery: Rob Magiera

392 **Advanced Technique: Illustrator with Photoshop:** Shape Shifting: *Exporting Paths to Shapes in Photoshop*

394–407 Galleries: Judy Stead, Timothy Donaldson, April Greiman, Lance Hidy, David Pounds, Ron Chan, Louis Fishauf, Filip Yip, Chris Spollen, Bryan Christie, Eliot Bergman, Tom Willcockson, Joe Jones

408 **Artists Appendix**

412 **Resources Appendix**

413 **General Index**

Important: Read me first!

Critical print resolution issues

Illustrator requires that you manually set the proper resolution for output of images that include transparency or live effects! For details, see the *Transparency & Appearances* chapter introduction.

Lots of artwork on the CD!

We're putting more of our *Illustrator Wow!* artists' artwork on our *Wow! CD*. You will find more than eighty examples of artwork from the book so you can follow along, or simply pick the art apart to see how it was constructed.

Additional Illustrator training

You'll find additional lessons in the "Ch02 The Zen of Illustrator" folder on the *Wow! CD*, including the *Zen Lessons* (which supplement *The Zen of Illustrator* chapter). These lessons walk you through some basics of working with the Pen tool, Bézier curves, layers, and stacking order. (If you're looking for more help with the Pen tool, look at the demo for zenofthepen.org on the *Wow! CD*). If you're new to Illustrator, you may even want to begin with a class. If you're teaching a class in Illustrator, look for the *IllustratorCS Wow! Course Outline* on the Web site: www.ssteuer.com/edu

This book has been fully updated, reworked, and expanded for Illustrator users of all levels to master the exciting (and sometimes perplexing) features of Adobe Illustrator CS. You'll find hundreds of essential production techniques, timesaving tips, and beautiful art generously shared by *Illustrator Wow!* artists worldwide. All lessons are deliberately kept short to allow you to squeeze in a lesson or two between clients, and to encourage the use of this book within the confines of supervised classrooms.

In order to keep the content in this book tantalizing to everyone—I've assumed a reasonable level of competence with basic Mac and Windows concepts, such as opening and saving files, launching applications, copying objects to the clipboard, and doing mouse operations. I've also assumed that you've read through "Learning about Adobe Illustrator" in the beginning of the *Adobe Illustrator CS User Guide* (*User Guide*), and understand the basic functionality of most of the tools.

I'd love to tell you that you can learn Adobe Illustrator just by flipping through the pages of this book, but the reality is that there is no substitute for practice. The good news is, the more you work with Illustrator, the more techniques you'll be able to integrate into your creative process.

Use this book as a reference, a guide for specific techniques, or just as a source of inspiration. After you've read this book, read it again, and you'll undoubtedly learn something you missed the first time. As I hope you'll discover, the more experienced you become with Adobe Illustrator, the easier it will be to assimilate all the new information and inspiration you'll find in this book. Happy Illustrating!

Sharon Steuer

How to use this book...

Before you do anything else, read the *Wow! Glossary* on the pull-out quick reference card at the back of the book. The Glossary provides definitions for the terms used throughout *The Illustrator CS Wow! Book* (for example, ⌘ is the Command key for Mac).

WELCOME TO *WOW!* FOR WINDOWS AND MAC

If you already use Adobe Photoshop or InDesign you'll see many interface similarities to Illustrator CS. The similarities should make the time you spend learning each program much shorter (especially if you're a newcomer to all three products). Your productivity should also increase across the board once you adjust to the new shortcuts and methodologies (see "Shortcuts and keystrokes" following, and the *Illustrator Basics* chapter).

Shortcuts and keystrokes

Because you can now customize keyboard shortcuts, we're restricting the keystrokes references in the book to those instances when it's so standard that we assume you'll keep the default, or when there is no other way to achieve that function (such as Lock All Unselected objects). We'll always give you Macintosh shortcuts first, then the Windows equivalent (⌘-Z/Ctrl-Z). For help with customizing keyboard shortcuts, and tool and menu navigation (such as single key tool access and Tab to hide palettes), see the *Illustrator Basics* chapter.

Setting up your palettes

In terms of following along with the lessons in this book, you'll probably want to enable the "Type Object Selection by Path Only" option (see Tip "Selecting type by accident" in the *Type* chapter). Next, if you want your palettes to look like our palettes, you'll need to set swatches to be sorted by name, choose "Sort by Name" and "List View" from the Swatches pop-up menu (at right).

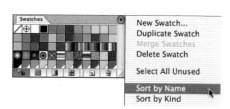

With the All Swatches icon selected choose "Sort by Name" then "List View" from the pop-up menu

The Swatches palette viewed with "Sort by Name" selected

Illustrator CS sets an application default that could inhibit the way Illustrator experts work. In order for your currently selected object to set all the styling attributes for the next object you draw (including brush strokes, live effects, transparency, etc.), you must open the Appearance palette (Window menu) and disable New Art Has Basic Appearance. You can disable (and re-enable) this default either by: 1) clicking on the bottom left icon in the Appearance palette (dark shows that it's enabled; see Tip at left), *or* 2) choosing New Art Has Basic Appearance from the Appearance palette pop-up menu (✔ shows it's enabled). Your new setting sticks even after you've quit.

HOW THIS BOOK IS ORGANIZED...

You'll find six kinds of information woven throughout this book—all of it up to date for Illustrator CS: **Basics, Tips, Exercises, Techniques, Galleries, and References.**

1

2 The CD icon indicates that related artwork can be found on the IllustratorCSWowCD

3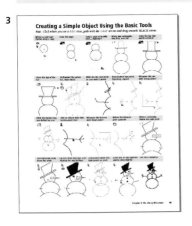

1 Basics. *Illustrator Basics* and *The Zen of Illustrator* qualify as full-blown chapters on basics and are packed with information that distills and supplements your Adobe Illustrator manual and disk. Every chapter starts with a general overview of the basics. These sections are designed so advanced Illustrator users can move quickly through them, but I strongly suggest that the rest of you read them very carefully. Please remember, this book is a supplement to, not a substitute for, your *User Guide*.

2 Tips. When you see this icon (◉), you'll find related artwork on the *IllustratorCSWowCD* (referred to hereafter as the *Wow! CD*) within that chapter's folder. Look to the information in the gray and red boxes for hands-on Tips that can help you work more efficiently. Usually you can find tips alongside related textual information, but if you're in an impatient mood, you might just want to flip through, looking for interesting or relevant tips. The red arrows ——▶, red outlines and **red text** found in tips (and sometimes with artwork) have been added to emphasize or further explain a concept or technique.

3 Exercises. (Not for the faint of heart.) We have included step-by-step exercises to help you make the transition to Illustrator technician extraordinaire. *The Zen of Illustrator* chapter and the *Zen Lessons* on the *Wow! CD* are dedicated to helping you master the mechanics (and the soul) of Illustrator. Take these lessons in small doses, in order, and at a relaxed pace. All of the Finger Dances are customized for Mac and Windows.

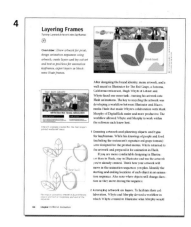

4 Techniques. In these sections, you'll find step-by-step techniques gathered from almost a hundred *Illustrator Wow!* artists. Most *Wow!* techniques focus on one aspect of how an image was created, though I'll often refer you to different *Wow!* chapters (or to a specific step-by-step technique, Tip, or Gallery where a technique is introduced) to give you the opportunity to explore a briefly-covered feature more thoroughly. Feel free to start with almost any chapter, but, since each technique builds on those previously explained, try to follow the techniques within each chapter sequentially. Some chapters include Advanced Technique lessons, which assume that you have assimilated all of the techniques found throughout the chapter. *Advanced Techniques* is an entire chapter dedicated to advanced tips, tricks, and techniques.

5 Galleries. The Gallery pages consist of images related to techniques demonstrated nearby. Each Gallery piece is accompanied by a description of how the artist created that image, and may include steps showing the progression of a technique detailed elsewhere. *Illustrator & Other Programs* consists almost entirely of Gallery pages to give you a sense of Illustrator's flexibility.

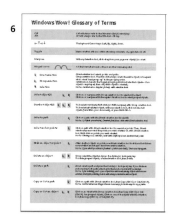

6 References. *Resources* and *Artists* appendixes, *Glossaries*, and *General Index* can be found in the back of this book and in the pull-out card. In addition, we will occasionally direct you to the *User Guide* when referring to specific information that's already well-documented in the *Adobe Illustrator CS User Guide.*

What's New in Illustrator CS?

By Dave Awl

Illustrator's new floral application icon. All of the Creative Suite applications have icons inspired by nature—Illustrator's flower corresponds to Photoshop CS's new feather and InDesign CS's butterfly

Adobe's Creative Suite is available in Standard and Premium versions

Still in love with Venus?

If you can't face life without Venus's lovely visage from previous versions of Illustrator, don't worry—she isn't gone entirely from Illustrator CS, she's just hiding. You can get her to make an appearance by typing the letters V-E-N-U-S (making sure the Type tool isn't active first); then take a look at the Toolbox.

Accessing the Welcome screen

One of the first things you might notice about the newest version of Adobe Illustrator is that numbers are out, and letters are in. Instead of the predictable "Illustrator 11," this release has been given the name "Illustrator CS." The CS stands for Creative Suite, and in fact it is a pretty suite deal (ouch).

"Creative Suite" refers to the fact that Illustrator is now engineered to function more closely than ever with its sibling applications, Photoshop and InDesign. All three are now available as a suite, akin to the way Microsoft Office bundles together Microsoft's most popular applications. (In addition to the Standard version of the Suite, which contains Illustrator, Photoshop, and InDesign, there's also a Premium version that includes Acrobat and GoLive.)

But Illustrator CS has plenty more excitement to offer than just sibling bonding. Read on for a quick tour of Illustrator CS's new capabilities.

SPEED, GLORIOUS SPEED

Adobe knows that getting it done on time is half the battle. So Illustrator CS has been blessed with speed enhancements in almost every area of the application. This means Illustrator can move faster than ever to keep up with your working pace and help you to sustain your creative momentum.

A WELCOME BEGINNING

Illustrator CS lays out the welcome mat for its users with a brand new Welcome screen that greets you at startup (and can be accessed at any time during your session via the Help menu). The Welcome screen lets you quickly choose from three handy options for getting started: creating a new blank document, creating a new document from a template, or opening an existing document. Illustrator's virtual welcome mat also gives you handy access to Illustrator tutorials, a guide to Illustrator CS's new features, and a PDF catalog of the "cool extras" included on the CD (such as fonts, templates, swatch and symbol libraries, and more).

JOURNEY ACROSS THE THIRD DIMENSION

The first of two exciting graphics effects Illustrator CS offers is the ability to render objects in glorious 3D—even if you're a beginner without a sophisticated knowledge of perspective. The 3D effect lets you transform type and shapes into 3D objects, and extrude, revolve, or rotate them in space. You can even customize their lighting and surface appearance.

This might sound familiar to users of Adobe Dimensions; but Illustrator's 3D shapes are live effects, so changes you make to your 2D original are automatically reflected in your 3D version. Even better, you can map artwork onto the 3D objects you create. So you can create, for example, a 3D wine bottle (as in the illustration at right)—and then it's a snap to create a label that wraps around it with perfect 3D perspective. You can learn lots more about the 3D effect and its various capabilities in the *Live Effects & Graphic Styles* chapter.

SCRIBBLING: NOT JUST KID STUFF

Illustrator CS's other new graphics effect lets you indulge your inner child's urge to scribble without any risk to your nice clean walls. Use Illustrator's Scribble effect to give your original artwork a friendly, hand-drawn feel; or add it to existing clip art or other objects for a dash of eye-catching personality. You can also use it to mask images, create scratchboard-like illustrations, add cross-hatching to a design, or create animated wiggly lines. Like the 3D effect described above, the Scribble effect is live, so you can edit your original object without having to reapply or modify the effect. Learn more about the Scribble effect in the *Live Effects & Graphic Styles* chapter.

Illustrator's new Welcome screen helps you get started quickly

Mordy Golding used Illustrator's 3D effect to create the wine bottle (left) from the half bottle segment (right). He then wrapped the label art around it. See the "Wine Bottle" Gallery in the Live Effects & Graphic Styles *chapter for details*

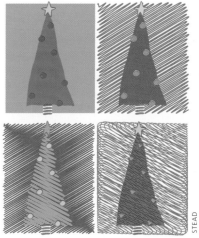

Judy Stead used Illustrator's Scribble effect to create this eye-catching holiday card. See the "Scribble Basics" lesson in the Live Effects & Graphic Styles *chapter for details*

One of several Web site templates included with
Illustrator CS

Left, one of the Illustrator's restaurant menu
templates; Right, one of Illustrator's newsletter
templates

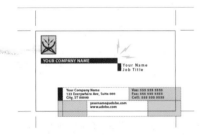

A business card template, from one of several
coordinated "Business Sets" included in Illustrator CS. Each includes templates for a variety of
items with a common design theme. See the
Illustrator Basics chapter for more

MS Office and transparency

Illustrator's new Save for
Microsoft Office command is useful, but it doesn't yet support
transparency. So, if you need to
move artwork with transparency
into an MS Office application, you
may be better off exporting to a
format like PNG.

TEMPLATES: NO MORE REINVENTING THE WHEEL

Illustrator's convenient new template file format makes
it easy for you to save finished designs that can be used
as the basis for new work. Templates come in handy any
time you've got an overall design that remains largely the
same, except for certain specific content that changes.
Templates can store Artboard dimensions, swatches,
character and paragraph styles, symbols, guides, and
other elements used to create the precise look and feel you
want for a particular client or project.

When you create a new file from a template, Illustrator
opens a new untitled document that's an exact duplicate
of the template. You can then make any changes you like
to the new file, while the original template file remains
unchanged, ready for the next time you need it.

But wait, there's more. Adobe has thoughtfully
included a selection of more than 200 professionally
designed templates to get you started, including CD and
DVD labels, booklets and tray cards to Web page layouts,
business cards, gift certificates, and just about anything
else you can think of. And, as mentioned above, Illustrator gives you easy access to your templates via the new
Welcome screen.

COMPATIBILITY: PLAYING WELL WITH OTHERS

Illustrator CS displays admirable team spirit by offering
increased compatibility with other important applications. For starters, as previously mentioned, Illustrator
CS is part of Adobe's new Creative Suite, along with
Photoshop CS and InDesign CS. All three applications
are designed to function work more closely together than
ever before.

In particular, the CS versions of Photoshop and Illustrator do a much better job of cooperating with each
other than previous releases. Illustrator is now better at
handling Photoshop's raster objects, and Illustrator's layers, text, slices, transparency, and image maps are more
likely to display correctly in Photoshop (though there
may still be some discrepancies).

Illustrator CS also offers increased compatibility with Microsoft Office. For example, it includes a new "Save for Microsoft Office" command that can make it easier to move artwork from Illustrator into a PowerPoint presentation, a Word document, or an Excel Spreadsheet. (Learn more about Illustrator's compatibility with other programs in the *Illustrator & Other Programs* chapter.)

The Adobe PDF Options dialog box

A FLEXIBLE RELATIONSHIP WITH ACROBAT AND PDF

While we're talking compatibility, Illustrator CS offers better support for the PDF format (including the new PDF 1.5 format, compatible with Acrobat 6), making it easy to save PDF files for use with Adobe Acrobat or the free Adobe Reader. You can choose to save your files as Acrobat 4, 5, or 6. Illustrator CS also includes many powerful features from Acrobat Distiller, giving you increased control over the process of making PDFs from your Illustrator documents.

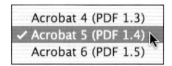

The Compatibility menu in the Adobe PDF Options dialog box lets you choose a specific version of PDF

Illustrator CS offers support for layers, printer's marks, and bleeds in PDF documents, as well as extensive security options. In addition, Illustrator's new time-saving PDF presets help you streamline production while ensuring consistency in the way transparency and layers are treated as you export or print PDFs.

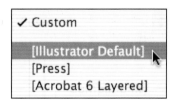

The Presets menu in the Adobe PDF Options dialog box offers three default presets as well as the option to create and save your own custom presets

For more details about working with PDFs in Illustrator CS, see the chapters *Illustrator Basics, Transparency & Appearances*, and *Illustrator & Other Programs*.

A BOLD NEW APPROACH TO TYPE

With Illustrator CS, Adobe's engineers brought Illustrator's type capabilities to a whole new level. The results include a redesigned text engine and a full-featured, exquisitely-detailed new set of controls that allow designers to design and set type with satisfying precision. Also, many of Illustrator's new features function similarly to their InDesign counterparts—part of the compatibility improvements of the Creative Suite.

Illustrator CS takes full advantage of the advanced layout features of the OpenType format, so you'll be able

PDF presets and transparency

Illustrator's new Transparency Flattener presets are particularly helpful in light of the fact that PDF file formats earlier than 1.5 (Acrobat 6) don't process transparency natively; yet, you may find yourself needing to save to the 1.3 (Acrobat 4) and 1.4 (Acrobat 5) formats. These controls can help you to find the right balance between quality and speed of output as you save to PDF.

OpenType fonts automatically set standard ligatures as you type. The type on the top row is set using a standard version of Adobe's Minion font. The bottom row is set using Minion Pro, one of the OpenType fonts included with Illustrator CS. Minion Pro supplies the ligatures for "ff" and "ffl", which give the type a more sophisticated look. See the Type chapter for more

Lorem ipsum dolor sit amet, consectetuer adipiscing elit. Sed at nibh. Nam ultrices erat nec pede. Vivamus est ante, aliquet vel, fermentum et, nonummy eget, ante. Morbi metus nisl, placerat ut, accumsan id, aliquet vel, nulla. Aenean scelerisque dapibus nunc. Proin augue. Vestibulum dictum. Morbi eget urna. Phasellus id augue. Nulla congue imperdiet dolor. Lorem ipsum dolor sit amet, consectetuer adipiscing elit. Sed at nibh.

Text composed using Single-line Composer

Lorem ipsum dolor sit amet, consectetuer adipiscing elit. Sed at nibh. Nam ultrices erat nec pede. Vivamus est ante, aliquet vel, fermentum et, nonummy eget, ante. Morbi metus nisl, placerat ut, accumsan id, aliquet vel, nulla. Aenean scelerisque dapibus nunc. Proin augue. Vestibulum dictum. Morbi eget urna. Phasellus id augue. Nulla congue imperdiet dolor. Lorem ipsum dolor sit amet, consectetuer adipiscing elit. Sed at nibh.

Here, the same text composed using Every-line Composer, which automatically creates less ragged-looking text blocks with more uniform line lengths. See the Type chapter for more

Working with legacy text

Because Illustrator CS's new type engine handles text differently than previous versions of Illustrator, text created in Illustrator 10 or earlier is considered *legacy text* and must be updated before it's editable in Illustrator CS. See the *Type* chapter for more on working with legacy text.

to make good use of the free OpenType fonts that come with the application. OpenType fonts make it easier to share documents between platforms, because both Windows and Mac OS use the same font file for OpenType. OpenType fonts also give you easy, context-sensitive access to special characters that let you design your type more elegantly and precisely.

When you type using any OpenType font, Illustrator CS automatically sets standard ligatures. There are also two new palettes to help you take advantage of OpenType's benefits: The OpenType palette gives you access to OpenType's special features, while the Glyphs palette gives you easy access to special characters.

Illustrator CS's new paragraph and character styles will help you achieve precise and consistent formatting, while saving you time by letting you apply multiple formatting attributes—ranging from simple to elaborate—with a single mouse click. Accessed via the new Paragraph and Character Styles palette, these styles can be updated live and can easily be shared among colleagues and team members.

Particular attention has been paid to Illustrator's ability to create blocks of text that are pleasing to the eye. Illustrator CS's new Every-line Composer allows you to create even, polished-looking text columns with minimal hyphenation and consistent spacing—without having to fine-tune line breaks by hand.

Illustrator CS also gives you increased control over multi-column layouts, with detailed Rows & Columns controls (in the Area Type Options dialog box) that allow you to precisely define the characteristics of the columns and rows in any text area. Optical Kerning and Optical Margin Alignment allow you to easily optimize the spacing between characters and the way characters align at the margins. The new Custom Tab leaders feature lets you customize the dot type and pattern for tab leaders (or even design your own graphics to be used as leaders).

Other benefits included in Illustrator CS's new approach to type are new, more flexible path type options;

improved controls for hyphenation and justification; on-screen highlighting of missing fonts; expanded language support (including the ability to spell-check and hyphenate in 29 languages); improved text linking and deletion; a WYSIWYG font menu so you can see what fonts look like before selecting them; and more. See the *Type* chapter for more about Illustrator CS's type capabilities.

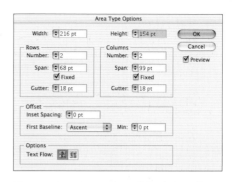

The new Area Type Options dialog box, with improved controls for rows and columns

A MORE PRECISE WAY TO PRINT

One of Adobe's top priorities for Illustrator CS was to refine the printing experience—to make Illustrator print jobs more efficient and reliable to output, no matter whether you're using a desktop printer or a high-end production printer.

The key to Illustrator's printing revolution is a streamlined, comprehensive Print dialog box that manages to simultaneously simplify the printing process and give you much more control over it. From the new Print dialog box, you can specify all print settings, from tiling and custom page sizes to printer's marks, color management output profiles, and transparency flattener settings—enhanced controls for flattening transparent artwork as you print or export it. You can even save transparency flattener settings as presets to save time and maximize consistency.

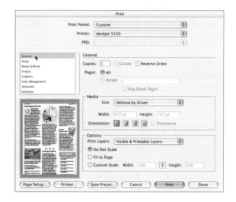

Illustrator's new full service, one-stop Print dialog box. Note the preview area in the lower left-hand corner

The new Print interface gives you a thumbnail-sized interactive Print Preview right in the dialog box, as well as convenient scaling options, intuitive tiling controls, the ability to create time-saving print presets, and more flexible printer's marks and bleed settings that can be specified independently of each other.

Illustrator CS also offers new separation options that can help you output jobs more quickly, and achieve better control over PostScript output (via the new Device Independent option).

Find out more about Illustrator CS's new Print interface in the *Illustrator Basics* chapter.

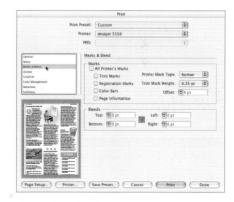

The Marks & Bleed section of the new Print dialog box gives you detailed control over flexible printer's marks and bleeds that can be set independently of each other

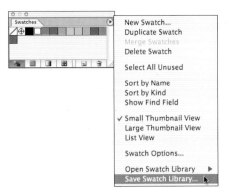

The Save Library command lets you save libraries directly from the Graphic Styles, Swatches, Brushes, and Symbols palettes

The Open Library command lets you open libraries from the Graphic Styles, Swatches, Brushes, and Symbols palettes

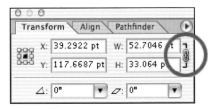

The new lock button in the Transform palette makes it easy to scale objects proportionately

IT'S THE LITTLE THINGS THAT MATTER

Illustrator CS offers a number of other enhancements to help make your life easier.

- **You can now open and save libraries** (including Graphic Style, Swatch, Brush and Symbol libraries) right from their respective palettes, thanks to the new Open Library and Save Library commands in the palette menus.

- **The Transform palette has a new lock button** that lets you scale objects proportionately. Just click the button and you can resize an object without fear of distorting it.

- **The Eyedropper now allows you** to choose how large an area to sample from (single point, 3 x 3, or 5 x 5 pixels), like you can in Photoshop.

- **You can now print and export** an Illustrator document containing linked EPS and PDF files that interact with transparency without having to embed the linked files first.

SCRIPTING: AUTOMATICALLY EASIER

Speaking of convenience, Illustrator CS lets you automate more tasks than ever with enhancements to its Scripting capabilities. All of Illustrator's new features can be automated with expanded scripting support, including the new printing interface.

WHAT ARE YOU WAITING FOR?

Now that you've had a quick tour of Illustrator CS's new features, it's time to learn more about how to use them (and the rest of Illustrator's great features). That's what the rest of this book is here to help you do.

Illustrator Basics

1

2 Introduction

2 Computer & System Requirements

2 Setting Up Your Page

5 Making Your Moves Easier

6 Working with Objects

8 Watch Your Cursor!

9 Bézier-Editing Tools

11 Geometric Objects

12 Selecting & Grouping Objects

14 Joining & Averaging

15 Working with Palettes

17 Graphing & Charting

19 Transformations

22 Working Smart

24 Changing Your Views

25 Zooming In & Out

26 Show/Hide Choices

28 Color in Illustrator

31 Saving as PDF

32 Image Formats

33 PostScript Printing & Exporting

35 Actions

36 Scripting and Variables

37 Data-driven graphics

Illustrator Basics

Don't start yet!

Before you begin this book, make sure you read both the "How to Use This Book" section in the front of the book, and the pullout *Glossary* at the back.

System requirements

Any improvements to these minimum system requirements will increase Illustrator's performance.
Macintosh:
- PowerPC G3, G4 or G5 processor
- Mac OS X, version 10.2.4 or later

Windows:
- Intel Pentium III or 4 processor
- Windows 2000 (SP3) or Windows XP

Both systems:
- 192 MB of RAM installed
- 470 MB of available hard drive space
- If using Adobe PostScript Printers: Adobe PostScript Level 2 or Adobe PostScript 3
- 1024 x 768 or better monitor resolution recommended
- CD-ROM drive for installation

Tool tips

When enabled (Illustrator > Preferences > General for Mac; Edit > Preferences > General for Windows), tool tips will display descriptive captions for all icons, tools, and certain functions.

This chapter is packed with tips and techniques chosen to help you use Adobe Illustrator with optimal ease and efficiency. Whether you're a veteran of Illustrator or a relative newcomer, you're likely to find information here that will greatly increase your productivity and help you get up to speed on the latest features. Remember, this chapter is an addendum to, not a replacement for, Adobe Illustrator's *User Guide*. (And be sure to heed the advice of the "Don't start yet!" Tip at left.)

COMPUTER & SYSTEM REQUIREMENTS

Creating artwork on the computer is as rewarding as it is challenging. Computer art tools, including Adobe Illustrator, have undergone great improvements in the past few years. In order to accommodate demands for faster and more powerful software, the more powerful upgrades might not run on older computers. For example, the minimum requirement is now at least 192 MB of RAM available to run Illustrator, and Adobe recommends 256 MB. You'll also need more hard disk space than ever before: at least 470 MB and probably much more, because Illustrator files containing live blends, brushes, raster images, gradient meshes, live effects, and transparency can be quite large. (Not to mention that the Adobe Illustrator CS CD contains lots of bonus content you'll want room for, including templates, libraries, and fonts.) Illustrator doesn't require a large monitor, but 1024 x 768 or larger is recommended to avoid feeling cramped. The best solution is two monitors. This allows you to keep your palettes on one monitor, while using the other to create your artwork.

SETTING UP YOUR PAGE
New Document

When you first launch Illustrator, you'll be greeted by a Welcome screen (new in Illustrator CS) that allows you to choose one of three possible options for getting started:

New document (which simply opens a new blank document), New from Template (which allows you to select a template file on which to base your document), and Open Document (while lets you choose a pre-existing file to open). After startup, New, New from Template, and Open are accessible from the File menu, and the Welcome screen remains available from the Help menu.

To create a new blank document, select New from the File menu or the Welcome screen. In the dialog box, select the Artboard Setup (the document dimensions and orientation) and the Color Mode (CMYK or RGB). For dimensions, the default page size is 612 pt x 792 pt, which is equivalent to 8.5" x 11." You can choose different page sizes from the pop-up menu (including common paper sizes for print purposes, and several common Web page sizes in pixels), and you can also choose your preferred measurement system. Pages can be as small as 1 pixel x 1 pixel, or as large as 227.5" x 227.5." For orientation, choose either Portrait or Landscape by clicking one of the two buttons. For color mode, Illustrator doesn't allow you to create new art that uses both CMYK and RGB colors in the same document, so you'll need to pick one or the other.

Templates

Illustrator CS takes convenience to a new level with its new template files. Illustrator's templates are actually a special file format (ending in .ait). When you choose New from Template (from either the File menu or the Welcome screen), Illustrator creates a regular Illustrator document (ending in .ai) based on the template, while the original .ait template file remains unchanged, no matter what changes you make to your new document.

When you create a new file from a template, Illustrator automatically loads the various settings associated with the template file (including details such as Artboard dimensions, swatches, character and paragraph styles, symbols, guides), as well as any content the template contains. This comes in handy any time you need to create a number of documents or pages with common design

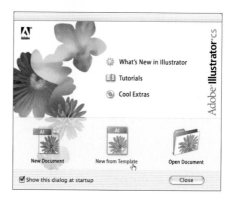

The Welcome screen offers you a number of options for starting your session, as well as convenient access to information and extras

If Welcome isn't welcome

If you don't want the Welcome screen to appear every time you launch Illustrator, don't worry. Just uncheck the "Show this dialog at startup" box in the Welcome screen's lower left corner and it will no longer appear automatically. (But it will remain available via the Help menu if you change your mind.)

The Templates folder inside the Illustrator application folder (accessed here via File > New from Template) contains more than 200 professionally designed templates to choose from, organized into helpful categories

Letterhead and Business card templates

Brochure template and CD label template

Web site template

Pictured above are items from one of several co-ordinated Business Sets included among Illustrator CS's free templates, each offering a variety of items sharing a common design theme

A zoomed-out view of the Artboard

elements, but specific content that changes.

You can create as many original templates as you need or want, and you can also take advantage of the more than 200 professionally designed templates included with Illustrator CS—everything from business cards to Web pages to restaurant menus.

The Artboard

A box with a solid black outline defines the Artboard dimensions and the final document size. Double-click the Hand tool to fit your image to the current window. One change you may notice from previous versions of Illustrator is that the dotted line indicating page tiling (and showing the current printable area) no longer displays on the Artboard by default. That's because page tiling is now displayed and controlled from the preview in the Print dialog box (as discussed below), so most users will never need to view page tiling on the Artboard. (That said, you can still use View > Show Page Tiling to display dotted lines if you want them, and View > Hide Page Tiling to conceal them. Use the Page tool to click-drag the dotted-line page parameters around the Artboard.)

Prior to Illustrator CS, only objects within the dotted line would print. However, with Illustrator's sophisticated new print controls, you can now make very precise choices about what to print: Using the Crop Artwork to menu in the Print dialog box's Setup options, you can choose to print all artwork in the file, everything within the preview area's dotted line, or everything within your own user-defined crop area.

The One-Stop Print Dialog Box

Thanks to Illustrator's new full-service Print dialog box, it's no longer necessary to use a Page Setup dialog box to change things like page size and orientation. You can now control all those settings and more from within the Print dialog box. (In fact, although the Mac version still has a Page Setup button, if you click on it you'll get a warning that the Page Setup dialog box is provided by the OS, and for best results you should set all options from within Illustrator's Print dialog box).

As previously mentioned, the preview area in the Print dialog box shows you the page's printable area. It also lets you scale artwork to order as you go to print it, while choosing exactly which artwork in the document you want to print. So you no longer have to worry about changing the size of the Artboard itself in order to print things at a different scale.

Illustrator CS also lets you save your Print settings as time-saving presets, so if you're designing billboards or other very large media sizes, you can set the appropriate scale and then save it as a Print preset for easy access.

Illustrator's one-stop Print dialog box—note the preview area in the lower left corner, which shows you the printable area of the page, and lets you adjust and scale your artwork to print

MAKING YOUR MOVES EASIER

Look over this section to make sure you're aware of the many ways to select tools and access features. Learning these simple techniques will free you from mousing to the toolbox or depending on the pull-down menus.

Mac users: It's recommended that you set all your options in Illustrator's Print dialog box, rather than through the OS-provided Page Setup dialog box. If you forget, Illustrator will remind you with the message shown above

Keyboard shortcuts for tools and navigation

Need to access a tool? Press a key. Press "T" to choose the Type tool, "P" for the Pen tool, and so on. Choose any tool in the toolbox by pressing its keyboard shortcut. (Each shortcut used to be a single key, but there are now so many tools that a few of them have double-key shortcuts.) To learn the default keyboard shortcuts for your tools, with Show Tool Tips enabled (this is on by default), hold the cursor over any tool in the toolbox, and its keyboard shortcut will appear in parentheses next to the tool name (toggle the Tool Tip option in General Preferences). **Note:** *Keyboard shortcuts won't work while you're in text editing mode. Press Escape to leave text editing mode and use a keyboard shortcut. Your text will remain unchanged, with edits preserved.*

Changing keyboard shortcuts

To change a shortcut for a tool or menu item, open the Keyboard Shortcut dialog box (Edit > Keyboard Short-

Custom keyboard shortcuts

To assign a shortcut to a menu item or tool, select Edit > Keyboard Shortcuts. Making any changes will rename the set "Custom." If you choose a shortcut already in use, you will get a warning that it is currently being used and that reassigning it will remove it from the item it is currently assigned to. When you exit the dialog box you will be asked to save your custom set. You can't overwrite a *preset*.

Resizing and stroke weight

If you double-click the Scale tool, you can resize your selection with or without altering line weights:

- To scale a selection, while also scaling line weights, make sure to enable the Scale Strokes & Effects checkbox.
- To scale a selection while maintaining your line weights, disable Scale Strokes & Effects.
- To decrease line weights (50%) without scaling objects, first scale the selection (200%) with Scale Strokes & Effects disabled. Then scale (50%) with it enabled. Reverse to increase line weights.

STEUER

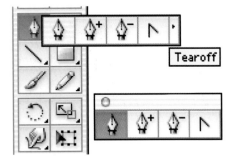

Tear off tool palettes

cuts). Making a change to a shortcut will change the Set name to "Custom." When you're finished making changes and want to exit the dialog box, you will be asked to save your shortcuts to a new file. This file will be saved in the Illustrator application folder and will end in ".kys". As long as these file types are located in the application folder, they will be available as choices in the Set pop-up menu. In addition, every time you make any changes to a saved set (not a default preset), you'll be asked if you want to overwrite that set. You can also use the Save button to create a new keyboard shortcut file. Click the Export Text button if you need a text file as a reference for a specific set of shortcuts or need to print them.

Note: *You can't change most palette items, but the few you can change are found at the bottom of the menu commands list in the Edit > Keyboard Shortcuts dialog box.*

Context-sensitive menus

If you're not already familiar with context-sensitive menus, you might find them a great time saver. Windows users merely click the right mouse button. If you're on a Mac with a single-button mouse, press the Control key while you click and hold the mouse button. In both cases a menu pops up (specific to the tool or item you are working with) providing you with an alternative to the regular pull-down menus.

Tear off palettes

The Illustrator Toolbox lets you tear *off* subsets of tools so you can move the entire set to another location. Click on a tool with a pop-up menu, drag the cursor to the arrow end of the pop-up, and release the mouse.

WORKING WITH OBJECTS
Anchor points, lines, and Bézier curves

Instead of using pixels to draw shapes, Illustrator creates objects made up of points, called "anchor points." They are connected by curved or straight outlines called "paths" and are visible if you work in Outline mode (formerly Artwork mode). (Choose View>Outline to enter Outline mode, and View>Preview to change back.) Illustrator describes information about the location and size of each path, as well as its dozen or so attributes, such as its fill color and its stroke weight and color. Because you are creating objects, you'll be able to change the order in which they stack. You'll also be able to group objects together so you can select them as if they were one object. You can even ungroup them later, if you wish.

If you took geometry, you probably remember that the shortest distance between two points is a straight line. In Illustrator, this rule translates into each line being defined by two anchor points that you create by clicking with the Pen tool, or drawing with the Line Segment tool.

In mathematically describing rectangles and ellipses, Illustrator computes the center, the length of the sides, or the radius, based on the total width and height you specify. For more complex shapes involving free-form curves, Adobe Illustrator allows you to use the Pen tool to create Bézier curves, defined by non-printing anchor points (which literally anchor the path at those points), and direction points (which define the angle and depth of the curve). To make these direction points easier to see and manipulate, each direction point is connected to its anchor point with a non-printing direction line, also called a "handle." The direction points and handles are visible when you're creating a path with the Pen tool or editing the path with the Direct Selection tool. While all of this might sound complicated, manipulating Bézier curves can become intuitive. Mastering these curves, though initially awkward, is the heart and soul of using Illustrator.

More about Bézier curves

If you're new to using Bézier curves, take some time to go through the Adobe training materials. The "Ch 02 The Zen of Illustrator" folder on the *Wow! CD* includes several "Zen" practice lessons that will help you fine-tune your Bézier capabilities.

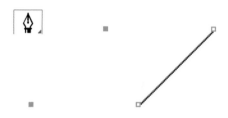

Clicking with the Pen tool to create anchor points for straight lines

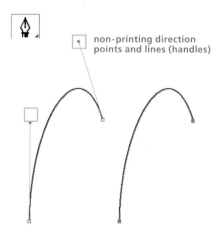

non-printing direction points and lines (handles)

Click-dragging with the Pen tool to create anchor points and pulling out direction lines for curves

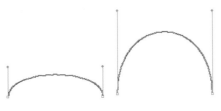

When direction handles are short, curves are shallow; when handles are long, curves are deep

The length and angle of the handles determine the gesture of the curves

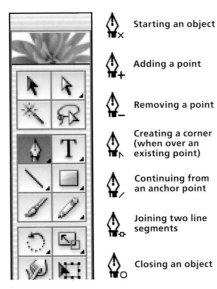

Starting an object

Adding a point

Removing a point

Creating a corner
(when over an
existing point)

Continuing from
an anchor point

Joining two line
segments

Closing an object

Basic cursor feedback for the Pen tool

Many graphics programs include Béziers, so mastering the Pen tool, though challenging at first, is very important. Friskets in Corel Painter, paths in Photoshop, and the outline and extrusion curves of many 3D programs all use the Bézier curve.

The key to learning Béziers is to take your initial lessons in short doses and stop if you get frustrated. Designer Kathleen Tinkel describes Bézier direction lines as "following the gesture of the curve." This artistic view should help you to create fluid Bézier curves.

Some final rules about Bézier curves

- The length and angle of the handles "anticipate" the curves that will follow.
- To ensure that the curve is smooth, place anchor points on either side of an arc, not in between.
- The fewer the anchor points, the smoother the curve will look and the faster it will print.
- Adjust a curve's height and angle by dragging the direction points, or grab the curve itself to adjust its height.

WATCH YOUR CURSOR!

Illustrator's cursors change to indicate not only what tool you have selected, but also which function you are about to perform. If you watch your cursor, you will avoid the most common Illustrator mistakes.

If you choose the Pen tool:

- **Before you start**, your cursor displays as the Pen tool with "×" indicating that you're starting a new object.

- **Once you've begun your object,** your cursor changes to a regular Pen. This indicates that you're about to add to an existing object.

- **If your cursor gets close to an existing anchor point,** it will change to a Pen with "–" indicating that you're about to delete the last anchor point! If you click-drag on top of that anchor point, you'll redraw that curve. If you hold the Option (Mac)/Alt (Win) key while you click-drag on top of the point, you'll pull out a new direction line, creating a corner (as in the petals of a flower). If you click on top of the point, you'll collapse the outgoing direction line, allowing you to attach a straight line to the curve.

- **If your cursor gets close to an end anchor point of an object,** it will change to a Pen with "o" to indicate that you're about to "close" the path. If you do close the path, then your cursor will change back to a Pen with "×" to indicate that you're beginning a new object.

- **If you use the Direct Selection tool to adjust the object as you go,** be sure to look at your cursor when you're ready to continue your object. If it's still a regular Pen, then continue to place the next point, adding to your object. If the Pen tool has "×" (indicating that you are about to start a new object), then you must redraw your last point. As you approach this last anchor point, your cursor will change to a Pen with "/"; click and drag over this last point to redraw the last curve. To form a hinged corner on the point as you draw, hold down Option (Mac) /Alt (Win) as you click-drag out a new direction line.

BÉZIER-EDITING TOOLS

The group of tools you can use to edit Illustrator paths are called Bézier-editing tools. To access them, click and hold the Pen, Pencil, or Scissors tool and drag to select one of the other tools. You can also tear off this palette. (To learn how to combine paths into new objects, read about the Pathfinder palette in the *Drawing & Coloring* chapter.)

- **The Pen tool** and **Auto Add/Delete** can perform a variety of functions. Auto Add/Delete (which is on by default, but can be disabled in General Preferences) allows the Pen tool to change automatically to the Add Anchor Point tool when the tool is over a selected path segment, or to the Delete Anchor Point tool when over an anchor point. To temporarily disable the Auto

Ways to "hinge" Bézier curves

A Bézier curve is "hinged" when it's attached to a line, or to another curve by a corner.

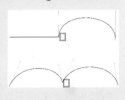

- **To hinge a curve as you draw #1:** While you are click-dragging to draw a curve, press Option/Alt to hinge the curve—pulling the handle in a new direction
- **To hinge a curve as you draw #2:** With the Pen tool, hold Option/Alt and click-drag over the last drawn anchor point to hinge the curve—pulling the handle in a new direction
- **To attach a curve to a line:** Place the Pen tool on a line's anchor point and click-drag to pull out a direction handle for your next curve.
- **Use the Convert Anchor Point Tool** to smooth hinged anchor points and hinge curves.

The hollow snap-to arrow

As long as Snap to Point is enabled (View menu), you can grab objects from any path or point and drag until they snap to a guide or another anchor point. Watch for the cursor to change to a hollow (white) arrow.

Avoid these common mistakes:

- If you try to deselect by clicking outside your object while you still have the Pen tool chosen, you'll scatter extra points throughout your image, causing possible problems later. If you're aware that you clicked by mistake, Undo. To remove stray points, choose Edit > Select > Stray Points and then press Delete. (Or, alternatively, you can choose Object > Path > Clean Up.) The best solution is to remember to hold down the Ctrl (Win) or ⌘ (Mac) key when you click; the cursor will temporarily toggle to the Selection tool and you can safely click to deselect.
- If you try to delete an object that you selected with the Direct Selection tool, you'll delete only the selected point or path. What remains of the object will now be fully selected. Press Delete again to remove the remaining portions of your object.

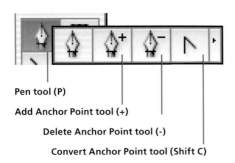

Pen tool (P)

Add Anchor Point tool (+)

Delete Anchor Point tool (-)

Convert Anchor Point tool (Shift C)

Add/Delete function of the Pen tool, hold down the Shift key. If you don't want the path to constrain to an angle, release the Shift key prior to releasing the mouse.

- **The Convert Anchor Point tool,** hidden within the Pen tool (default is Shift-C), converts an anchor point from a smooth curve to a corner point by simply clicking on it. To convert a corner point to a smooth curve, click-drag on the anchor point counterclockwise to pull out a new direction handle (or twirl the point until it straightens out the curve). To convert a smooth curve to a hinged curve (two curves hinged at a point), grab the direction point and hold Option/Alt as you drag out to the new position. With the Pen tool selected, you can temporarily access the Convert Anchor Point tool by pressing Option or Alt.

- **The Add Anchor Point tool,** accessible from the Pen pop-up menu or by pressing the + (plus) key, adds an anchor point to a path at the location where you click.

- **The Delete Anchor Point tool,** accessible from the Pen pop-up menu or by pressing – (minus), deletes an anchor point when you click directly on the point. **Note:** *If you select the Add/Delete Anchor Point tools by pressing + or –, press P to get back to the Pen tool.*

- **The Pencil tool** reshapes a selected path when Edit selected paths is checked in the tools preferences. Select a path and draw on or close to the path to reshape it. (For a Pencil lesson, see "Tracing Details" in the *Layers* chapter.)

- **The Smooth tool** smooths the points on already-drawn paths by smoothing corners and deleting points. As you move the Smooth tool over your path, it attempts to keep the original shape of the path as intact as possible.

- **The Erase tool** removes sections of a selected path. By dragging along the path you can erase or remove portions of it. You must drag along the path—drawing perpendicular to the path will result in unexpected effects. This tool adds a pair of anchor points to the remaining path, on either side of the erased section of the path.

- **The Scissors tool** cuts a path where you click by adding two disconnected, selected anchor points exactly on top of each other. To select just one of the points, deselect the object, then click with the Direct Selection tool on the spot where you cut. This will allow you to select the upper anchor point and drag it to the side in order to see the two points better.

- **The Knife tool** slices through all unlocked visible objects and closed paths. Simply drag the Knife tool across the object you want to slice, then select the object(s) you want to move or delete.

GEOMETRIC OBJECTS

The Ellipse, Rounded Rectangle, Polygon, and Star tools create objects called "geometric primitives." These objects are mathematically-described symmetrical paths grouped with a non-printing anchor point, which indicates the center. Use the centers of the geometric objects to snap-align them with each other, or with other objects and guides. You can create these geometric objects numerically or manually. Access the tools in the pop-up palette from the Rectangle tool in the Toolbox. (See the *Zen of Illustrator* chapter for exercises in creating and manipulating geometric objects, and Tip at right.)

- **To create a geometric shape manually,** select the desired geometric tool, and click-drag to form the object from one corner to the other. To create the object from the center, hold down the Option (Mac)/Alt (Win) key and drag from the center outward (keep the Option/Alt key down until you release the mouse button to ensure that it draws from the center). Once you have drawn the geometric objects, you can edit them exactly as you do other paths.

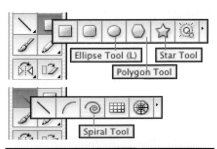

Serious fun with shapes

The Ellipse (select by typing "L"), Polygon, Star, and Spiral are simple, but powerful, tools. Used with these key combinations, you may find them indispensable:

- **Spacebar-drag** allows you to re-position your object.
- **Shift** constrains the object's proportions.
- **Up-arrow (↑)** increases points on a star, sides on a polygon, and coils on a spiral.
- **Down-arrow (↓)** removes points from a star, sides from a polygon, and coils from a spiral.
- **Option (Mac)/Alt (Win)** increases the angle of the star's points.
- **⌘-drag** changes the inside and outside radius of a star, or increases or decreases the decay in a spiral.
- **~-drag (tilde-drag)** creates multiple objects based on the speed and length of your drag. Try it using the Star tool with stroke, but no fill.
- **Combinations**: Experiment with all the keys separately and in combination with the other keys. Doing so is the only way to fully understand these fun tools.

Drawing freehand while holding a mouse or even a digital pen can be less than elegant. The Pencil, Smooth, and Brush tools contain options that can help you to create more types of paths, ranging from very realistic to more shapely and graceful ones, without the constant need to adjust anchor points. Double-click on the tool to view the options.

- **Fidelity:** Increases or decreases the distance between anchor points on the path created or edited. The smaller the number, the more points that will make up the path and vice versa.
- **Smoothness:** The smoothness option varies the percentage of smoothness you'll see as you create and edit paths. Use a lower percentage of smoothness for more realistic lines and brush strokes, and a higher percentage for less realistic but more elegant lines.

Note: *Closing Pencil and Brush tool paths is a bit awkward. If you hold down the Option (Mac)/Alt (Win) key when you are ready to close a path, a straight line segment will be drawn between the first and last anchor points. If you hold down the Option/Alt key and extend slightly past the first anchor point, the path will close automatically. Set the tool preferences to low numbers to make closing easier. — Sandee Cohen*

- **To create a geometric object with numeric input,** select a geometric tool and click on the Artboard to establish the upper left corner of your object. Enter the desired dimensions in the dialog box and click OK. To create the object numerically from the object's center, Option-click (Mac)/Alt-click (Win) on the Artboard.

To draw an arc, select the Arc tool and then click and drag to start drawing the arc. Press the "F" key to flip the arc from convex to concave, and use the up and down Arrow keys to adjust the radius of the arc. Pressing the "C" key will "close" the arc by drawing the perpendicular lines that form the axes, and pressing the "X" key will flip the arc without moving these axes ("F" flips both the arc and the axes). Release the mouse to finish the arc.

To draw a grid, select either the Rectangular Grid tool or the Polar Grid tool and click-drag to start drawing the grid. You can control the shape of the grid by pressing various keys as you draw (see the *User Guide* for details). Release the mouse to finish the grid.

SELECTING & GROUPING OBJECTS
Selecting

The Select menu gives you easy access to basic selection commands, including the ability to select specific types of objects and attributes. You can use the Selection tools to select individual or multiple objects. You can use the target indicators in the Layers palette to select and target objects, groups, and layers. Targeting a group or layer selects everything contained within it, and makes the group or layer the focus of the Appearance and Graphic Styles palettes. (For more on targeting and selecting via the Layers palette, see the *Layers* chapter.)

Use the Lasso tool to select an entire path or multiple paths by encircling them. Option (Mac)/Alt (Win) + the Lasso tool subtracts entire paths from a selection. Shift + Lasso tool adds entire paths to a selection.

You can also use the Lasso tool to select individual anchor points or path segments by encircling them with the tool. Option (Mac)/Alt (Win) + Lasso tool subtracts anchor points from a selection. Shift + Lasso tool adds anchor points to a selection.

Grouping and selecting

Many programs provide you with a grouping function so you can act upon multiple objects as one unit. In Illustrator, grouping objects places all the objects on the same layer and creates a <group> container in the Layers palette; remember don't choose group if you want your objects on different layers. (For more on layers and objects, see the *Layers* chapter.) So, when *do* you want to group objects? Group objects when you need to select them *repeatedly* as a unit or want to apply an appearance to the entire group. Take an illustration of a bicycle as an example. Use the Group function to group the spokes of a wheel. Next, group the two wheels of the bicycle, then group the wheels with the frame. We will continue to refer to this bicycle below.

- **With the Direct Selection tool.** Click on a point or path with the Direct Selection tool to select that point or portion of the path. If you click on a spoke of a wheel, you'll select the portion of the spoke's path you clicked on.

- **With the Selection tool.** Click on an object with the Selection tool to select the largest group containing that object. In our example, it would be the entire bicycle.

- **With the Group Selection tool.** Use the Group Selection tool to select sub groupings progressively. The first click with the Group Selection tool selects a single object. The next click selects the entire spoke path. The third click selects the entire wheel, the fourth selects both wheels, and the fifth, the entire bicycle.
Note: *To grab and move objects selected with the Group Selection tool, you must change to one of the other selection tools or, during a selection, drag without releasing the mouse. When you continually click with the Group Selection tool, you're always selecting the next group up.*

If you can't group...

If you try to group objects and get the message "Can't make a group of objects that are within different groups":

- Make certain that the objects to be grouped are fully selected.
- Cut the objects.
- Use Paste in Front or Paste in Back to paste the objects back into your image in exactly the same location (see introduction to the *Layers* chapter). While the objects are still selected, select Object > Group.

Selection tool	Direct Selection tool	Group Selection tool

Efficient ungrouping

To select an object in a group, you don't need to ungroup it; just use the Group Selection tool. To group, select the objects and ⌘-G (Mac)/Ctrl-G (Win). If you want to ungroup, select the group with the Selection tool and Ungroup once for each level of grouping you wish to remove. For the example of the bicycle (given in the "Grouping and Selecting" section), selecting the entire bicycle and pressing ⌘-Shift-G (Mac)/Ctrl-Shift-G (Win) the first time would remove the last grouping applied; typing it four times would remove all the groupings.

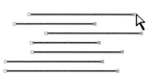

- **See the "Finger Dance" lessons in the Zen chapter.** This section includes a variety of selection exercises.

JOINING & AVERAGING

Two of Illustrator's most useful functions are Average and Join (both found under the Object > Path menu or in the Context-sensitive menu). Use the Average function to sandwich two endpoints on top of each other. Use the Join function to join two endpoints. The Join function will operate differently depending on the objects.

Averaging also allows you to align selected *points*. (To align objects, use the Align palette.) To average, use the Direct Selection tool or Lasso tool to marquee-select or Shift-select any number of points belonging to any number of objects. Then use the Context-sensitive menu (for the Mac hold the Control key, use the right mouse button for Windows) to average, aligning the selected points horizontally, vertically, or along both axes.

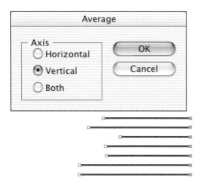

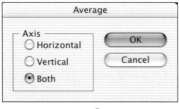

Using the Average command to align selected endpoints vertically, then choosing Both

- **If the two open endpoints are exactly on top of each other,** then Join opens a dialog box asking if the join should be a smooth point or a corner. A smooth point is a curved Bézier anchor that smoothly joins two curves, with direction handles that always move together; a corner point is any other point connecting two paths. Once you've clicked OK in the dialog box, both points will fuse into a single point. However, keep in mind that a true smooth point will only result if the proper conditions exist: namely, that the two curves that you are trying to join have the potential to join together into a smooth curve. Otherwise, you'll get a corner point, even if you chose Smooth in the dialog box.

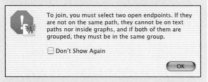

Joining warning

If you get an error message that you can't join points, do the following—in addition to the conditions in the warning:

> To join, you must select two open endpoints. If they are not on the same path, they cannot be on text paths nor inside graphs, and if both of them are grouped, they must be in the same group.
>
> ☐ Don't Show Again
>
> OK

- Make sure you've selected only two points (no third stray point selected by mistake).
- Make sure you've selected *end-points*, not midpoints.

- **If the two open endpoints are not exactly on top of each other,** then Join will connect the two points with a line. If you try to Join two points to fuse as one but don't get a dialog box, then you've merely connected your points with a line! Undo (⌘-Z for Mac/Ctrl-Z for Windows) and see "Averaging & Joining in one step" below.

- **If you select an open path** (in this case, you don't need to select the endpoints), then Join closes the path.

- **If the two open endpoints are on different objects,** then Join connects the two paths into one.

- **Averaging & Joining in one step.** Use the following keyboard command: ⌘-Option-Shift-J (Mac)/Ctrl-Alt-Shift-J (Win); there is no menu equivalent! The command forms a corner when joining two lines, or a hinged corner when joining a line or curve to a curve.

WORKING WITH PALETTES

Most of Illustrator's palettes are accessible via the Window menu. Each palette is unique, but they all share common features:

- **You can regroup tabbed palettes to save desktop space.** Reduce the space that palettes require by nesting the palettes together into smaller groups. Grab a palette's tab and drag it to another palette group to nest it. You can also drag a tab to the *bottom* of a palette to dock the palettes on top of one another.

- **You can make most palettes smaller or larger.** If there's a sizing icon in the lower right corner, click and drag it to shrink or expand the palette. Palettes also have pop-up menus offering additional options. If a palette contains more options, it will have an double arrow to the left of the palette name. Click on the arrows to cycle through the various options. Click the square (minimize box), on the top of the title bar to shrink all palettes docked or nested together down to just title bars and tabs. Click the right square again, and the palettes will re-expand. Double-click the title bar to cycle through the states, from maximum to collapsed.

- **Reset palettes easily.** Certain palettes (including the Character, Paragraph and OpenType palettes) contain a

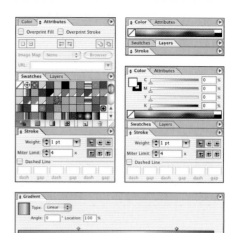

Modes of expansion for docked palettes; lower figure is Gradient palette, alone and expanded

Typing units into palettes

To use the current unit of measurement, type the number, then Tab to the next text field or press Return. To use another unit of measurement, *follow* the number with "in" or " (inch), "pt" (point), "p" (pica), or "mm" (millimeter) and Return. To resume typing into an image text block, press Shift-Return. You can also enter calculations in palettes: for example, if you were specifying the size of a rectangle, you could type 72 pt + 2 cm for the height. Illustrator would then perform the calculation and apply the result. Partial calculations work as well; if you type + 2, Illustrator will add two of whatever unit you're currently using. Try it!

Teeny tiny palettes

Double-click the tab name or the space to the right of the tab, or single-click the double arrows on the tab to cycle through expanded and collapsed views of the palette. Only palettes with more options have double arrows on the palette tab.

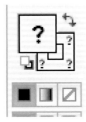

The original objects

Objects selected (the bottom of the Toolbox indicates different strokes and fills are selected)

Palette be gone!

If you want to get rid of the various palettes on your screen temporarily, it's easy to do. Just press Tab to hide the palettes and Toolbox; then press Tab when you want to toggle them into view again. If you'd rather keep the Toolbox visible and just hide the other palettes, use Shift-Tab.

Reset Palette command that allows you to easily restore the palette's default settings.

- **You must select your object(s) before you can make changes.** With your objects selected, you can click on the label or inside any edit box in the palette containing text and begin typing. If you're typing something that has limited choices (such as a font or type style), Illustrator will attempt to complete your word; just keep typing until your choice is visible. If you're typing into a text field, use the Tab key to move to other text fields within the palette. **IMPORTANT:** *When you've finished typing into palette text fields, you must press Return (or Enter). This action signals the application that you are ready to enter text somewhere else or to resume manipulating your artwork.*

- **There are many ways to fill or stroke an object.** Focus on a selected object's fill or stroke by clicking on the Fill or Stroke icon near the bottom of the Toolbox, or toggle between them with the X key. To set the stroke or fill to None, use the / (slash) key. Set your color by: 1) adjusting the sliders or sampling a color from the color ramp in the Color palette, 2) clicking on a swatch in the Swatches palette, 3) sampling colors from the color picker, or 4) using the Eyedropper to sample from other objects in your file. In addition, you can drag color swatches from palettes to selected objects or to the Fill/Stroke icon in the Toolbox.

- **Objects, groups of objects, or layers can have appearances associated with them.** *Appearance attributes* are properties that affect the look of an object without affecting its underlying structure—such as strokes, fills, transparency and effects. The term *appearance* is used in this book to refer to an object's appearance attributes collectively. All objects have an appearance, even if that appearance is no stroke and no fill.

- **You can apply a graphic style to an object, group of objects, or a layer.** The total sum of applied characteristics can be saved as a style in the Graphic Styles palette. *Graphic styles* are "live" (updatable) combinations of fills, strokes, blending modes, opacity, and effects. For details about working with the Graphic Styles palette, see the *Live Effects & Graphic Styles* chapter, especially the chapter introduction and the "Scratchboard Art" lesson.

GRAPHING & CHARTING

Using the Graph tools, Illustrator allows you to create charts and graphs in nine different styles. If you're new to charts or graphs, be sure to read "Creating Graphs" in the "Advanced Drawing Chapter" of the *User Guide*. Please keep in mind that the purpose of a chart or graph is clear communication of numeric information as a visual aid. A properly selected chart design will accomplish this. If you create a lot of charts or graphs, look into a specialty graphic application. Before you begin, set a default chart or graph style by double-clicking on a Graph tool and choosing the style you want. To produce your graph, use the Graph tool you've chosen as you would use the Rectangle tool: either click-drag to create a rectangular object from corner to corner, or click with the tool to numerically specify the dimensions of your graph.

After you establish the dimensions, the Graph dialog box opens, awaiting input of numeric data. Enter labels and numbers by highlighting the desired cell and typing into the entry line along the top. Tab to enter text in the next horizontal cell. See the PDF version of the *User Guide* on the application CD to determine how you should enter data for the specific graph style you want. **Note:** *It's very easy to enter text into the wrong field by mistake; so be meticulous. Mistakes are difficult to correct.*

Alternatively, you can import data that's been saved in *Tab-delineated* text format. Most word processing, spreadsheet, or charting programs let you save or export data and labels as text, separated by Tabs and Returns.

To change the style of an existing graph, select the entire graph with the Selection tool and double-click on the current Graph tool in the Toolbox. Choose another

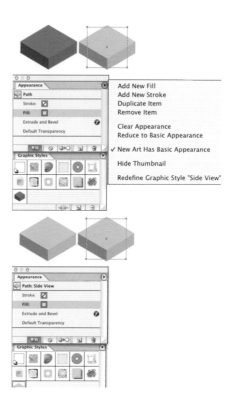

To update or replace a graphic style throughout the entire document, select an object and apply the style you want to modify and update. With the object selected, make changes to its appearance and choose Replace Graphic Style from the Appearance palette menu. The name of the style will display next to the replace command. This will globally update all objects using this named graphic style. To change the name of the style, double-click on the proxy in the Graphic Styles palette and rename it.

If you want to continue to work with your graph numerically, *don't*, under any circumstances, ungroup your graph; it will make numerical data changes impossible. To avoid losing the special graph formatting, follow these special precautions:

- Using the Selection tool, select the entire graph for changes in style. With the graph selected, 1) Double-click the current Graph tool to change the graph style; or 2) Choose Object > Graph > Data to change numeric data; or 3) To apply shaped design elements, see "Customizing graph designs" in this section.
- Use the Group Selection tool to select a category of data, then restyle or recolor as desired.
- Use the Direct Selection tool to select individual elements to change their styling.
- Use the Direct Selection tool or Type tool to select and change individual text elements.

Once you're *completely* finished numerically adjusting a graph, you may wish to delete some objects. Select the graph (with the Selection tool) and Ungroup (⌘-U/Ctrl-U). Once ungrouped, the objects are no longer part of a graph and can be deleted.

style and click OK. Be aware that some types of charts may not be translatable to all other formats.

To re-access a graph's numeric data, save your graph, then select your graph with the Selection tool and choose Object > Graph > Data. There is no Cancel command in data entry, but you can always use Undo (⌘-Z/Ctrl-Z).

Customizing graph designs

Being able to insert design elements into a graph is a snazzy—but overused—aspect of the graphing feature. Illustrator allows you to define graph designs, which can be used as substitutes for rectangular column bars and line markers. For instance, using the "scaling" option, you can take a heart-shaped design and incorporate it into a graph by stretching (vertically scaling) or enlarging (uniformly scaling) the heart to the correct height. A variant of this technique allows you to define a portion of the heart to be scaled (called the "Sliding" Design). By using the "repeating" option, you can stack the hearts on top of each other until they reach the correct height.

Here's how to define a graph design element. After creating the object(s) you wish to use as a design element, select the object(s) and choose Object > Graph > Design. In the dialog box, click the New Design button; your creation will appear in the list of designs with the name "New Design." To give it a distinctive name, make sure "New Design" is selected in the list, click the Rename button, and name your design. To apply the design, use the Selection tool to select a previously created graph, and choose Object > Graph > Column. In the Graph Column dialog box, select your new design from the list and choose from the options that determine how your design will be adapted to the column size (e.g. whether it's scaled or repeating, how many units each incidence of the design represents, how fractions of that amount are represented, etc.) You can also use design elements to serve as "markers" (indicating plotted points) for line and scatter graph styles. Follow the above procedure to create and name your design, select your graph, and choose Object >

Graph > Marker to select the previously defined design that will be used as a marker in the graph.

Some of the nation's busiest newspapers and periodicals say that even though they may finish their charts and graphs in Illustrator, most use other programs to translate numbers into graphics. Fortunately for those using Mac OS X, documents from other programs (like Microsoft Excel) can be easily converted to Illustrator documents using OS X's built-in support for PDF format. The Print dialog box in many OS X applications contains a Save as PDF button, and/or a Preview option that can be saved as a PDF. The resulting PDF can be opened in Illustrator.

TRANSFORMATIONS

Moving, scaling, rotating, reflecting, and shearing are all operations that transform selected objects. Begin by selecting what you wish to transform. If you don't like a transformation you've just applied, use Undo before applying a new transformation—or you'll end up applying the new transformation on top of the previous one. In Illustrator, you can perform most transformations manually (see the *Zen of Illustrator* chapter for exercises), through a dialog box for numeric accuracy, with the Free Transform tool (as an effect), or with the Transform palette. In addition, you can select more than one object and choose Object > Transform > Transform Each. Illustrator remembers the last transformation you performed, storing those numbers in the appropriate dialog box until you enter a new transform value or restart the program. For example, if you previously scaled an image and disabled Scale Strokes & Effects, the next time you scale (manually or numerically), your strokes and effects won't scale.

The bounding box

The bounding box should not be confused with the Free Transform tool (which allows you to perform additional functions; see discussion of the Free Transform tool below). The bounding box appears around selected objects when you are using the Selection tool (solid

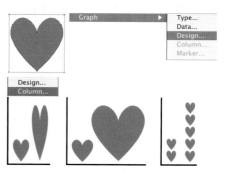

Defining a design; using the heart to create columns vertically scaled; uniformly scaled; forming a repeating design

Using graphs as templates

Designers use the Graph tools to plot points and generate the scale and legend. They create an illustration that uses the placement of the graph as a guide. See the *Brushes & Symbols* chapter for help in locking the graph for use as a template.

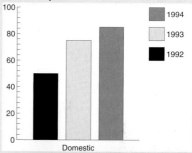

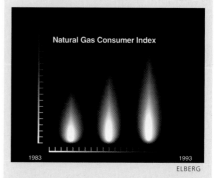

Eve Elberg used this bar graph as a template to plot the basic points in this illustration. For the glowing effect, she used blends and gradients (see the Blends, Gradients & Mesh *chapter)*

Try defining a graph design element using a symbol. Then you can update your graph easily just by redefining the symbol. (See the *Brushes & Symbols* chapter for more info on symbols.)

Moving complex images

If the Transform palette fails, create a proxy rectangle closely surrounding the objects you wish to move. Move the proxy in one motion to the desired location, and delete. To apply the move, select your objects, double-click the Selection arrow, and click OK.

Free Transform variations

With the Free Transform tool you can apply the following transformations to selected objects:

- **Rotate**—click outside the bounding box and drag.
- **Scale**—click on a corner of the bounding box and drag. Option-drag/Alt-drag to scale from the center and Shift-drag to scale proportionally.
- **Distort**—click on a corner handle of the bounding box and ⌘-drag/Ctrl-drag.
- **Shear**—click on a side handle of the bounding box and ⌘-drag/Ctrl-drag the handle.
- **Perspective**—click on a corner handle of the bounding box and ⌘-Option-drag/Ctrl-Alt-Shift-drag.

arrow), and can be useful for quick moving, scaling, rotating, or duplicating objects. With the bounding box, you can easily scale several objects at once. Select the objects, click on a corner of the bounding box and drag. To constrain proportionally while scaling, hold down the Shift key and drag a corner. By default, the bounding box is on. Toggle it on/off via the View > Hide/Show Bounding Box, or switch to the Direct Selection tool to hide the bounding box. To reset the bounding box after performing a transformation so it's once again square to the page, choose Object > Transform > Reset Bounding Box.

Note: *Holding down the Option or Alt key when you transform with the bounding box will not create a duplicate, but will instead transform from the center.*

Moving

In addition to grabbing and dragging objects manually, you can specify a new location numerically: Double-click the Selection arrow in the Toolbox or use the Context-sensitive menu to bring up the Move dialog box (select the Preview option). For help determining the distance you wish to move, click-drag with the Measure tool the distance you wish to calculate. Then *immediately* open the Move dialog box to see the measured distance loaded automatically, and click OK (or press Return/Enter).

The Free Transform tool

The Free Transform tool can be an easy way to transform objects once you learn the numerous keyboard combinations to take advantage of its functions. In addition to performing transformations such as rotate, scale, and shear, you can also create perspective and distortions (see the Tip "Free Transform variations" at left, and the "Distort Dynamics" lesson in the *Drawing & Coloring* chapter). Bear in mind that the Free Transform tool bases its transformations on a fixed center point that can not be relocated. If you need to transform from a different location, use the individual transformation tools, Transformation palette, or the Transform Each command.

The Transform palette

From this palette, you can determine numeric transformations that specify an object's width, height, and location on the document and how much to rotate or shear it. You can also access a palette pop-up menu that offers options to Flip Horizontal and Vertical; Transform Object, Pattern, or Both; and to enable Scale Strokes & Effects. The current Transform palette is a bit odd: You can Transform Again once you've applied a transformation, but the information in the text fields is not always retained. To maintain your numeric input, apply transformations through the transform tool's dialog box, discussed on the next page.

Individual transformation tools

For scaling, rotation, reflection, and shearing of objects with adjustable center points, you can click (to manually specify the center about which the transformation will occur), then grab your object to transform it. For practice with manual transformations see the *Zen* chapter. Each transformation tool has a dialog box where you can specify: the parameters for the tool, whether to transform the object or make a copy with the specified transform applied, and whether to transform just the objects and/or any patterns they may be filled with. (For more on transforming patterns see the *Drawing & Coloring* chapter.)

Here are three additional methods you can use to apply the individual transformation tools to objects:

- **Double-click on a transformation tool** to access the dialog box. This allows you to transform the objects numerically, originating from an object's center.

- **Option (Mac)/Alt (Win)-click on your image with a transformation tool** to access the dialog box that allows you to transform your objects numerically, originating from where you clicked.

Transform again

Illustrator remembers the last transformation you performed—from simple moves to rotating a *copy* of an object. Use the Context-sensitive menu to repeat the effect (Transform Again).

Transform palette modifiers

To modify your transformations when you press Return, hold down Option (Mac)/Alt (Win) to transform and make a copy. Click a point in the Transform palette to select a reference point.

Scaling objects to an exact size

- *The Transform palette way:* Type the new width or height in the palette and press ⌘-Return (Mac)/Ctrl-Return (Win). (Click the lock icon in the palette to scale proportionately.)

- *The proxy way:* Create a proxy rectangle the size of your image, then from the upper left corner of the proxy, Option/Alt-click to create another rectangle in the target dimensions. With your proxy selected, click with the Scale tool in the upper left and grab-drag the lower right to match the target. (Hold Shift to scale in only one dimension.) Delete these rectangles, select you objects, double-click the Scale tool and apply settings.

- **Click-drag on your image with a transformation tool** to transform the selected objects, originating from the center of the group of selected objects.

Reshape & Shear

The Reshape tool is quite different from the other transformation tools. Start by Direct-selecting the paths you wish to reshape. If you use the Selection tool by mistake, the entire path will move, and if you haven't made any selection you won't be able to use the tool. Next, choose the Reshape tool from the Scale tool pop-up menu. With this tool, marquee or Shift-select all points you wish to affect, then drag the points to reshape the path. The selected points move as a group, but instead of all moving the same distance, as they would if you dragged with the Direct Selection tool, the points closer to the cursor move more, and the ones farther away move less.

You will also find the Shear tool hidden within the Scale tool. It's used to slant objects.

Transform Each

To perform multiple transformations at once, open the Transform Each dialog box (Object > Transform > Transform Each). You can perform the transformations on several objects or on a single one. Additions to this dialog box include the ability to reflect objects over the X and Y axes, and to change the point of origin. If you want to apply a transformation, but you think you might want to change it later, try a Transformation Effect (see the *Transparency & Appearances* chapter).

WORKING SMART
Saving strategies

Probably the most important advice you'll ever get is to save every few minutes. Whenever you make a substantial change to your image, use File > Save As and give your image a new name.

It's much more time-efficient to save incremental versions of your image than it is to reconstruct an earlier version. Back up your work at least once a day before you shut down. Just think to yourself, "If this computer never starts up again, what will I need?" Develop a backup system using CDs, DVDs, Zip or Jaz drives, DATs (digital audio tapes), or opticals so you can archive all of your work. Use a program such as Dantz's Retrospect to automatically add new and changed files to your archives.

Get in the habit of archiving virtually everything, and develop a file-naming system that actually helps you keep track of your work in progress—simplifying your recovery of a working version if necessary. A good system involves three components. First, start with a meaningful description of your current image ("hearts compound"), and second, add a numerical notation of the version ("1.0"). Keep your numbering system consecutive, regardless of the label, throughout the entire project. Keep the number in a decimal sequence when you make an incremental change to your image ("1.1, 1.2, 1.3…"). Change to the next numeric sequence when you make a substantive change ("2.0"). Don't start numbers at 1.0 for each phase of the project or you'll be unable to figure out which came first: "Sky 1.0" or "Heart 1.0." Instead, if labels are "Sky 1.0" and "Heart 4.0," then the creation order is self-explanatory. Third, add a suffix to indicate its file type (.ai for Illustrator, .psd for Photoshop, .eps for Encapsulated PostScript file). Also, make sure that you keep all files in a named and dated folder that distinguishes them from other projects. (For saving in other formats see "Image Formats" later in this chapter.)

Multiple Undos

Some programs give you only one chance to undo your last move. Illustrator CS allows "unlimited undos," which, practically speaking, means that the number of undos you can perform is limited only by how much memory you have available.

Even *after* you save a file, your Undos (and Redos) will still be available (as long as you haven't closed and reopened the file), making it possible for you to save the

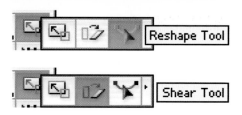

Reshape Tool

Shear Tool

The selected area indicated in red

Direct-selected and dragged wing objects

HESS

For Eric Hess's "Soaring Hearts Futons" logo, he roughly Direct-selected, then with Reshape he marqueed as indicated above, and dragged

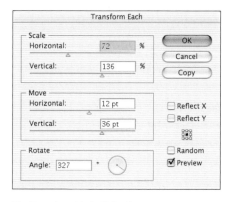

The Transform Each dialog box (Object >Transform >Transform Each)

current version, undo it to a previous stage and save it, or continue working from an earlier state. But once you close your file, your undos are cleared from memory, so they won't be available the next time you open the file.

You can also revert the file to the most recently saved version by choosing File > Revert, but you can't undo a revert, so you'll want to be careful.

Note: *Not all operations are undoable. For example, changes to Preferences aren't affected by Undo.*

CHANGING YOUR VIEWS
Preview and Outline

To control the speed of your screen redraw, learn to make use of the Preview mode and the Outline mode (formerly Artwork mode), which can be toggled in the View menu. In Preview mode, you view the document in full color; in Outline mode you see only the wire frames of the objects.

Illustrator CS also adds a great new way to control the speed and quality of your screen redraws when using the Hand Tool. In the Units & Display Performance area of Preferences, there's a Display Performance slider for the Hand Tool that lets you set your own preferred balance between speed and quality of redraws.

New View

New View (View > New View) allows you to save your current window viewpoint, remembering also your zoom level and which layers are hidden, locked, or in Preview mode. Custom views are added to the bottom of the View menu to let you easily recall a saved view. You can rename a view, but the views themselves are not editable—if you need to make a change to a view, you'll have to make a New View.

New Window

Illustrator gives you the ability to display different aspects of your current image simultaneously. This allows you to separately view different Proof Setups, Overprint or Pixel Previews, and zoom levels. You can resize them, have edges hidden or visible, or hide or lock different *layers* in Preview or Outline (see the *Layers* chapter and "Hide/ Show Edges" later in this chapter). Most window configurations are saved with the file.

Window controls

There are three small icons at the very bottom of the Toolbox. One is always selected; this is the default in which Illustrator displays your file window. Starting at the far left, choose from Standard Screen mode (desktop showing around the edges of your file), Full Screen mode with menu bar (file window visible, but confined to the center of the screen with no desktop showing; you can access your menu bar) and Full Screen mode (same as above, but you cannot access your menu bar). You can toggle among the views by pressing the "F" key.

ZOOMING IN & OUT

Illustrator provides many ways to zoom in and out.

- **From the View menu.** Choose Zoom In/Out, Actual Size, or Fit in Window.

- **With the Zoom tool.** Click to zoom in one level of magnification; hold down the Option (Mac)/Alt (Win) key and click to zoom out one level. You can also click-drag to define an area, and Illustrator will attempt to fill the current window with the area that you defined.

- **Use the shortcut ⌘ (Mac)/Ctrl (Win) for Zoom.** With any tool selected, use ⌘-hyphen (Mac)/Ctrl-hyphen (Win)—think "minus to zoom out"—and ⌘+ (Mac)/ Ctrl+ (Win)—think "plus to zoom in".

- **Use Context-sensitive menus.** With nothing selected, Control-click (Mac) or use the right mouse button (Windows) to access a pop-up menu so you can zoom in and out, change views, undo, and show or hide guides, rulers, and grids.

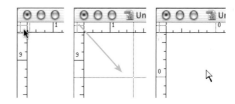

Grabbing and dragging the ruler corner to recenter the ruler origin (zero point)

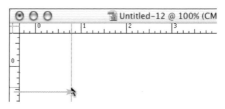

Clicking inside the ruler and dragging into your image to create a vertical or horizontal guide

The Navigator palette (always in Preview mode) offers many ways to zoom in and out of documents:

- Double-click the mountain icons along the bottom edge of the palette window to increase or decrease the amount of zoom in 200% increments.
- Hold the ⌘ (Mac)/Ctrl (Win)-key drag to marquee the area in the palette thumbnail that you want to zoom into or out from.
- Enable View Artboard Only to keep your view limited to the Artboard area. This is helpful if you are working on a large document with objects on the pasteboard that are distracting your focus.

Change the color of the border around the thumbnail in the View Options dialog box (found in the Navigator palette pop-up menu).

Note: *Navigator might slow down files with a lot of text objects. The Navigator creates a thumbnail view of the document; every time you zoom or scroll, the Navigator must redraw its thumbnail. Unless you need to view the Navigator palette, close it.*

If you have many file windows open, simply select the file you want to bring to the front from the list of files at the bottom of the Window menu.

- **Navigator palette.** With the Navigator palette, you can quickly zoom in or out and change the viewing area with the help of the palette thumbnail (see Tip "The Navigator palette & views" at left).

SHOW/HIDE CHOICES

From the View menu, you can show and hide several items, such as grids, guides, smart guides, transparency grid, edges, Artboard, and page tilings.

Rulers, Guides, Smart Guides, and Grids

Toggle Illustrator's Show/Hide Rulers, or use the ⌘-R / Crtl-R shortcut, or use the Context-sensitive menu (as long as nothing in your document is selected). The per-document ruler units are set in Document Setup. If you want all new documents to use a specific unit of measurement, change your preferences for Units (Preferences > Units & Display Performance).

In some previous versions of Illustrator, the ruler origin (where 0,0 is) was in the lower right corner of the image. In Illustrator CS, the location of the ruler origin depends on the tiling options you've chosen in the Setup area of the Print dialog box. Generally, if you've chosen either Single Full Page or Tile Full Pages, the origin will be in the lower left corner. To change the ruler origin, grab the upper left corner (where the vertical and horizontal rulers meet) and drag the crosshair to the desired location. The zeros of the rulers will reset to the point where you release your mouse (to reset the rulers to the default location, double-click the upper left corner). But beware—resetting your ruler origin will realign all patterns and affect alignment of Paste in Front/Back between documents (see the *Layers* chapter for more on Paste in Front/Back).

To create simple vertical or horizontal ruler guides, click-drag from one of the rulers into your image. A guide appears where you release your mouse. You can define guide color and style in General Preferences. Guides automatically lock after you create them. To release a guide quickly, ⌘-Shift-double-click/ Ctrl-Shift-double-click on the guide. You can lock and unlock guides with the Context-sensitive menu in Preview mode. You should note that locking or unlocking guides affects *every* open document. If you have too many guides visible in your document, simply choose View > Guides > Clear Guides. This only works on guides that are on visible, unlocked layers. Hiding or locking layers retains any guides you have created (see the *Layers* chapter). To learn how to create custom guides from objects or paths, see the "Varied Perspective" lesson in the *Layers* chapter.

Smart Guides can be somewhat unnerving when you see them flash on and off as you work. However, with practice and understanding of each option, you'll be able to refine how to incorporate them into your work flow. Illustrator also has automatic grids. To view grids, select View > Show Grid, or use the Context-sensitive menu. You can adjust the color, style of line (dots or solid), and size of the grid's subdivisions from File > Preferences > Guides & Grid. As with guides, you can also enable a snap-to grid function. Toggle Snap to Grid on and off by choosing View > Snap to Grid (see Tip "Glorious grids" at right). **IMPORTANT:** *If you adjust the X and Y axes in Preferences > General > Constrain Angle, it will affect the drawn objects and transformations of your grid, as they will follow the adjusted angle when you create a new object. This works out well if you happen to be doing a complicated layout requiring alignment of objects at an angle.*

Transparency Grid & Simulate Color Paper

Now that Illustrator can use transparency, you might want to change the background of the Artboard to the transparency grid, or better yet, to a color. Both the transparency grid and simulated color paper are non-printable attributes.

To view the transparency grid, select View > Show Transparency Grid. Change the grid colors in the Transparency panel of the Document Setup dialog box. If you change both grid colors to the same color, you can change

Zippy zooming

Current magnification is displayed in the bottom left corner of your document. Access a list of percentages (3.13% to 6400%) or Fit on Screen from the pop-up, or simply select the text and enter any percentage within the limit.

Glorious grids

Customize your grids in Illustrator. Select a grid style and color.

- View > Show Grid, use the Context-sensitive menu or ⌘ (Mac)/ Ctrl (Win)-' *apostrophe.*
- Toggle Snap to Grid on and off from the View menu or use the shortcut ⌘ (Mac)/Ctrl (Win)-Shift-' *apostrophe.*
- Set the division and subdivision for your grid in Preferences > Guides & Grid and choose either dotted divisions or lines and the color of those lines.
- To toggle the grid display in front or in back of your artwork, check or uncheck the Grids In Back checkbox (Preferences > Guides & Grid).
- Tilt the grid on an angle by choosing Preferences > General and then changing the Constrain Angle value.

Note: *The Constrain Angle affects the angle at which objects are drawn and moved. (See the **Drawing & Coloring** chapter on how to adjust it for creating isometrics.)*

There are a multitude of Smart Guide preferences. Here's what each one does:

- Text Label Hints provide information about an object when the cursor passes over it—helpful for identifying a specific object within complicated artwork.
- Construction Guides are the temporary guidelines that help you align between objects and anchor points.
- Transform Tools help with transformations.
- Object Highlighting enables the anchor point, center point, and path of a deselected object to appear as your cursor passes within a specified tolerance from the object. This can be very useful for aligning objects. For best alignment results, select an object's anchor point or center point.

Note: *Smart Guides will slow you down when working on very large files. Also, you can't align using Smart Guides if View > Snap to Grid is enabled.*

When you toggle to Hide Edges and have Show Bounding Box enabled (both in the View menu), the bounding box will remain visible while the anchor points and paths of objects will be hidden.

the white background to a color (see the Transparency chapter).

Hide/Show Edges

If looking at all those anchor points and colored paths distracts you from figuring out what to do with selected objects in your current window, choose View > Hide/Show Edges to toggle them on or off. (Or use the shortcut: ⌘-H/Crtl-H.) Once you hide the edges, all subsequent path edges will be hidden until you show them again. Hide/Show Edges is saved with your file.

COLOR IN ILLUSTRATOR

Consumer-level monitors, which display color in red, green, and blue lights (RGB), cannot yet match four-color CMYK (cyan, magenta, yellow, black) inks printed onto paper. Therefore, you must retrofit the current technology with partial solutions, starting with calibrating your monitor.

Some programs (such as the Apple Display Calibrator, found in the Apple Displays control panel) provide some degree of control over the way your monitor displays colors. ColorSync (Mac) and Kodak Digital Science Color Management (Windows) are the two main systems. The colors displayed on the screen will be closer to the color you output if you follow a few key steps (see the *User Guide* for more information on using color management).

In addition to color management through software calibration, methods of hardware calibration are available that actually adjust the beams of the cathode-ray tube emitting the RGB lights. Generally, the larger the monitor, the more likely the colors will vary in different areas of the screen. Monitor color is also affected by the length of time your monitor is on and the ambient light in your workroom.

In order to produce an accurate proof (if a printing press is your target), Illustrator needs to support printing profiles for both composite (your printer) and separation (the final printing device) ICC(M) printers. Illustrator now supports ICC(M) profiles for both types of printing, although it is still not possible to emulate the separation printer on the composite printer. It is, however, possible to use Illustrator for proofing directly on your screen and for printing a more accurate proof to your printer when you are not soft proofing to the screen. If you are creating art for placement into QuarkXPress, InDesign, or Page-Maker, there is no application-level color management module currently supporting the EPS file format. Always consult with your pre-press house and run a proof prior to printing an entire job.

Working in RGB or CMYK

Illustrator offers you the flexibility of working and print-ing in either RGB or CMYK color. This is a mixed bless-ing, because the printing environment cannot accurately capture vibrant RGB colors. As a result, the RGB colors are usually muddy or muted when printed. If your final artwork is going to be printed, work in CMYK!

Work in an RGB color space when creating artwork that will be displayed on-screen, or to simulate a spot color (such as a day-glo color) on your printer. (For more on working in RGB, see the *Web & Animation* chapter.)

Single color space

When you open a new document, you select a color model (or color space). Illustrator no longer allows you to work in multiple color spaces at the same time. If you work in print, always check your files to make certain they are in the appropriate color model before you output. The document's color model is always displayed next to the file name, on the title bar. You can change the document's color mode at any time by choosing File > Document Color Mode > CMYK Color or RGB Color.

Opening legacy documents (documents created with older versions of Illustrator) with objects containing mixed color spaces will invoke a warning asking you to decide which color space (RGB or CMYK) the docu-ment should open in. Currently, linked images are not

CMY Color Model   RGB Color Model

CMY (Cyan, Magenta, Yellow) **subtractive** col-ors get darker when mixed; RGB (Red, Green, Blue) **additive** colors combine to make white

Whiter whites/blacker blacks

If your whites or blacks seem to be taking on an undesirable color cast, look to your color manage-ment system as the possible source of the problem. (See the *User Guide* for more details on color management in this version of Illustrator.) Also, check your Proof Setup or preview modes.

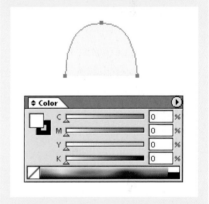

Converting RGB to CMYK

Although Illustrator can make conversions from RGB to CMYK (and vice versa), File > Document Color Mode > CMYK/RGB, such conversions may result in undesir-able color shifts. Consult the *User Guide*, your service bureau, and/ or printer for detailed directions based on your job specifications.

Continuous-tone, anti-aliased bitmapped images naturally form "traps" to hide misregistration of CMYK inks, but hard, crisp PostScript edges are a registration nightmare. Some products globally trap pages. If you know the exact size and resolution of your final image, you can rasterize Illustrator files (or specific objects) into raster images by using Object > Rasterize and Flatten Transparency or rasterize in Photoshop. If your image is not rasterized:

- Construct your images so overlapping shapes having common inks form natural traps.
- Set individual colors to Overprint in the Attributes palette.
- Globally set blacks to Overprint (Filter > Colors > Overprint Black).
- See the *User Guide* for details on setting traps in *solid* objects using Pathfinder palette: Trap.
- For trapping patterns and gradients, (see Tip "Manual Trapping..." in the *Drawing & Coloring* chapter).

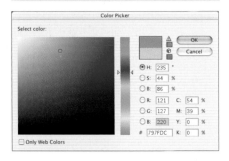

Adobe Color Picker

converted to the document's color space. If you open the Document Info palette and select Linked Images, the "Type" info is misleading. For example, if you have a CMYK document with a linked RGB image, the linked image type is Transparent CMYK. The linked image has not been converted, but the image preview has been converted to CMYK.

There are some effects (and graphic styles that use them) that work only in RGB mode. If you start off in RGB mode and use some of the default RGB graphic styles, they won't be rendered correctly if you then convert your document to CMYK mode.

Enabling color management

The default color setting for Illustrator is "Emulate Adobe Illustrator 6.0," which is all color management *off*. To start color managing your documents, select Edit > Color Settings. Choose a setting from the pop-up menu, or customize your own setting. Depending on how you set up color management, you might get several warnings about colors, such as when you open documents or paste colors between documents. The *User Guide* offers detailed explanations about these warnings and what to do.

Color systems and libraries

Besides creating colors in RGB, HSB, or CMYK, you can also select colors from other color matching systems, such as the 216-color Web color palette or the color picker. You can access Focoltone, Diccolor, Toyo, Trumatch, and Pantone libraries or the Web palette by choosing Window > Swatch Libraries, then selecting it from the menu. (Also, new in Illustrator CS, you can access the swatch libraries through the menu in the Swatches palette itself.) Keep in mind that color libraries open as separate uneditable palettes, but once you use a color swatch, it will automatically load into your Swatches palette, where you can then edit it. The default for the Swatches palette is to open with swatches—not view by name. Use the palette menu to change to List View if you prefer. Holding down

Option/Alt while you choose a view will set that view for each of the types of swatches. To access styles, brushes, or swatches in other documents, either choose Window > Graphic Style, Brush, Symbol, or Swatch Libraries > Other Library. You can also use the new Open Library command in the Graphic Styles, Brushes, Symbols or Swatches palettes. Then select the file that contains the item you want. This opens a new palette with that document's components. To store a component from an open library in your current document, just use the graphic style, brush, symbol or swatch—or drag the swatch from its library palette to the document's palette.

SAVING AS PDF

Illustrator CS makes it easy to save your document as a PDF (portable document format) file, and even lets you choose what version of PDF you'd like to save as, while providing handy PDF presets that let you quickly save PDFs with different settings for different circumstances.

To save a document as a PDF, choose File > Save or File > Save As, and choose Illustrator PDF from the Format menu. In that next Adobe PDF Options dialog box, you can choose from a variety of options and settings, including compatibility (PDF version), compression, printer's marks and bleeds, security settings, and more.

The Compatibility menu lets you choose from a number of versions of PDF. Illustrator CS's default is PDF 1.4, which is compatible with Acrobat 5. You can also choose to save in the new PDF 1.5 format, which is compatible with Illustrator 6 and preserves advanced features, such as PDF layers. However, these files may not be compatible with earlier versions of Acrobat, so if you're going to be distributing the file widely, you may want to save as PDF 1.4 or even 1.3 (the menu's third option) to maximize compatibility. PDF 1.3 is compatible with Acrobat 4 and will be viewable and printable by the widest range of users, but it doesn't support transparency.

You can choose a PDF preset from the Preset menu to quickly access frequently used PDF settings. You can

Links are manageable

The Links palette keeps a running (and updatable) list of all images in your document, whether they are linked or embedded. The key features of this palette are:

• You can quickly find out if you are missing a link (stop sign icon on the link layer) or need to update a link (exclamation icon).

• You can replace a link, update a link, go to a link, or edit a link with the click on an icon.

• You can change a linked image into an embedded image through the pop-up menu.

• You can find out information about the link (file name, location, size, kind, date modified, and transformations made) by double-clicking on a link layer to open the Link information dialog box (not all information is available for all formats).

Note: *Until the Links palette provides information on the color mode (RGB, CMYK, Grayscale, or raster images), be careful to check your links manually!*

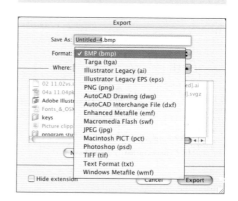

The Adobe PDF Options dialog box (choose Illus-trator PDF in the Format menu of the File > Save or File > Save As dialog box)

create your own custom presets by choosing Custom from the menu, adjusting your settings, and then clicking the Save Preset button at the bottom of the dialog box. Additionally, Illustrator ships with the following three predefined presets:

- **Illustrator Default** uses PDF 1.4 and creates a PDF in which all Illustrator data is preserved.

- **Press** uses PDF 1.3 and is best for creating a high-qual-ity file for imagesetters or placesetters at a commercial printer or service provider. Use this preset when file size is not an issue and the primary consideration is to pre-serve the maximum amount of information needed to print the document correctly.

- **Acrobat 6 Layered** uses PDF 1.5 and creates a file where top-level Illustrator layers are saved as PDF layers.

For more detailed information on PDF settings and presets, see the *User Guide.*

IMAGE FORMATS

You might need to open a document created in an earlier version of Illustrator (FreeHand, CorelDraw, and some 3D programs allow you to save images in older Illustra-tor formats). To open any file saved in an earlier version (known as a *legacy file*), drag it onto an Illustrator alias, or open the older formatted file from within Illustra-tor by choosing File > Open and selecting the document you want to open. Your document will be converted to Illustrator CS format, and "[Converted]" will be added to the file name. If you want to save it back to any pre-Illus-trator CS format, you'll need to export it by choosing the Illustrator Legacy format in the File > Export dialog box.

If you open any legacy file containing type, you'll get a dialog box asking you how to handle the conversion, because Illustrator CS's new type engine handles things very differently. See the *Type* chapter (as well as the *User Guide*) for details on working with legacy type.

EPS (Encapsulated PostScript)

EPS is a universal format, which means that a wide variety of programs support importing and exporting EPS images for printing to PostScript printers. As in most programs, when saving an image in EPS format you can choose to include a Preview. This preview is an on-screen PICT or TIFF representation of your image. When an EPS image is placed into another program without a preview, it will print properly, but it cannot be viewed. In order to import an EPS image into Illustrator, choose File > Place (see the *Layers* and *Illustrator & Other Programs* chapters to learn more about EPS).

Other image formats

Illustrator supports many file formats (such as SWF, SVG, GIF, JPEG, TIFF, PICT, PCX, Pixar, and Photoshop). You can also open and edit PDF documents, and even "raw" PostScript files, directly from within Illustrator. If you place images into a document, you can choose whether these files will remain *linked* (see Tip "Links are manageable" in this chapter) or will become *embedded* image objects (see the *Illustrator & Other Programs* chapter for specifics on embedding, and the *Web & Animation* chapter for details on Web-related formats). If you use File > Open, then images become embedded. (See the *User Guide* and *Read Me* files for lists of supported formats that shipped with this version.) Check Adobe's Web site (www.adobe.com) for the latest information on supported formats, as well as other file format plug-ins. (For more on file format issues, see the *Other Programs* chapter.)

POSTSCRIPT PRINTING & EXPORTING

When you're ready to print your image (to a laser or ink-jet printer, imagesetter, or film recorder), you should use a PostScript printing device. Adobe owns and licenses the PostScript language, making PostScript printers somewhat more expensive than non-PostScript printers. Some companies produce PostScript-compatible printers or provide PostScript emulation. Although Illustrator

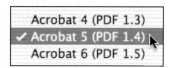

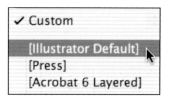

The Compatibility menu in the Adobe PDF Options dialog box

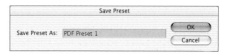

The Preset menu in the Adobe PDF Options dialog box

The Save Preset dialog box that results when you click the Save Preset button at the bottom of the Adobe PDF Options dialog box

Illustrator adds the "[Converted]" tag to file names in the title bars of legacy files

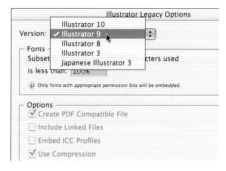

The Illustrator Legacy Options dialog box lets you export to a number of earlier Illustrator formats (choose Illustrator Legacy format in the File > Export dialog box)

Get into the habit of proofing all your images to a laser printer to gauge whether your image will take a long time to print. The higher your printing resolution, the longer your PostScript image will take to print. Based on your laser test, if you know that your image will require hours to print, you might be able to arrange for your service bureau to print your image overnight or on a weekend to save extra charges.

Hand tool while typing

First press ⌘/Ctrl + spacebar, then release the ⌘/Ctrl key to access the Hand tool, even while typing.

Clean Up stray paths & points

Select Object > Path > Clean Up and check the items you want to delete from your document. Choose Stray Points, Unpainted Objects, and/or Empty Text Paths. Click OK and all of those items are removed.

New levels of PostScript

Adobe's PostScript 3 language is full of new features that improve printing time, deliver truer colors, and provide Web-Ready printing. For details on PS3, refer to Adobe's "white paper" on PS3 on the Web at www.adobe.com.

images often print just fine to these printers, sometimes you can run into problems. In general, the newer the PostScript device, the faster and less problematic your printing will be. PostScript Level 2 and Level 3 printers provide better printing clarity and even some special effects, such as Illustrator's integration of PostScript Level 3's "smooth shading" technology (which should greatly enhance gradients and reduce banding problems). Finally, the more memory you install in your printer, the quicker your text and images will print. For crucial jobs, develop good relations with your service bureau, and get into the habit of running test prints to identify possible problems. (Also see the Tip "Proofing your prints" at left.)

Correcting and avoiding printing problems

If you have trouble printing, first make sure your placed images are linked properly and the fonts needed to print the document are loaded. Second, check for any complex objects in the document (e.g., objects with many points, compound masks or shapes, or gradient meshes). (See the *Blends, Gradients & Mesh* chapter for issues regarding printing gradient mesh objects.) Use Save a Copy (to retain the original file), remove the complex object(s), and try to print. If that doesn't work, make sure File > Document Setup and the File > Print dialog box have the correct settings for your output device.

Keep in mind that Illustrator CS's new comprehensive Print dialog box takes on many of the functions that belonged to the Page Setup and Separation Setup dialog boxes in previous versions of Illustrator. But the new Print dialog box gives you much more control over every part of the printing process.

If you're using transparency, or effects that contain transparency, you might want to preview how your art will print using the Flattener Preview palette (Window > Flattener Preview). For information on the Flattener Preview palette, and other ways to control flattening settings, see the *Transparency & Appearances* chapter. Printing results will vary depending on these settings.

More about controlling the size of your files

The major factors that can increase your file size are the inclusion of image objects, path pattern, brushes and ink pen objects, complex patterns, a large number of blends and gradients (especially gradient mesh objects and gradient-to-gradient blends), linked bitmapped images, and transparency. Although linked bitmaps can be large, the same image embedded as an image object is significantly larger. If your Illustrator file contains linked images, and you need to save the entire file in EPS (for placement and printing in other programs), you have the option Include Linked Files. Most service bureaus highly recommend this option, as it will embed placed images in your Illustrator file and make printing from page layout programs and film recorders much more predictable (be sure to see the Tip "Proofing your prints" at left). However, since including placed images will further increase the file size, wait until you've completed an image and are ready to place it into another program before you save a copy with placed images embedded. Whether or not you choose to embed linked images, you must collect all of the files that have been linked into your Illustrator documents and transport them along with your Illustrator file. Illustrator makes your task easier if you choose File > Document Info > Linked Images, which outputs a text file of all images in your document. Press Save to create a text file that you can keep for future reference or give to your service bureau as a record of the images included in your files.

ACTIONS

Actions are a set of commands or a series of events that you can record and save as a set in the Actions palette. Once a set is recorded, you can play back an action in the same order in which you recorded it, to automate a job you do repeatedly (such as a production task or special effect).

Select the action in the Actions palette and activate it by clicking the Play icon at the bottom of the palette,

In a jam? There's help available

Adobe provides many ways to help you learn Illustrator and troubleshoot problems. Find

Help
Illustrator Help... F1
Welcome Screen...
Tutorials...
System Info...
Online Support...
Updates...
Registration...
Illustrator Online...

help under the Help menu, along with instant access to Adobe Online. You can also access Adobe Online by clicking the flower icon on top of the Toolbox.

Is Raster the answer?

Most printing problems in Illustrator CS involve transparency and flattening. The optimal setting for the Raster/Vector slider in your flattening settings is all the way to Vector, but if you're having trouble printing, you can try setting it all the way to Raster which may help in some cases. The flattening settings can be accessed via the Print dialog box and the new Flattener Preview palette, among other places. See the *Transparency & Appearances* chapter for details about the many ways to control flattening settings in Illustrator.

The proof is in the Preview

Want the best on-screen preview for your art? Choose View > Overprint Preview for the best way to proof color on your screen and to see how your art will look when printed.

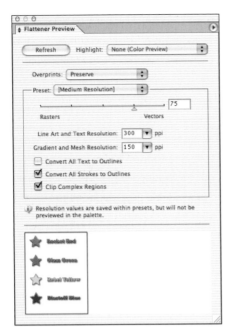

Illustrator's new Flattener Preview palette

Resolution templates

If you're saving a batch of documents, and want them all to have the same resolution settings, Illustrator's new Templates feature makes it easy. Just set up a new document with the settings you want, and then save it as a template (.ait) file (File > Save as Template). Then you can base as many new documents on your template as you like, and they'll have your preferred resolution settings.

Selecting objects in an action

When recording an action, use the Attributes palette (Show Note) to name an object, and Select Object (Action pop-up) to type in the object's name (note) to select it.

by choosing Play from the pop-up menu, or by assigning the action to a keyboard "F key" (function key) so you can play the action with a keystroke. You can select an action set, a single action, or a command within an action to play. To exclude a command from playing within an action, disable the checkbox to the left of the command.

In order to play some types of actions, you may have to first select an object or text. Load action sets using the pop-up menu. (You can find sets of actions on the Adobe Illustrator CS CD in the Illustrator Extras folder, and in the "WOW Actions" folder on the *Wow! CD.*)

Since you must record actions and save within an action set, begin a new action by clicking the Create New Set icon or by choosing New Set from the pop-up menu. Name the action set and click OK. With the new set selected, click the Create New Action icon, name the action, and click Record. Illustrator records your commands and steps until you click Stop. To resume recording, click on the last step, choose Begin, and continue adding to the action. When you've finished recording, you'll need to save the action file by selecting the action set and choosing Save Actions from the pop-up menu.

When you are recording, keep in mind that not all commands or tools are recordable. For example, the Pen tool itself is not recordable, but you can add the paths the Pen tool creates to an action by selecting a path and choosing Insert Selected Paths from the pop-up menu. Recording actions takes some practice, so don't get discouraged, always save a backup file, and refer to the *User Guide* for more details on Actions.

SCRIPTING AND VARIABLES

Illustrator CS offers expanded scripting support to let you automate more tasks than before. Illustrator supports AppleScript (for Mac), Visual Basic scripting (for Windows), and JavaScript (for both platforms). If you're familiar with any of these scripting languages, you can use them to your advantage to save time in Illustrator. For more information on scripting in Illustrator, see the

"Adobe Illustrator CS Scripting Guide," found on the Adobe Illustrator CS CD.

Illustrator also supports XML variables. You can specify variables using the Variables palette, found in the Window menu. With variables, you can hook up an Illustrator file to a database, using any of the scripting languages mentioned above, to automatically generate versions of artwork. For example, you can create a business card and then link that card to a database that contains a list of names. A script could then generate a separate card for each name in the database. For more information on this, see the *User Guide* on Data-Driven Graphics, and the "Illustrator CS XML Grammar Guide" on the Adobe Illustrator CS CD.

Variables palette and mockups

Illustrator's Variables palette can help create useful design mockups within Illustrator. It's helpful not only for trying out different sets of data for a design, such as localizing content, but also for showing the same set of data within multiple designs. It's handy for being able to test out different kinds of data simultaneously in various comps. It can also be used as a communication tool between the front end (designers) and the back end (engineers): one can specify the things that will change in the design and share that variable set (XML file) with the other to either make sure that the variable names and types are in synch, the data is in synch, or both. One of the biggest concerns for many Web designers is preserving their designs, and having this intermediate step can help them do so.

DATA-DRIVEN GRAPHICS

To see an example of data-driven graphics in action, take a look at the Travel Ads.ai sample file included in the Illustrator CS Sample Art folder.

Saving time and space

Note: *Before you attempt to minimize the size of your file, make certain that you're working on a copy.* To minimize the size of your file, first remove all your unused colors, patterns, and brushes. You can do this easily using a handy set of Actions, included by default, in the Illustrator CS Actions palette. Open the palette (Window > Actions) and choose Delete Unused Palette Items, which will automatically select and delete all unused graphic styles, brushes, swatches, and symbols. (Click the triangle next to Delete Unused Palette Items to choose specific Actions.) You should minimize the time it takes to print an Illustrator file, even if it's been placed into another program, such as QuarkXPress or PageMaker (see the *Other Programs* chapter for details on exporting). If you've scaled or rotated an Illustrator image once it's been placed into another program, note the numeric percentages of scaling and the degrees of rotation. Next, reopen the file in Illustrator, perform the identical scale or rotation, then place this pre-transformed version back into the other program. Make sure you reset scaling and rotation to zero. **Note:** *Be certain to scale line weight, objects, and pattern tiles when you perform these transformations in Illustrator.*

The Zen of Illustrator

2

40 Introduction

42 Building Houses: *Sequential Object Construction Exercises*

48 A Classic Icon: *Five Ways to Re-create Simple Shapes*

50 Zen Scaling

52 Zen Rotation

53 Creating a Simple Object Using the Basic Tools

54 A Finger Dance: *Turbo-charge with Illustrator's Power-keys*

The Zen of Illustrator

You're comfortable with the basic operations of your computer. You've read through "An Overview of Adobe Illustrator" in the *User Guide*. You've logged enough hours to Illustrator to be familiar with how each tool (theoretically) functions. You even understand how to make Bézier curves. Now what? How do you take all this knowledge and turn it into a mastery of the medium?

As with learning any new artistic medium (such as engraving, watercolor, or airbrush), learning to manipulate the tools is just the beginning. Thinking and seeing in that medium is what really makes those tools part of your creative arsenal. Before you can determine the best way to construct an image, you have to be able to envision at least some of the possibilities. The first key to mastering Illustrator is to understand that Illustrator's greatest strength comes not from its many tools and functions but from its extreme flexibility in terms of how you construct images. The first part of this chapter, therefore, introduces you to a variety of approaches and techniques for creating and transforming objects.

Once you've got yourself "thinking in Illustrator," you can begin to *visualize* how to achieve the final results. What is the simplest and most elegant way to construct an image? Which tools will you use? Then, once you've begun, allow yourself the flexibility to change course and try something else. Be willing to say to yourself: How else can I get the results that I want?

* Adapted from *Webster's New World Dictionary of the English Language*

The second key to mastering Illustrator (or any new medium) is perfecting your hand/eye coordination. In Illustrator, this translates into being proficient enough with the "power-keys" to gain instant access to tools and functions by using the keyboard. With both eyes on the monitor, one hand on the mouse, and the other hand on the keyboard, an experienced Illustrator user can create and manipulate objects in a fraction of the time required otherwise. The second part of this chapter helps you to learn the "finger dance" necessary to become a truly adept power-user.

The ability to harness the full power of Illustrator's basic tools and functions will ultimately make you a true master of Adobe Illustrator. Treat this chapter like meditation. Take it in small doses if necessary. Be mindful that the purpose of these exercises is to open up your mind to possibilities, not to force memorization. When you can conceptualize a number of different ways to create an image, then the hundreds of hints, tips, tricks, and techniques found elsewhere in this book can serve as a jumping-off point for further exploration. If you take the time to explore and absorb this chapter, you should begin to experience what I call the "Zen of Illustrator." This magical program, at first cryptic and counterintuitive, can help you achieve creative results not possible in any other medium.

Building Houses

Sequential Object Construction Exercises

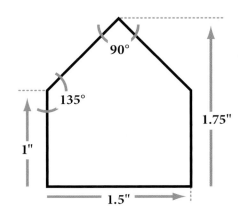

Overview: *Explore different approaches to constructing the same object with Illustrator's basic construction tools.*

This sequence of exercises explores different ways to construct the same simple object, a house. The purpose of these exercises is to introduce you to the flexibility of Illustrator's object construction, so don't worry if some exercises seem less efficient than others. In Preferences > Units & Display Performance, set Units > General for Inches (so you can use the numbers provided and the measurements above). And read through the recommendations below for preparing your working environment.

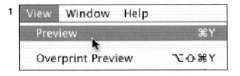

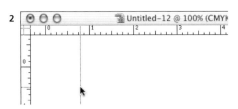

Dragging out a guide from the Ruler, and choosing Window > Info to open the Info palette if it's not open before you begin

1 Work in Outline mode. Doing so keeps you from being distracted by fills or line weights, and lets you see the centers of geometric objects (marked by "×").

2 Use Show Rulers and Show Info. Choose Show Rulers (View menu) so you can "pull out" guides. Use the Info palette to view numeric data as you work, or ignore the numeric data and just draw the houses by eye.

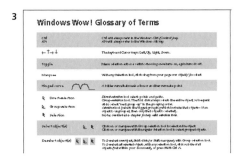

3 Read through the *Wow! Glossary.* Please make sure to read *How to use this book* and the *Glossary* pull-out card.

Hold down the Shift key to constrain movement to horizontal/vertical direction. For more modifier key help, see the end of this chapter for the "Finger Dance" lesson.

4 Use "modifier" keys. These exercises use Shift and Option (Opt) or Alt keys, which you must hold down until *after* you release your mouse button. If you make a mistake, choose Undo and try again. Some functions are also accessible from the Context-sensitive menu. Try keyboard shortcuts for frequently-used menu commands.

Exercise #1:

Use Add Anchor Point tool

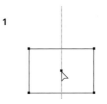
1

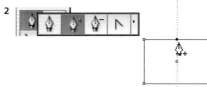
2

3

1 Create a rectangle and a vertical guide. Create a wide rectangle (1.5" x 1") and drag out a vertical guide that snaps to the center.

2 Add an anchor point on the top. Use the Add Anchor Point tool to add a point on the top segment over the center guide.

3 Drag the new point up. Use the Direct Selection tool to grab the new point and drag it up into position (.75" for a total height of 1.75").

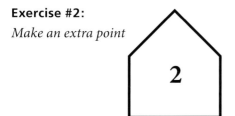

Exercise #2:

Make an extra point

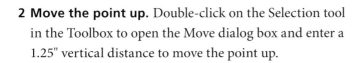

1

2

3

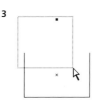

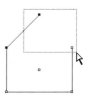

1 Create a rectangle, delete the top path and place a center point. Create a wide rectangle (1.5" x 1"). With the Direct Selection tool, select the top path segment and delete it. With the Pen tool, place a point on top of the rectangle center point.

2 Move the point up. Double-click on the Selection tool in the Toolbox to open the Move dialog box and enter a 1.25" vertical distance to move the point up.

3 Select and join the point to each side. Use the Direct Selection tool to select the left two points and Join (Object > Path > Join) them to the top point. Repeat with the right two points.

1

2

3

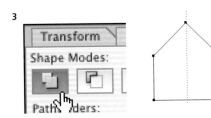

1

2

3

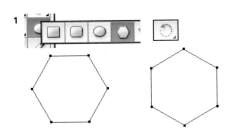

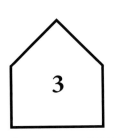

Exercise #3:
Rotate and Add

1 Create two rectangles, one centered on the other. Create a wide rectangle (1.5" x 1") and drag out a vertical guide, snapping it to the center. Hold down Opt/Alt and click with the Rectangle tool (Opt/Alt-click) on the center guide (on the top segment). Enter 1.05" x 1.05".

2 Rotate one rectangle. Double-click the Rotate tool to rotate the new rectangle around its center and enter 45°.

3 Select and Add the rectangles. Marquee-select both objects, choose Widow>Pathfinder and click the Add icon. Switch to Preview mode to see the single shape!

Exercise #4:
Make a six-sided polygon

1 Create a six-sided polygon. With the Polygon tool selected, click once and enter 6 sides and a .866" Radius. Then double-click the Rotate tool and enter 30°.

2 Delete the bottom point. With the Delete Anchor Point tool, click on the bottom point to delete it.

3 Move the two bottom points down, then the two middle points. Use the Direct Selection tool to select the bottom two points. Then grab one of the points and Shift-drag in a vertical line (down .423"). Lastly, Direct-select, grab and Shift-drag the middle two points down vertically into position (down .275").

Exercise #5:

Use Add Anchor Points filter in a three-sided polygon

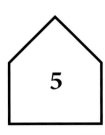

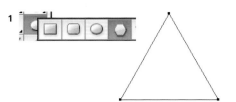

1 Create a three-sided polygon. With the Polygon tool selected, click once, then enter 3 sides and a 1.299" Radius.

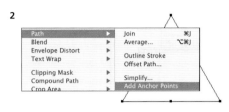

2 Use the Add Anchor Points filter. With the polygon still selected, choose Object > Path > Add Anchor Points (use the default keyboard shortcut, or create your own).

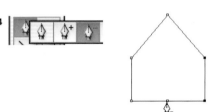

3 Average the two left points, then Average the two right points. Direct-select the two left points and Average them along the vertical axis (Context-sensitive: Average, or Object > Path > Average), then repeat for the two right points.

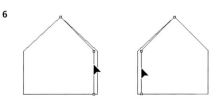

4 Delete the bottom point. With the Delete Anchor Point tool, click on the bottom point to delete it.

5 Move the top point down. Use the Direct Selection tool to select the top point, then double-click on the Direct Selection tool itself (in the Toolbox) to open the Move dialog box and enter a –.186" vertical distance.

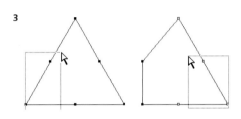

6 Slide in the sides towards the center. Use the Direct Selection tool to click on the right side of the house and drag it towards the center until the roofline looks smooth (hold down your Shift key to constrain the drag horizontally). Repeat for the left side of the house. Alternatively, select the right side and use the ← key on your keyboard to nudge the right side towards the center until the roofline looks smooth. Then, click on the left side to select it, and use the → key to nudge it towards the center. (If necessary, change your Keyboard Increment setting in the Preferences > General dialog.)

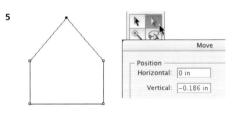

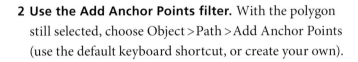

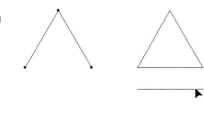

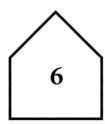

Exercise #6:
Cut a path and Paste in Front

1 Cut, paste, then move the bottom of a triangle. With the Polygon tool selected, click once and enter 3 sides and a .866" Radius. With the Direct Selection tool, select and Cut the bottom path to the Clipboard, choose Edit > Paste in Front, then grab the bottom path and drag it into position (down .423").

2 Create the sides and move middle points into place. Direct-select the two right points and join them, then repeat for the two left points. Finally, select the two middle points, and grab one to drag *both* up (.275").

Exercise #7:
Join two objects

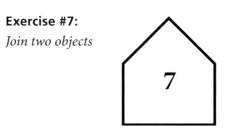

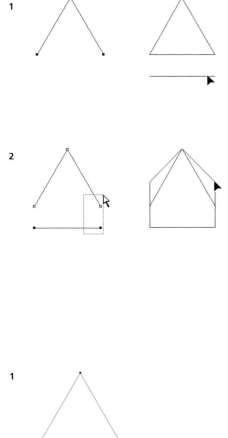

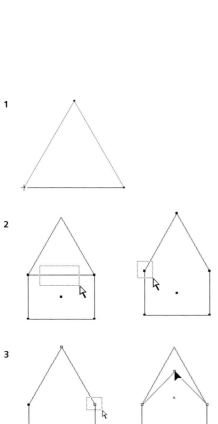

1 Make two objects. Click once with the Polygon tool, enter 3 sides and a .866" Radius. Zoom in on the lower left corner and, with the Rectangle tool, click exactly on the lower left anchor point. Set the rectangle to 1.5" x 1" .

2 Delete the middle lines and join the corners. Direct-select marquee the middle bisecting lines and delete. Select the upper-left corner points and Average-Join by either Averaging and then Joining the points (see exercises #5 and #6 above) or by pressing ⌘-Shift-Option-J/ Ctrl-Shift-Alt-J to average and join simultaneously. Select and Average-Join the upper right points.

3 Drag the top point down. Grab the top point, hold the Shift key and drag it into position (down .55").

Exercise #8:

Use Add Anchor Points filter, then Average-Join

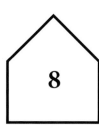

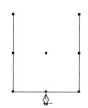

1

1 Make a tall rectangle, delete top path, add anchor points, remove bottom point. Create a tall rectangle (1.5" x 1.75") and delete the top path. Choose Add Anchor Points (Object > Path) and use the Delete Anchor Point tool to remove the bottom point.

2

2 Select and Average-Join the top points and move middles into position. Direct-select the top two points and Average-Join (see Exercise #7, step 2). Then Direct-select the middle points, grab one, and with the Shift key, drag them both into position (up .125").

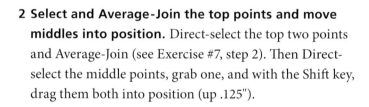

Exercise #9:

Reflect a Pen profile

1

1 Create a house profile. Drag out a vertical guide, then reset the ruler origin on the guide. To draw the profile, use the Pen tool to click on the guide at the ruler zero point, hold down Shift (to constrain your lines to 45° angles) and click to place the corner (.75" down and .75" to the left) and the bottom (1" down).

2

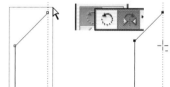

2 Reflect a copy of the profile. Select all three points of the house profile With the Reflect tool, Option/Alt-click-on the guide line. Enter an angle of 90° and click Copy.

3

3 Join the two profiles. Direct-select and Join the bottom two points. Then Direct-select the top two points and Average-Join (see Exercise #7, step 2).

A Classic Icon

Five Ways to Re-create Simple Shapes

Overview: *Finding different ways to construct the same iconic image.*

McSHANE, ADIGARD/M.A.D.

1

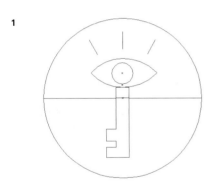

The Outline view of the original logo

The original logo, constructed from a stroked line and a solid circle

You can construct even the simplest of iconic images in many ways. Patricia McShane and Erik Adigard of the M.A.D. graphics firm designed this classic logo for the *Computers Freedom & Privacy* annual conference. This conference addresses the effects of computer and telecommunications technologies on societal and personal freedom and privacy. This simple iconic representation of an eye is a perfect example of how you can explore different ways to solve the same graphics problem.

1 First, construct your logo in the way that seems most logical to you. Everybody's mind works differently, and the most obvious solutions to you might seem innovative to the next person. Follow your instincts as to how to construct each image. If design changes require you to rethink your approach (for instance, what if the client wanted a radial fill instead of the black fill?), try something slightly, or even completely, different.

Viewed in Outline mode, the original *Computers Freedom & Privacy* logo is clean and elegant with a minimum number of anchor points and lines. The M.A.D. team constructed the eye from a stroked line (made with the Pen tool) and a filled, black circle.

2 Make the outer eye shape. Create the solid black, almond-shaped object in any way you wish: Draw it with the Pen tool like M.A.D. did, or convert an ellipse into the correct shape by clicking on the middle points with the Convert Anchor Point tool from the Pen tool pop-up.

3 Try using solid objects. Starting with your base object, construct the eye with overlapping solid objects. Scale a version of the outline for the green inset and place a black circle on the top.

4 Try making a compound object. Use the objects that you created in the previous version to make a compound object that allows the inner part of the eye to be cut out. Select the outer black outline and the inner green inset and choose Object>Compound Paths>Make.

5 Try using compound shapes. Compound shapes are powerful tools that let you combine shapes or create knockouts (see the *Drawing & Coloring* chapter for details on compound shapes). To create the back of the eye, start by creating an ellipse. With the ellipse still selected, switch to the Selection tool. Now hold Option-Shift (Mac)/Alt-Shift (Win) keys, grab the center of the ellipse and drag downward until the center of the new ellipse is at the bottom of the original ellipse. Select both shapes and click the Intersect button on the Pathfinder palette. To create the shape that will become the white of the eye, select the back of the eye, open the Object>Transform> Transform Each dialog box and enter: 70 % H, 50% V, then click Copy. To use this shape to knockout the white of the eye, first put it behind the back of the eye by using Object>Arrange>Send to Back, then select both objects and click on the Exclude button on the Pathfinder palette. Next, create the circle for the pupil over the knocked out eye shape, select them both, and click on the Vertical Align Center and Horizontal Align Center buttons on the Align palette. To finish, click on the Add button on the Pathfinder palette.

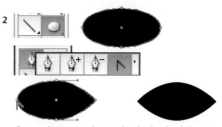

2

Converting an oval to make the back of the eye

3

Constructing the logo with three solid objects

4

Constructing the logo from an outer compound object and an inner solid circle

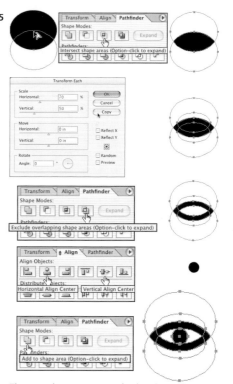

5

The same logo constructed using Copy, Compound Shape modes, and Transform Each

Zen Scaling

Note: *Use the Shift key to constrain proportions.* ***Zen Scaling*** *practice is also on the* ***Wow! CD.***

1 Scaling proportionally towards the top Click at the top, grab lower-right (LR), drag up

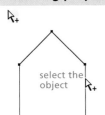 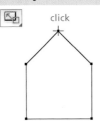 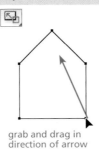 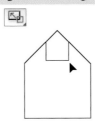

select the
object

click

grab and drag in
direction of arrow

2 Scaling horizontally towards the center Click at the top, grab LR, drag inwards

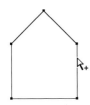    

3 Scaling vertically towards the top Click at the top, grab LR, drag straight up

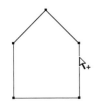   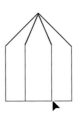

4 Scaling vertically and flipping the object Click at the top, grab LR, drag straight up

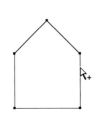  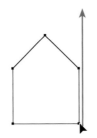 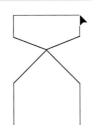

Zen Scaling *(continued)*

Note: *Use the Shift key to constrain proportions.* ***Zen Scaling*** *practice is also on the* ***Wow! CD***.

5 Scaling proportionally towards lower-left (LL) Click LL, grab upper-right, drag to LL

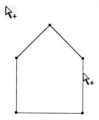  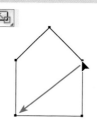 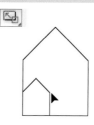

6 Scaling horizontally to the left side Click LL, grab lower-right (LR), drag to left

7 Scaling vertically towards the bottom Click center bottom, grab top, drag down

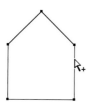  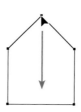 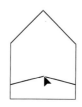

8 Scaling proportionally towards the center Click the center, grab corner, drag to center

   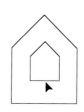

Or, to scale about the center, use the Scale tool to click-drag outside the object towards the center

Zen Rotation

Note: *Use the Shift key to constrain movement.* **Zen Rotation** *practice is also on the* **Wow! CD.**

1 Rotating around the center Click in the center, then grab lower-right (LR) and drag

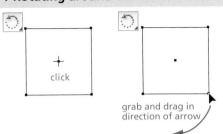 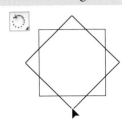 

click

grab and drag in
direction of arrow

Or, to rotate about the center, use the Rotate tool to click-drag outside the object towards the center

2 Rotating from a corner Click in the upper left corner, then grab LR and drag

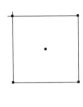 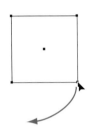 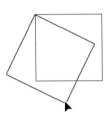 

3 Rotating from outside Click above the left corner, then grab LR and drag

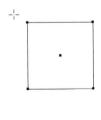  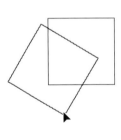 

4 Rotating part of a path Marquee points with the Direct Selection tool, then use Rotate tool

Marquee the forearm with Direct Selection tool   *With the Rotate tool, click on the elbow, grab the hand and drag it around*

Creating a Simple Object Using the Basic Tools

Key: *Click where you see a* RED *cross, grab with the* GRAY *arrow and drag towards* BLACK *arrow.*

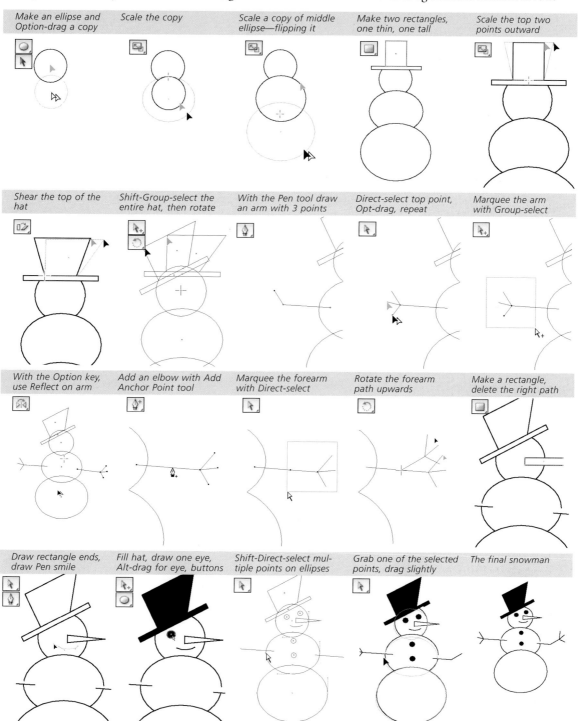

Make an ellipse and Option-drag a copy	Scale the copy	Scale a copy of middle ellipse—flipping it	Make two rectangles, one thin, one tall	Scale the top two points outward

Shear the top of the hat	Shift-Group-select the entire hat, then rotate	With the Pen tool draw an arm with 3 points	Direct-select top point, Opt-drag, repeat	Marquee the arm with Group-select

With the Option key, use Reflect on arm	Add an elbow with Add Anchor Point tool	Marquee the forearm with Direct-select	Rotate the forearm path upwards	Make a rectangle, delete the right path

Draw rectangle ends, draw Pen smile	Fill hat, draw one eye, Alt-drag for eye, buttons	Shift-Direct-select multiple points on ellipses	Grab one of the selected points, drag slightly	The final snowman

A Finger Dance
Turbo-charge with Illustrator's Power-keys

Overview: *Save hours of production time by mastering the finger dance of Illustrator's power-keys.*

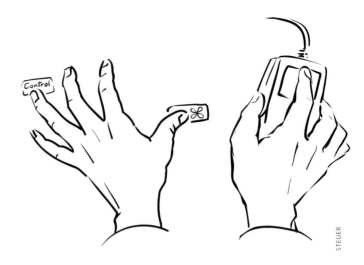

STEUER

Find a summary of Finger Dance power-keys on the pull-out quick reference card

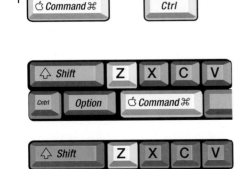

If you are using the mouse to choose your selection tools from the Toolbox, then you need this lesson. With some time and patience, you'll be able to free up your mouse so that practically the only thing you do with it is draw. Your other hand will learn to dance around the keyboard accessing all of your selection tools, modifying your creation and transformation tools, using your Zoom and Hand tools, and last but not least, providing instant Undo and Redo.

This "Finger Dance" is probably the most difficult aspect of Illustrator to master. Go through these lessons in order, but don't expect to get through them in one or even two sittings. When you make a mistake, use Undo (⌘/Ctrl-Z). Try a couple of exercises, then go back to your own work, incorporating what you've just learned. When you begin to get frustrated, take a break. Later—hours, days, or weeks later—try another lesson. And don't forget to breathe.

Rule #1: Always keep one finger on the ⌘ key (Ctrl for Windows). Whether you are using a mouse or a pressure-sensitive tablet, the hand you are not drawing with should be resting on the keyboard, with one finger (or thumb) on the ⌘ key. This position will make that all-important Undo (⌘-Z/Ctrl-Z) instantly accessible.

Rule #2: Undo if you make a mistake. This is so crucial an aspect of working in the computer environment that I am willing to be redundant. If there is only one key combination that you memorize, make it Undo (⌘-Z/Ctrl-Z).

Rule #3: The ⌘ (Ctrl) key turns your cursor into a selection tool. In Illustrator, the ⌘/Ctrl key does a lot more than merely provide you with easy access to Undo. The ⌘/Ctrl key will convert any tool into the selection arrow that you last used. In the exercises that follow, you'll soon discover that the most flexible selection arrow is the Direct Selection tool.

Rule #4: Watch your cursor. If you learn to watch your cursor, you'll be able to prevent most errors before they happen. And if you don't (for instance, if you drag a copy of an object by mistake), then use Undo and try again.

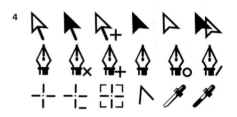

Rule #5: Pay careful attention to when you hold down each key. Most of the modifier keys operate differently depending on *when* you hold each key down. If you obey Rule #4 and watch your cursor, then you'll notice what the key you are holding does.

Rule #6: Hold down the key(s) until after you let go of your mouse button. In order for your modifier key to actually modify your action, you *must* keep your key down until *after* you let go of your mouse button.

Rule #7: Work in Outline mode. When you are constructing or manipulating objects, get into the habit of working in Outline mode. Of course, if you are designing the colors in your image, you'll need to work in Preview, but while you're learning how to use the power-keys, you'll generally find it much quicker and easier if you are in Outline mode.

Universal Access conflict (Mac)

When you're using Illustrator, you should probably disable Universal Access, which is a feature developed for those with limited manual dexterity (System Preferences > Universal Access > Allow Universal Access Shortcuts). It can interfere with Illustrator's normal functioning. If you have limited manual dexterity, try using CE Software's QuicKeys to simplify menu selection, keystrokes, and object creation.

Before you begin this sequence of exercises, choose the Direct Selection tool, then select the Rectangle tool and drag to create a rectangle.

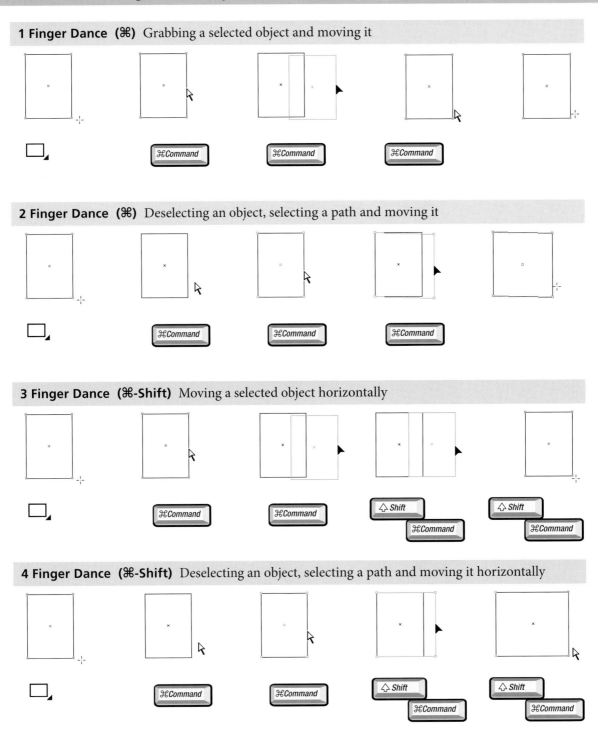

1 Finger Dance (⌘) Grabbing a selected object and moving it

⌘ Command ⌘ Command ⌘ Command

2 Finger Dance (⌘) Deselecting an object, selecting a path and moving it

⌘ Command ⌘ Command ⌘ Command

3 Finger Dance (⌘-Shift) Moving a selected object horizontally

⌘ Command ⌘ Command ⬆ Shift / ⌘ Command ⬆ Shift / ⌘ Command

4 Finger Dance (⌘-Shift) Deselecting an object, selecting a path and moving it horizontally

⌘ Command ⌘ Command ⬆ Shift / ⌘ Command ⬆ Shift / ⌘ Command

Before you begin this sequence of exercises, choose the Direct Selection tool,
then select the Rectangle tool and drag to create a rectangle.

1 Finger Dance (Ctrl) Grabbing a selected object and moving it

2 Finger Dance (Ctrl) Deselecting an object, selecting a path and moving it

3 Finger Dance (Ctrl-Shift) Moving a selected object horizontally

4 Finger Dance (Ctrl-Shift) Deselecting an object, selecting a path and moving it horizontally

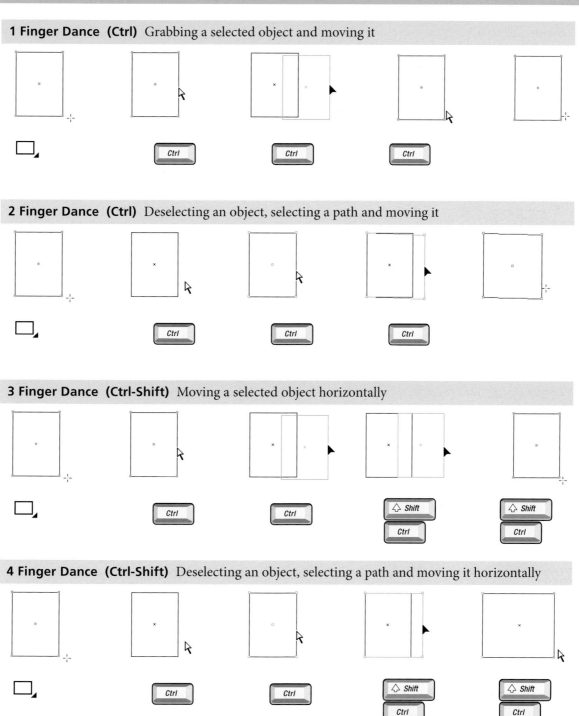

Before you begin this sequence of exercises, choose the Direct Selection tool, then select the Rectangle tool and drag to create a rectangle.

5 Finger Dance (⌘, then ⌘-Option) Moving a copy of a selected object

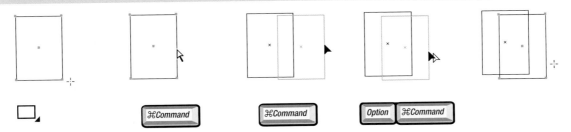

6 Finger Dance (⌘, then ⌘-Option) Deselecting an object, moving a copy of a path

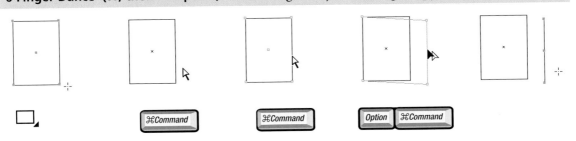

7 Finger Dance (⌘, then ⌘-Shift-Option) Moving a copy of a selected object horizontally

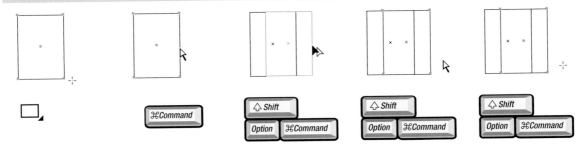

8 Finger Dance (⌘, then ⌘-Shift-Option) Deselecting, moving a copy of the path horizontally

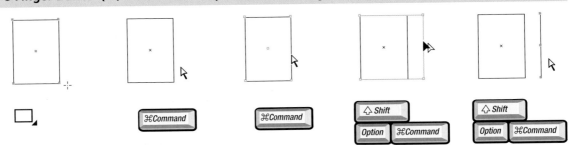

WINDOWS FINGER DANCES

Before you begin this sequence of exercises, choose the Direct Selection tool,
then select the Rectangle tool and drag to create a rectangle.

5 Finger Dance (Ctrl, then Ctrl-Alt) Moving a copy of a selected object

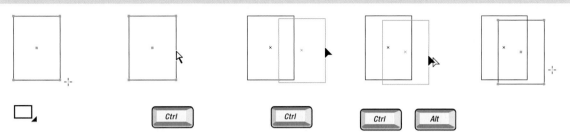

6 Finger Dance (Ctrl, then Ctrl-Alt) Deselecting an object, moving a copy of a path

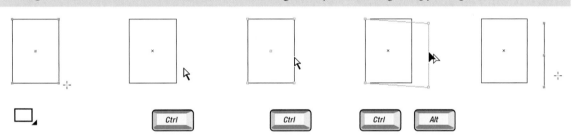

7 Finger Dance (Ctrl, then Ctrl-Shift-Alt) Moving a copy of a selected object horizontally

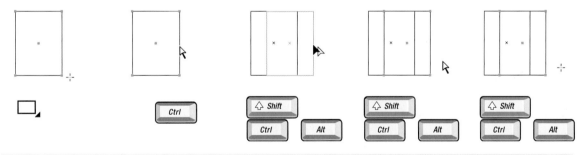

8 Finger Dance (Ctrl, then Ctrl-Shift-Alt) Deselecting, moving a copy of the path

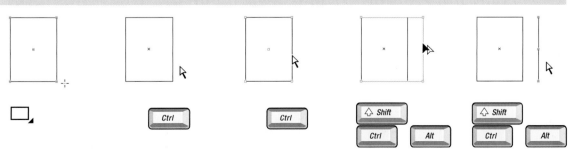

MACINTOSH FINGER DANCES
*Before you begin this sequence of exercises, choose the Direct Selection tool,
then select the Rectangle tool and drag to create a rectangle.*

9 Finger Dance (⌘-Option, then ⌘-Option) Deselecting, Group-selecting, moving a copy

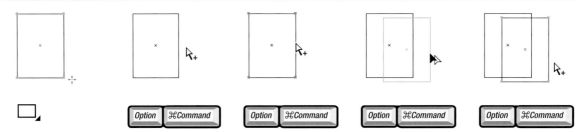

10 Finger Dance (⌘-Option, ⌘-Shift) Group-selecting, moving an object horizontally

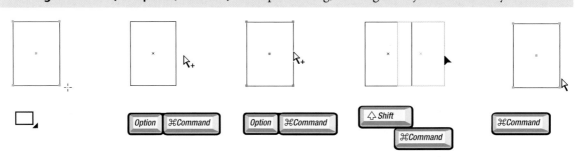

11 Finger Dance (⌘-Option, ⌘-Option-Shift) Moving copies horizontally, adding selections

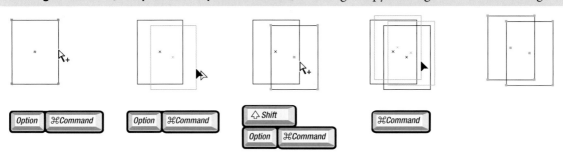

12 Finger Dance (⌘-Option, ⌘-Option-Shift, ⌘) Moving a copy, adding a selection, moving

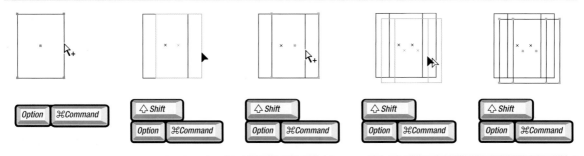

Before you begin this sequence of exercises, choose the Direct Selection tool, then select the Rectangle tool and drag to create a rectangle.

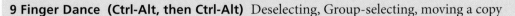

9 Finger Dance (Ctrl-Alt, then Ctrl-Alt) Deselecting, Group-selecting, moving a copy

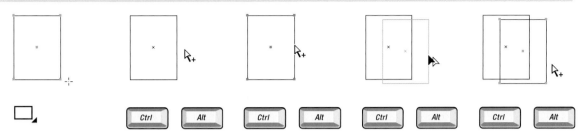

10 Finger Dance (Ctrl-Alt, Ctrl-Shift) Group-selecting, moving an object horizontally

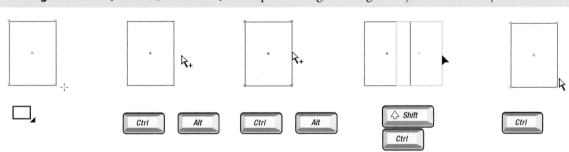

11 Finger Dance (Ctrl-Alt, Ctrl-Alt-Shift) Moving copies horizontally, adding selections

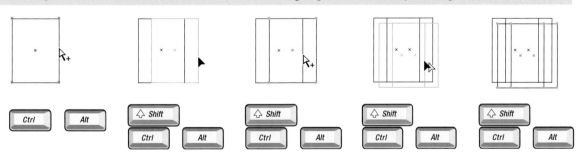

12 Finger Dance (Ctrl-Alt, Ctrl-Alt-Shift, Ctrl) Moving a copy, adding a selection, moving

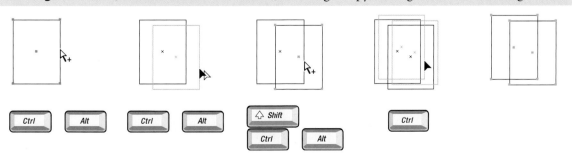

Drawing & Coloring

3

64 Introduction

64 Basic Drawing & Coloring

69 Expanding Your Drawing & Coloring Toolset

72 Pathfinder Palette

78 Simple Realism: *Realism from Geometry and Observation*

81 Gallery: Mark Fox

82 Cutting & Joining: *Basic Path Construction with Pathfinders*

86 Add & Expand: *More Pathfinder Palette Basics*

88 Divide & Color: *Applying Pathfinder Divide & Subtract*

90 Cubist Constructs: *Creative Experimentation with Pathfinders*

92 Isometric Systems: *Arrow Keys, Constrain Angles & Formulas*

94–95 Galleries: Rick Henkel, Kurt Hess, Jared Schneidman

96 Objective Colors: *Custom Labels for Making Quick Changes*

98–105 Galleries: Jean Tuttle, Clarke Tate, Christopher Burke, Dorothy Remington, Karen Barranco, Filip Yip, Gary Ferster

106 Distort Dynamics: *Adding Character Dynamics with Transform*

108 Distort Filter Flora: *Applying Distort Filters to Create Flowers*

111 Gallery: Laurie Grace

112 Vector Photos: *Pen and Eyedropper Technique*

115 Gallery: Brad Hamann

116 Advanced Technique: Intricate Patterns: *Designing Complex Repeating Patterns*

118 Gallery: Tiffany Larsen

Drawing & Coloring

Illustrator allows you to fill open paths. When you fill an open path (left) the fill is applied as though the two endpoints were connected by a straight line (right)

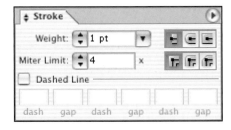

Left, same object as above with Stroke set to None; Right, same object with Fill set to None

Stroke palette

Drawing and coloring are the heart and soul of creating with Illustrator. This chapter continues the discussion of basic techniques that began in the first two chapters, rounding out the essential knowledge you'll need to work with Illustrator's drawing and coloring tools.

After reading this chapter, you'll be ready to move on to the more advanced techniques in the chapters that follow. Once you've mastered the techniques in this book, Illustrator offers unlimited possibilities for creating quick, simple, and elegant images.

The first part of this chapter, "Basic Drawing & Coloring," defines the basic tools and terms you'll need in order to understand the material in the rest of the book. The second part of the chapter, "Expanding Your Drawing & Coloring Toolset," is intended as a reference that you can consult as you work in Illustrator.

BASIC DRAWING & COLORING

In this section, you'll learn the fundamentals of strokes and fills, as well as the ins and outs of the Color palette and the Swatches palette. You'll also learn how to use those handy tools—the Eyedropper and Paint Bucket—to pick up and deposit color (plus other functions).

Fill

Fill is what goes inside of a path (hence the name). The fill you choose might be a color, a gradient, or a pattern. You can even choose a fill of None, in which case there will be no fill. When you fill an open path (where the endpoints aren't connected), the fill is applied as though the two endpoints were connected by a straight line.

Stroke

The *stroke* refers to the basic "outline" of your path. While the fill gives you control over the space enclosed by a path, you can think of the stroke as the way you "dress up" the path itself to make it look the way you want. You do this by assigning various attributes to the stroke, including weight (how thick or thin it looks), whether the line is solid or dashed, the dash sequence (if the line is dashed), and the styles of line joins and line caps. You can also assign your path a stroke of None, in which case it won't have a visible stroke at all. (Dashed lines, joins, and caps are covered in the following section, "Expanding Your Drawing & Coloring Toolset.")

The many ways to fill or stroke an object

To set the fill or stroke for an object, first select the object and then click on the Fill or Stroke icon near the bottom of the Toolbox. (You can toggle between fill and stroke by pressing the X key.) If you want to set the object's stroke or fill to None, use the / key, or click the None button on the Toolbox or the Color palette (the little white box with a red slash through it).

You can set the fill or stroke color you want using any of the following methods: 1) adjusting the sliders or sampling a color from the color bar in the Color palette; 2) clicking on a swatch in the Swatches palette; 3) using the Eyedropper tool to sample color from other objects in your file; or 4) sampling colors from the Color Picker. (To open the Adobe Color Picker, double-click the Fill or Stroke icon in the Toolbox or the Color palette.) In addition, you can drag color swatches from palettes to selected objects, or to the Fill/Stroke icon in the Toolbox.

Color palette

The Color palette is a collection of tools that allows you to mix and choose the colors for your artwork. In addition to the sliders and edit fields for locating precise colors, this palette includes a None button so you can set your Fill or Stroke to no color at all. The Color palette also sometimes displays a Last Color proxy; this allows you to easily return to the last color you used before choosing a pattern, a gradient, or setting None. The Color palette's menu options include Invert and Complement. Invert

Swapping fill and stroke

When you press the X key by itself, it toggles the Stroke or Fill box to active (in front of the other) on the Tools and Color palettes. If you press Shift-X it swaps the actual *attributes* or contents of the Stroke and Fill boxes. For example, if you start with a white fill and a black stroke, after you press Shift-X you will have a black fill and a white stroke. **Note:** *Because gradients are not allowed on strokes, Shift-X will not work when the current fill is a gradient.*

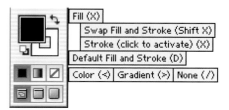

Fill and Stroke section of the Tools palette

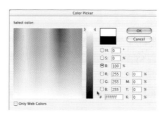

The Adobe Color Picker

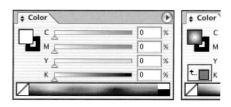

The Color palette. The sliders show the settings of the Fill or Stroke color—whichever is in front. Shown on the right is the Last Color proxy (outlined in red); when it appears you can click it to return to the last color used before choosing a pattern or gradient, or setting a style of None

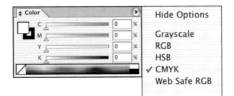

Color palette and pop-up menu

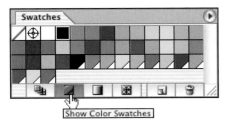

Swatches palette showing only the color swatches

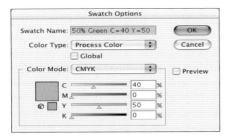

Swatch Options dialog box

Global colors in gradients

CATER (©INMOTION 2003)

By using just two global colors in the definition of his gradients, David Cater was able to easily change the color of this Mini Cooper as his clients required. See the David Cater/InMotion Gallery in the *Advanced Techniques* chapter for details

converts a color to its negative color (as in photographic negative). Complement locates the Adobe color complement of a selected color (the complements don't seem to match art school color wheels).

If you're doing print work in CMYK mode, you'll know you've chosen a non-CMYK color if an exclamation point appears on the Color palette. Illustrator will automatically correct your color to the nearest CMYK equivalent. Click the exclamation point to move the sliders—this will show you the corrected color settings.

If you're creating artwork for the Web, you can choose Web safe RGB from the Palette menu, which displays the hexadecimal values for colors in the Color palette. If a non-Web-safe color is selected, an out-of-gamut Web color icon displays (it looks like a 3D cube). If you want to stay aware of the CMYK gamut while working in RGB mode, watch for the exclamation point mentioned in the preceding paragraph. It displays when you choose a non-CMYK color, and you can click it to correct the color.

Swatches palette

To save colors you've mixed in the Color palette, drag them to the Swatches palette from the Color palette, the Toolbox, or the Gradient palette. You can also save your current color as a swatch by clicking the New Swatch button at the bottom of the Swatches palette. If you want to name the Swatch and set other options as you save it, either hold Option/Alt as you click the New Swatch button, or choose New Swatch from the palette menu.

Whenever you copy and paste objects that contain custom swatches or styles from one document to another, Illustrator will automatically paste those elements into the new document's palettes.

The Swatch Options dialog box (which you can open by double-clicking any swatch) lets you change the individual attributes of a swatch—including its name, color mode, color definition, and whether it's a process or spot color. (For pattern and gradient swatches, the only attribute in the Swatch Options dialog box is the name.)

There's also a check box that lets you decide whether changes you make to the swatch will be Global (in which case they'll be applied to all objects using the swatch color throughout the document) or not. The Global check box is off by default.

Saving custom swatch libraries

Once you've set up your Swatches palette to your satisfaction, you can save it as a custom swatch library for use with other documents. This can help you avoid having to duplicate your efforts later on. Saving a swatch library is easier than ever in Illustrator CS, thanks to the new Save Swatch Library command in the palette menu. Use this command to name and save your swatch library to the Adobe Illustrator CS > Presets > Swatches folder. The next time you launch Illustrator, the name you gave your file will appear in the Window > Swatch Libraries menu.

This is the most efficient method in most cases, but there are other ways to make your custom Swatches palette accessible to other documents. If you want, you can choose to save the custom Swatches palette as part of your own custom Template (.ait) file, in which case it will be available when you base new files on the Template (see the *Illustrator Basics* chapter for more on Illustrator's new Templates feature). Or, you can simply save your file wherever you'd like, and use the Other Library menu command (available either through the palette menu's Open Swatch Library command, or via Window > Swatch Libraries) to open your custom Swatches palette.

Of course, you can always open the original document when you need to access its Swatches palette—but saving it as a custom swatch library, as described above, will save you the trouble.

The Eyedropper and Paint Bucket tools

Two extremely useful Illustrator tools are the Eyedropper (which *picks up* stroke, fill, color, and text attributes) and the Paint Bucket (which *deposits* stroke, fill, color, and text attributes). These tools allow you to easily borrow

Using the libraries

The Swatch Library palettes (Window > Swatch Libraries) let you open Swatch palettes for specific color systems (such as Pantone or Trumatch). Or choose Other Library to access saved colors from any document.

The Save Swatch Library command in the Swatches palette menu makes it easy to save custom swatch libraries

When deleting swatches

When you click the Trash icon in the Swatches palette to delete selected swatches, Illustrator does *not* warn you that you might be deleting colors used in the document. Instead Illustrator will convert global colors and spot colors used to fill objects to non-global process colors. To be safe, choose Select All Unused and then click the Trash.

Note: *You will also not be warned when deleting graphic styles that might be used in the document.*

Eyedropper, Paint Bucket, and Measure tools

Using the Eyedropper and Paint Bucket options, you have complete control over what is picked up and/or deposited. In addition to Stroke, Fill, color, and text formatting, the Eyedropper and Paint Bucket tools can also be used to copy styles and type attributes (which are discussed later in the book). See the User Guide for more about using the Eyedropper and Paint Bucket to copy those attributes

attributes from one object and add them to another.

To set the default color for your next object, use the Eyedropper tool to click on an object that contains a color you want to sample. The Eyedropper will pick up the color of the object you clicked on. Then you can apply that color to another object just by clicking on it with the Paint Bucket tool.

With one tool selected, you can access the other by holding down Option (Mac) or Alt (Win). In addition to sampling color from objects, the Eyedropper can sample colors from a raster image if you hold down the Shift key.

Keep in mind that, by default, a regular click with the Eyedropper picks up all fill and stroke attributes, including whole patterns and gradients. But if you hold down the Shift key as you click, you'll not only be able to sample color from any type of object, you'll switch to sampling color *only* (as opposed to other attributes). Another effect of Shift-clicking is that the color you sample will be applied to only one or the other of the stroke or the fill, whichever is active in the Toolbox at the time you click.

You can control which attributes the Eyedropper picks up by using the Eyedropper/Paint Bucket Options dialog box (accessed by double-clicking the Eyedropper or Paint Bucket in the toolbox). You can also control how large an area the Eyedropper samples from raster images by using the Raster Sample Size menu at the bottom of the dialog box. Choosing Single Point will sample from a single pixel; 3 x 3 will pick up a sample averaged from a 3 pixel grid surrounding the point you click on; and 5 x 5 will do so for a 5 pixel grid. (This will help you get a more accurate color sample in many cases, since it can be difficult to get the colors that the eye "blends" from many pixels by clicking on a single point.)

The Pathfinders

It's often easier to create an object by combining two or more relatively simple shapes than it would be to draw the more complex result directly. Pathfinder operations let you easily combine objects to get the result you want. For examples of the Pathfinders in action, take a look at the Pathfinder palette chart on the following pages.

There are two effective ways to combine objects using the Pathfinders: 1) compound shapes, which remain "live" and editable; and 2) Pathfinder commands, which become "destructive" (permanent), and can't be returned to their original editable state except by using Undo.

See the "Add & Expand" lesson for a lesson that helps you to see compound shapes in action. The "Cutting & Joining" and "Divide & Color" lessons illustrate some uses of Pathfinder commands.

EXPANDING YOUR DRAWING & COLORING TOOLSET

This section provides more detail about compound shapes and related concepts, and explores some of the technical details involved with creating simple objects in Illustrator. If you're new to Illustrator you may want to experiment a bit with the lessons and Galleries later in this chapter to solidify what you've learned before continuing with this section. Consider "Expanding Your Drawing & Coloring Toolset" a reference section that is available when you're ready to delve deeper into the details of object creation in Illustrator. Topics covered include the Simplify command, color modification filters, and Illustrator's new "Liquify" set of tools.

Compound paths

A compound path consists of one or more simple paths that have been combined so that they behave as a single unit. One very useful aspect of compound paths is that a hole can be created where the original objects overlapped. These holes are empty areas cut out from others (think of the center of a donut, or the letter **O**), through which objects below can be seen.

To create a compound path, e.g., the letter **O**, draw an oval, then draw a smaller oval that will form the center hole of the **O**. Select the two paths, and then choose Object > Compound Path > Make. Select the completed letter and apply the fill color of your choice, and the hole

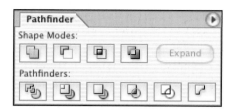

Pathfinder palette

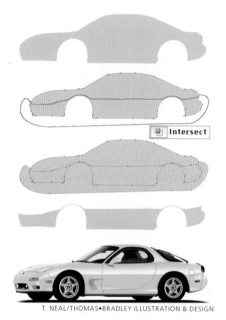

T. NEAL/THOMAS•BRADLEY ILLUSTRATION & DESIGN

Using the Intersect Pathfinder to cut out the lower part of the car body. Bottom, the finished illustration

Tim Girvin used the Divide Pathfinder to create the logo for the film The Matrix. *See his Gallery in the* Type *chapter*

Left to right: two ovals (the inner oval has no fill, but appears black because of the black fill of the larger oval behind it); as part of a compound path the inner oval knocks a hole into the outer one where they overlap; the same compound path with inner oval, which was Direct-selected and moved to the right to show that the hole is only where the objects overlap

Compounds operate as a unit

Compound shapes and compound paths don't have to overlap to be useful; apply a "compound" to multiple objects whenever you want them to operate as a unit, as if they were one object.

NEWMAN

Example of a compound path used here to make the letters operate as a unit (see Tip above); from the Gary Newman Gallery in the Type *chapter*

Compound paths or shapes?

The quick answer to this question is to use compound paths on simple objects for simple combining or cutting holes. Use compound shapes on more complex objects (such as live type or effects) and to more fully control how your objects interact. See the section "The pros and cons of compound shapes and paths" (opposite) for details on when to use which.

Learn to use Compound Shapes

The **Minus Back** Pathfinder command is the reverse of the **Subtract** shape mode. You can create the same effect using the Subtract Shape mode by simply reversing the stacking order of the elements in your compound shape. See the *Layers* chapter for more about object stacking order.

will be left empty. To adjust one of the paths within a compound path, use the Direct Selection tool. To adjust the compound path as a unit, use the Group Selection or Selection tool.

In addition to creating holes in objects, you can use compound paths to force multiple objects to behave as if they were a single unit. An advanced application of this is to make separate objects behave as one unit to mask others. For an example of this using separate "outlined" type elements (see figures at left extracted from Gary Newman's "Careers" Gallery in the *Type* chapter).

Holes and fills with compound paths

For simple holes, the Compound Path > Make command will generally give the result you need. If your compound path has multiple overlapping shapes, or you're not getting the desired holes in the spaces, see "Fill Rules.pdf" on the *Wow! CD*. Or try using compound shapes (described in the next section), which give you complete control. Certain results can be obtained only by using compound shapes.

Compound shapes

As mentioned earlier, sometimes it's easier to create an object by combining simpler objects, rather than trying to draw the complex result directly. A *compound shape* is a live combination of shapes using the Add, Subtract, Intersect, and/or Exclude Pathfinder operations. See the first four rows of the Pathfinder Commands chart on the pages following for a look at the various command functions, as well as examples of how they can be used.

Compound shapes can be made from two or more paths, other compound shapes, text, envelopes, blends, groups, or any artwork that has vector effects applied to it. To create a compound shape, choose Window > Pathfinder to display the Pathfinder palette. Then select your objects, and choose Make Compound Shape from the Pathfinder palette menu. To assign a particular Shape Mode, select one of the components of your compound shape and click on the corresponding Shape mode button on the top row of the Pathfinder palette.

Note: *Simply selecting your objects and pressing one of the Shape Mode buttons creates a compound shape and applies the shape mode you've chosen to the objects.*

The pros and cons of compound shapes and paths

Compound paths can be made only from simple objects. In order to make a compound path from more complex objects (such as live type or "envelopes") you have to first convert them into simpler objects (see the *Type* and *Live Effects & Graphic Styles* chapters for details on how to do this), and you'll only be able to edit them as paths. You can, however, combine complex objects using *compound shapes* and have them remain editable.

As you know by now, compound shapes allow you to combine objects in a variety of ways using Add, Subtract, Intersect, and Exclude. While keeping these Shape modes live, you can also continue to apply (or remove) Shape modes, or a wide variety of effects, to the compound shape as a unit. In later chapters, as you work with live effects such as envelopes, warps, and drop shadows, remember that you can integrate effects into your compound shapes while remaining able to edit your objects—even if your objects are editable type! Compound shapes can also help you bring objects into Photoshop (see the "Shape Shifting" lesson in the *Illustrator & Other Programs* chapter).

The power of compound shapes does come at a cost. Compound shapes require Illustrator to perform many calculations on your behalf, so as a result, too many compound shapes, or too many operations or effects applied to compound shapes, can slow down the screen redraw of your image. Although compound paths are much less powerful or flexible, they won't slow down your redraw. So if you're working with simple objects, it's best to use compound paths instead.

Starting objects: the word Sub is a compound shape ("Subtract" is subtracted from "Sub")

The starting objects from above, after Make Compound Shape and the corresponding shape modes have been applied, i.e., "intr" has the Intersect shape mode applied

In a compound shape all the original objects remain editable. Here the word "excl" was expanded to "Exclude," then a gradient and drop shadow were applied to the compound shape as a whole

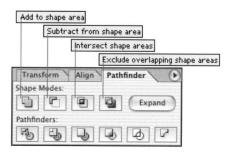

Shape Modes

The default settings for were used unless otherwise noted. Artists' work may use custom settings.

 Add
(Unite)

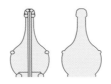

Before and after Unite

 Subtract
(Minus Front)

Before Minus Front

After Minus Front

 Intersect

Two objects, then overlapping and selected, then after choosing Intersect

Copies of intersection

 Exclude

Two objects

Both objects selected

YOU'RE IN BUSINESS
PRODUCTS FOR LEASE

 Minus Back

Green objects selected and made compound paths

After Minus Back, objects can then be filled separately

KINGSLAND

 Divide

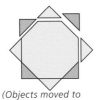
(Objects moved to show results)

Four objects

Objects divided

Each newly divided object filled

The default settings for were used unless otherwise noted. Artists' work may use custom settings.

Outline

Before Outline

After Outline, and re-setting line weight

STEUER

(Objects moved and line weights in-creased to .5 pt to show results)

Trim

(Objects moved to show results)

Before Trim; in Pre-view and Outline

After Trim; overlaps are reduced, BUT strokes are lost

SHIELDS DESIGN

Merge

(Objects moved to show results)

Before Merge in Outline

After Merge; like fills are united, BUT strokes are lost

STAHL

Crop

A copy of the fish in front to use for Crop

After Crop; objects are now separated

DROBLAS GREENBERG

Hard Mix

Same color objects don't mix, so over-lapping objects were colored differently

After Hard filter. Each overlap is now a separate object

After using the Eye-dropper to switch the colors in the front objects

MARGOLIS PINEO (digitized by Steuer)

Note: The Hard Mix filter is available in the Pathfinder Filters action set on the Wow! CD

Soft Mix

Before Soft filter; the blue waves over-lap and obscure the detail along the bot-tom of the rocks

After Soft filter: see "SandeeCs Soft Mix Chart.ai" in SandeeCs WOW Actions folder on the Wow! CD

FERSTER

Note: The Soft Mix filter is available in the Path-finder Filters action set on the Wow! CD

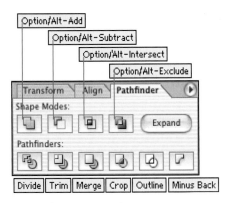

The Pathfinder Commands

The Adjust Colors filter (Filter > Colors)

Pathfinder commands

The Pathfinder commands consist of Option/Alt-Add, Option/Alt-Subtract, Option/Alt-Intersect, Option/Alt-Exclude, Divide, Trim, Merge, Crop, Outline, and Minus Back, all of which you can use to combine or separate shapes. See the preceding Pathfinder chart for a guide to what the various commands do and examples of how they can be used.

Unlike objects you create using compound shapes, the results you get when you apply the Pathfinder commands are destructive (they alter your artwork permanently). When working with complicated objects, it's best to use compound shapes instead of Pathfinders (see the Tip "Compound paths or shapes?" and the section "The Pros and Cons of Compound Shapes and Paths" earlier in this chapter).

The Divide, Trim, Merge, Crop, and Outline Pathfinder commands are used to separate (not combine) shapes—think of them as an advanced form of cookie cutters. The Trim and Merge commands require that your objects be filled before you use them.

Hard Mix and Soft Mix

You may notice that Hard Mix and Soft Mix are shown on the chart but no longer included on the Pathfinder palette. To restore these Pathfinders, install the *WOW Actions* "Pathfinder Filters.aia" from the *Wow! CD* (in "SandeeCs *Wow* Actions" folder in the "*WOW Actions*" folder), or apply them from Effect > Pathfinder, then choose Object > Expand Appearance (for more on Effects see the "Hard and Soft Mix" section in the *Live Effects & Graphic Styles* chapter introduction).

Color modification filters

Located in the Filter > Colors menu, the Adjust Colors filter lets you adjust the tint of Global colors in selections. Illustrator no longer allows multiple color spaces in a single document, so some color spaces will be unavailable. The Saturate filter (which integrates Saturate, Saturate More, Desaturate, and Desaturate More filters) lets you adjust the saturation of objects and images either by using sliders or by entering numerical values.

End of Lines

An aspect of Illustrator that often mystifies newcomers is the way endpoints of stroked lines are drawn. You may discover that although a set of lines seem to match up perfectly when viewed in Outline mode, they may visibly overlap when previewed. Solve this problem by changing the end caps in the Stroke palette.

Select one of the three end cap styles described below to determine how the endpoints of your selected paths will look when previewed.

The first (and default) choice is called a Butt cap; it causes your path to stop at the end anchor point. Butt caps are essential for creating exact placement of one path against another. The middle choice is the Round cap, which rounds the endpoint in a more natural manner. Round caps are especially good for softening the effect of single lines or curves, making them appear slightly less harsh. The final type is the Projecting cap, which extends lines and dashes at half the stroke weight beyond the end anchor point.

In addition to determining the appearance of path endpoints, cap styles affect the shape of dashed lines (see illustration at right).

Corner Shapes

The shape of a stroked line at its corner points is determined by the Join style in the Stroke palette. Each of the three styles determines the shape of the outside of the corner; the inside of the corner is always angled.

The default Miter join creates a pointy corner. The length of the point is determined by the width of the stroke, the angle of the corner (narrow angles create longer points, see illustration at right) and the Miter limit setting on the Stroke palette. Miter limits can range from 1x (which is always blunt) to 500x. Generally the default

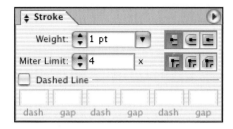

The Stroke palette

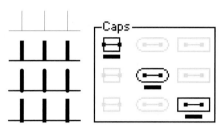

The same lines shown first in Outline, then in Preview with Butt cap, Round cap and Projecting cap

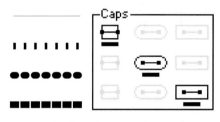

A 5 pt dashed line with a 2 pt dash and 6 pt gap shown first in Outline, then Preview with a Butt cap, Round cap, and Projecting cap

A path shown first in Outline, then in Preview with a Miter join, Round join, and Bevel join

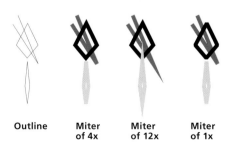

| Outline | Miter of 4x | Miter of 12x | Miter of 1x |

Objects with 6 pt strokes and various Miter limits, demonstrating that the angles of lines affects Miter limits

The Free Transform tool

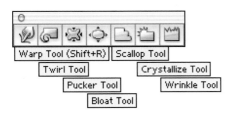

The Liquify Distortion tools' tear off palette can be accessed from the Warp tool: see "Tear off palettes" in the Illustrator Basics *chapter*

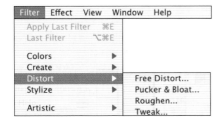

The Distort Filter menu

Miter join with a miter limit of 4x looks just fine.

The Round join creates a rounded outside corner for which the radius is half the stroke width. Illustrator's Round join option looks like Photoshop's Stroke layer effect. See the *Illustrator & Other Programs* chapter for more about Illustrator and Photoshop.

The Bevel join creates a squared-off outside corner, equivalent to a Miter join with the miter limit set to 1x.

Patterns

The *User Guide* has a very informative section on "Creating and Working with Patterns." For an example of working with patterns, see the lesson "Intricate Patterns: Designing Complex Repeating Patterns" in this chapter.

Free Transform & Liquify tools, and Distort filters

You can use Illustrator's Free Transform tool to distort the size and shape of an object by dragging the corner points of the object's bounding box. The shape of the object distorts progressively as you drag the handles.

One of the more recent additions to Illustrator is the suite of "Liquify" Distortion tools that arrived with Illustrator 10. They allow you to distort objects manually, by dragging the mouse over them. The Warp, Twirl, Pucker, Bloat, Scallop, Crystallize, and Wrinkle tools work not only on vector objects, but on embedded raster images as well. Use the Option/Alt key to resize the Liquify brush as you drag. These tools are a step beyond the Distort filters Illustrator had prior to version 10—they're more interactive, more intuitive, and more fun to use.

But the Distort filters Illustrator had prior to version 10 aren't gone—they can still be found under both the Filter menu (choose the topmost of the two Distort submenus in the Filter menu) and the Effect menu (choose Effect > Distort & Transform). They do have their uses. For instance, the ability to control distortion numerically via the filters' dialog boxes can allow for greater precision. They can also be used to create in-betweens for animations in cases where blends might not give the desired results or might be too cumbersome.

The Distort filters include Free Distort, Pucker & Bloat, Roughen, Tweak, Twist, and Zig Zag. All of these filters distort paths based on the paths' anchor points. They move (and possibly add) anchor points to create distortions. Checking the Preview box in the dialog box lets you see and modify the results as you experiment with the settings.

Many of the Free Distort functions can also be performed with the Free Transform tool (for a lesson using the Free Transform tool, see the "Distort Dynamics" lesson later in this chapter).

Path Simplify command

More is not better when it comes to the number of anchor points you use to define a path. The more anchor points, the more complicated the path—which makes the file size larger and harder to process when printing. The Simplify command (Object > Path > Simplify) removes excess anchor points from one or more selected paths without making major changes to the path's original shape. You might want to apply this command after using the Auto Trace tool, opening a clip art file, or using Adobe Streamline.

Two sliders control the amount and type of simplification. Enable Show Original and turn on the Preview option to preview the effect of the sliders as you adjust them. The Preview option also displays the original number of points in the curve and the number that will be left if the current settings are applied. Adjust the Curve Precision slider to determine how accurately the new path should match the original path. The higher the percentage, the more anchor points will remain, and the closer the new path will be to the original. The endpoints of an open path are never altered. The Angle Threshold determines when corner points should become smooth. The higher the threshold, the more likely a corner point will remain sharp.

Need more points?

Use the Add Anchor Point tool to add points at specific locations along your path. Or use the Object > Path > Add Anchor Points command to neatly place one point between each existing pair of points on your path.

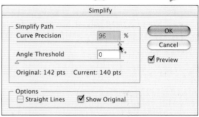

The Object > Path > Simplify dialog box can be used to reduce the number of points and to stylize type

More Simplify Commands

- Use Object > Path > Clean Up to remove stray points, unpainted objects, or empty text paths.
- If you want to see the stray points before deleting them, use Select > Object > Stray Points to select them, then press the Delete key to remove them.

Simple Realism

Realism from Geometry and Observation

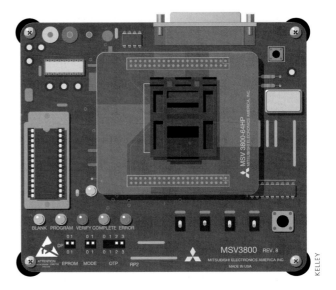

Overview: *Draw a mechanical object using the Rectangle, Rounded Rectangle, and Ellipse tools; use tints to fill all of the paths; add selected highlights and offset shadows to simulate depth.*

1

The default Fill and Stroke in the Tools palette; setting the default stroke weight for objects

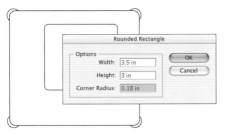

Creating rounded rectangles and ellipses to construct the basic forms

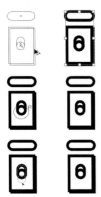

Option-Shift/Alt-Shift dragging a selection to duplicate and constrain it to align with the original; using the Lasso tool to select specific points; Shift-dragging to constrain and move the selected points

Many people believe the only way to achieve realism in Illustrator is with elaborate gradients and blends, but this illustration by Andrea Kelley proves that artistic observation is the real secret. Using observation and some simple Illustrator techniques, Kelley drew technical product illustrations of computer chip boards for a handbook for her client, Mitsubishi.

1 Recreating a mechanical object with repeating geometric shapes by altering copies of objects. Most artists find that close observation, not complex perspective, is the most crucial aspect to rendering illustrations. To sharpen your skills in observing the forms and details of objects, select a simple mechanical device to render in grayscale. First, create a new Illustrator document. Then experiment with the Ellipse, Rectangle, and Rounded Rectangle tools to draw the basic elements of the device. After you've made your first object—with the object still selected—click on the Default Fill and Stroke icon in the Tool palette, open the Stroke palette (Window > Stroke), and choose a stroke weight of 0.75 pt using the Weight pop-up menu. All objects you make from that point on will have the same fill and stroke as your first object.

Because mechanical and computer devices often have similar components, you can save time by copying an object you've drawn and then modifying the shape of the copy. You can easily align your copy with the original by holding the Opt-Shift/Alt-Shift keys while dragging out the copy from the selected object to the desired location.

To illustrate a series of switches, Kelley dragged a selected switch (while holding Option-Shift/Alt-Shift to copy and constrain its movement), stretched the switch copy by selecting one end of the switch knob with the Lasso and dragged it down (holding the Shift key to constrain it vertically). She repeated this process to create a line of switches with the same switch plate width, but different switch knob lengths.

2 **Using tints to fill the objects.** At this point, all the objects are filled with white and have a stroke of black. Select a single object and set the Stroke to None and the Fill to black using the Color palette (Window>Color). Open the Swatches palette (Window>Swatches) and Option/Alt-click on the New Swatch icon to name it "Black Spot," and set the Color Type to Spot Color. Click OK to save your new spot color. Then create a tint using the Tint slider in the Color palette. Continue to fill individual objects (be sure to set their Stroke to None) using Black Spot as the fill color, and adjust the tints for individual objects using the Tint slider until you are happy with their shades. Kelley used percentages from 10–90%, with most of the objects being 55–75% black.

3 **Creating a few carefully placed highlights.** Look closely at the subject of your drawing and decide where to place highlights. For lines that follow the contour of your object, select part or all of your object's path with the Direct Selection tool, copy (Edit>Copy) and Paste in Front (Edit>Paste in Front) that path or path section. Using the Color palette, change the Fill of your path to None and use the tint slider to change the Stroke to a light value of gray. While the highlight's path is still selected, you can reduce or increase the width of your stroke using the Weight field of the Stroke palette. If you

2

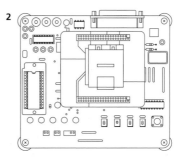

The drawn object prior to filling selected paths with gray

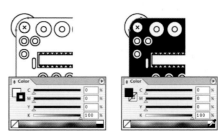

Left, the selected path set to the default stroke and fill colors; right, the selected object set to a fill of Black and a stroke of None

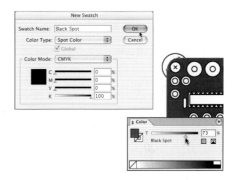

Creating a new custom spot color that will then appear in the Swatches palette; setting the selected path to a fill of 73% Spot Black using the Tint slider in the Color palette

Individual paths filled with tints of Black Spot in a range from 10% to 90%

3

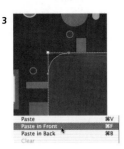

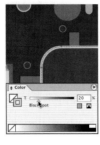

Using *Paste in Front* on a selected, copied path to duplicate it directly on top; changing the Stroke and Fill of the duplicate path to create a highlighted outline

Using the Stroke palette Weight field to increase or decrease the width of the highlight path

Placing small circles with a Fill of 0% black (white) and a darker inset curved path to simulate depth; Option-Shift/Alt-Shift dragging a selected path to duplicate the path and constrain its movement

4

Copying a dial and choosing *Paste in Back*; using Arrow keys to offset the copy; setting the Fill "T" tint to 87% black to create a shadow from the copy

need to trim the length of a highlight, cut its path with the Scissors tool and then select the unwanted segments with the Direct Selection tool and delete them.

For some of the knobs and dials on her chip, Kelley used circular highlights with a value of 0% black (white) and an inset curved path with a darker value to simulate depth. Once you are satisfied with the highlights on a particular knob, select the paths (both the highlights and the knob) and hold down the Option/Alt key while dragging the objects in order to duplicate them (hold down Option-Shift/Alt-Shift to copy and constrain the paths as you drag them).

For her highlights, Kelley used lines that varied in weight from .2 to .57 pt and colors that varied in tint from 10–50%. She also used carefully placed white circles for some of the highlights. Try experimenting with different Cap and Join styles in the Stroke palette; see "End of Lines" section and figures in the introduction to this chapter for more on Caps and Joins.

4 Creating shadows. Follow the same procedure as above, but this time use darker tints on duplicated paths pasted behind in order to create shadows. Select a path to make into a shadow, copy it, and use Edit > Paste in Back to place a copy of the path directly behind the original path. Use your Arrow keys to offset the copy, and change the Fill to a darker tint using the Color palette.

Consider using Effects to create shadows and highlights. See the *Live Effects & Graphic Styles* chapter for information on building multi-stroke appearances and saving them as styles that you can use on other artwork.

Symbols

Use Symbols instead of copies of artwork if you want to export the illustration as a Shockwave Flash file (Symbols result in a smaller file). See the *Brushes & Symbols* chapter to learn more about creating and modifying Symbols, and about the benefits of using them.

© 1989 BLACKDOG

FOX / BLACKDOG (Art Director: Neal Zimmermann, Zimmermann Crowe Design)

Mark Fox/BlackDog

Using techniques similar to those shown in the next lesson, Mark Fox redesigned this eagle decal for Bianchi USA—the American branch of the Italian bicycle manufacturer—under the art direction of Neal Zimmermann (Zimmermann Crowe Design).

Cutting & Joining
Basic Path Construction with Pathfinders

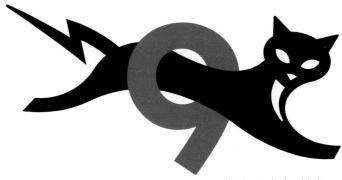

FOX / BLACKDOG (Art Director: Jeff Carino, Landor Associates)

Overview: *Design an illustration using overlapping objects; use the Pathfinder palette to join and intersect objects, join lines to circles, and cut objects from other objects.*

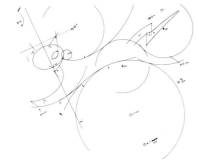

Fox's inked sketch drawn with a compass
NOTE: Fox created his image in reverse. As a last step, he used the Reflect tool to flip the final image (see the *Zen* chapter for help reflecting).

Using the Tools palette to set the Fill to None before starting to draw

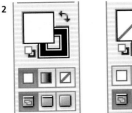

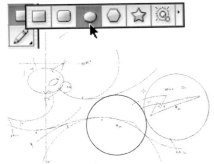

Drawing constrained circles from the center with the Ellipse tool (while holding Option-Shift/ Alt-Shift) to trace over the placed template

To redesign the classic "9 Lives" cat symbol that has appeared on Eveready batteries for over 50 years, Mark Fox began with a hand-drawn sketch. Once his sketch was approved, he inked the sketch with a Rapidograph pen and a compass, and then reconstructed the ink image in Illustrator using permanent (destructive) Pathfinder commands. To permanently apply the top row of Pathfinders, you'll have to hold Option (Mac)/Alt (Win) when you click these icons. The bottom row of Pathfinder icons are always permanent. *Especially* when you work with permanent Pathfinders, make sure you save incremental versions of your image as you work.

1 Creating a sketch and placing it as a template. Fox used a compass to create a precise drawing constructed of fluid curves. Using his inked sketch as a template, Fox then used the Ellipse tool to recreate his compass circles in Illustrator. Create your own sketch using traditional materials and then scan it, or sketch directly into a painting program (such as Painter or Photoshop). Save your sketch as a TIFF or your preferred raster format, and place it into a new Illustrator document as a template. To do this, choose File > Place to locate the image you wish to use as a template, then enable the Template option and click Place (see the *Layers* chapter for more on templates).

2 Tracing your template using adjoining and overlapping objects. In order to see what you're doing as you work, use the Fill/Stroke section of the Tools palette to set your Fill to None and Stroke to black before you begin drawing. Now use the Ellipse and Rectangle tools to create the basic shapes that will make up your image. Fox used some circles to form the shapes themselves (like the rump of the cat), and others to define the areas that would later be cut from others (like the arc of the underbelly). To create perfect circles or squares hold the Shift key while you draw with the Ellipse and Rectangle tools. By default, ellipse and rectangles are drawn from a corner—in order to draw these objects from a center point, hold down the Option (Mac) or Alt (Win) key as you draw. To create a circle from its center point, you'll need to hold down the modifier keys Shift+Option (Mac), or Shift+Alt (Win) as you draw—don't release the modifier keys until after you release your mouse button. Because Fox measured everything in millimeters in his inking stage, he created his circles numerically. With the Ellipse tool, Fox Option-clicked (Alt clicked for Win) on each center point marked on his template, entered the correct diameter for Width and Height, and clicked OK.

3 Constructing curves by combining parts of different circles. Once your paths are drawn and in position, use the Pathfinder palette (Window > Pathfinder) to combine portions of different circles to create complex curves. After drawing basic circles, use the Line Segment tool to draw a line through the circles at the point where you want to join them, and choose Object > Path > Divide Objects Below. Then select the sub-sections of the divided circles that you don't want and delete. To join separate adjoining curves, select them, hold Option/Alt, and click the Add to Shape Area Pathfinder icon.

4 Constructing objects using the Intersect Pathfinder command. If the area you wish to keep is the portion where objects overlap, use the Intersect command. Fox used Intersect to create the eyes and the nose of the cat. To make the eye shape, he drew a circle and then dragged off a duplicate by holding Option/Alt as he moved it with

3

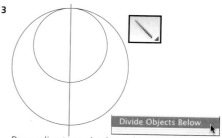

Draw a line to mark where objects will be joined and apply Object >Path >Divide Objects Below

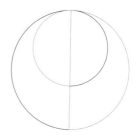

Select and delete unwanted portions of objects that won't be part of the final curve

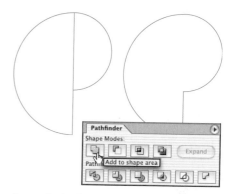

Once only the elements you wish to be joined remain, select them, hold Option/Alt and click on the Add to Shape Area Pathfinder icon

4

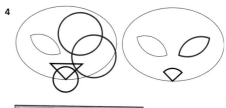

Constructing the eyes and nose using the Intersect Shape Areas Pathfinder command

5

Drawing one line from an anchor point on the circle and another angled line slightly removed

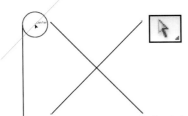

Creating a perpendicular copy of the angled line by double-clicking the Rotate tool, specifying a 90° Angle, and clicking copy

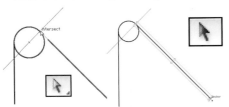

Moving the perpendicular copy to the circle's center and then making it into a guide

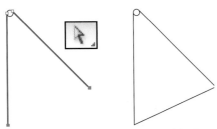

Moving the angled line tangent to the circle using the guide, then lengthening the line

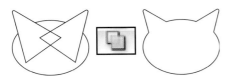

Selecting the two end anchor points of the lines and closing using Join to connect the lines

Using the Add to Shape Pathfinder command to attach the circle to the angled shape, then the completed ears to the cat-head ellipse

the Selection tool. He then positioned the two circles so the overlap created the desired shape, selected both circles, and held down Option/Alt while he clicked the Intersect Shape Areas Pathfinder icon.

5 Attaching lines to circles. Fox connected angled lines to a tiny circle to form the cat's ear. To smoothly attach lines to circles, the lines need to lie "tangent" to the circle (touching the circle at only one anchor point). To work with precision, turn on Smart Guides (View menu).

Start with the Ellipse tool and draw a small circle. To create the first tangent line, choose the Line Segment tool, and place the cursor over the left side anchor-point of the circle. When you see the word "anchor point" click-drag downward from that anchor point to draw a vertical line (hold the Shift key to constrain your line to vertical).

Creating a tangent line that doesn't begin at an anchor point is trickier. Start by drawing another line slightly apart from the circle, but at the angle you desire (holding the Shift key constrains your line to horizontals, verticals, and 45° angles). To help you find the tangent point for this line, you need to create a line perpendicular to it. With your angled line selected, double-click the Rotate tool, enter 90°, and click Copy. Use the Direct selection tool to grab this perpendicular copy of your line near the middle and drag it toward the center of your circle; release the mouse when you see the word "center." With this line still selected, make it into a guide with View > Guides > Make Guides. Now select your angled line (marquee it with the Direct selection tool, or click it with the Selection or Group selection tool). Finally, with the Direct selection tool, grab the top anchor point and drag it to where the perpendicular guide meets the circle; release the mouse when you see the word "intersect."

To adjust the length of either line, switch to the Selection tool, select the line, and drag the bounding box from the middle end handle at the open anchor point.

The Add to Shape Pathfinder ignores lines, so to attach the lines to the circle, first connect the lines together to form a two-dimensional shape. Using the Direct Selection tool, marquee the two open anchor points and choose Object > Path > Join (⌘-J/Ctrl-J) to connect the points with a line.

Finally, to unite your angled shape with the circle, select them both, hold Option/Alt, and click the Add to Shape Area Pathfinder icon. Fox also used Add to Shape Area to join the ears to the head (he rotated the first ear into position, and used the Reflect tool to create a copy for the other ear—see the *Zen of Illustrator* chapter for help with rotation and reflection).

6 Cutting portions of paths with another object. To create the rear flank of the cat, Fox used a large object to cut away an area (subtract) from another circle. Use the Selection tool to select the path you'll use as the cutter and bring it to the top of the stacking order (in the exact position) either by choosing Object > Arrange > Bring to Front, or Edit > Cut and then Edit > Paste in Front (⌘-F/Ctrl-F). Marquee or Shift-select to select the cutter object as well as the objects you want to cut. To apply the cut, hold Option/Alt and click the Subtract from Shape Area Pathfinder icon. If you want a different result—Undo, make adjustments and reapply the Pathfinder.

6

Better to see Pathfinders...

If your objects are styled with  a stroke and no fill, you can swap the Fill and Stroke styling to better see the effects of a Pathfinder command. To do this, with objects selected, click on the Swap Fill and Stroke arrows in the bottom section of the Tools palette. Click again to swap it back.

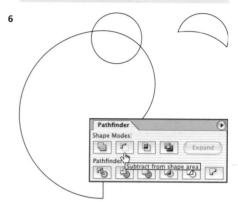

Using the Subtract from Shape Area to cut one object from others

Manually cut with Scissors

Although it's not as precise as using a line and "Divide Objects Below," you *can* use the Scissors tool to cut any path, including open paths. Turn on Smart Guides (View menu) and click with the Scissors tool when the word "Path" appears to place two coinciding points on the path. To separate the points, first deselect the path entirely. Then, with the Direct Selection tool, click on top of the new points to select only the top point. Then you can move or delete the selected point.

Joining open paths & closing paths smoothly

Pathfinder > Add to Shape will close open paths, joining them with a straight line. Use the following method to manually join two open paths or to close a path smoothly. Since you can only join two points at a time, start by deleting any stray points (Select > Object > Stray Points). Before you can join points with a smooth curve, you need to ensure the points are exactly on top of each other. Use the Direct Selection tool or Lasso to select one pair of end anchor points and choose Object > Path > Average (Both) and click OK, then Object > Path > Join and click OK. To Average/Join in one step, press ⌘-Shift-Option-J (Mac)/Ctrl-Shift-Alt-J (Win)—there isn't a menu command for this.

Add & Expand
More Pathfinder Palette Basics

Overview: *Create and position overlapping objects; use the Pathfinder palette to unite the paths into an editable Compound Shape, then consolidate the paths with Expand.*

1

Assembling the basic elements for creating the beaver lodge

Positioning the stick paths to overlap the lodge path—the final assemblage

2

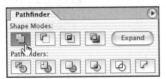

Applying Add in the Pathfinder palette to the selected paths to create a Compound Shape
Note: The Compound Shape will take on the Fill and Stroke attributes of the topmost object.

The design team of Diane and John Kanzler used the Pathfinder palette to create a logo and vehicle signage for the Urban Wildlife Program of the Fund for Animals. When the illustration was completed and approved by the client, the Kanzlers used the Expand feature of the Pathfinder palette as the final step to prepare the file for sending to the sign company.

1 Creating and positioning overlapping objects. The Kanzlers wanted their logo's final lodge to look like it was made of sticks, like a real beaver lodge. To achieve this effect, begin by using the Pen tool to draw a basic lodge form. Set the lodge path's Fill to Black and the Stroke to None, then adjust the Black to a gray value using the K slider in the Color palette. (For more on using the Color palette, see the "Simple Realism" lesson earlier in this chapter.) Draw a series of jagged logs and branches with a Fill of Black and a Stroke of None; this will make placement of the individual branch and log paths easier to view over the gray lodge shape. Next, use the Selection tool to position the log and branch paths so they overlap the lodge path. When you are satisfied with the placement of the logs and branches, choose Select > All to select all the paths you want to be united.

2 Using the Pathfinder palette to Add. Open the Pathfinder palette (Window > Pathfinder) and click on the

Add button in the top row of palette choices. The result is a fully editable Compound Shape that unites all of the selected paths. You should note that the paths within the Compound Shape will take on the Fill and Stroke attributes of the topmost path. To reposition any path within the Compound Shape, select and move it with the Group Selection tool, or use the Direct Selection tool to click within a filled path to select and reposition it. You can use the Direct Selection tool to edit the shape of any path within the Compound Shape.

3 Using Expand to convert Compound Shapes into a single path. The Kanzlers maintained the beaver lodge as a "live" editable Compound Shape during the client approval process, which made modifications easier.

When their final sign was approved, the Kanzlers needed to prepare the file to send to the signage contractor. The design was to be output directly to the contractor's vinyl-cutting equipment using an older version of Illustrator on the Windows platform. In order to minimize the possibility of problems in printing their image with an earlier version of Illustrator, and to reduce the potential for their illustration to be inadvertently modified, they chose to apply the Expand command to permanently unite the separate beaver lodge shapes into one continuous path. Once you apply Expand to Compound Shape artwork, the separate paths will be united and you will no longer be able to move the individual stick shapes independently. Therefore, if you think you may need to edit the silhouette sometime in the future, be sure to save a copy of your artwork before you apply Expand.

To Expand your live Compound Shapes (in a copy of your file), use the Selection tool to select your Compound Shape. Then, in the Pathfinder palette, click the Expand button to permanently apply your Pathfinder—in this case, to unite your paths. You can also access Expand by choosing "Expand Compound Shape" from the Pathfinder palette's pop-up menu.

The beaver lodge as a Compound Shape

Using the Group Selection tool to move individual paths within the Compound Shape

Expanding the Compound Shape to consolidate all of the individual paths into a single path

(Top) The final, expanded path; (bottom) the final logo and signage

Divide & Color

Applying Pathfinder Divide & Subtract

Overview: *Design an illustration using overlapping elements; create individual paths using Divide, and delete unnecessary paths; using Subtract to cut "holes" and create Compound Paths; Divide again and assign colors to divided objects.*

1

Creating the basic elements using the Rectangle and Ellipse tools

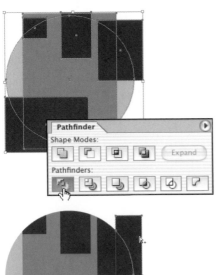

(Top) Selecting all paths and clicking on Divide in the Pathfinder palette; (bottom) selecting and deleting unnecessary paths

Illustrator's Pathfinder palette provides many ways to combine objects. To create this disco clock for a World-studio Foundation's "Make Time" benefit, John Pirman used the Divide and Subtract Pathfinder options to permanently alter his objects. This allowed him to adjust colors within each of the divided areas in his illustration.

1 Creating and positioning paths; dividing overlapping paths. Pirman created a circle and a number of rectangles to serve as the background (and later as the objects to Divide his figure shapes) for his clock face design. In a new Illustrator document, draw a filled circle with no Stroke using the Ellipse tool (hold the Shift key to constrain the ellipse to a circle). Then use the Rectangle tool to draw a few rectangles filled with different gray values, and Stroke of None. Use a selection tool to move the rectangles around until you are satisfied with an arrangement of rectangles in relationship to the circle. Next, choose Select > All, then open the Pathfinder palette (Window > Pathfinder) and click the Divide button (in the palette's bottom row). All overlapping paths will split into separate, editable objects. To delete the extra paths outside of this "divided circle" shape, first choose Select > Deselect, then select them, and press Delete.

2 Using Subtract to create "holes" and Divide again. Next, Pirman drew a series of silhouetted human figures with the Pen and Pencil tools and arranged them in relation to the background. For figures that included enclosed "negative space" (such as an arm partially touching another part of the body) he used Pathfinder Subtract to cut the areas as "holes," so objects behind would show through. To cut enclosed areas into permanent holes, first make sure that your enclosed paths are on top of the rest of the figure. Next, set solid fills for all the objects, with no strokes. Then select your figure and the enclosed spaces and hold Option (Mac)/Alt (Win) while you click on Subtract in the Pathfinder palette (holding Option (Mac)/Alt (Win) while applying a Pathfinder in the upper row of the palette makes that Pathfinder action permanent). Your figure with holes has now become a Compound Path. Use the Selection tool to reposition the complete figure, the Group Selection tool to reposition the holes, or the Direct Selection tool to edit the paths.

Pirman created a palette of blues, greens, and white to apply to his figures. He then positioned each figure over his "divided circle" background and used his background objects to divide the figures. To do this, choose different color fills for your figures and arrange them in front of your divided background (the stacking order doesn't matter). Next, select all your paths (Select > All) and click Divide in the Pathfinder palette. As before, all of the overlapping paths will now be split into individual paths. Use the Group Selection tool to select and delete paths outside of your background shape, and then to select individual sections of the figures in order to change the fill color. Pirman used colors of similar value to visually integrate the divided figures.

With his figures divided, Pirman then used his palette colors to recolor the various divided sections of the figures and continued to make adjustments to the background. To do this, color all of the paths that make up the fully divided illustration using your color palette. Using the Group Selection tool, click on the individual paths within the circle shape (hold Shift to select multiple paths) and style with any Fill color you like.

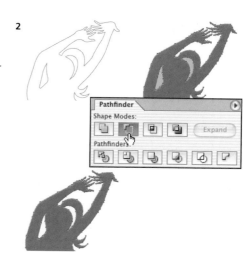

Drawing a figure that includes enclosed objects defining "negative space" (top left), selecting all the objects that create the figure and applying Pathfinder > Subtract while holding Option/Alt (top right), the figure now as a Compound Path

Filled figures; positioning the colored figure paths over the divided circle background

The process of styling individual objects with different colors.

Cubist Constructs

Creative Experimentation with Pathfinders

Overview: *Create objects as the basis for Pathfinder commands; use commands on different sets of objects; make color and object adjustments.*

The scanned sketch placed as a template

Before and after circles are cut and joined

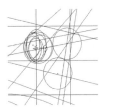
On the left, three objects (shown with different stroke colors); on the right, the objects with colored fills (no stroke) prior to running the Soft Mix command

Soft Mix applied, then objects recolored

CHAN

To build his geometrically complex style, Ron Chan depends on Illustrator's drawing tools and the Pathfinder palette commands. Many different ways exist to achieve similar effects. Here are some that Chan has perfected.

1 Preparing the basic objects you will work from.
Create the objects that will form the basis for your filtering. Chan used methods discussed elsewhere in the book to prepare the initial objects, including scanning a sketch to use as a template (see "Digitizing a Logo" in the *Layers* chapter), creating a custom drawing grid (*Type* chapter) in its own layer, and making a masking layer (*Advanced Techniques* chapter). He cut and joined circles to form elements such as the head shown at left (see "Cutting & Joining," earlier in this chapter).

2 Selecting overlapping objects and applying Soft Mix. After creating a few overlapping objects, you might choose to see how those objects "cut into" each other. First, select the objects with any selection tool. Then use the Pathfinder commands (Window > Pathfinder). The previous lesson "Divide & Conquer" uses the Divide Pathfinder to create separate objects for each area in which the objects intersect. Chan preferred to use the Soft Mix Pathfinder. Soft Mix creates new colors where objects overlap, making the intersections easy to . In this way, Chan could use the Direct Selection tool to choose particular divided objects for recoloring. (If your version of Illustrator doesn't include Soft Mix and Hard Mix in the Pathfinder palette, see the Tip at right.) To recolor all like-colored objects together, Chan Direct-selected one color and used Select > Same > Fill Color, to select all objects of that color.

3 Outlining and offsetting paths. Turning paths into outlined shapes gives you flexibility in styling and aligning lines. Chan stroked the jaw path and then outlined it using Object > Path > Outline Stroke. This allowed him to align the bottom edge of the line to the chin object. If you outline a path, you can fill it with gradients (see the *Blends, Gradients & Mesh* chapter) or patterns (for a lesson in patterns, see "Intricate Patterns" later in this chapter). Another way to turn a path into a fill able shape is to offset a copy of a selected path (Object > Path > Offset) and then join the endpoints of the copy and the original.

4 Cropping copies for an inset look. To create the look of an inset or lens of your image, first select and copy all the objects that will be affected, and then use Paste in Front and Group on the copy you just made. Using any method you wish, create a closed object to define the inset area. With the object still selected, press the Shift key and use the Selection tool to select the grouped copy and click the Crop icon in the Pathfinder palette. You can then use the Direct Selection tool to choose individual objects so you can change color or opacity, or apply effects from the Effect menu. Also, try experimenting with the Colors > Adjust Colors filter (Filter menu) until you achieve a color change you like.

Where's Soft Mix Pathfinder?
Illustrator no longer includes Hard Mix and Soft Mix in the Pathfinder palette. To restore Mix functionality, either install the *Wow! Actions* "Pathfinder Filters.aia" from the *Wow! CD* (in "SandeeCs WOW Actions," in the "WOW Actions" folder), or apply them from Effect > Pathfinder, then choose Object > Expand Appearance.

3

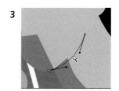

Selecting a path and then applying Object > Path > Outline Stroke

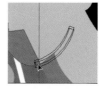
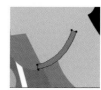

The outlined path was moved up (Smart Guides are turned on), then recolored

4

Artwork copied and pasted in front, then circle drawn for inset shape

After Pathfinder > Crop, the circle was recolored

Isometric Systems

Arrow Keys, Constrain Angles & Formulas

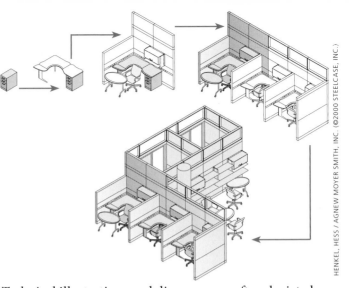

Overview: *Create detailed views of an object from front, top and side; use an isometric formula to transform the objects; set "Constrain-angle" and "Keyboard Increment;" use Lasso and Arrow keys with Snap to Point to adjust and assemble objects.*

Stubborn snapping-to-point

Sometimes if you try to move an object just slightly, it will annoyingly "snap" to the wrong place. If this happens, move it away from the area and release. Then grab the object again at the point you'd like to align and move it so that it snaps into the correct position. If you still have trouble, zoom in. As a last resort, you can disable "Snap to Point" in the View menu.

1

Top, front and side faces with more than one component are grouped

2

Scaling, skewing and rotating

Technical illustrations and diagrams are often depicted in isometrics, and Adobe Illustrator can be the ideal program both for creating your initial illustrations, and for transforming them into this projection. The artists at Agnew Moyer Smith (AMS) created and transformed the diagrams on these pages using their three-step iso projection. For both the initial creation and manipulation of the isometric objects in space, AMS custom-set "Keyboard Increment" and "Constrain Angle" (in Illustrator > Preferences > General) and made sure that View > Snap to Point was enabled.

1 Creating detailed renderings of the front, side and top views of your object to scale. Before you begin a technical illustration, you should choose a drawing scale, then coordinate the settings Preferences > General to match. For instance, to create a file drawer in the scale of 1 mm = 2″, set the Units to millimeters and "Keyboard Increment" to .5 mm, and make sure that the "Snap to Point" option is enabled. With these features enabled and matching your drawing scale, it's easy to create detailed views of your object. To easily keep track of your object sizing as you work, choose Window > Info. If a portion of the real object is inset 1″ to the left, you can use the ← key to move the path one increment (.5 mm) farther left. Finally, Snap to Point will help you align and assemble your various components. Select and group all the components of the front view. Separately group the top and side so you'll be able to easily isolate each of the views for transformation and assembly. AMS renders every internal detail, which allows them to view "cut-aways" or adjust individual elements, or groups of elements—for instance, when a drawer is opened.

2 Using an isometric formula to transform your objects, then assembling the elements.

The artists at AMS created and transformed the diagrams on these pages using their three-step process, which is fully demonstrated on the *Wow! CD*. To transform your objects, double-click on the various tools to specify the correct percentages numerically. First, select all three views and scale them 100% horizontally and 86.6% vertically. Next, select the top and side, shear them at a –30° angle, and then shear the front 30°. Rotate the top and front 30° and the side –30°. The movement chart shows angles and directions.

To assemble the top, front and side, use the Selection tool to grab a specific anchor-point from the side view that will contact the front view, and drag it until it snaps into the correct position (the arrow turns hollow). Next, select and drag to snap the top into position. Finally, select and group the entire object for easy reselection.

3 Using selection, Constrain Angle and Arrow keys to adjust objects and assemble multiple components.

Try using the Lasso tool to select a portion of an object (Shift-Lasso adds points to a selection; Option-Lasso/Alt-Lasso deletes points from a selection), setting Constrain Angle to 30°, then slide your selection along the isometric axes using alternating Arrow keys. Select entire objects and snap them into position against other objects. Also, look at the movement chart (top of the page) to determine the direction in which to move, then double-click the Selection tool in the toolbox to specify a numeric movement for selections or objects.

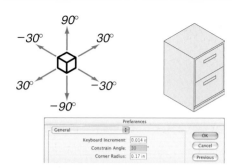

An arrow key movement chart based on a Constrain Angle of 30°; AMS groups fully transformed and assembled objects for easy selection; setting Constrain Angle in Preferences > General

3

You can use the Lasso to select the points you want to move.

To lengthen the cart, select the points indicated and move in the direction of the arrow (–30°)

To widen the cart, select the points indicated, and either double-click on the Selection tool in the Toolbox to specify a Move numerically, or use your Arrow keys

Transforming one object into the next, by Direct-selecting the appropriate anchor points and using the Move command, or by setting and using a custom Constrain Angle and Arrow keys

Automated Isometric Actions!
Rick Henkel of AMS created *WOW Actions* that automate formulas for isometrics (on the *Wow! CD*).

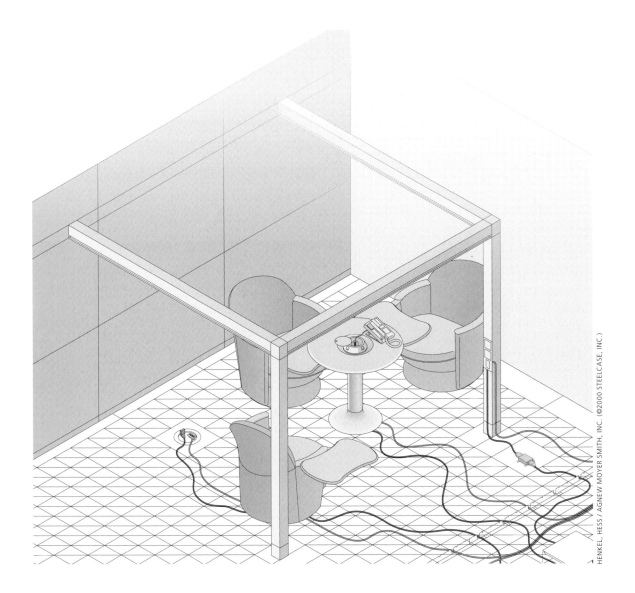

Rick Henkel, Kurt Hess /
Agnew Moyer Smith, Inc.

Agnew Moyer Smith's artists use Illustrator not only to create discrete elements, but also because it provides so much flexibility in composing an environment with those elements. Objects can be saved in separate files by category and used as "libraries" when constructing different scenes.

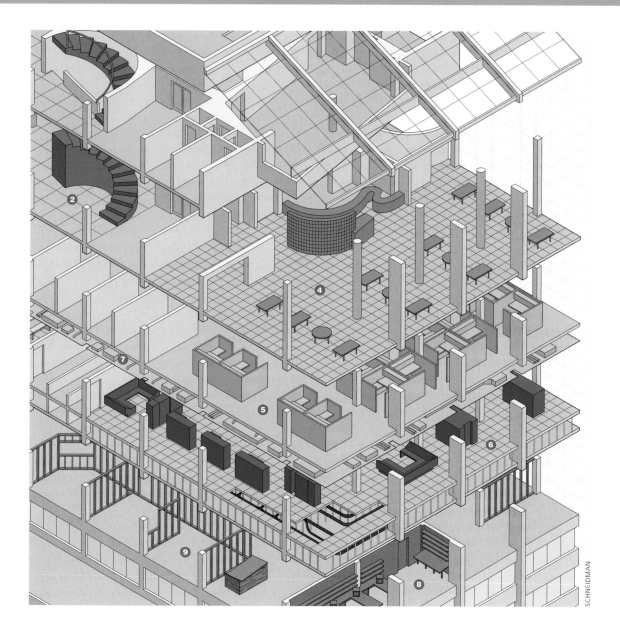

Jared Schneidman

Jared Schneidman illustrated this building for a capabilities brochure for Structure Tone, an interior construction company. Schneidman traced a scan of an architectural drawing of the building, rendered originally in an isometric view. While drawing, Schneidman set the

Constrain Angle (Preferences > General) to 30°, so he could edit objects by dragging selected points or lines along the same angles as the isometric view (he held down the Shift key while dragging to constrain movement to the set angles).

Objective Colors

Custom Labels for Making Quick Changes

Overview: *Define custom spot or global colors, naming colors by the type of object; repeat the procedure for each type of object; use Select commands to select types of objects by spot or global color name to edit colors or objects.*

1

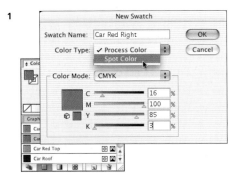

Option-clicking on the New Swatch icon to directly access Swatch Options; naming the color, then setting the color to be a Spot Color or choosing the Global option, which allows global changes and tinting

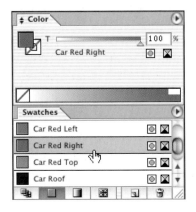

A spot color swatch with its custom label

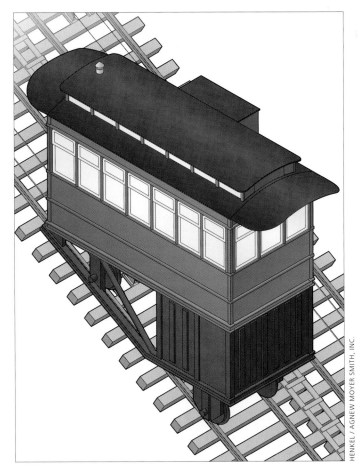

When you need to frequently adjust the colors of an illustration, it's essential to find a way of organizing your colors. This illustration by Rick Henkel demonstrates how his firm, Agnew Moyer Smith (AMS), uses colors to label different categories of objects, making it simple to isolate and update colors. This method also makes it easy to find all objects in a category in order to apply any other global changes, such as changing the stroke weight or scaling, or adding transparency or effects.

1 Creating custom spot or global colors. AMS uses spot colors, even for process color jobs, to allow easy access to tints. (You can also use Process colors by checking the Global option in the Swatches palette.) In the Swatches palette, Option-click/Alt-click on the New Swatch icon.

If you have premixed a color in the Color palette, this color will be loaded in the color mixer. You can then edit it using the color sliders. Now give your color a name that conveys the kind of object you plan to fill with the color and either choose Spot Color from the Color Type pop-up, or choose Process, and enable the Global option. Rick Henkel used labels such as "CamRight" and "DriveLeft" to label the colors he would use in his illustration of the Duquesne Incline. To help his selection of reliably reproducible colors, Henkel used the Agfa PostScript Process Color Guide to look up the color he actually wanted and then entered the CMYK percentages.

2 Repeating the procedure for all colors and labels, and changing color definitions as necessary. Create colors for each type of object to be styled differently, naming each color for the objects it will fill (to speed creation of swatches, see the Tip below right). Henkel created spot colors, properly labeled, for each type of object included in this incline railroad illustration.

The spot and global color systems makes it easy to change definitions of colors. From the Swatches palette, double-click on the color you want to change in order to open Swatch Options, where you can change the color recipe. Click OK to apply the changes to all objects containing that color.

3 Using the labels to find all like objects. To select all like objects—for example, those colored with "CamRight"—click on that color name in your Swatches palette list and choose Select > Same > Fill Color. Once selected, you can edit other attributes besides color (like stroke width, layer position and alignment).

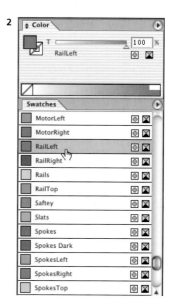

2

Creating custom spot color swatches for each category of object to be styled differently

3

With a color swatch label selected, choosing Select > Same > Fill Color to find the objects filled with that color

After selecting the next color swatch, using the Select > Reselect command to select all objects colored with that swatch

Spot colors for four-color-process jobs

If you choose to define your swatches as spot colors, and you intend to print four-color-process separations from the Print dialog box, be sure to enable the "Convert All Spot Colors to Process" Output option.

From one swatch to another

When defining swatches with custom parameters in Swatch Options, such as Spot colors or Global process colors, instead of having to continually set similar parameters, simply select a swatch that is close to the color you want, then Option-click/Alt-click the New Swatch icon to redefine and name the Swatch.

TUTTLE

Jean Tuttle

As any colorist knows, an organized palette helps facilitate the creative process. Artist Jean Tuttle constructed a color chart file that made it easy to create several illustrations using the same palette and allowed her to work with colors in an intuitive manner. In order to reliably predict the colors she'd get in print, Tuttle used tear-out swatches from a Pantone Color Specifier to choose the beginning colors for her base palette. In Illustrator, she then constructed a palette of rectangles filled with the Pantone colors she'd chosen (from the Libraries option in the Swatches pop-up menu). Each time she chose a Pantone color from the Pantone library it was automatically added to her Swatches palette. She renamed these swatches based on their colors (a color containing yellow would include "yel" in its new name). To rename a

color swatch in the Swatches palette, first deselect all objects (Select > Deselect), then double-click a swatch name in the Swatches palette to display the Swatch Options dialog box. In Options, you can rename your swatch in the Swatch Name field and adjust the color recipe if you wish.

Saturating and desaturating with sliders

With the Shift key held down, grab one color slider to move all sliders together. Grabbing the right-most slider gives the greatest control. Drag to the right to 100% for full color saturation. Drag left to desaturate.

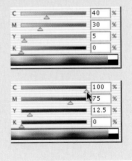

TATE (©1999 UNITED FEATURE SYNDICATE, INC.)

Clarke Tate

Setting the familiar characters, Woodstock and Snoopy, in famous locations, Clarke Tate illustrated this scene for a McDonald's Happy Meal box designed for Asian markets. Tate produced a palette of custom colors with descriptive names. View color names by selecting Name

View from the Swatches palette pop-up menu.

	Bamboo Or Tan 2	⊠
	Bamboo Y Hlite 1	⊠
	Bamboo Shadow	⊠

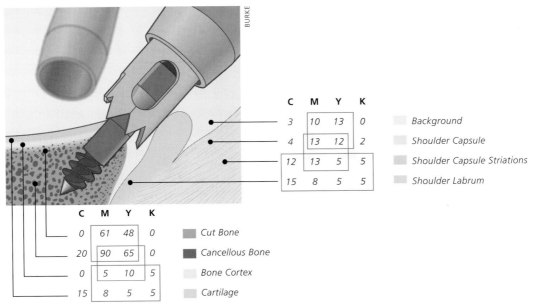

C	M	Y	K	
3	10	13	0	Background
4	13	12	2	Shoulder Capsule
12	13	5	5	Shoulder Capsule Striations
15	8	5	5	Shoulder Labrum

C	M	Y	K	
0	61	48	0	Cut Bone
20	90	65	0	Cancellous Bone
0	5	10	5	Bone Cortex
15	8	5	5	Cartilage

Christopher Burke

When printed in CMYK, Illustrator's smooth, crisp edges can be a registration nightmare. Even the slightest misregistration of inks can create visually disturbing white gaps between colors. So, although you shouldn't have to worry about what happens to your illustration once it's completed, the reality is that you still have to help your printer along. "Trapping" is a technique of printing one color over the edge of another—usually achieved by creating overprinting strokes that overlap adjacent objects. Christopher Burke uses a work-around where the colors in his images contain at least one (preferably two) of the color plates in every region of his image. As long as adjacent objects share at least 5% of at least one color, no white gaps can form, and trapping will naturally occur. This technique ensures "continuous coverage" of ink and maintains a full spectrum palette while keeping just enough in common between adjacent colors. (See Tip "Trapping Issues" in the *Basics* chapter) The background image is a rasterized Illustrator drawing with an applied blur effect; raster images are free of trapping problems (see the *Illustrator & Other Programs* chapter for more on rasterizing).

Manual trapping of gradients and pattern fills

Since you can't style strokes with gradients or patterns, you can't trap using the Pathfinder Trap filter either. To trap gradients and patterns manually, first duplicate your object and stroke it in the weight you'd like for a trap. Then use Object > Path > Outline Stroke to convert the stroke to a filled object and style this the same as the object you'd like to trap. Lastly, enable the Overprint Fill box in the Attributes palette. If necessary, use the Gradient tool to unify gradients (see "Unified Gradients" in the *Blends, Gradients & Mesh* chapter), and replicate pattern transformations.

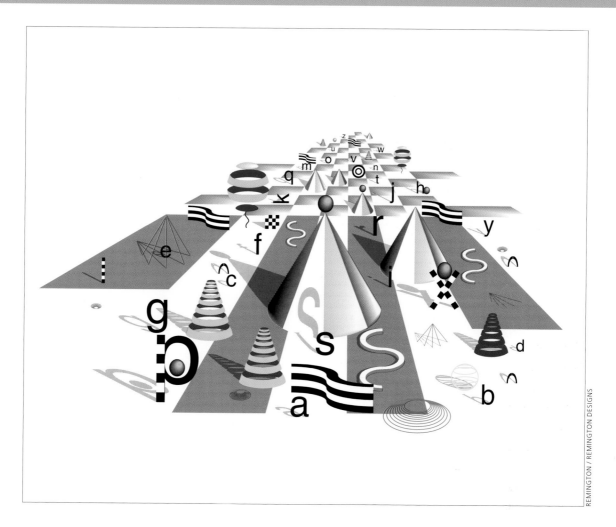

Dorothy Remington / Remington Designs

Color printers are notoriously unpredictable in terms of color consistency, so Dorothy Remington developed a method to increase consistency from proof to final output. When Remington constructs an image, she freely chooses colors from any of the CMYK process color models (such as Pantone Process, TruMatch, Focoltone, Toyo, etc.) that come with Illustrator, provided that she has the matching color swatchbooks. Whenever she sends the computer file to the service bureau for proofing or final output, she also sends along the matching color swatches representing the colors she used in the image. Remington then asks the service bureau to calibrate the printer to match her swatches as closely as possible. Although requesting such special attention might result in a small surcharge, it can save you an immense amount of time with the service bureau, and can save you the expense of reprinting the image because colors did not turn out as expected.

Karen Barranco / Evenson Design Group

Karen Barranco was hired to design a versatile, stylized version of the original Warner Brothers shield for a sports apparel line. It's important to remember that often the simplest techniques can be used to make the most sophisticated logo. Here, Barranco used only the Pen tool and Bézier editing tools to modify the original version of the logo to create the current one. Simple changes in fill color allow the logo to be adapted for a wide variety of applications (T-shirt and sneaker shown below).

S P O R T

BARRANCO

Karen Barranco / Special Modern Design

In order to create a logo, it is often important to try out a wide range of designs in order to capture the essential elements of the idea the logo is to represent. To design this logo for the Jennifer Diamond Foundation, Karen Barranco created variations of the dragonfly by first placing photo references of the dragonfly on a locked layer of the artboard, which she used as a template. She then traced the photos with the Pen tool until she was satisfied with the overall shape. Barranco continued to refine the dragonfly image, experimenting with many styles, as shown above. She used the most basic of Illustrator tools, the Pen, to create each of her trial designs. With the addition of color and variations of opacity, a multitude of elegant dragonflies were created, until the final design was achieved.

Filip Yip

The green perimeter in the background of this Illustration consists of multiple copies of a rough-edged oval (shown above) grouped together, along with other artwork. First, Filip Yip drew a rough-edged, oval-shaped line with charcoal on rough watercolor paper. He then scanned it into Adobe Photoshop, saved the image as a TIFF, and autotraced it in Adobe Streamline. The sketch was brought back into Photoshop (where the edges were cleaned up), saved as a path, and exported to Illustrator (File > Export > Paths to Illustrator). In Illustrator, Yip drew a solid oval shape to fit the rough textured path, selected both, and chose Object > Compound Path > Make to preserve the transparency around the edges of the textured path. Yip copied the compound path (a green oval with a jagged edge) several times and in various sizes, and grouped the resulting objects together to make up the jagged-edged perimeter. Once he was satisfied with the overall shape of the green background, he chose Effect > Pathfinder > Merge to make the background into one object. He created jagged shapes manually instead of using brushes (see the *Brushes & Symbols* chapter), because he preferred the consistent, jagged edge he could achieve by hand. The distortions that occur when brushes "stretch" felt too unpredictable to Yip.

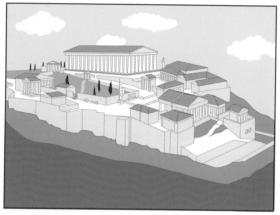
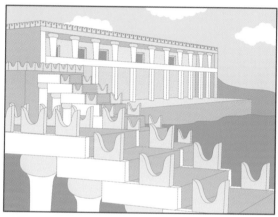
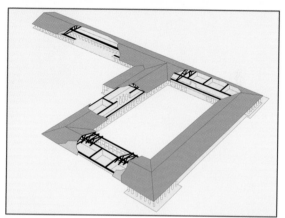

FERSTER

Gary Ferster

Using only simple filled and stroked objects, Gary Ferster was able to create this series of illustrations on Roman Life for a children's educational CD-ROM titled "Ancient 2000". For help making perspective guidelines, see "Varied Perspective" in the *Layers* Chapter.

Distort Dynamics

Adding Character Dynamics with Transform

Overview: *Create characters and group them; use the Free Transform tool to drag one corner to exaggerate the character; draw a sun and use the Free Transform tool to add dynamics to circles.*

1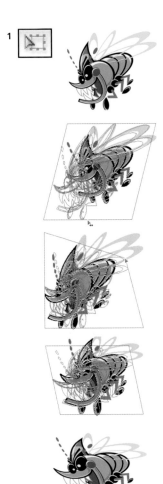

The original bug (top); then with the Free Transform tool the jaw is enlarged, the back is squashed and the entire character is skewed forward

After John Kanzler creates the cast of characters in his scenes, he often uses the Free Transform tool on each of the characters one at a time in order to add energy, movement, dynamics and action.

1 Creating and grouping a character, then applying the Free Transform tool. After building his bug one object at a time, Kanzler thought it needed a more menacing look, and wanted the bug to appear as if it was charging forward. By grabbing and moving various handles, he was able to enlarge the jaws while squashing the body. Then he skewed the bug to the left to give a sense of forward motion and more energy than the original. Select your objects and choose the Free Transform tool (E key). Now, this is essential throughout this lesson: grab a handle and *then* hold down ⌘ (Mac)/Ctrl (Win) to pull only that selected handle to distort the image. Look carefully at what results from movement of each of the Free Transform handles. For his hovering wasp, Kanzler used the Free Transform tool to give the wasp a little more "personality" by pulling a corner out to one side. Notice that as you pull a *corner* sideways to expand in one direction, the opposite side distorts and compresses—if you pull a *center* handle, you will merely skew the objects, elongating them toward the pulled side.

The effect of Free Transform on the hovering wasp

2 Applying the Free Transform tool to regularly shaped objects to add perspective and dynamics. In creating an "action line" for his illustration, Kanzler used the Free Transform tool to make an arc of dots skew out of uniformity, while constraining the arc of the skewed path to that of the original, unskewed path. First, he applied a custom dotted Pattern Brush to a curved path (see the *Brushes & Symbols* chapter for help). Then he chose Object > Expand Appearance to turn the brushed path into a group of oval objects. By carefully tucking and pulling with the Free Transform tool, Kanzler was able to add flair to the arc while keeping the same general size.

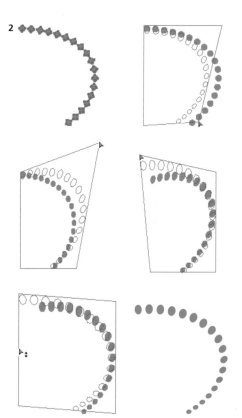

Using the Free Transform tool, pull different handles to create action and perspective effects

3 Making a sun, then creating extreme perspective using the Free Transform tool. To make the sun object, draw a circle (hold Shift as you draw with the Ellipse tool). In Outline mode (View menu), place your cursor over the circle centerpoint, hold Option/Alt *and* the Shift key while drawing a second, larger concentric circle and make it into a Guide (View > Guides > Make Guides). With the Pen tool, draw a wedge-shaped "ray" that touches the outer-circle guide. Select the wedge, and with the Rotate tool, Option/Alt-click on the circle's center point. Decide how many rays you want, divide 360 (the degrees in a circle) by the number of rays to find the angle to enter in the dialog box and click Copy. To create the remaining rays, keep repeating Transform Again, ⌘-D (Mac)/Ctrl-D (Win). Select all sun objects and choose Object > Group. Then, with the Free Transform tool, grab one single corner handle to skew the sun's perspective.

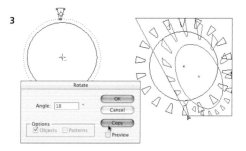

The sun object shown in Outline mode, before the process of Transform Again; and while pulling a Free Transform handle

Distort Filter Flora

Applying Distort Filters to Create Flowers

Overview: *Create rough circles; resize and rotate copies of the circles to construct a rose; fill with a radial gradient; apply the Roughen filter; apply other Distort filters to copies.*

1

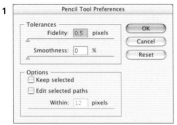

Setting the Pencil Tool Preferences; drawing two rough circular paths

Using the Scale tool dialog window to create a reduced-size pair of circles nested within the first pair of circles

(Left) Using the Rotate tool to rotate the last-created pair of circles; (right) the complete construction of the flower before coloring—the flower center consists of a few small circles

GRACE

Artist Laurie Grace used two roughly drawn circular paths and a series of Distort filters to construct the delicate flowers in her illustration, which she colored with various radial gradients. (See the *Live Effects & Graphic Styles* chapter for examples of artwork created using "live" versions of filters, called "effects.")

1 Drawing circular paths; resizing and rotating path copies. Grace drew two rough circular paths, then resized and duplicated the two paths as the first steps in creating each rose. In a new Illustrator document, double-click on the Pencil tool to bring up the Pencil Tool Preferences window. In the Tolerances section, set Fidelity to 0.5 pixels and Smoothness to 0. In the Options section, disable "Keep selected" and "Edit selected paths." Using the Color palette, set a Fill of None and a Stroke of Black. Draw a roughly circular path, holding the Option (Mac)/ Alt (Win) key as you near the end of the circle to automatically close the path. Then draw another rough circle just within the first circle. Overlapping is okay.

Use the Selection tool or Lasso tool to select the two paths. To create a duplicate pair of circles that is smaller

than and nested within the first pair, double-click on the
Scale tool again (you should note that the previously used
reduction setting is saved) and click the Copy button.
With the last pair still selected, choose the Rotate tool and
click-drag on the image in the direction of the rotation
you want. Continue to resize/copy and rotate selected
pairs of circles until the flower form you are building is
almost filled with circles.

To vary the petal placement in the final rose, you can
continue to rotate some of the pairs after you've created
them. Then, for the center of the rose, click on the Pencil
tool and draw a few small, nested circles. Use the Lasso
tool or the Selection tool to select all the paths that make
up the rose construction, and choose Object > Group,
then deselect all paths by choosing Select > Deselect.

2 Coloring the flower using a radial gradient. To give
the final rose illustration a color effect that mimicked
the petals of real flowers, Grace created a radial gradient color swatch and applied it to her rose construction.
Open the Swatches palette (Window > Swatches), and
click on the "Show Gradient Swatches" button. Next, click
on the "Black, White Radial" swatch. To change the colors of the gradient, open the Color and Gradient palettes
(Window > Color and Window > Gradient), click once on
the leftmost gradient slider (the beginning point of the
gradient) in the Gradient palette, and adjust the color
sliders in the Color palette. Grace chose 100% M for the
beginning slider. Next, click on the rightmost gradient
slider (the ending point of the gradient) and adjust the
color sliders; Grace chose 34% M and moved the K slider
to 0%. To increase the amount of 100% magenta in your
filled objects, drag the left slider to the right and release it
where you like (Grace used a Location setting of 45.51%).
Finally, create your new Gradient swatch by Option-
clicking (Mac)/Alt-clicking (Win) on the "New Swatch"
button in the Swatches palette. Name your swatch (Grace
chose "Pink Flower Gradient") and click OK. Select the
rose illustration and then set the Fill to "Pink Flower

2

Choosing a radial gradient swatch to adjust

*Adjusting the color settings of the beginning
point gradient slider*

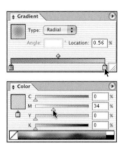

*Adjusting the color settings of the ending point
gradient slider*

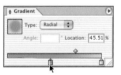

Repositioning the beginning gradient slider

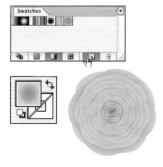

*(Top) Creating a new Gradient swatch; (bottom,
left and right) setting Fill to the "Pink Flower
Gradient" swatch and Stroke to None*

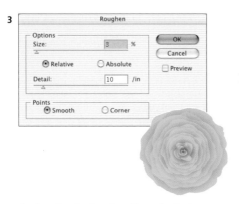

3

Settings for the Roughen filter; the final rose

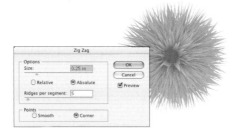

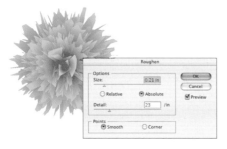

Applying additional distortion filters to copies of the final rose illustration.

Gradient" and the Stroke to None. For more on Gradients, see the *Blends, Gradients & Mesh* chapter.

3 Applying the Roughen filter. To give her rose a realistic rough-edged petal effect, Grace applied the Roughen filter to the illustration. Use the Selection tool to select the rose, then choose Filter > Distort > Roughen. In the Roughen dialog box, enable the Preview checkbox to see the effect of the filter before you apply it. In the Roughen Options, set Size to 3%, Detail to 5/in, and Points to Smooth. Click OK to apply your chosen settings.

Grace used her final rose to create some of the other flowers in her illustration by applying more Distort filters to copies of the rose (be sure to enable the Preview checkbox for each as you work). Select the entire rose and duplicate it by holding down the Option (Mac)/Alt (Win) key as you drag the rose to a new location. With the duplicate still selected, choose Filter > Distort > Pucker & Bloat, enable Preview, and set the Bloat to 33%. Click OK to apply. On another copy of the rose, apply a Pucker & Bloat setting of –40 Pucker. With a third copy of the rose selected, choose Filter > Distort > Zig Zag and set Size to .25 in, choose Absolute, set Ridges to 5 and choose Corner in the Points section. With a fourth copy of the rose, apply an additional roughening by choosing Filter > Distort > Roughen. Set Size to .21 in, choose Absolute, set Detail to 23/in, and select Smooth in the Points section.

You can easily change the colors of the radial gradient for each of your flowers using the three-palette combination of Color, Swatches, and Gradient. Select the flower you want to change and modify the color and positioning of the sliders in the Gradient palette. When you change any attributes of your flower's Fill, it will disassociate from your "Pink Flower Gradient" swatch in the Swatches palette. In order to save any new gradient you create (that you may want to apply later to other flowers), Option-click (Mac) or Alt-click (Win) on the New Swatch button in the Swatches palette while you have your new gradient-filled object selected, name the swatch, and click OK.

Laurie Grace

Continuing with the flower theme she created in the previous lesson, Laurie Grace made some adjustments to color and size used for some of the flowers. She created variations on the other flowers by using Filter > Distort > Roughen. She created more flowers using the pen tool to draw individual pedals and then adding color using gradient mesh. She option clicked on the rotate tool to bring up a dialog box, typed in 30° and chose Copy. She then used ⌘-D/Alt-D to continue the rotation around 360°. To add to the decorative design for the greenery, she used the Pen and Pencil tools to draw the stems and leaves. She then used Filter > Distort > Zig Zag or Twist on some of the pen lines and leaves. (See the *Blends, Gradients & Mesh* chapter for help with blends.)

Vector Photos

Pen and Eyedropper Technique

Overview: *Trace object outline using template; create contour paths then divide using Pathfinder; select and fill each object with Eyedropper tool.*

The original photographic composite image placed as a template

The Place dialog box with the Link and Template checkboxes enabled

Brashear's building outline (a closed object) on the left; two open paths drawn on the right (Brashear used the open paths to divide the building outline)

Reproducing a pixel image as a vector composition is usually done by auto-tracing the image in a program like Adobe Streamline. Tracing it manually in Illustrator, however, allows greater control in organizing layers and eliminating unwanted detail. For this scene from Gothenburg, Sweden, artist Bruce Brashear traced shapes from an imported image, used the Pathfinder filters to create the detailed elements of buildings and figures, and sampled image colors with the Eyedropper tool to apply to vector objects he had created.

1 Starting a new document, placing an image, and modifying image visibility. Start your reproduction by creating a new document (File > New). Import the image you'll trace by choosing File > Place. In the Place dialog box, select the image and enable the Template checkbox to automatically create a template layer for the image. If you want to change the opacity of the layer, so the image doesn't obscure the vector objects you will create, double-click the template layer's name in the Layers palette and key in a percentage in the Dim Images field. (See the *Layers* chapter for more information on creating and working with the Layers palette and with template layers.)

2 Drawing shapes of buildings and creating compound shapes with the Pathfinder palette. To reproduce the buildings in his image, Brashear drew overlapping paths and relied on the Divide Pathfinder to create adjoining objects (like the sunlit and shadowed parts of a wall) whose edges aligned perfectly (thus alleviating the need to meticulously draw adjoining edges so that there were no gaps between them). To divide a closed path (like the roof of a building) with open paths, first draw a closed path and give it a stroke but no fill. Then draw a line that divides the closed path into light and shadow, extending your path beyond the closed object. Select both the closed object and the open path and click on the Divide icon in the Pathfinder palette. As a result, Illustrator divides the roof object into two closed objects (one representing the sunlit part of the roof and the other the shadowed part).

You may need to divide one closed path with another closed path. To create the building's window balconies, Brashear drew overlapping rectangles, one for the window and one for the balcony. After selecting both objects, he applied the Divide Pathfinder, which created three objects. To remove the object created where the window and balcony overlap, select both objects and Option-click/Alt-click the Add to Shape Area icon in the Shape Modes from the Pathfinder palette. Both objects are then combined into one object. (If you don't remember to Option-click/Alt-click, simply click the palette's Expand button after using the Shape Mode.)

Instead of using the Pathfinders to divide an object, consider using the Knife tool. To access the Knife tool, click and hold the mouse button down on the Scissors tool icon. Select an object and then draw a freehand line with the Knife (press the Option/Alt key *before* you drag it across an object to constrain the direction that the Knife moves). When you release the mouse button, Illustrator will automatically divide the selected object into two separate objects.

Your goal is to make as many closed objects as necessary to reproduce the different shapes you see in the placed image. The more objects you make, the more closely your vector reproduction will match the detail and realism of the image.

Left, result of using the Divide Pathfinder; right, the three objects (colored for demonstration)

Top left, portion of template image; top right, two rectangles drawn over the template image; bottom, Pathfinder palette with Divide icon being selected

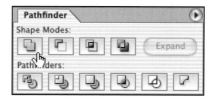

Top left, the result of using the Divide Pathfinder, the two rectangles that need to be merged; top right, the two remaining rectangles after using the Add to Shape Area Pathfinder; bottom, the Pathfinder palette with the Add to Shape Area icon selected

The Knife tool accessed by holding the cursor down on the Scissors icon in the toolbox

Left, the placed image that Brashear sampled with the Eyedropper tool; Right, objects filled with sampled colors (including a radial gradient created from sampled colors)

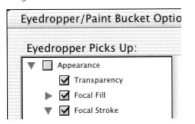

Default Eyedropper tool's options dialog box; these settings require a Shift-click to sample an image

Eyedropper/Paint Bucket Optio

Eyedropper Picks Up:

▼ ☐ Appearance
  ☑ Transparency
  ▶ ☑ Focal Fill
  ▼ ☑ Focal Stroke

By disabling the Appearance checkbox, the Eyedropper tool can be clicked instead of Shift-clicked to sample an image

Changing the shape of a cut

Whether you cut an object with the Divide Pathfinder or with the Knife tool, the result will be two objects that share adjoining edges. While these two edges look like one line, they are two coinciding paths. To change the shape of two unfilled edges at the same time, so that they remain coincidental, be sure to select points using the Direct Selection tool before moving the points. That way you'll move points on *both* of the paths simultaneously.

3 Using the Eyedropper tool to fill objects with colors selected from the image. After creating his objects, Brashear filled them with colors he sampled from the placed image. First, select an object you want to fill (make sure the Fill icon in the toolbox is active so you color the fill, not the stroke). Next, find a representative color in the placed image and Shift-click on it with the Eyedropper tool to fill the object with the sampled color.

You can create a color gradient with colors that are sampled from the image. To learn about producing a gradient fill, see the *Blends, Gradients & Mesh* chapter. Because a gradient will obscure the image underneath it as you create and edit it, see the *Layers* chapter to learn how to toggle a layer or object from Preview to Outline view before you begin sampling image colors.

From Shift-click to click

Can't remember to Shift-click with the Eyedropper tool when sampling a color from an image? Just change the tool options. Double-click the Eyedropper icon in the toolbox. Then, uncheck the Appearance checkbox in the Eyedropper Picks Up portion of the Eyedropper's options dialog box. Now just click to sample a color from an image.

Two tools at once

You can toggle between a selection tool and the Eyedropper tool using the ⌘/Ctrl key. First, click on the selection tool you'll use to select objects (the Selection, Direct Selection, or Group Selection tool). Then click on the Eyedropper tool. Now, when you're using the Eyedropper and want to select an object, the ⌘/Ctrl key will toggle to the selection tool you clicked on previously. See *The Zen of Illustrator* chapter for additional keyboard shortcuts ("Finger dances") that can save you time as you work.

HAMANN

Brad Hamann

Brad Hamann created this travel sticker for a Honda Corporation ad campaign for one of its cars (the Passport). He placed a photo of Niagara Falls into his document as a template and then traced over it using the Pencil tool. Using the Eyedropper tool, he held the Shift key to sample color from the photo to fill his pencil-drawn shapes. To finalize his image he created a clipping mask in the shape of a circle and added type (see the *Advanced Techniques* and *Type* chapters for help with masks and type).

Intricate Patterns

Designing Complex Repeating Patterns

Advanced Technique

Overview: *Design a rough composition; define a confining pattern boundary and place behind all layers; use the box to generate crop marks; copy and position elements using crop marks for alignment; define and use the pattern.*

1

Left, arranging pattern elements into a basic design; right, adding the pattern tile rectangle behind the pattern elements

Creating crop marks based on selection of the pattern tile rectangle

Included with Illustrator are many wonderful patterns for you to use and customize, and the *User Guide* does a good job of explaining pattern-making basics. But what if you want to create a more complex pattern?

A simple trick with crop marks can help to simplify a tedious process of trial and error. With some help from author and consultant Sandee Cohen, Alan James Weimer used the following technique to design an intricate tile that prints seamlessly as a repeating pattern.

1 Designing your basic pattern, drawing a confining rectangle, then creating crop marks for registration.
Create a design that will allow for some rearrangement of artwork elements. ***Hint:*** *You can't make a pattern tile that contains rasterized or placed images, or unexpanded and unmasked patterns, gradients, blends, or brushes.*

Use the Rectangle tool to draw a box around the part of the image you would like to repeat. This rectangle defines the boundary of the pattern tile. Send the rectangle to the bottom of the Layers palette or to the bottom of your drawing layer (Object > Arrange > Send to Back). This boundary rectangle, which controls how your pattern repeats, must be an unstroked, unfilled, nonrotated, nonskewed object. Make certain this rectangle is selected, and select Filter > Create > Crop Marks. Last, Ungroup these marks (in the next step, you'll use the crop marks to align elements that extend past the pattern tile).

2 Developing the repeating elements. If your pattern has an element that extends beyond the edge of the pattern tile, you must copy that element and place it on the opposite side of the tile. For example, if a flower blossom extends below the tile, you must place a copy of the remainder of the blossom at the top of the tile, ensuring that the whole flower is visible when the pattern repeats. To do this, select an element that overlaps above or below the tile and then Shift-select the nearest horizontal crop mark (position the cursor on an endpoint of the crop mark). While pressing the Shift-Option or Shift-Alt keys (the Option key copies the selections and the Shift key constrains dragging to vertical and horizontal directions), drag the element and crop mark upward until the cursor snaps to the endpoint of the upper horizontal crop mark. (For any element that overlaps the left or right side of the tile, select the element and the vertical crop mark and hold down Shift-Option/Shift-Alt as you drag them into position.)

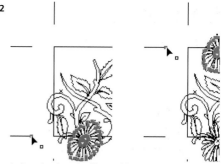

Left, selecting the flower blossom and horizontal crop mark; right, after dragging a copy of the flower blossom and crop mark into position at the top of the pattern tile artwork

Finished artwork for the pattern tile, before turning into a pattern swatch in the Swatches palette

3 Testing and optimizing your pattern. To test your pattern, select your pattern elements (including the bounding rectangle), and either choose Edit > Define Pattern to name your pattern, or drag your selection to the Swatches palette (then double-click the swatch to customize its name). Create a new rectangle and select the pattern as your fill from the Swatches palette. Illustrator will fill the rectangle with your repeating pattern. If you redesign the pattern tile and then wish to update the pattern swatch, select your pattern elements again, but this time Option-drag/Alt-drag the elements onto the pattern swatch you made before.

Optimize your pattern for printing by deleting excess anchor points. Select pattern elements and use the Simplify command (Object > Path > Simplify).

Making a new swatch using Edit > Define Pattern

Speeding redraw with patterns

After filling an object with a pattern, speed up screen redraw by setting View to Outline mode, or by rasterizing a copy of the object (keep the original object unfilled in case you need to use it later).

Tiffany Larsen

Tiffany Larsen used custom patterns to dress the Big Bad Wolf in realistic fabric textures. The gingham dress pattern was created by drawing a checkerboard of squares with the Rectangle tool. Within the checkerboard, Larsen drew smaller squares of various sizes to simulate a mottled appearance. She then masked the grouped checkerboard into the size she wanted and dragged it to the Swatches palette to create a pattern. To make the lace (shown above on a black background), Larsen drew several circles (white Fill, no Stroke)

within a square (white Fill, no Stroke). With the Direct Selection tool, she selected the square and circles and made the selection into a compound path (Object > Compound Path > Make) to create transparent holes (see the *Advanced Techniques* chapter for more on masks). Larsen made the selection into a pattern by choosing Edit > Define Pattern. Using the Stroke palette, Larsen made the stitching a 1 pt dashed line with a 2 pt gap.

Brushes & Symbols

120 Introduction

120 Brushes

123 Symbols

124 Symbols vs. Scatter Brushes

125 Gallery: Chris Bucheit

126 Ink Brush Strokes: *Making Naturalistic Pen and Ink Drawings*

128–131 Galleries: Sharon Steuer, Lisa Jackmore, Jen Alspach, Ellen Papciak-Rose

132 Preparing Art: *Adding Brushes to Existing Artwork*

134 Pattern Brushes: *Creating Details with the Pattern Brush*

136–139 Galleries: Bert Monroy, Shayne Davidson, Steve Spindler, Jacqueline Mahannah

140 Building Brushes: *Building Brushes for Lettering*

142 Advanced Technique: Map Techniques: *Simplifying Complex Image Creation*

145 Gallery: Joe Lertola

146 Symbol Basics: *Creating and Working with Symbols*

149 Gallery: Sandee Cohen & Sharon Steuer

150 Advanced Technique: Organic Creation: *Painting with Brushes, Symbols, and Mesh*

152 SPECIAL BRUSHES SUPPLEMENT *by Sandee Cohen*

Brushes & Symbols

These custom brushes created by Lisa Jackmore, plus others, can be found on the Wow! CD

Find two more brushes lessons in the Transparency & Appearances chapter: "Transparency 101" (top) and "Transparent Color" (above)

Brushes and Symbols blur the boundaries between Strokes, Fills, and Patterns. Using these tools and effects, you can create strokes made of fills or patterns, and fills made from strokes and other artwork.

Using Brushes and Symbols, you can create the equivalents of many traditional illustration tools, such as pens and brushes that drip and splatter, colored pencils and charcoals, calligraphy pens and brushes, and spray cans that can spray anything—from single color spots to complex artwork. You can use these tools with a pen and tablet, or with a mouse or trackball.

BRUSHES

There are four basic types of Brushes: Calligraphic, Art, Scatter, and Pattern. You can use Brushes for everything from mimicking traditional art tools to painting with complex patterns and textures. You can either create brush strokes with the Brush tool, or you can apply a brush stroke to a previously drawn path.

Use Calligraphic Brushes to create strokes that look like they're from a real-world calligraphy pen or brush, or to mimic felt pens. You can define a degree of variation for the size, roundness, and angle of each "nib." You can also set each of the above characteristics to be Fixed, Pressure, or Random. See the "Ink Brush Strokes" lesson, and the "Special Brushes Supplement" later in this chapter for a complete description of the tool and its settings.

Art Brushes consist of one or more pieces of artwork that get stretched evenly along the path you create with them. You can use Art Brushes to imitate drippy, splattery ink pens, charcoal, spatter brushes, dry brushes, watercolors, and more. See the "Building Brushes" lesson, and the "Special Brushes Supplement" later in this chapter to learn how to create your own brushes.

The artwork you use to create an Art Brush can represent virtually anything: the leaves of a tree, stars, blades of grass, and so on. This flexibility is explored in the "Organic Creation" lesson, and in the "Special Brushes Supplement" later in this chapter.

Use Scatter Brushes to scatter copies of artwork along the path you create with them: flowers in a field, bees in the air, stars in the sky. The size, spacing, scatter, rotation, and colorization of the artwork can all vary along the path. See the "Organic Creation" lesson, and the "Special Brushes Supplement" later in this chapter for more examples.

Pattern Brushes are related to the Patterns feature in Illustrator. You can use Pattern Brushes to paint patterns along a path. To use a Pattern Brush, you first define the tiles that will make up your pattern. For example, you can create railroad symbols on a map, multicolored dashed lines, chain links, or grass. These patterns are defined by up to five types of tiles—side, outer corner, inner corner, start, and end—that you create, and one of three methods of fitting them together (Stretch to Fit, Add Space to Fit, and Approximate Path). See the "Pattern Brushes," "Map Techniques," and "Organic Creation" lessons for more on how to create Pattern Brushes.

In addition to the Brushes examples in this chapter, you'll find numerous step-by-step lessons and Galleries involving Brushes throughout the book. In particular, see the "Brushed Type" lesson in the *Type* chapter, and the "Scratchboard Art" lesson in the *Live Effects & Graphic Styles* chapter.

Artwork for Creating Brushes

Art, Scatter, and Pattern Brushes can only be made from simple lines and fills, and groups of objects created from them. Gradients, live effects, raster art, and other more complex artwork cannot be used.

Working with Brushes

Double-click the Paintbrush tool to set application-level preferences for all brushes. When using Fidelity and Smoothness, lower numbers are more accurate, and

Closing a brush path

To close a path using the Brush tool, hold down the Option (Mac)/Alt (Win) key *after* you begin creating the path, then let go of the mouse button just before you're ready to close the path. Border brushes work best on closed paths.

Constraining a brush

You can't use the Shift key to constrain a Brush tool to draw a straight path, so draw the path first with the Pen tool, *then* select the desired brush in the Brushes palette. —*Robin AF Olson*

Naming Brushes

If you create more than just a few brushes, incorporate the more important brush characteristics into the names of your brushes. This is especially helpful with calligraphy brushes—otherwise you can easily end up with the same icon for different brushes in the palette. Use the List View to group and show the brush names.

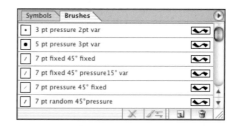

Including brush characteristics in brush name; using List View to make brushes easier to find

Brushes to layers

Scatter Brush artwork can be easily separated onto individual layers for use in animation. For details about distributing artwork to layers, see the "Release to Layers" section in the *Web & Animation* chapter introduction.

Scaling brushes

To scale artwork that contains paths with applied brushes:

- Expand the brushed path first (Object > Expand Appearance), then scale the artwork.
- Scale the artwork after placing it into a page layout program.

Note: *When you apply a scale transformation to brushed paths, enabling Scale Strokes & Effects (Preferences > General) will also scale the brush art.*

More about brushes

- Pasting a path that contains brushes will add them to the Brushes palette.
- Convert an applied brush into editable artwork by selecting the path and choosing Object > Expand Appearance.
- Drag a brush out of the Brushes palette to edit the brush art.
- To create a brush from an applied brush path, blend, gradient, or gradient mesh, expand it first (Object > Expand).

higher numbers are smoother. Check the "Fill new brush strokes" option if you want the brush path to take on the fill color in addition to the stroke color. When Keep Selected and Edit Selected Paths are both enabled, the last drawn path stays selected, and drawing a new path close to the selected path will redraw that path. Disabling either of these options will allow you to draw multiple brush strokes near each other, instead of redrawing the last drawn path. Disabling Keep Selected deselects paths as they are drawn, while disabling Edit Selected Paths turns off the adjusting behavior of the Brush tool even when it is near selected paths. If left enabled, the Edit Selected Paths slider determines how close you have to be in order to redraw the selected path, as opposed to drawing a new path. The lower the number, the closer you have to be to the selected path to redraw it.

To edit a brush: double-click it in the Brushes palette to change Brush options, or drag it out of the Brushes palette to edit the brush and then drag the new art into the Brushes palette. To replace a brush, press the Option (Mac)/Alt (Win) key and drag the new brush over the original brush slot in the Brushes palette. Then in the dialog, choose either to replace all instances of the applied brush already used in the document with the newly created brush, or to create a new brush in the palette.

There are four colorization methods (None, Tints, Tints and Shades, and Hue Shift) you can use with Brushes. None uses the colors of the brush as they were defined and how they appear in the Brushes palette. The Tints method causes the brush to use the current stroke color, allowing you to create any color brush you like, regardless of the color of the brush depicted in the Brushes palette. Click on the Tips button in the Art Brush Options dialog box for detailed explanations and examples of how all four color modes work.

When drawing with a pressure-sensitive stylus (pen) and tablet, using the Calligraphic Brush tool and a pressure setting in the options dialog, you'll be able to draw with varying stroke thickness according to the pressure you apply to the tablet. For Scatter brush pressure settings, vary the size, spacing, and scatter of the brush art. If you don't have a tablet, try choosing Random settings for Calligraphic and Scatter brush options.

SYMBOLS

Symbols consist of artwork that you create and store in the Symbols palette. From this palette, you then apply one or more copies of the symbols (called *instances*) into your artwork.

Artwork for Creating Symbols

Symbols can be made from almost any art you create in Illustrator. The only exceptions are a few kinds of complex groups (such as groups of graphs) and placed art, which has to be embedded (not linked).

Working with Symbols

There are eight Symbolism tools. Use the Symbol Sprayer tool to spray selected symbols onto your document. A group of symbols sprayed onto your document is called a *symbol instance set* and is surrounded by a bounding box (you cannot select individual instances inside a set with any of the selection tools). Then use the Symbol Shifter, Scruncher, Sizer, Spinner, Stainer, Screener, or Styler tools to modify symbols in the symbol instance set.

To add symbols to an existing instance set, select the instance set. Then, from the Symbols palette, select the symbol to be added—which can be the same as or different from the symbols already present in the instance set—and spray. If you are using the default Average mode, your new symbol instances can inherit attributes (size, rotation, transparency, style) from nearby symbols in the same instance set. Use ⌘-click (Mac) or Ctrl-click (Win) to add or delete symbols to your current symbol selection in the Symbols palette. See the *User Guide* for details about the Average versus User Defined modes.

When you add or modify symbol instances, make sure that you have both the symbol instance set and the cor-

Symbols and the Web

Because Illustrator Symbols are fully supported in SWF and SVG, using multiple instances of symbols in your document will result in file size savings on the Web.

Symbols to layers

Symbol artwork can be easily separated onto individual layers for use in animations. Select and target the Symbol artwork layer, then choose Release to Layers (Sequence) from the Layers palette menu. For more see "Release to Layers" in the *Web & Animation* chapter introduction.

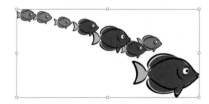

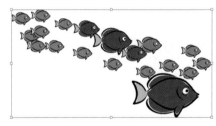

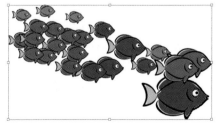

Top, symbols sprayed, sized, and stained. Middle, symbols added using User Defined mode; new symbols are all same color and size. Bottom, symbols added using Average mode; new symbols inherit average color and size from symbols nearby (as defined by the brush radius)

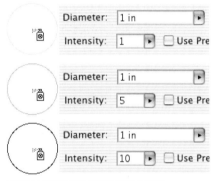

☑ Show Brush Size and Intensity

When Show Brush Size and Intensity is enabled, the intensity of the Symbolism tool is indicated by the shade of gray of the brush size circle

responding symbol(s) in the Symbols palette selected. If you don't, the Symbolism tools can easily appear to be broken.

To remove symbols from an existing instance set, hold down the Option (Mac)/Alt (Win) key and click on the symbols with the Symbol Sprayer tool.

Details on how to create and modify symbols are covered in the "Symbol Basics" lesson found later in this chapter.

SYMBOLS VS. SCATTER BRUSHES

In general, Symbols are much more flexible than Scatter Brushes. Symbols can be made from almost anything you can create using Illustrator, whereas brushes are limited to simple lines and fills.

Symbols are also more flexible regarding the types of changes you can make to them after they are applied. Using the Symbolism tools, you can change many attributes (such as size, rotation, and spacing) to individual symbols in an instance set. Using Scatter Brushes attributes will be applied to the whole set—you cannot change attributes for single objects in a set.

With Symbols, you can redefine the original artwork stored in the Symbols palette and have all the instances on the Artboard reflect those changes. Using Scatter Brushes, the original artwork in the Brushes palette cannot be changed.

Using Symbols you can remove individual instances from a symbolism instance set. You cannot delete Scatter Brush objects without first expanding the artwork.

Unlike other types of vector artwork, the art objects inside Symbols are not affected by the Scale Strokes & Effects preference. Scatter Brush artwork responds in its own unique way. For details see the file "Scaling & Scatter Brushes.ai" on the *Wow! CD*.

BUCHEIT / DESIGNTIME

Chris Bucheit / DesignTime

Musician and artist Chris Bucheit decided to show his graphic design class the step-by-step process of creating the CD packaging for his group's latest album. Bucheit began with pencil sketches that he scanned and placed in Illustrator. To lend a painterly look to the artwork, Bucheit used gradient meshes, gradients, and transparency. For the mermaid's hair, Bucheit created custom art brushes that tapered at both ends. To do this, he drew a lens shape with the Pen that he copied and pasted to produce four objects. He filled the objects

with gold, brown and reddish-brown colors, and then used the Direct Selection tool to select and move points on each lens object so that all four objects were of different shapes. He moved the objects together to adjoin or slightly overlap and then dragged the artwork to the Brushes palette. In the New Brush dialog box he specified Art Brush and in the Art Brush Options dialog he gave the new brush a descriptive name. After making several custom brushes, he drew strands of hair with the Pen tool and applied the art brushes to them.

Ink Brush Strokes

Making Naturalistic Pen and Ink Drawings

STEUER

SYLVIE   STEUER

Overview: *Adjust the Paintbrush tool settings; customize a Calligraphic brush; trace or draw your composition; experiment by using other brushes to stroke the paths.*

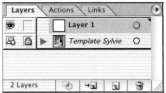

The composite photo of Sylvie saved as TIFF and placed as an Illustrator template layer

Maintaining your pressure

Only brush strokes *initially* drawn with pressure-sensitive settings can take advantage of pressure-sensitivity. Also be aware that reapplying a brush after trying another may alter the stroke shape.

It's easy to create spontaneous painterly and calligraphic marks in Illustrator—perhaps easier than in any other digital medium. And then after creating these highly variable, responsive strokes (using a graphics tablet and a pressure-sensitive, pen-like stylus), you can edit those strokes as *paths*, or experiment by applying different brushes to the existing paths. This portrait of Sylvie was drawn using one custom Calligraphic Brush and a pressure-sensitive Wacom tablet.

1 If you are tracing or referencing artwork, prepare your template layer. You can draw directly into Illustrator, but if you want to trace a scanned photo or sketch, you'll need to prepare an image to use as a template layer. For her template image, Steuer scanned a few photos of Sylvie and composited them together in Photoshop. She then saved the composite in TIFF format, and placed the TIFF as a template layer in Illustrator. To place a TIFF or Photoshop image as a template layer, choose File > Place, locate your file when prompted, enable the Template check box, and click the Place button. Toggle between hiding and showing the template layer using ⌘-Shift-W

(Mac)/Ctrl-Shift-W (Win), or by clicking in the visibility column in the Layers palette (the icon for a template layer is a tiny triangle/circle/square, instead of the Eye icon).

2 Setting your Paintbrush Tool Preferences and customizing a Calligraphic brush. In order to sketch freely and with accurate detail, you'll need to adjust the default Paintbrush tool settings. Double-click the Paintbrush tool in the Tools palette to open Paintbrush Tool Preferences. Drag the Fidelity and Smoothness sliders all the way to the left and disable the "Fill new brush strokes" and "Keep Selected" options.

To create a custom brush, select a Calligraphic brush (one of the first brushes in the default Brushes palette). Then click the New Brush icon at the bottom of the palette and click OK for a New Calligraphic Brush. Experiment with various settings, name your brush, and click OK. For this portrait, Steuer chose the following settings: Angle=90°/Fixed; Roundness=10%/Fixed; Diameter=4 pt/Pressure/Variation=4 pt. If you don't have a pressure-sensitive tablet, try Random as a setting for any of the three Brush Options, since Pressure won't have any effect. The Paintbrush uses your current stroke color (if there isn't a stroke color, it will use the previous stroke color or the fill color). Now draw. If you don't like a mark: 1) choose Undo to delete it, or 2) use the Direct Selection tool to edit the path, or 3) select the path and try redrawing it using the Paintbrush (to hide or show selection outlines, choose View>Hide/Show Edges). To edit a brush, double-click it in the Brushes palette, or drag it to the New Brush icon to duplicate it, then edit the copy.

3 Experimenting with your artwork. Save any versions of your artwork that you like. Now try applying different brushes to specific strokes and to the entire piece. To access more Adobe-made Calligraphic Brushes, choose Window>Brush Libraries>Artisitic_Calligraphic (at right, see two default Adobe brushes applied to the same strokes as the custom paths).

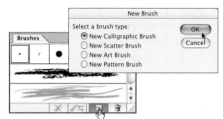

Customizing the Paintbrush Tool Preferences

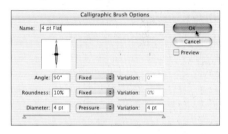

Creating a new Calligraphic brush

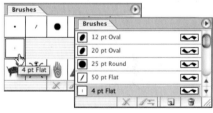

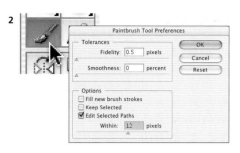

Angle, Roundness, and Diameter can be set to respond to pressure, to vary randomly, or to remain fixed; the new brush in the Brushes palette viewed with tool tips and in List View

Strokes made with Steuer's customized 4 pt flat brush (left); applying Adobe's default 3 pt Round brush (center), then the 1 pt Oval brush

STEUER

Sharon Steuer

Using the same Calligraphic Brush as in her preceding lesson, Sharon Steuer drew the seashells in black. On layers below (for help see the *Layers* chapter), she created a background gradient (see the *Blends, Gradients & Mesh* chapter), and then used the Pencil tool to draw enclosed areas of flat color (shown alone below right). On a layer above, she drew a few details in color with the Calligraphic Brush. To create the textured background, she made two copies of the gradient layer, then transformed the first gradient copy into a gradient mesh

(Object > Expand, Gradient Mesh) so she could select a few interior points and add highlights (see the *Blends, Gradients & Mesh* chapter for more details about mesh).

JACKMORE

Lisa Jackmore

Lisa Jackmore often begins her Illustrator paintings by making smaller versions of the default Calligraphic Brushes. Although she often prefers more rounded brushes and draws in black for the initial sketch, sometimes she just makes a variety of brushes, then "doodles until the shape of a line inspires" her. Occasionally Jackmore will even save a doodle and figure out later how to incorporate it into the artwork.

She constructs her illustration, then colors the brush strokes toward the end of the project. To make a custom charcoal Art Brush, Jackmore used Adobe Streamline to turn a scanned charcoal mark into an Illustrator object. Jackmore opened the object in Illustrator and dragged it into the Brushes palette, then used the new brush to create the marks under the notepaper and in the framed painting.

ALSPACH

Jen Alspach

Jen Alspach started with a digital photograph of her cat Static, which she placed into a template layer (see the *Layers* chapter). In a new layer above, she traced over the photo, using brushes, with a Wacom "Pen Partner" 4" x 5" tablet. Alspach used darker, heavier brushes to draw the basic outline and the important interior lines like the eyes, ears, and neck (all attributes set to Pressure with a 2 pt Diameter and a 2 pt variation). In another pressure-sensitive brush, she set a Fixed Angle and Roundness (diameter of 6 pt), while in a third brush she set all attributes to Random. Using the Wacom tablet with the pressure-sensitive Calligraphic Brushes, she was able to use very light hand pressure to draw the fine lines around the eyes and the whiskers.

PAPCIAK-ROSE

Ellen Papciak-Rose / In The Studio

In this magazine illustration for *Newsweek International*, Ellen Papciak-Rose used a scratchboard technique to capture the hip-hop feel of Kwaito music, in South Africa. She began by creating several variations of a default charcoal brush found in the (Window > Brush Libraries > Artistic_ChalkCharcoalPencil brush library. After importing the "Charcoal Rough" brush into the Brushes palette, Papciak-Rose made a copy of the brush by dragging it to the New Brush icon. Papciak-Rose double-clicked on the brush copy and in the

Art Brush Options dialog box she altered the new brush by clicking on the direction arrows and entering a percentage to change the width. She then painted the strokes of the drawn objects using various custom-built rough charcoal brushes. Papciak-Rose drew all the letters in her illustration with the Pen tool and applied graphic styles made of multiple brush strokes. (See the "Scratchboard Art" lesson in the *Live Effects & Graphic Styles* chapter for more about her scratchboard techniques.)

Preparing Art

Adding Brushes to Existing Artwork

Overview: *Modify existing art-work; change closed paths to open paths; apply Art Brushes to modified artwork.*

COHEN (from Dynamic Graphics/Designer's Club clip art)

1

Red outlines indicate the type of closed paths to change in the original clip art

2

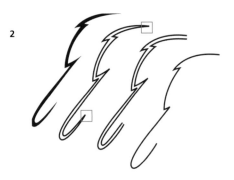

Use the Scissors tool to cut a closed path into two paths, swap the fill and stroke, then delete one path

Sandee Cohen, a vector expert and *Illustrator Wow!* consultant, enjoys working with Illustrator's brushes to modify existing art. This lesson shows how Cohen changed ordinary clip art into more sophisticated artwork. Her technique can be used to give both commercial clip art, and any of your own existing artwork, a bit more pizzaz.

1 Examine the clip art shapes. First, Cohen examines the artwork in the Outline mode in order to plot her steps. She typically ignores open paths because they take brush strokes very well. She also does not worry about closed paths if they have large areas. She is most interested in finding thin closed paths that mimic the look of brush strokes. These paths are often found in artwork created by previous versions of Illustrator.

2 Split closed paths and delete segments. So they will accept the brush strokes, Cohen splits thin closed paths with the Scissors tool. She swaps the fill and stroke colors of selected paths by pressing Shift-X to make it easier to see each path. (You can also change from Preview to Outline View to see paths without fills.) After cutting a path, she deletes one of the cut paths, usually the smaller one.

3 Apply natural-looking brush strokes to simplified paths. Once the artwork is cleaned up, the simplified paths are ready to have brushes applied to them. Many different types of looks can be created without moving or deleting any more of the paths in the illustration. Cohen applies her choice of brushes to the simplified, open paths. Among Cohen's favorite brushes is Charcoal, one of the natural-looking brushes found in Illustrator's default set. She also uses brushes found in the Artistic brush libraries under Window > Brush Libraries.

4 Apply brushes to large closed paths. In most cases, Cohen leaves large, closed paths filled with solid color. Some of the large, closed paths could be made to look more organic by applying Art brushes to their strokes. For instance, Cohen applies natural-media brushes, such as Chalk Scribbler and Fire Ash to the large, closed shapes. **Warning:** *These natural brush forms contain hundreds of points in each brush stroke. While there may be few points in each path, use of these brushes can add dramatically to the file size—a consideration if your computer is slow, or if you need a small file size for storage or to transfer by email.*

5 Experiment with Calligraphic brushes. Cohen also uses Calligraphic brushes set to thin roundness and various angles to replicate the feeling of the original artwork. She creates several Calligraphic brushes, each set at a different angle, to apply various appearances to the paths. Cohen accesses the Brush Options in the Brushes palette menu and chooses the Random setting for the Angle, Roundness, and Diameter options. She then experiments with the numeric settings of each option.

If you alternate between applying a Calligraphic brush with Random settings and another brush, each time you return to the randomized Calligraphic brush the results will be different. Cohen often applies the same brush several times to the same object until she achieves the appearance she likes.

Once the artwork has been cleaned up, you are ready to apply brushes

3

The Charcoal brush (shown in black) gives the art more of a hand-rendered appearance

4

The Chalk Scribbler (top left) and Fire Ash (bottom right) brushes applied to large closed shapes create a more organic look

5

A Calligraphic brush set to an angle of 90 degrees, roundness of 10%, and diameter of 9 points brings back the look of the original art

Pattern Brushes
Creating Details with the Pattern Brush

MONROY

Overview: *Create interlocking chain links by drawing and cutting duplicate curve sections; select the link artwork and create a new Pattern brush; draw a path and paint it with the new brush.*

1

At the left, the ring drawn with the Ellipse tool and given a thick stroke; in the middle, the ellipse cut into four curve sections shown in Outline view (sections are separated to show them better); on the right, the four curve sections shown in Outline view, after using the Object > Path >Outline Stroke command

On the left, the two left curve sections copied and pasted, and colors changed to light brown in the middle; on the right, the two sections are slid to the right to form the right half link

*On the left, the half-link selected and reflected using the Reflect tool (the **X** in the middle of the guide ellipse served as the axis); on the right, both half-links in position*

One look at a Bert Monroy image and you will immediately recognize the intricacy and rich realism of his style of illustration. When crafting an image like the Rendezvous Cafe (see the Gallery image that follows for the complete image), Monroy travels between Illustrator and Photoshop, stopping long enough in Illustrator to construct the intricate shapes and details that turn his scenes into slices of life in Photoshop. The easel chain is one such detail that Monroy created in Illustrator using a custom-made Pattern brush.

1 Drawing, cutting, copying, and reflecting curves.
To build a chain-link Pattern brush, Monroy first created one link that was interconnected with half-links on either side (the half-links would connect with other half-links to form the chain once the Pattern brush was applied to a path). To create the pattern unit with the Ellipse tool, begin the center link by drawing an ellipse with a thick stroke. Copy the ellipse, Paste in Back; then turn the ellipse into a guide (View >Guides >Make Guides). You'll use this guide later when making the half-links. Now select the original ellipse and use the Scissors tool to cut the ellipse near each of the four control points (choose

View > Outline to better see the points). Shift-select the four curved paths with the Direct Selection tool and select Object > Path > Outline Stroke. Illustrator automatically constructs four closed-curve objects.

To make the right half-link, select the left two curve objects and duplicate them to make the right half-link by dragging the two objects to the right while holding down the Opt/Alt key; then change the color of the copies. For the left half-link, select the two curves you just dragged and colored, choose the Reflect tool, hold down the Opt/Alt key and click in the center of the ellipse guide (the center point is an **X**). In the Reflect dialog box, click the Vertical Axis button and click Copy to create a mirror-image of the right half-link for the left half-link. **Note:** *The center link must be aligned exactly in-between the two half-links, so that the half-links join when applied to a path as a Pattern brush.*

2 Finishing the link. The two adjoining half-links should look like they're entwined with the link. Monroy selected the top objects of both the left and right half-links and moved them behind the center link (Object > Arrange > Send to Back). You can create a different look by selecting the top of the left half-link, and the bottom of the right half-link, and moving them to the back.

3 Making and using a Pattern brush. To make the brush, select the artwork and drag it into the Brushes palette. Choose New Pattern Brush in the New Brush dialog box; in the next dialog box, name the brush and click OK (leave the default settings as you find them). You can now apply the chain pattern to a path by selecting the path and clicking on the brush in the Brushes palette.

Depending on the size of your original links artwork, you may need to reduce the size of the brush artwork to fit the path better. You can do this by reducing the original artwork with the Scale tool and making a new brush, or by double-clicking the brush in the Brushes palette and editing the value in the Scale field of the dialog box.

2

Finished link artwork; at the left, the links as Monroy created them; at the right, an alternative version of the interconnected links

3

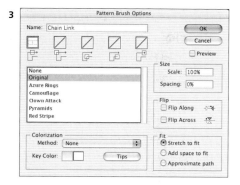

The Pattern Brush Options dialog box showing default settings

Original path on top; below, path painted with Chain Link Pattern brush

Drop Shadows

Even if your artwork is destined for Photoshop, you can make a drop shadow for it in Illustrator. Select the artwork, then choose Effect > Stylize > Drop Shadow. Copy the object (which automatically copies all of its appearances) and paste in Photoshop (Edit > Paste > Paste as Pixels). (See the *Transparency & Appearances* chapter for more on appearances, and the *Illustrator & Other Programs* chapter for more on using Photoshop with Illustrator.)

MONROY

© Bert Monroy 1999

Bert Monroy

Artist Bert Monroy incorporates elements he draws in Illustrator into the detailed realism he paints in Photoshop. In this cafe scene, Monroy used Illustrator Pattern brushes for the sign post and the easel chain. For the leaves in the foreground, Monroy first drew one leaf object and made it into a Scatter brush (he used Random settings for the brush parameters). He brought resulting foliage into Photoshop where he detailed it further. (See the *Illustrator & Other Programs* chapter to learn more techniques for using Illustrator with Photoshop.)

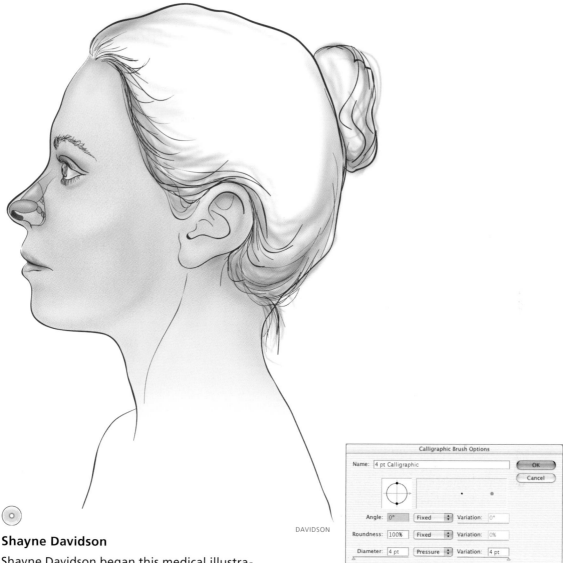

DAVIDSON

Shayne Davidson

Shayne Davidson began this medical illustration by airbrushing the soft background colors in Photoshop. After placing the image in Illustrator, she used custom-made Calligraphic brushes to draw the outlines and details. To create a brush, she opened the Brushes palette, selected New Brush from the palette's menu and picked New Calligraphic Brush from the New Brush dialog. This brought up the Calligraphic Brush Options dialog, where she left the brush Angle at 0° (Fixed), Roundness at 100% (Fixed), and specified a Diameter (she used diameters between 0.8 and 4 points). She also set Diameter to Pressure, and Variation to the same point size as the Diameter (this establishes the maximum width of the stroke on either side of the path), and clicked OK. She repeated this process to create brushes with different diameters.

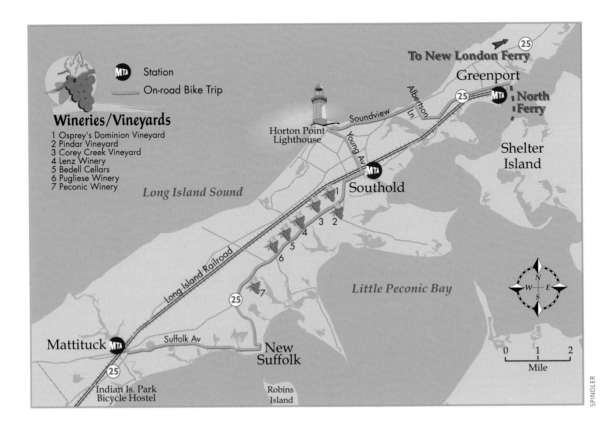

Steve Spindler / Bike Maps

When cartographer Steve Spindler begins using a new version of Illustrator, he quickly adopts its new features to his method of making maps. In this bike map of part of Long Island, New York, Spindler created Art brushes for the bike route and railroad track. He placed scanned photographs on a template layer to draw the vineyard grapes and lighthouse. For the grapes, he used the Tapered Stroke brush for the outlines of the leaves and the Marker brush to draw the stems (both brushes are installed with Illustrator CS, access them from the Brushes palette pop-up menu by choosing

Open Brush Library >Artistic_Ink). To create a Scatter brush from the grapes, Spindler first expanded the artwork (because Illustrator cannot build a brush from artwork that already contains a brush), then dragged the artwork into the Brushes palette. For the compass rose, Spindler imported a custom brush library (Brush Library >Other Library...) containing a collection of his own cartographic Art and Scatter brushes.

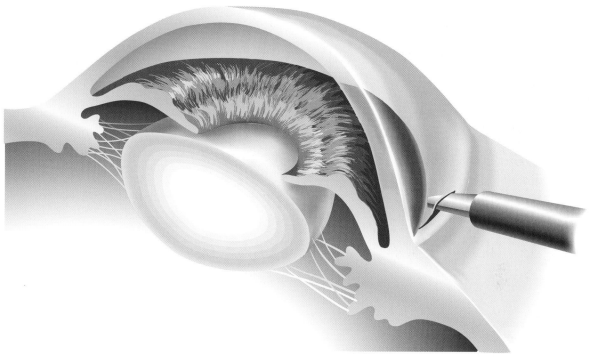

MAHANNAH

Jacqueline Mahannah

Drawing the delicate structure of the iris of the human eye to illustrate glaucoma surgery, artist Jacqueline Mahannah combined Illustrator brushes with the pressure-sensitivity of a Wacom tablet. For the iris structure, Mahannah used the Marker brush from the Ink Brushes library (found on the Adobe Illustrator Application CD, in Illustrator Extras > Brush Libraries > Artistic). She adjusted the width setting of this brush by double-clicking the brush in the palette, then editing the Width field in the Art Brush Options dialog. Mahannah chose a light blue color for the brush and drew the innermost strokes. Then she chose a darker color and drew the next set of strokes, letting them overlap the first strokes. She continued working outward, sometimes overlapping dark brush strokes with lighter ones to suggest highlights and texture.

Building Brushes

Building Brushes for Lettering

Overview: *Draw and shape letterforms; create and vectorize brush strokes in Photoshop; bring brush paths into Illustrator and edit them; add brushes to the Brushes palette; adjust color and layering, and apply effects and transparency.*

DONALDSON

1

Hand-drawn letterform paths using Pen and Pencil tools

Donaldson hand-drew two different sets of letterforms and positioned them on two different layers; each was then painted with a different brush (see Step 4 at right)

2

Brush stroke created in Photoshop using the Paintbrush tool; below, brush stroke edited with Eraser and Airbrush tools

Timothy Donaldson's style of abstract calligraphy challenges the lettering artist to look beyond Illustrator's default brushes (like the brushes sets found under Window > Brush Libraries) to paint programs like Photoshop and Painter, where he develops brush strokes with the look of traditional art tools.

1 Drawing, smoothing and shaping letterform paths. Donaldson began the composition "abcxyz" by drawing letterform paths with the Pen and Pencil tools, going back over the paths with the Pencil to smooth them. (Use the Pencil Tool Preferences menu's Smoothness Tolerance to control how the Pencil will simplify and smooth a line you've drawn.) Once you draw the letterforms, refine them further with the Shear and Scale tools until you are satisfied with their shapes.

2 Creating brush strokes in a paint program. To build a custom brush, open any paint program that offers paintbrushes (Donaldson works in Painter and Photoshop). Start a new file in the paint program, specifying a resolution of 72 ppi and a transparent background. Set the foreground and background colors to black and white (this will make it easier when vectorizing the brush stroke in the paint program later). Next, select the Paint brush tool and edit the brush settings or preferences (opacity, blending mode, textures, pressure-sensitivity and others). (See *The Photoshop Wow! Book* by Linnea Dayton and Jack Davis, or *The Painter Wow! Book* by Cher Threinen-Pendarvis for more about painting with brushes.)

Now you're ready to paint a brush stroke. Hold down the Shift key (to constrain the cursor to straight movements) and make a stroke with the brush tool. Modify the look of the brush stroke with the Eraser or other painting tools, or with filters (but avoid filters that blur or otherwise anti-alias the brush stroke edge). If your paint program can export vector paths as an EPS or Illustrator file, then select the pixels of the brush stroke with the Magic Wand, or other selection tool, and convert the pixels to paths. Otherwise, save the image as a TIFF.

3 Opening, then editing brush strokes in Illustrator. Bring your brush stroke into Illustrator by opening the EPS or placing the TIFF image. Use Illustrator's Auto Trace tool to vectorize the raster brush stroke, or manually trace over it using the Pen and Pencil tools. You can reshape the brush artwork using the selection tools or the Pencil tool. (See the *Drawing & Coloring* chapter for more on modifying paths.) Convert your brush stroke artwork into an Illustrator brush by selecting the artwork and dragging it into the Brushes palette. Select New Art Brush from the New Brush dialog and set various brush parameters in the Art Brush Options dialog box.

4 Applying different brushes. Donaldson created multiple brushed letterforms by duplicating the layer with the paths (drag the layer to the New Layer icon in the Layers palette). For each layer with letterforms, select the paths and click on a custom brush in the Brushes palette. Alter the look of your composition by changing colors or brushes, adjusting the stacking order of layers in the Layers palette, or applying effects to modify transparency and blending (see the *Transparency & Appearances* and *Live Effects & Graphic Styles* chapters for details).

3

Top, work path based on selection made in Photoshop before being saved as an Illustrator file; bottom, path in Illustrator after editing and being filled with black

4

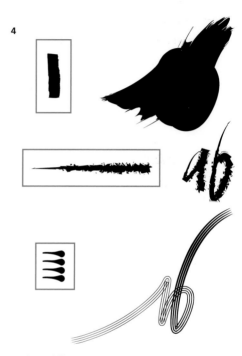

Three different brushes (outlined here in red) applied to the hand-drawn letterforms "ab"

In the background, Feather Effect applied to gray letterforms; in the middle, an 80% transparency and Multiply blending mode assigned to greenish letterforms; in foreground, red letters given a Screen blending mode with 65% transparency

Map Techniques

Simplifying Complex Image Creation

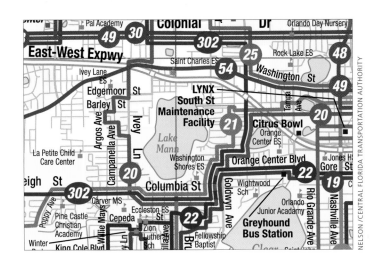

Advanced Technique

Overview: *Use Simplify to reduce points in paths; create and select Scatter Brushes; create multicolored dashes, tapered lines and self-adjusting scales; import brushes from another document.*

1

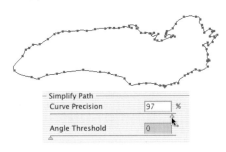

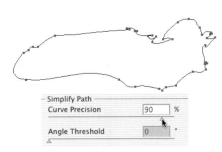

Top, the original lake shape, created from imported geographical data (195 points); middle, using Simplify reduces the lake to 89 points without noticeable distortion of shape; bottom, Simplify reduces the lake to 38 points but with some distortion of shape

From line simplification to brushes that solve many problems, Illustrator now offers professional illustrators and map makers many tools and features that help streamline the creation and updating of complex artwork. In creating a city bus map for Orlando, Florida, cartographer David Nelson was able to take advantage of dozens of recently added Illustrator features.

1 Simplifying paths. When you trace detailed lines such as rivers and roads, or bring clip-art or geographical data into Illustrator, you will likely have paths with too many points. To remove unnecessary points while preserving an accurate path shape, first select a line and choose Object > Path > Simplify. In the Simplify dialog, click to enable Preview and use the Curve Precision control to reduce points (a lower percentage results in fewer points but more distortion to the shape of the path). Use the Angle Threshold setting to make minute changes to some of the curves in the path by smoothing the curve at corner points with angles larger than those specified in the setting.

2 Making, placing and selecting Scatter brush "symbols." Scatter brushes are an ideal way to help manage map symbols. Create symbols for such features as schools, airports, parks, museums, golf courses, and the like.

When you've finished making a symbol, drag it into the Brushes palette. In the New Brush dialog, choose New Scatter Brush, then in the Scatter Brush Options dialog, specify 0% Fixed in the Scatter field and select None for the Colorization Method. To place symbols on the map, click once with the Pen tool and select a Scatter brush you made.

While Illustrator doesn't provide a way for you to select all strokes made with a particular Scatter brush, it can locate and select objects by color, so you can "cheat." Simply set a unique color as a stroke or fill, then click with the Pen tool to create the points to which you'll apply a particular Scatter brush. If you need to select all of the points you painted with a brush, click on a brush stroke on the map and choose Select > Same > Fill Color. Illustrator will select all brushes whose points have the same fill or stroke color as the brush you chose.

3 Creating complex dashed lines. In Illustrator you can even make custom graphic styles for applying complex multicolored dashed lines to paths. Draw stroked paths and color each stroke with a different color. Arrange the paths end-to-end. One way to accomplish this is to make sure you've enabled View > Snap to Point, then position the cursor over the endpoint of one segment and drag it so it snaps on the endpoint of another segment. After you've arranged the colored paths, select and drag them into the Brushes palette. In the New Brush dialog, choose New Pattern Brush. Then in the Pattern Brush Options dialog, choose the "Stretch to fit" option. (See "Pattern Brushes" lesson earlier in this chapter for details.)

If your dashes are uneven or gapped when applied to a path, select the path and use the Smooth tool (from the Pencil tool pop-up palette) to "iron out" the problems (see Nelson's "Zooming more means smoothing less" Tip in the "Tracing Details" lesson in the *Layers* chapter).

4 Creating tapered brushes. You can use custom brushes to create elements that taper, like creeks. Draw a color-

2

North

Mapping Services
Denver, Colorado

On the top and the bottom-left, Scatter brushes representing map symbols and north arrow; on the bottom-right, the New Brush dialog

Selecting a Fill color on the left; in the middle, the points created with the Pen tool; on the right, the points after applying a Scatter brush

3

End-to-end strokes (shown enlarged) are made into a Pattern brush

Pattern brush dashes on a path shown before (left) and after being adjusted with the Smooth tool

4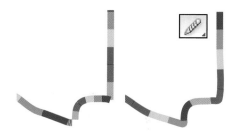

Two of the objects made into tapered brushes

Auto-replacing brush objects

To replace all applications of a brush, hold Option/Alt and drag one brush over another in the Brushes palette (you may wish to duplicate the brush being re-placed first!). —*David Nelson*

Reversing Brush strokes

To change the direction of a brush stroke on an open path, first select the path and then click on an endpoint with the Pen tool to establish the new direction toward that point. —*David Nelson*

5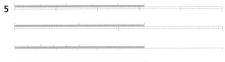

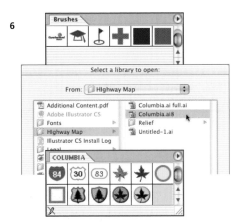

Three "self-adjusting scale" brushes and a map legend that includes a scale drawn with one of the brushes

6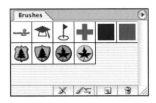

The active document's Brushes palette (top); Window > Brush Libraries > Other Library dialog and the selected document's Brushes palette (middle); the active document's default Brushes palette after importing four new Scatter Brushes

filled rectangle; Nelson's was about 4 inches long and 2–3 points wide. Select the right pair of anchor points and Average (Object > Path > Average), creating a triangle. Drag this path into the Brushes palette and define it as an Art brush, using the point-width in the name of the brush. Select the path that you wish to make into a tapered object and choose your new brush (if the path tapers the wrong way, see "Reversing Brush strokes," at the left). To create a brush that tapers at a different rate, adjust the shape of the triangular object (adding or editing points) and create a new brush with that version.

5 **Making a "self-adjusting" scale.** Create a scale, using evenly-spaced divisions to represent miles, kilometers or another unit of measure. (One way of creating evenly spaced tick marks is by creating a blend between the two end marks on the scale; see the *Blends, Gradients & Mesh* chapter for more on setting up a blend with the Specified Steps option.) Because you are making a multi-purpose brush that you'll use on different maps, don't add text or numbers to your scale artwork. Now, select your artwork and drag it to the Brushes palette. In the New Brush dialog, choose New Art Brush. On your map, draw a horizontal line whose length represents X units of measure in your document (miles, kilometers, etc.) and apply your new brush—which will adjust proportionately to the length of the line. Add numbers for the units and other necessary text.

6 **Sharing custom brushes between documents.** You can bring custom brushes into a document by choosing Window > Brush Libraries > Other Library. In the dialog, select a document that contains the brushes you'd like to import. After you select the document and click Open, a palette containing that document's brushes appears with the name of the document in the palette tab. To move brushes, drag from this document palette to your active document's Brushes palette, or apply brushes from the document palette to objects in your active document.

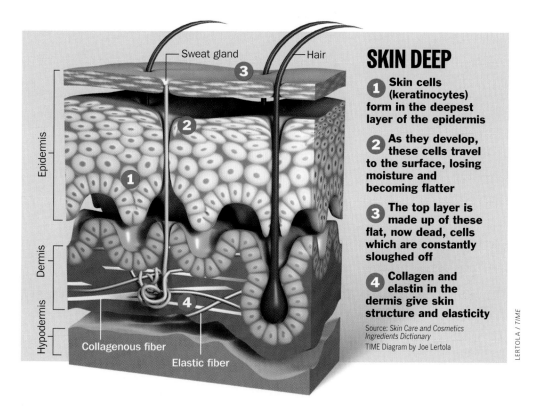

SKIN DEEP

1 Skin cells (keratinocytes) form in the deepest layer of the epidermis

2 As they develop, these cells travel to the surface, losing moisture and becoming flatter

3 The top layer is made up of these flat, now dead, cells which are constantly sloughed off

4 Collagen and elastin in the dermis give skin structure and elasticity

Source: *Skin Care and Cosmetics Ingredients Dictionary*
TIME Diagram by Joe Lertola

LERTOLA / TIME

Labels in diagram: Sweat gland — Hair — Epidermis — Dermis — Hypodermis — Collagenous fiber — Elastic fiber

Joe Lertola / TIME

For this medical infographic, artist Joe Lertola relied on the suppleness of Illustrator's Art brushes to show closely packed skin cells. To begin the top layer of cells (**1** and **2** in the illustration above), Lertola built a single cell from two blends, stacking the smaller brown blend on top of the lighter skin-colored blend. Selecting both blends, Lertola chose Object > Expand. Then he dragged the expanded artwork into the Brushes palette and selected New Art Brush from the New Brush dialog. Next, Lertola developed three more cells, varying the oval shape of each cell before turning it into an Art brush. To make the cells, Lertola drew short paths and

painted each with one of the four cell brushes. Lertola finished the illustration by rasterizing the skin cells in Photoshop and exporting a color and grayscale version of the cells. He imported the grayscale cells into the Lightwave 3D modeler software, where he built a model of the cells and applied the color version of the cells as a color map. (To learn more about using Illustrator artwork with other software, see the *Illustrator & Other Programs* chapter.)

Symbol Basics

Creating and Working with Symbols

Overview: Create background elements; define symbols; use Symbolism tools to place and customize symbols.

The concept sketch

1

The background and symbol artwork

HOLLIN

Kaoru Hollin created this Tropical Card for Adobe to use as sample art that would show the power and variety of effects possible using the new Symbolism tools. After creating a concept sketch, Hollin defined a library of symbols and then used the Symbolism tools to place and customize the symbols, almost as though they were brushes.

1 Creating the Background art. Based on her sketch, Hollin created the background art using eight simple layered objects, filled with gradients. To create the luminous colors, Hollin applied varying amounts of transparency to each of the objects. Hollin then added depth and richness to the water by applying Effect > Stylize > Inner Glow to the upper water curve, and Outer Glow to the lower water curve. Gradients, transparency, and effects are discussed in detail later in the book.

2 Creating symbols. Hollin created the artwork for each of the 20 symbols that she would use to create the piece. The simplest way to turn a piece of artwork into a symbol is to select the artwork and drag it onto the Symbols palette.

To make your artwork on the Artboard become a symbol instance at the same time you create a symbol, hold down the ⌘ key (Mac) or Ctrl key (Win) as you drag the artwork onto the Symbols palette.

3 Applying symbols. After creating a new layer for the fish, Hollin selected the fish symbol in the Symbols palette and created the school of fish with a single stroke of the Symbol Sprayer tool. You can experiment with the Symbol Sprayer by adjusting the Density and Intensity settings (double-click on any Symbolism tool to access the Symbolism Tool Options), and the speed of your spray strokes. Don't worry about getting an exact number or precise placement for each symbol as you spray; you can fine tune those and other symbol attributes using other Symbolism tools.

4 Resizing symbols. To create a sense of depth, Hollin used the Symbol Sizer tool to make some of the fish smaller. By default, the Sizer tool increases the size of symbols within the tool's brush radius. To make a symbol smaller, hold down the Option (Mac)/Alt (Win) key as you brush over it with the Symbol Sizer tool.

To make the diameter of a Symbolism tool visible, double-click on any Symbolism tool and enable the Show Brush Size and Intensity option. As for brushes, use the] key to make the Symbolism tool diameter larger and the [key to make it smaller.

5 Modifying symbol transparency and color. To modify the appearance of symbols, use the Symbol Screener,

2

The artwork for the 20 symbols that were used to complete the piece

3

The raw fish after being sprayed on with the Symbol Sprayer tool

The Symbolism tools tear off palette, see "Tear-off palettes" in the Illustrator Basics *chapter*

To access the other Symbolism tools, hold down Control-Option-click (Mac) or Alt-right-click (Win) and drag toward the tool you want to use until the Tool icon changes. —Mordy Golding

4

Hollin used the Symbol Sizer tool to make some of the fish smaller and to add depth

5

The Symbol Stainer tool set to random was used to vary the color of the fish

6

Use the Symbol Spinner tool to adjust the rotation of symbols

7

After using the Symbol Shifter tool with a smaller brush size to adjust the fish positions

8

The final fish after more fine tuning with the Symbol Sizer, Shifter, and Spinner tools

Symbols Stacking Order

To change the stacking order for your symbols, use the Symbol Shifter tool and:

• Shift-click the symbol instance to bring it forward.

• Option (Mac) or Alt (Win) shift-click to push the symbol instance backward.

Stainer, and Styler tools. The Screener tool adjusts the transparency of symbols. The Stainer tool shifts the color of the symbol to be more similar to the current fill color, while preserving its luminosity. The Styler tool allows you to apply (in variable amounts) styles from the Graphic Styles palette. See the *User Guide* for details about the coloring modes and application methods of these tools.

Hollin used the Symbol Stainer tool, set to Random, to tint the fish a variety of colors with just one stroke. Later, she also used the Stainer tool on the hibiscus and starfish, and the Screener tool on the butterflies.

6 Rotating symbols. To make the first rough adjustment to the orientation of the fish, Hollin used the Symbol Spinner tool set to User Defined (which sets the spin based on the direction that the mouse is moved). See "Working with Symbols" in the Introduction to this chapter and the *User Guide* for an explanation of the User Defined and Average modes.

7 Moving symbols. Hollin used the Symbol Shifter tool with a smaller brush size to adjust the position of the fish.

The Shifter tool was not designed to move symbols large distances. To maximize symbol movement, first make the brush size as large as you can—at least as large as the symbol you wish to move. Then drag across the symbol, as though you were trying to push the symbol with a broom.

8 Deleting symbols. At this point, Hollin felt there were too many fish in the school. To remove the unwanted fish, Hollin used the Symbol Sprayer tool with the Option (Mac)/Alt (Win) key held down. She chose a narrow brush size and clicked on the fish to be removed.

Finally, in order to make the school of fish conform more to the shape of the waves in the background, Hollin used the Symbol Sizer, Shifter, and Spinner tools to make further adjustments.

STEUER / COHEN

Sandee Cohen & Sharon Steuer

Starting with Sharon Steuer's illustration in the "Organic Creation" lesson (following), Sandee Cohen created only four symbols to add the grass, stars, and water you see above. After spraying the stars onto the sky, Sandee then used the Symbol Screener tool to mute the intensity of some stars in order to create a sense of depth. After spraying the foreground grass symbol (which includes the grass shadow), Sandee used the Symbol Sizer tool to vary the grass heights. One symbol was used to create the grass between the dunes. Sandee used the Symbol Stainer tool to vary the color of the grass, and the Symbol Spinner tool to vary the angles of some of the grass. For the water, Sandee used one wave of dark blue as the symbol, which she then sprayed over the gradient background, which goes from almost white under the moon to dark blue at the sides of the artwork. To finish the water, Sandee used the Symbol Stainer tool to make some of the waves lighter shades of blue.

Organic Creation

Painting with Brushes, Symbols, and Mesh

Advanced Technique

Overview: *Create Scatter brushes of stars; draw with a "hue-tinted" Art brush; create bark textures with Art brushes; automate drawing of grass with Pattern brushes; add symbols and gradient mesh.*

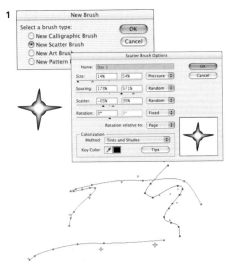

Dragging the star objects into the Brushes palette to specify Scatter brush; the settings for one of the four stars; three selected paths with different star Scatter brushes applied

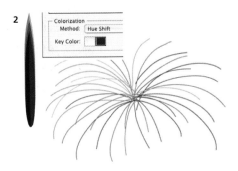

The leaf Art brush (left) with the Hue Shift Colorization option; the final color strokes for the leaves shown without the Art brush applied

Sharon Steuer painted these stars, trees, and grasses using a variety of brushes, with gradients, symbols, and mesh. Please see the *Blends, Gradients & Mesh* chapter for help with the blend, gradient, or mesh portions of this lesson.

1 Defining a star Scatter brush. Create a star. Steuer created her stars using Guilbert Gates's "Glowing Starshine" instructions (*Advanced Techniques* chapter), then expanded those blends (Object > Expand). Drag your star to the Brushes palette, and choose Scatter Brush. In Options, name the star and try various settings, but keep "Rotation relative to" Page. Set Colorization to Tints and Shades. With the Brush tool and new Star Brush selected, draw some paths—your stroke color will tint the star. For brush variations, drag your brush to the New Brush icon, then double-click that brush to rename and edit it.

2 Drawing leaves. Make a straight leaf. Drag it into the Brushes palette, choose Art Brush, then name the brush and choose Hue Shift for Colorization. With the Brush tool and this brush loaded, choose a stroke color (hue) that this brush will be based on and draw. Steuer first mixed and stored about a dozen colors, then drew leaves with a Wacom tablet. Though she chose stroke colors as she worked, she also edited the paths (with Direct Selection) and changed stroke colors as the piece developed.

3 Creating tree trunks. Create objects to use as a trunk. In order to make a brush of blends or gradients, choose Object > Expand. In the case of a gradient, apply Divide from the Pathfinder palette to eliminate the Clipping Mask that results from using the Expand command. Drag the trunk into the Brushes palette and choose Art Brush. Apply this trunk brush to a path. To change the thickness of the path, double-click the brush and change the Size %. Steuer made a second trunk brush—slightly narrower and paler—and gave it a different scaling percentage. She applied the thinner trunk to a slightly offset copy of the first trunk path. For texture, draw some strokes and make an Art brush of the strokes with Hue Shift colorization. Selecting a path styled as you want sets the default for the next path.

4 Creating a Pattern brush to generate grass. Design a pattern tile with 20–30 blades of grass. Drag the grouping of grass into the Brushes palette and choose Pattern Brush. Set the direction to be perpendicular to the grass and Tints and Shades Colorization. Draw a curvy path and select the grass Pattern brush to apply it.

5 Creating water, sand, and moon effects. To create the water, first lay down an unstroked gradient as the background. Then draw a small set of wavelet shapes and drag them to the Symbols palette. Spray the symbol across the background. Edit the wavelets using the Symbol Shifter, Symbol Sizer, Symbol Scruncher, and Symbol Stainer tools. For the sand, Steuer converted a linear gradient into a gradient mesh (Object > Expand). For the moon, she used a gradient mesh circle over the moon-glow gradient.

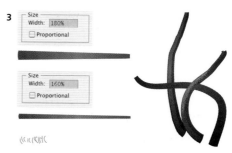

The three Art brushes used in the trunks (the top two with size scaled in Options); the trunks shown (from left to right) with one, two, and all three brushes applied

The Grass objects that make up the Pattern brush; then the brush applied to a path

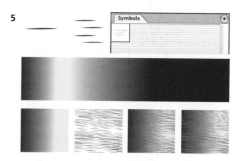

The unstroked background gradient; the wavelet shapes, turned into a symbol, sprayed across the background; then edited using the Shifter, Sizer, Scruncher, and Stainer tools

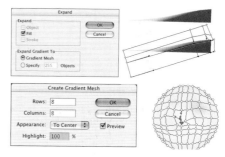

Expanding a gradient-filled object into a mesh (which was then adjusted to curve around the slope of the hill); for the moon, choosing Object > Create Gradient Mesh to convert a circle into a mesh (which was then manipulated using the Direct Selection tool and colored)

Calligraphic brushes allow you to create strokes that resemble those drawn with traditional pen and ink. You can control the angle, roundness and diameter of the brush, and brushes can be set to vary from the pressure of a drawing tablet or "randomly." Multiple calligraphic brushes allow you to create more sophisticated effects. In each of these illustrations, the hair has been changed only by applying different calligraphic brushes. (See "Calligraphic brushes.ai" on the *Wow! CD*.)

Calligraphic brush: *angle = 0°; roundness = 100%; diameter = 1 pt*

Calligraphic brush: *angle = 0°; roundness = 100%; diameter = 1 pt, variation = 1 pt*

Calligraphic brush: *angle = 0°, variation = 101°; roundness = 26%, variation = 14%; diameter = 3 pt*

Dark brown calligraphic brush: *angle = 136°, variation = 180°; roundness variation = 26%; diameter = 12 pt, variation = 3 pt*
Light brown calligraphic brush: *angle = 65°; roundness = 13%, variation = 3%; diameter = 2 pt, variation = 2 pt*

Dark calligraphic brush: *angle = 0°; roundness = 100%; diameter = 1 pt, variation = 1 pt*
Light calligraphic brush: *angle = 0°; roundness = 100%; diameter = 0.5 pt*

Dark calligraphic brush: *angle = -90°, variation = 180°; roundness = 10%, variation = 10%; diameter = 1.5 pt*
Medium calligraphic brush: *angle = 60°, variation = 180°; roundness = 60%, variation = 40%; diameter = 1.5 pt*
Light calligraphic brush: *angle = 120°, variation = 180°; roundness = 10%, variation = 10%; diameter = 0.5 pt*

Art Brushes can create distortions that can be used in animation. Each original silhouette (the left column) was defined as an art brush. The shape and direction of the brush stroke (gray line) then created different positions of the athlete. (See the "Art Brush Motions.ai" on the *Wow! CD*.)

Brushes can be used to create textures. The brush strokes (shown in the lower right corner of each figure), were applied to the outline and stripes of the sweater (original by Lisa Jackmore). None of the artwork was moved or otherwise altered. (See "SweaterTextures.ai" on the *Wow! CD*.)

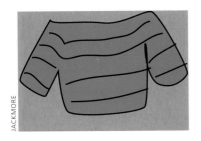

JACKMORE

The original shirt *Plain green with a black outline and black stripes*

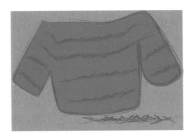

Sketched shirt *Art brush of crossed lines was applied to the outline and stripes. Notice that the brush is distorted along the outside path*

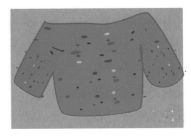

Funky t-shirt *Art brush of small circles was applied to the stripes*

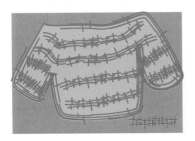

Sketched shirt 2 *An art brush of crossed lines was applied to the outline. This brush was scaled up 150%. The same brush objects, but scaled down 75% with a tighter spacing was applied to the stripes*

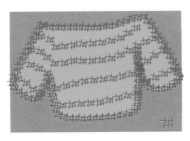

Sketched shirt 3 *Art brush of crosses was applied to the outline and strokes. Notice the distortion along the outside*

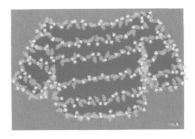

Fuzzy sweater *Small circles, set with different opacities, were defined as a scatter brush. This brush was then applied to the outline and stripes with varying rotations and spacings*

Fuzzy sweater 2 *Small circles were defined as a scatter brush and then applied to the outline and stripes with varying rotations and spacings*

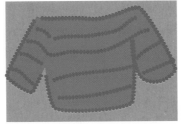

Knitted sweater *One small circle was defined as a pattern brush, then applied to the outline and stripes*

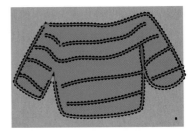

Knitted sweater 2 *One small circle was defined as a pattern brush. Using multiple strokes (see the Transparency & Appearances chapter), the brush was applied first in black, then in green at a smaller size*

Layers

5

156 Introduction

160 Controlling the Stacking Order of Objects

162 Making Selections using the Layers Palette

163 Gallery: David Nelson/Mapping Services

164 Digitizing a Logo: *Controlling Your Illustrator Template*

166 Tracing Details: *Tracing Intricate Details with the Pencil*

168 Colors with Layers: *Coloring Black & White Images with Layers*

170 Organizing Layers: *Managing Custom Layers and Sublayers*

173 Gallery: Nancy Stahl

174 Nested Layers: *Organizing with Layers and Sublayers*

176 Advanced Technique: Varied Perspective:
Analyzing Different Views of Perspective

Layers

Layers palette navigation

- To hide a layer, click the Eye icon. Click again to show it.
- To lock a layer, click in the column to the right of the eye (a lock displays). Click again to unlock.
- To Lock/Unlock or Show/Hide all *other* layers, Option-click (Mac) or Alt-click (Win) on a layer's Lock or Eye icon.
- To duplicate a layer, drag it to either the Create New Layer or Create New Sublayer icon.
- To select multiple contiguous layers, click one layer, then Shift-click the other. To select (or deselect) *any* multiple layers, ⌘-click (Mac) or Ctrl-click (Win) a layer in any order.
- Double-click any layer to open Layer Options for that layer.

Layer Options (double-click a layer name)

Used wisely, layers can ease your workflow by dramatically improving organization of complicated artwork. Think of layers as sheets of clear acetate, stacked one on top of the other, allowing you to separate dozens of objects and groups of objects. New documents begin with one layer, but you can create as many layers and sublayers as you wish. You can also re-arrange the stacking order of the layers; lock, hide, or copy layers; and move or copy objects from one layer to another. You can even open a layer to view and identify and select individual paths or groups contained within a layer!

A few shortcuts will help when you're adding layers to the Layers palette. Click the Create New Layer icon to add a layer in numeric sequence above the current layer. Hold Option/Alt when you click this icon to open Layer Options as you add the layer. To add a layer to the top of the Layers palette, hold ⌘/Ctrl when you click the Create New Layer icon. To make a new layer below the current layer and open the Layer Options, hold ⌘-Option/Ctrl-Alt when you click the Create New Layer icon. Finally, you can easily duplicate a layer, sublayer, group, or path by dragging it to the Create New Layer icon at the bottom of the Layers palette. To delete selected layers, click on the Trash icon or drag the layers to the Trash. (See Tip at left.)
Note: *To bypass the warning that you're about to delete a layer containing artwork, drag the layer to the Trash or hold Option (Mac)/Alt (Win) when you click the Trash. If you're not sure whether a layer has artwork or guides you may need, select the layer and click the Trash so you'll only get the warning if there is something on the layer.*

Sublayers can help you to stay organized. Sublayers are contained within the layer listed above them, if you delete a container layer, all of its sublayers will be deleted as well.
WARNING: *Sublayers may not export properly to other programs (see the "Shape Shifting" lesson in the* Illustrator & Other Programs *chapter for one instance).*

Using Layer Options

You can double-click on any group, path, compound path, clipping path, blend, mesh, guide, type, object, placed object, or raster object in the Layers palette to set Options such as the Name, Show and/or Lock status. If you would like to know what the items are once you've re-named them, retain the name of the subcomponent. For example, you can rename a group to help organize your layer list, but keep the bracket description as part of the renaming of the layer: e.g. *floral <Group>*.

Double-click a layer name to access the Layer Options discussed below:

- **Name the layer.** When creating complicated artwork, giving layers descriptive names keeps your job, and your brain, organized.

- **Change the layer's color.** A layer's color determines the selection color for paths, anchor points, bounding boxes, and Smart Guides. Adjust the layer color so selections stand out against artwork (see the Tip "Color-coding groups of layers" to the right).

- **Template layer.** Illustrator's template layers are special layers that don't print or export. They're useful when-ever you want to base new artwork on existing art—for example, you can place the existing art on a non-printing template layer, and then trace over it on a regular print-ing layer. There are two recommended ways to create a template layer: You can select Template from the Layers pop-up menu, or check Template when placing an image in Illustrator. By default, Template layers are locked. To unlock a Template in order to adjust or edit objects, click the lock icon to the left of the layer name.

Note: *Template layers shouldn't be confused with Illustra-tor CS's new Templates feature.* Templates *are a special file format ending in .ait; whereas* template layers *are simply a special kind of layer. For more about* Templates, *see the* Illustrator Basics *chapter.*

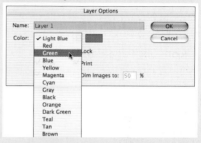

```
New Layer...
New Sublayer...
Duplicate "Layer 1"
Delete Selection

Options for "Layer 1"...

Make Clipping Mask

Locate Object

Merge Selected
Flatten Artwork
Collect in New Layer

Release to Layers (Sequence)
Release to Layers (Build)
Reverse Order

Template
Show All Layers
Outline All Layers
Lock All Layers

Paste Remembers Layers

Palette Options...
```

Layers palette pop-up menu

- **Show/Hide layer.** This option functions the same way as the Show/Hide toggle, which you access by clicking the Eye icon (see the Tip "Layers palette navigation" on the opposite page). By default, hiding a layer sets that layer *not* to print.

- **Preview/Outline mode.** If you have objects that are easier to edit in Outline mode, or objects that are slow to redraw (such as complicated patterns, live blends, or gradients), you may want to set only those layers to Outline mode. Uncheck Preview to set selected layers to Outline mode in Layer Options, or toggle this option on and off directly by ⌘-clicking (Mac) or Ctrl-clicking (Win) the Eye icon in the view column.

- **Lock/Unlock layer.** This option functions the same way as the Lock/Unlock toggle, which you access by clicking the lock column of the layer (see the Tip "Layers palette navigation" at the beginning of this chapter).

- **Print.** When you print from Illustrator you can use this feature to override the default, which sets visible layers to print. If you need to ensure that a layer will never print in any circumstance (for instance, when placed into a page layout program), make it into a Template layer.

- **Dim Images.** You can only dim raster images (not vector Illustrator objects) from 1% to 99% opacity.

The Layers pop-up menu

You can perform the first six functions in the Layers palette menu via the Layer palette icons, or Layer Options (see above). With the ability to nest sublayers within other layers and create group objects comes the potential for confusion about how to find objects when they become buried in the layer list. Use Locate Object, or Locate Layer when Show Layers Only is checked in Palette Options, to find selected objects. Merge Selected is available when two or more layers are selected and will place *visible* objects in the topmost layer. You can consolidate all visible items in your artwork into a single layer using the Flatten Artwork command in the Layers palette menu. (An alternative method is to Select > All, then Cut and Paste, with Paste Remembers Layers unchecked.)

Paste Remembers Layers is a great feature: When it's enabled, pasted objects retain their layer order; when unchecked, pasted objects go into the selected layer. If the layers don't exist, Paste Remembers Layers will make them for you! This feature can be turned on and off even after the objects have been copied—so if you paste, and wish that the toggle were reversed, you can Undo, toggle the Paste Remembers Layers option, then paste again. IMPORTANT: *There is one significant problem with this feature. If you target a top-level layer and apply strokes, fills, effects, or transparency and then copy/paste that layer into a new document, all appearance attributes that were applied to that layer will be lost in the new document, even when Paste Remembers Layers is enabled.*

Try this workaround by Jean-Claude Tremblay (it also works to maintain a Clipping Mask applied to the layer): Since the attributes of a top-level layer are not retained and you get no warning when pasting into the new document, you need to nest the top-layer into another layer, making it a sublayer. Then copy/paste this sublayer into the new document to retain the appearance attributes.

Collect in New Layer moves all of the selected objects, groups or layers into a new layer. Release to Layers (Build) or Release to Layers (Sequence), allows you to make individual object layers from a group of objects, such as a blend, a layer, or art created by using a brush. (This can be useful when creating animations; see the *Web & Animation* chapter.)

Reverse Order reverses the stacking order of selected layers within a container layer. Hide All Layers/Others, Outline All Layers/Others, and Lock All Layers/Others all perform actions on unselected layers or objects.

Last, Palette Options customizes the layer display. This is a great help to artists who have complicated files

If you can't select an object...

If you have trouble selecting an object, check/try the following:
- Is the object's layer locked?
- Is the object locked?
- Are the edges hidden?
- Is the Object Selection by Path Only box enabled (Preferences > General)?
- Locate the thumbnail in the layer list and click on the target indicator.

If you keep selecting the wrong object, try again after you:
- Switch to Outline mode.
- Zoom in.
- Try to locate the thumbnail in the layer list and click on the target indicator.
- Hide the selected object; repeat if necessary.
- Lock the selected object; repeat if necessary.
- Put the object on top in another layer and hide that layer, or select Outline for the layer.
- Use the Move command: Option-click (Mac) or Alt-click (Win) the Selection tool in the Toolbox to move selected objects a set distance (you can move them back later).
- Check for objects with transparency. Overlapping transparency inhibits selection.
- Try enabling the Type Object Selection by Path Only checkbox (Preferences > Type and Auto Tracing).

with many layers. Show Layers Only hides the disclosure arrow so you only see the container layer thumbnail. Adding sublayers reveals the arrow, but you still can't target groups or individual paths in this mode. Row Size defines the size of the thumbnail for a layer. You can specify a thumbnail size from Small (no thumbnail) to Large, or use Other to customize a size up to 100 pixels. Thumbnail lets you individually set thumbnail visibility for the Layers, Top Level Only (when Layers is checked), Group, and Object.

CONTROLLING THE STACKING ORDER OF OBJECTS

Layers are crucial for organizing your images, but controlling the stacking order of objects *within* a layer is just as essential. The intuitive layers and sublayers disclose their hierarchical contents when you open the disclosure arrow. Following is a summary of the functions that will help you control the stacking order of objects within layers and sublayers.

Sublayers and the hierarchical layer structure

In addition to regular layers, there are sublayers and groups, both of which act as containers for objects or images. When you click on the sublayer icon, a new sublayer is added inside the current layer. Artwork that you add to the sublayer will be underneath the art contained on the main layer. Clicking the Create New Layer icon with a sublayer selected will add a new sublayer above the current one. Adding subsequent layers adds the contents at the top of the stacking order or puts the artwork above the current layer. Clicking the Create New Sublayer icon creates a new sublayer level nested within the first one.

Grouping objects together automatically creates a container "layer" named *<Group>*. Double-click the *<Group>* layer to open its options. Group layers are much like sublayers. You can target them to apply appearances that affect all the objects within the group. In some cases, such as when Pathfinder effects are applied, objects have to be grouped and the group layer must be targeted in order to apply the effect.

Note: *If you rename your <Group>, you might get confused when it doesn't behave like a regular layer. Instead of removing <Group> from the name appended to it, leave <Group> as part of the renaming of the layer.*

Paste in Front, Paste in Back (Edit menu)

Illustrator doesn't merely reposition an object in front of or behind all other objects when you choose Paste in Front/Back; it aligns the object *exactly* on top of or behind the object you copied. A second, and equally important, aspect is that the two functions paste objects that are Cut or Copied into the exact same location—in relation to the *ruler origin*. This capability transfers from one document to another, ensuring perfect registration and alignment when you copy and use Edit > Paste in Front/Back. (See the *Wow! CD* for a lesson using paste commands: 2a Zen-Layers-Moving_Pasting.ai.)

Lock/Unlock All (Object menu)

In the days before it was possible to open layers up in Illustrator and select the individual items they contain, the Lock/Unlock All commands were essential. They're a little less important now, but can still be useful if you can't locate your path from within the layer contents.

When you're trying to select an object and you accidentally select an object on top of it, try locking the selected object (Object > Lock) and clicking again. Repeat as necessary until you reach the correct object. When you've finished the task, choose Unlock All to release all the locked objects.

Note: *Use the Direct Selection tool to select and lock objects that are part of a group (see the section "Selecting within groups" in the* Illustrator Basics *chapter)—but if you select an unlocked object in the group with the Group Selection or other selection tools, the locked objects can become selected. Hidden objects stay hidden even if you select other objects in the same group.*

○ *Target icon for any layer or subcomponent*

◎ *Selection is also currently targeted*

■ *Selection indicator for a container layer*

■ *Selection indicator when all objects are selected*

If layers are too slow to open

When opening a file created by an older version of Illustrator, it can take a long time for the Layers palette to draw all the thumbnails for each path. Before you attempt to open layers to view their contents, you'll save a lot of time if you choose Palette Options from the Layers palette pop-up menu and uncheck the Objects option in the Thumbnails grouping. Once you've reorganized your paths in the Layers palette, be sure to re-enable the Objects checkbox in the Palette Options to view the thumbnails for your paths.

Problem with New Views

There are unpredictable situations when using sublayers and New Views in which the view doesn't save the state of the sublayer.
Note: *You should think of views as a way to control top-level layers only (and not sublayers).*

A Group command bug...

A bug in the Group command can reorder the relative stacking order of your objects when you group (Object > Group, or ⌘-G/Ctrl-G)! This can occur if you group objects that aren't within any sublayer with objects that are on a sublayer. In order to avoid this, before you group make sure that all of your objects are within sublayers, or that none are in sublayers.

Hide/Show All (Object menu)

Another way to handle objects that get in the way is to select them and choose Object > Hide > Selection. To view all hidden objects, choose Object > Show All.
Note: *Hidden objects may print if they're on visible layers.*

Bring Forward/Bring to Front and more

These commands work on objects within a layer. Bring Forward (Object > Arrange) stacks an object on top of the object directly above it; Bring to Front moves an object in front of all other objects on its layer. Similarly, Send to Back sends an object as far back as it can go in its stacking order, whereas Send Backward sends an object behind its closest neighbor.
Note: *Bring Forward and Send Backward may not work on large files. In cases where they don't, use the Layers palette to reorder items by moving the selection indicator to the right of the layer name up or down in the layer list.*

MAKING SELECTIONS USING THE LAYERS PALETTE

There are several ways to make selections. Click the layer's target icon or Option-click (Mac)/Alt-click (Win) the layer name to select all unlocked and visible objects on the layer, including sublayers and groups. Click the sublayer's target icon to select everything on the sublayer, including other sublayers or groups. Clicking the *group's* target icon will also select all grouped objects. Shift-click the target icons to select multiple objects on different layers, including sublayers and groups. Always use the *target* icon to make a selection when applying an appearance to a layer, sublayer, or group.

If you have selected artwork on the Artboard, click on the small square to select all of the objects on the layer or in the group. A larger square means that all of the objects on that layer or group are already selected. Clicking in the small space to the right of the target indicator will also make a selection of all objects on the layer, sublayer, or group.

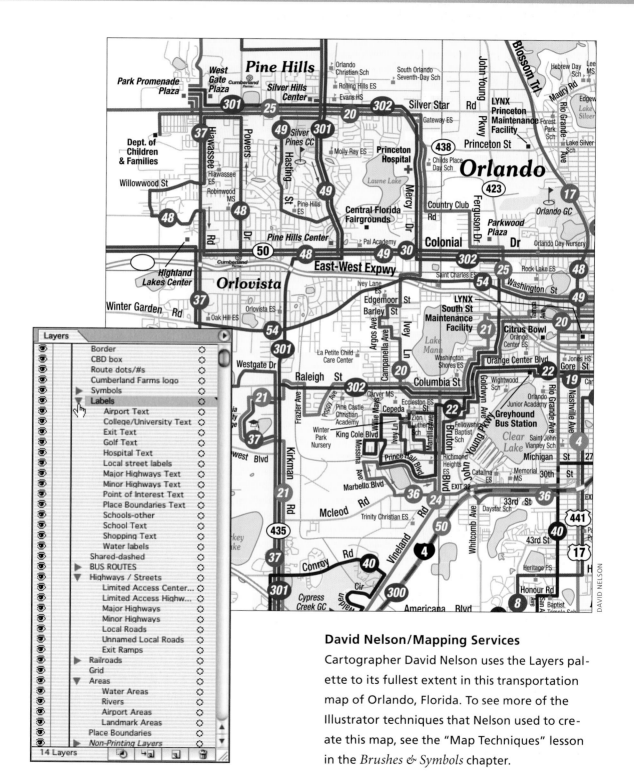

DAVID NELSON

David Nelson/Mapping Services

Cartographer David Nelson uses the Layers palette to its fullest extent in this transportation map of Orlando, Florida. To see more of the Illustrator techniques that Nelson used to create this map, see the "Map Techniques" lesson in the *Brushes & Symbols* chapter.

Digitizing a Logo
Controlling Your Illustrator Template

Overview: *Scan a clean version of your artwork; place the art as a template in Illustrator; trace the template; modify the curve of drawn lines to better fit the template image by manipulating points and by using the Pencil tool.*

A large, clean scan of the artwork

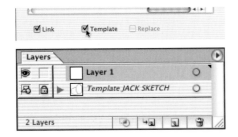

Creating the template and a drawing layer

You can easily use Illustrator's Template layer to re-create traditional line art with the computer—easily, that is, if you know the tricks. San Francisco artist Filip Yip was commissioned to modernize the classic Cracker Jack sailor boy and dog logo, and to digitize the logo for use in a variety of media. Yip scanned the original logo artwork and several sketches he drew and used the scans as sources in developing the new logo.

1 Placing a scanned image as a template and using Filters to modify the image. Select a high-contrast copy of the original artwork that is free of folds, tears, or stains. Scan the image at the highest resolution that will provide the detail you need for tracing. Open a new file in Illustrator (File > New), select File > Place, click the Template option, then choose your scan, thus placing it into a new template layer. Template layers are automatically set to be non-printing and dimmed layers.

If you need to improve the quality of your scanned image to better discern details, you can edit the image with a program like Photoshop prior to placing it in Illustrator. Alternatively, if you've already brought the image into Illustrator, use the Filter menu to change focus or color. (If you placed the image on a Template layer, you'll need to double-click the layer name in the Layers palette and disable the Template option; this will then allow you to edit the image.) Select the image and select Filter >Sharpen to make the image more crisp. Choose the Filter >Colors menu and select options like Convert to Grayscale, Saturate, or Adjust Colors to modify image properties.

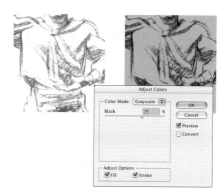

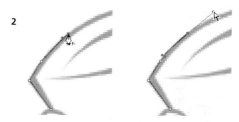

Darkening a scanned grayscale image using the Filter >Colors >Adjust Colors dialog box

2 Tracing the template. With the template as an on-screen tracing guide (and the original scanned artwork handy as an off-screen reference), select the Pen or Pencil tool and begin tracing over the scanned image. To reduce visual clutter in small areas of the drawing, try viewing your active layer in Outline mode (while pressing ⌘-D [Mac] or Ctrl-D [Win], click on the visibility icon next to the layer's name in the Layers palette). Don't worry too much about how closely you're matching the template as you draw. Next, zoom close (with the Zoom tool, drag to marquee the area you wish to inspect) and use the Direct-selection tool to adjust corner or curve points, curve segments, or direction lines until the Bézier curves properly fit the template. (See the *Drawing & Coloring* chapter for more on working with Bézier curves.)

2

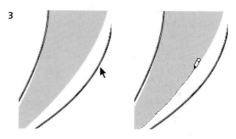

Modifying the fit of a drawn line using the Direct-selection tool to move a direction handle

3

On the left, electing a previously drawn line, and on the right, redrawing the selected line with the Pencil tool

3 Refining lines with the Pencil tool. To modify a line that doesn't follow the template, click the line to select it, then choose the Pencil tool and draw over the template with the Pencil. Illustrator automatically reshapes the selected line (instead of drawing a brand new line). You may need to edit the Pencil tool's settings (double-click the Pencil tool icon and edit the Pencil Tool Preferences dialog box) to control the smoothness of the revised line or the pixel distance from the selected line in which the Pencil tool will operate. (Learn more about using the Pencil tool in "Tracing Details" lesson in this chapter.)

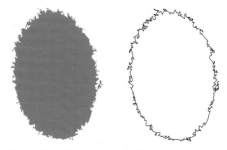

Manually tracing an intricate object may be more tedious and time-consuming than autotracing it; Yip drew the rough-edged parts of the sailor uniform with chalk on watercolor paper, which he then scanned, saved as a TIFF, and autotraced in Adobe Streamline

Tracing Details

Tracing Intricate Details with the Pencil

Overview: *Scan a photo and place it into a Template layer in Illustrator; adjust Pencil Options; trace the photo with the Pencil; create new layers; adjust layer positions and modes.*

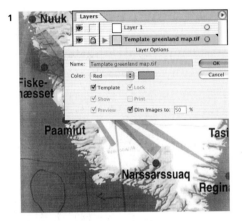

Double-clicking the Template layer to access Layer Options where "Dim Images" percentages can be customized

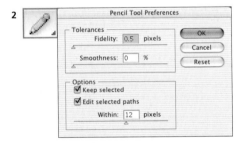

Double-clicking on the Pencil tool to set Options

Saving images for tracing

While EPS was once the preferred format for placed images (see the *Illustrator & Other Programs* chapter), saving images in TIFF will display more detail for tracing.

Laurie Grace loves the way the Pencil tool permits her to trace details with precision. Using the Pencil with custom settings and additional layers, she created this map of Greenland for a *Scientific American* article.

1 Scanning and placing the image into a Template layer. Scan the image you wish to use as a tracing template and save it in grayscale TIFF format. In a new Illustrator document, place your TIFF as a template (see "Digitizing a Logo" in this chapter). Your template will automatically be dimmed to 50%; to customize the percentage at which the template is dimmed, double-click the Template layer.

2 Setting up your Pencil Options for tracing. To draw with precision, you'll need to adjust the Pencil tool's default settings. Double-click the Pencil tool and drag the Fidelity slider all the way to the left, to 0.5 pixels, keeping Smoothness at 0% (higher numbers in Fidelity and Smoothness result in less accurate, smoother lines). For this lesson, keep "Keep Selected" enabled, so you can redraw lines and easily connect a new line to the last.

3 Drawing with the Pencil tool into Layer 1. It's very simple to attach one line to the next, so don't worry about tracing your entire template in one stroke. Zoom in on your work (see the *Illustrator Basics* chapter for Zoom help) and trace one section. When you finish drawing that section (and it's still selected), move the Pencil tool aside until you see "×", indicating that the Pencil would be drawing a new path. Next, move the Pencil close to the selected path and notice that the "×" disappears, indicating that the new path will be connected to the currently selected one, then continue to draw your path. To attach a new path to an unselected path, select the path you wish to attach to first. To draw a closed path with the Pencil (like the islands in Grace's map), hold the Option/Alt key down as you approach the first point in the path.

Note: *With Option/Alt down, if you stop before you reach the first point, the path will close with a straight line.*

4 **Creating and reordering new layers.** To add the background water and the coastline terrain details, Grace had to create additional layers. To create additional layers, click on the New Layer icon in the Layers palette. Clicking on a layer name activates that layer so the next object you create will be on that layer. To reorder layers, grab a layer by its name and drag it above or below another layer. Click in the Lock column to Lock/Unlock specific layers.

5 **Hiding and Previewing layers.** Toggle Hide/Show Template layers from the View menu. To toggle any layer between Hide and Show, click on the Eye icon in the Visibility column for that layer to remove or show the Eye. To toggle a non-template layer between Preview and Outline mode, ⌘-click/Ctrl-click the Eye icon. (To move objects between layers, see Tip "Moving an object from one layer to another" later in this chapter.)

3

After drawing part of the coastline it remains selected (top left); moving the Pencil close to the selected path then allows the next path to be connected (top right); continuing the path with the Pencil tool (directly above)

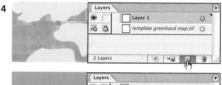

Drawing with the Pencil tool and holding the Option key to close the path

4

Making a New Layer; a blue object created in the new Layer 3 which is moved below Layer 1; Layer 1 locked with Layer 3 activated

5

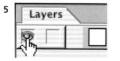
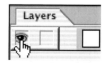

Toggling between Outline and Preview mode for a specific layer by ⌘/Ctrl-clicking the Eye icon

Colors with Layers

Coloring Black & White Images with Layers

Overview: *Create a sketch; scan and save it as a bitmap TIFF; set up layers in Illustrator for the TIFF and colored objects; place bitmap TIFF into the upper layer; color the image; group TIFF with its colors; add background.*

1

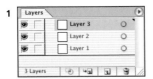

Setting up basic layers in Illustrator

2

A bitmap outline sketch

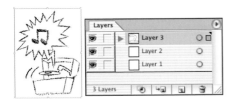

The scanned sketch placed into the top layer

Overprinting 1-bit TIFF problem

It's usually best to set black TIFFs to Overprint Fill in the Attributes palette. If Overprint is disabled, check www.adobe.com/illustrator for possible corrective updates.

While the most obvious way to trace an image in Illustrator is to place the image on a lower layer and use an upper layer to trace the new Illustrator objects, in some cases you'll want your tracing layer to be *below* a placed image. When creating an illustration for a children's magazine, John Kanzler placed his sketch on an upper layer. This way, he could add color using Illustrator and maintain a hand-sketched look by keeping the scanned sketch in the file.

1 **Setting up your Illustrator layers.** In Illustrator, create at least three layers for the elements of your image. You'll need to have a top layer for placing your sketches, a middle layer (or layers) for coloring your sketches, and a base layer for background objects. (For help making layers, see "Digitizing a Logo" and "Tracing Details" in this chapter.) Illustrator assigns a different color to each layer name—this helps you keep track of the objects in each layer (selected paths and anchor points will be color-coded to match their layer name).

2 **Sketching and scanning a black-and-white drawing; placing the image into the top layer in Illustrator.** Scan a hand-drawn sketch as a 1 bit bitmap format (black

and white only), or draw directly in a painting program set to a black-and-white (bitmapped) mode. Save your image as a TIFF file. Kanzler sketched his figure with a soft pencil on rough paper, scanned it, then saved it as a bitmap TIFF file. Next, in the Layers palette of your Illustrator file, make the top layer active (click on the layer name) and use the Place command (from the File menu) to place one of your drawings into the top layer.

3 Coloring your drawings. To make coloring your drawings easier, it helps to lock all but the layer in which you will be drawing. You must first unlock and activate the chosen layer (to the left of the layer you should see the Eye icon but no Lock icon; to activate a layer, click on its name in the Layers palette). Then, lock the top layer. Now, using filled colored objects without strokes, trace *under* your placed sketch. To view the color alone, hide the top layer by clicking on the Eye icon in the visibility column for that layer in the left side of the Layers palette.

4 Grouping your drawing with its colors; adding a background. When you have finished coloring the figure, unlock the top layer, select the placed TIFF with the objects that colorize that figure, and group them together (while selected, choose Object > Group). The grouped figure automatically moves to the top layer.

To add background elements, activate the bottommost layer and draw on it. Your grouped images can be easily repositioned within your composition by selecting and moving them with the Selection tool.

Changing layers by selecting an object

Instead of changing the active layer by selecting a new layer in the Layers palette, let Illustrator make the change for you. When you select an object from an unlocked layer, its layer automatically becomes active. The next object you create will use the same paint style as the last selected object and will be placed on that same active layer.

3

Drawing into layers below the top layer, which contains the scanned sketch

The colorized drawing with the sketch visible and the sketch hidden

4

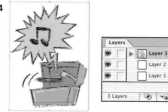

Selected objects that are on different layers, then grouped, automatically move to the layer where the topmost selected object resides

The background for the illustration, created in the bottom layer

Moving a grouped, colorized figure around the composition

Organizing Layers

Managing Custom Layers and Sublayers

Overview: *Sketch and scan a composition; set up basic, named layers in Illustrator for the objects you will create; place art into temporary sublayers; trace the placed art; delete the temporary sublayers.*

1

The initial concept for the illustration, used to set up a photo shoot; the assembled photographic collage

Hand-traced sketch scanned

Beginning your illustration with well-organized layers and sublayers can be a lifesaver when you're constructing complex illustrations. Using these layers to isolate or combine specific elements will save you an immense amount of production time by making it easy to hide, lock, or select related objects within layers. When American Express commissioned Nancy Stahl to design a cover for its internal magazine, *Context*, she saved time and frustration by creating layers and using sublayers for tracing and arranging various components of the cover illustration.

1 Collecting and assembling source materials. Prepare your own source materials to use as tracing templates in Illustrator. For the AmEx illustration, Stahl took

Polaroids of herself posed as each of the figures in her planned composition and scanned them into Adobe Photoshop, where she scaled them, composited some elements, and moved them into position. She then printed out the assembled "collage," roughly sketched in the other elements by hand and, with tracing paper, created a line drawing version of the full composition to use as an overall template. She then scanned it into the computer.

2 Setting up illustration layers. Before you begin to import any photos or drawings, take a few moments to set up layers to help you isolate the key elements in your illustration. For the cover illustration, before she actually started drawing in Illustrator, Stahl set up separate layers for the background, the sky, the rays of light, and the building in the background, which she called "OZ," as well as a character layer for each of the figures. Name a layer while creating it by Option-clicking/Alt-clicking on the Create New Layer icon in the Layers palette. You can also name or rename an existing layer or sublayer by double-clicking on it in the Layers palette.

3 Placing art to use as templates. Click on the layer in which you plan to trace your first object, then click on the Create New Sublayer icon in the Layers palette to create a sublayer for your template (Option-click/Alt-click on the icon to name your sublayer as you create it). Use File > Place to select the scan or artwork to be placed into this sublayer. The template sublayer should now be directly below the object layer upon which you will be tracing. Lock the template sublayer and draw into the layer above using the Pen, Pencil, or other drawing tools.

Stahl activated a character layer by clicking on it in the Layers palette, then created a sublayer that she named "JPEG Images". She placed the hand-traced figures image into her sublayer, locked it, and traced her first character into the layer above. Using the Layers palette, she freely moved the locked JPEG Images template sublayer below each character's layer as she drew.

2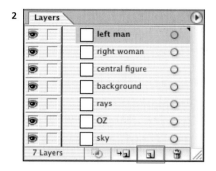

Setting up layers to isolate key elements

3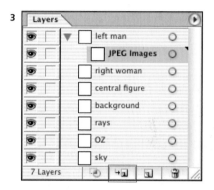

The temporary sublayer before placing the scan

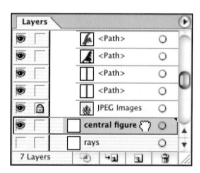

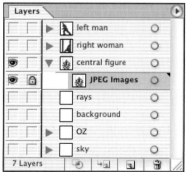

Moving the sublayer and setting up the Lock and Show options for tracing

4

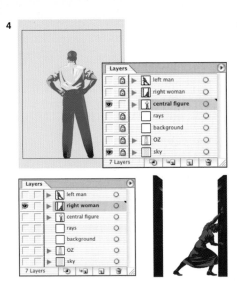

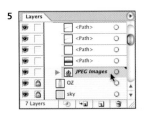

Viewing only the essential layers for each task

5

Clicking on a visible and unlocked sublayer to make it active for placing new art

6

New Layer...
New Sublayer...
Duplicate "JPEG Images"
Delete "JPEG Images"

Clicking on or dragging the sublayer to the Trash icon, or choosing Delete from the Layers palette pop-up menu

Changing placed art

Select the image you wish to replace. Next open the Links palette (Window menu) and click on the Replace Link icon (the bottom left icon) or choose Replace from the Links palette pop-up menu. In the dialog box, locate the replacement image and click Place.

4 Drawing into your layers. Now you can begin drawing and tracing elements into your compositional layers and sublayers. Activate the layer or sublayer in which you want to draw by clicking on the layer's name, make sure the layer or sublayer is unlocked and visible (there should be an Eye in the Visibility column and an empty box in the Lock column), and start to work. Use the Layers palette to lock, unlock, or hide layers or sublayers, as well as to toggle between Preview and Outline modes, switch your active layer, or add a new layer or sublayer. By maneuvering in this way, Stahl could easily trace a sketch of basic background elements, create rays against a locked background or develop one character at a time.

5 Adding new placed art to a layer or sublayer. If you need to import art into an existing layer or sublayer, first make sure the layer is visible and unlocked, then make it the active layer by clicking on it. For the AmEx cover, when Stahl needed additional references, she viewed and unlocked the JPEG Images template sublayer, clicked on it to make it active, and then used the Place command to bring the new scan or art into the template sublayer.

6 Deleting layers or sublayers when you are finished using them. Extra layers with placed art can take up quite a bit of disk space, so you'll want to delete them when you are done with them. When you finish using a template, first save the illustration. Then, in the Layers palette, click on the layer or sublayer you are ready to remove and click on the Trash icon in the Layers palette, choose the Delete option from the Layers palette pop-up menu, or drag the layer or sublayer to the Trash icon in the Layers palette. Finally, use Save As to save this new version of the illustration with a meaningful new name and version number (such as "AmEx no JPEG v3.ai"). Stahl eventually deleted all the sublayers she created as templates so she could save her final cover illustration with all the illustration layers but none of the template sublayers or placed pictures.

STAHL

Nancy Stahl

Using the same techniques as in "Organizing Layers," Nancy Stahl created this image for the interior of American Express's internal magazine, *Context*. When she wanted to move selected objects to another layer, she used the technique shown in the Tip below.

Moving an object from one layer to another

To move a selected object to another layer: open the Layers palette, grab the colored dot to the right of the object's layer, and drag it to the desired layer (see near right). To move a copy of an object: hold down the Option/Alt key while you drag (see far right).

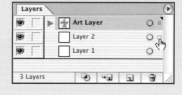

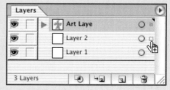

Nested Layers

Organizing with Layers and Sublayers

Overview: *Plan a layer structure; create layers and sublayers; refine the structure by rearranging layers and sublayers in the Layer palette's hierarchy; hide and lock layers; change the Layers palette display.*

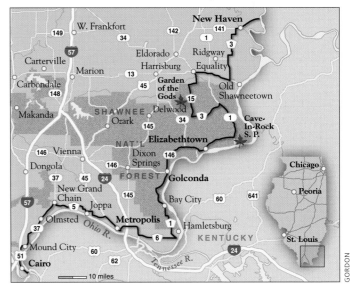

GORDON

1

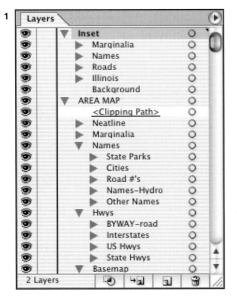

The completed layer structure for the map showing layers and two levels of sublayers

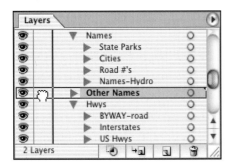

Selecting and dragging the BYWAY-road sublayer up and out of the Hwys sublayer, placing it on the same level in the hierarchy as Hwys

Layers have always been a great way of organizing artwork. Now with Illustrator, you can organize your Layers palette as a nested hierarchy, making it easier to navigate and manipulate. For this map of the Great River Scenic Byway in Illinois, Steven Gordon relied on nested layers and sublayers to organize the artwork he developed.

1 Planning, then creating and moving layers and sublayers. Gordon began by planning a layer structure for the map in which layers with similar information would be nested within several "master" layers, so he could easily navigate the Layers palette and manipulate the layers and sublayers. After planning the organization of your layered artwork, open the Layers palette (Window>Layers) and begin creating layers and sublayers. (Illustrator automatically creates a Layer 1 every time a new document is created—you can use or rename this layer.) To create a new layer, click the Create New Layer icon at the bottom of the palette. To create a new sublayer that's nested within a currently selected layer, click on the palette's Create New Sublayer icon.

As you continue working, you may need to refine your organization by changing the nesting of a current layer or sublayer. To do this, drag the layer name in the Layers palette and release it over a boundary between layers. To convert a sublayer to a layer, drag its name and release it above its master layer or below the last sublayer of the master layer (watch the sublayer's bar icon to ensure that it aligns with the left side of the names field in the Layers palette before releasing it). Don't forget that if you move a layer in the Layers palette, any sublayer, group, or path it contains will move with it, affecting the hierarchy of artwork in your illustration.

2 Hiding and locking layers. As you draw, you can hide or lock sublayers of artwork by simply clicking on the visibility (Eye) icon or edit (Lock) icon of their master layer. Gordon organized his map so that related artwork, such as different kinds of names, were placed on separate sublayers nested within the Names layer, and thus could be hidden or locked by hiding or locking the Names layer.

If you click on the visibility or edit icon of a master layer, Illustrator remembers the visibility and edit status of each sublayer before locking or hiding the master layer. When Gordon clicked the visibility icon of the Names layer, sublayers that had been hidden before he hid the master layer remained hidden after he made the Names layer visible again. To quickly make the contents of all layers and sublayers visible, select Show All Layers from the Layers palette's pop-up menu. To unlock the content of all layers and sublayers, choose Unlock All Layers. (If these commands are not available, it's because all layers are already showing or unlocked.)

3 Changing the Layers palette display. As you utilize the Layers palette, change its display to make the palette easier to navigate. Display layers and sublayers (and hide groups and paths) in the palette by choosing Palette Options from the palette menu and in the Layers palette Options dialog box, clicking Show Layers Only. To view tiny thumbnails of the artwork on each layer or sublayer, select a Row Size of Medium or Large, or select Other and set row size to 20 or more pixels in the dialog.

2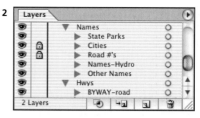

Top, a "master" layer with two sublayers locked; bottom, after the master layer is locked, the two sublayers' edit icons are not dimmed, indicating that they will remain locked when the layer is unlocked

3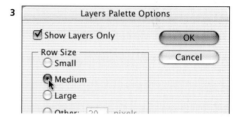

Selecting a row size in the Layers palette Options dialog box

Another way to unlock layers

A quick way to unlock all the contents of a layer: Make sure the layer itself is unlocked (the lock icon is gone) and then choose Unlock All from the Object menu.

Let Illustrator do the walking

Illustrator can automatically expand the Layers palette and scroll to a sublayer that's hidden within a collapsed layer. Just click on an object in your artwork and choose Locate Layer or Locate Object from the Layers palette's menu.

Varied Perspective

Analyzing Different Views of Perspective

Advanced Technique

Overview: *Draw and scan a sketch; create working layers using your sketch as a template; in each "guides" layer, draw a series of lines to establish perspective; make the perspective lines into guides; draw elements of your image using the applicable perspective guides.*

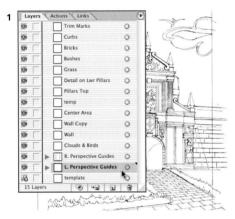

Portion of the original pencil sketch placed on a template layer with a custom layer ready for creation of guides

Locking and unlocking guides

- When guides are unlocked (uncheck View > Guides > Lock Guides), you can select any guide as an object and move or delete it.
- When a layer with guides is locked, the guides lose their "snap to" property—yet another good reason for you to keep guides on separate layers.

While any object can be made into a guide, converting lines into guides is indispensable when adding perspective to an image. To illustrate this McDonald's packaging design, Clarke Tate constructed several sets of vanishing point guides, enabling him to draw a background scene (Fort Santiago in the Philippines) that would contrast with the flat cartoon figures of Snoopy and Woodstock.

1 Setting up the layers. Sketch a detailed layout of the illustration on paper, shaping main elements like Tate's brick walk and wall with a perspective view. Scan your sketch and save the scan as a TIFF, then place the TIFF in Illustrator and choose Template from the Layers palette's pop-up menu. Analyze the image to determine the number of vanishing points in your illustration (points along the scene's horizon where parallel lines seem to converge). Create new layers (click the Create New Layer icon in the Layers palette) for compositional elements; add a layer for each vanishing point in the illustration.

2 Establishing the location of vanishing points. In the Layers palette, select the first layer you'll use for developing a set of perspective guides. Referring to your template, mark the first vanishing point and use the Pen tool to draw a path along the horizon and through the vanishing point. (Some or all of your vanishing points may need to extend beyond the picture border.) With the Direct-selection tool, select the anchor point from the end of the line that is away from the vanishing point. Grab the point, then hold down Option/Alt and swing this copy of the line up so it encompasses the uppermost object that will be constructed using the vanishing point. You should now have a **V** that extends along your horizon line through your vanishing point, then to an upper or lower portion of your composition.

To create in-between lines through the same vanishing point, select both of the original lines, use the Blend tool to click first on the outer anchor point of one of the lines, and then on the outer anchor point of the other line. (If you need to specify more or fewer steps, you can select the blend and edit the number of steps in the Spacing > Specified Steps field of the Object > Blend > Blend Options dialog box.) For each different vanishing point, repeat the above procedure.

3 Making and using the guides. Because Illustrator cannot create guides from blended objects, you must first select each blend with the Selection tool and then expand it (Object > Blend > Expand). Next, transform the blends into guides by choosing View > Guides > Make Guides. Now pick an area of the illustration and begin drawing. You may want to lock the layers containing guides for other vanishing points so you don't accidentally snap objects to the wrong perspective.

Top, dragging a perspective line to the uppermost object from the vanishing point; bottom, paths blended to create in-between perspective lines

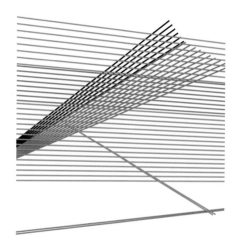

Perspective line blends before being transformed into guides

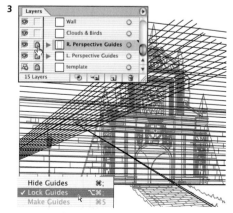

Turning off the "snap to" function for guides by locking the layer (left); locking guides in place by using the Lock/Unlock toggle in the View > Guides submenu

Type

6

180 Introduction

184 Working with Threaded Text

185 Wrapping Text Around Objects

185 Character and Paragraph Styles

186 Taking Advantage of OpenType

187 The Glyphs Palette

188 The Every-line Composer

188 More Type Functions (Type & Window menus)

189 Converting Type to Outlines

191 Using the Appearance Palette with Type

193 Exporting Illustrator Type

194 Custom Text Paths: *Trickling Type with Variations of Type Style*

196 Stretching Type: *Fitting Type by Converting to Outline*

198–199 Galleries: John Burns, Hornall Anderson

200 Masking Letters: *Masking Images with Letter Forms*

201 Gallery: Gary Newman

202 Book Cover Design: *Illustrator as a Stand-alone Layout Tool*

204 Brushed Type: *Applying Brushes to Letterforms*

206–211 Galleries: Joachim Müller-Lancé, Tim Girvin, Jennifer Bartlett, Louis Fishauf, Ellen Papciak-Rose, Bjørn Akselsen, Pattie Belle Hastings, Frank Jonen

212 Crunching Type: *Transforming Type with Warps & Envelopes*

214 Advanced Technique: Offset Fills: *Covering a Pattern with an Offset Fill*

216 Advanced Technique: Antiquing Type: *Applying Scribble in an Opacity Mask*

218 Gallery: Steven Gordon

Type

The Type tool, Area Type tool, Path Type tool, Vertical Type tool, Vertical Area Type tool, and Vertical Path Type tool. Select a Type tool and press Shift to toggle the tool between a horizontal and vertical orientation

Selecting type by accident

If you keep accidentally selecting type when you're trying to select an object with the Selection tool, enable Type Object Selection by Path Only (Preferences > Type & Auto Tracing). With this option turned on, you won't select type objects unless you click directly on the baseline or path of the type. (If you have trouble finding the path, you can select the text object in the Layers palette, or marquee at least a full letterform with a selection tool or the Lasso tool.)

It's Greek to me!

You can specify a size at which type will be "greeked" on screen (which means it will appear as gray bars rather than readable text). Set the greeking size by choosing Preferences > Type & Auto Tracing, and entering a size in the Greeking field. Text at or below that size will be greeked. Note that greeked text *prints* normally.

With the arrival of Illustrator CS, Illustrator users have taken a big step forward in terms of the control and sophistication with which they can design type. In addition to Illustrator's new Type engine itself, the most momentous new developments are the arrival of paragraph and character styles; increased support for OpenType fonts that allows you to take full advantage of their superior capabilities; and new features that help you create more aesthetically pleasing text layouts by increasing your control over text blocks, columns and rows, and the spacing and alignment of characters. Adobe rounds out the package with a wealth of smaller and less easily categorizable features that will help make the experience of designing type in Illustrator more satisfying.

Although you'll probably still prefer a page layout program such as QuarkXPress, InDesign, or PageMaker for multi-page documents like catalogues and long magazine articles, and Dreamweaver or GoLive for Web page layout, this chapter will demonstrate many reasons to stay within Illustrator for single-page documents. The Type chapter of the *User Guide* covers the creation and manipulation of type in great detail, so this introduction will focus on essentials, what's new and production tips.

For creating and manipulating type, Illustrator CS offers no less that seven palettes, all accessible from the Window > Type submenu. Nested in with the old Paragraph and Character palettes is the new OpenType palette, which gives you convenient access to the options of OpenType fonts. The new Glyphs palette lets you choose quickly from a wide range of special characters. The new Character Styles and Paragraph Styles palettes, nested together, are where you'll manage Illustrator's new automatic text formatting capabilities. And the new, improved Tabs palette replaces the old Tab Ruler.

When you first open the Character and Paragraph palettes, they may appear in a collapsed view. To cycle through display options for either palette, click the double arrow on the Palette tab.

There are three type options in Illustrator that are accessible through the Type tool: *Point type, Area type,* and *Path type.* The flexible Type tool lets you click to create a Point type object, click-drag to create an Area type object, click within any existing type object to enter or edit text, or click on a path to create Path type (discussed a bit further on). You can gain access to type created in other applications by using the File > Open or File > Place commands (and of course by using the Copy and Paste commands).

Select letters, words or an entire block of text by dragging across the letters with the Type tool, or use a selection tool to select text as an *object* by clicking on or marqueeing the text baseline (the baseline is the line that the type sits on).

- **Point type:** Click with the Type tool or the Vertical Type tool anywhere on the page to create Point type. Once you click, a blinking text-insertion cursor called an "I-beam" indicates that you can now type text using your keyboard. To add another line of text, press the Return/Enter key. When you're finished typing into one text object, click on the Type tool in the Toolbox to simultaneously select the current text as an object (the I-beam will disappear) and be poised to begin another text object. To just select the text as an object, click on a selection tool.

- **Area type:** Click and drag with the Type tool to create a rectangle, into which you can type. Once you've defined your rectangle, the I-beam awaits your typing, and the text automatically wraps to the next line when you type in the confines of the rectangle.

Another way to create Area type or Vertical Area type is to construct a path (with any tools you wish) forming a shape within which to place the type. Click and hold on the Type tool to access other tools, or press the Shift key to toggle between horizontal and vertical orientations

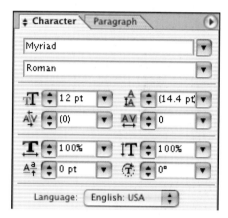

Ports illustrated

Each type object in Illustrator CS has an *in port* (a small box at the upper left side) and an *out port* (a small box at the lower right side). If both ports are empty, all the text is displayed and the object isn't currently linked (or *threaded*) to any other text objects. You may also see the following symbols in the ports:

- A red plus sign in the out port means the object contains *overflow text* (additional text that doesn't fit)
- An arrow in the in port means the object is threaded to a preceding text object, and text is flowing into the current object
- An arrow in the out port means the object is threaded to a subsequent text object, and text is flowing out of the current object.

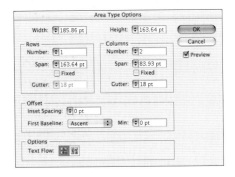

Area Type Options dialog box

Tabs palette

of *like* tools (see Tip "Type tool juggling" later in this chapter introduction). Choose the Area Type or Vertical Area Type tool and click on the path itself to place text within the path. Distort the confining shape by grabbing an anchor point with the Direct Selection tool and dragging it to a new location, or reshape the path by adjusting direction lines. The text within will reflow.

Note: *If you use the Vertical Area Type tool, you'll see that your text will flow automatically, starting from the right edge of the area flowing toward the left! Those of you who use Roman fonts and typographic standards won't have much use for this tool since Roman type flows from left to right (see the Tip "Multinational font support" later in this chapter.)*

Illustrator's new Area Type Options dialog box (Type > Area Type Options) gives you precise control over a number of important aspects of Area type. You can set numerical values for the width and height of the selected Area type; set precise values for Rows and Columns (i.e. you can divide a single Area type object into multiple columns or rows that will reflow as you type), and choose whether or not those values remain fixed as you scale; specify Offset options, including the amount of inset (defined as the margin between the text and the bounding path) and the alignment of the first baseline of text; and a Text Flow option that determines how text flows between rows or columns.

To set tabs for Area type, select the text object and choose Window > Type > Tabs. The Tabs palette (new in Illustrator CS) will open aligned with the text box. As you pan or zoom, you'll notice the Tab ruler doesn't move with the text box. No sweat: If you lose your alignment, just click the little Magnet button on the Tabs palette, and the palette will snap back into alignment.

One new feature that arrives with the Tabs palette is the ability to create your own *tab leaders*. A tab leader is a repeated pattern of characters (such as dots or dashes) between a Tab and the text that follows it. Select a tab stop on the ruler in the Tabs palette, type a pattern of up to eight characters in the palette's Leader box, then hit Return/Enter. You'll see your customized Leader pattern repeated across the width of the tab. (For more on using the Tabs palette, see the *User Guide*.)

• **Path type:** The Path type tool allows you to click on a path to flow text along the perimeter of the path (the path will then become unstroked or unfilled).

Illustrator CS adds a new level of control over Path type. When you select a Path type object, you'll see three brackets appear: one at the beginning, one in the center, and one at the end of the Path type. The beginning and end brackets carry an in port and an out port, respectively, which can be used to thread text between objects (see the Tip "Ports illustrated"). The center bracket is used to control the positioning of the Path type. Hold your cursor over it until a small icon that looks like an upside down T appears. You can now drag the center bracket to reposition the type. Dragging the bracket across the path will flip the type to the other side of the path. (For example, type along the outside of a circle would flip to the inside.) Dragging the bracket forward or backward along the direction of the path will move the type in that direction.

As with Area type, use the Direct Selection tool to reshape the confining path; the type on the path will automatically readjust to the new path shape.

The new Type on a Path Options dialog box (Type > Type on a Path > Type On a Path Options) lets you set a number of Path type attributes. You can choose from five different Path Type Effects (Rainbow, Skew, 3D Ribbon, Stair Step, and Gravity); a Flip checkbox that will automatically flip type to the other side of the path; a menu that lets you set the alignment of type relative to the path; and a Spacing control that lets you adjust the spacing of type as it moves around a curve. (The Path Type Effects are also available via the Type > Type on a Path submenu.) See the *User Guide* for in-depth info.

Object rows and columns

Wondering how to create rows and columns from non-type objects? Just select the object(s) and choose Object > Path > Split into Grid.

Rectangle rule relaxed

One nice improvement in Illustrator CS is that when you use the Area Type Options dialog box to create rows and columns, your type container won't get automatically converted to a rectangle (as was the case with the Rows and Columns function in previous versions of Illustrator).

To manually flip type on a path to the other side of the path, select the type and drag the center handle (the thin blue line perpendicular to the type) across the path, as indicated by the red arrow above. Note the tiny T-shaped icon that appears next to the cursor as you position it near the handle

The same type, after dragging across the path, but before releasing the mouse. After release, the type will be in the position indicated by the blue type above the path. You can then drag the center handle from side to side to adjust the position of the text—just don't drag across the path again or you'll flip the type back. You can also flip type across a path automatically by choosing Type > Type on a Path > Type on a Path Options, checking the Flip box (as shown on the following page), and clicking on OK

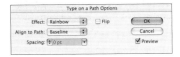

The Type on a Path Options dialog box

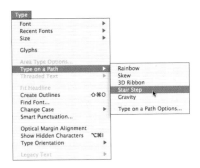

The Type on a Path submenu

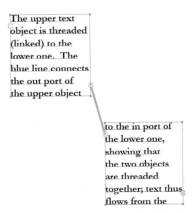

The upper text object is threaded (linked) to the lower one. The blue line connects the out port of the upper object to the in port of the lower one, showing that the two objects are threaded together; text thus flows from the first object to the second. The red plus sign in the out port of the lower object indicates that there is still more overflow text, which could flow into a third threaded object

WORKING WITH THREADED TEXT

If a text object contains more text than it has room to display, you'll see a plus sign in the small box along its lower right side. (This box is called the *out port*; see the Tip "Ports illustrated," earlier in this chapter.) To enlarge the object to allow for more text, use the Selection tool to grab the object by a bounding side and drag to resize it (hold down the Shift key if you want to constrain proportions as you resize).

To add a new text object that can receive overflow text, use the Selection tool to select the first text object. Next, click on the red plus sign in the out port. The cursor will change to the "loaded text" cursor, which looks like a miniature text block. Then you can either click on the Artboard to create a new text object the same size and shape as the original; or drag to create a text object of any size. Either way, the new text object will be *threaded* (linked) to the original, and the text that wouldn't fit in the first object will flow into the second.

Note: *Make sure Type Object Selection by Path Only is unchecked in the Type & Auto Tracing area of Preferences, or the above process won't work.*

Similarly, you can link existing text objects together by clicking the plus sign on the first object, and then clicking on the path of the object that is to receive the overflow text. (Keep your eye on the cursor, which will change to indicate valid "drop" locations.) You can also link objects using a menu command: Select the first object with the Selection tool, then Shift-click to select the second object as well. Choose Type > Threaded Text > Create, and *voilà*, the objects are linked.

Of course, the threads between objects can be broken as easily as they're created. If you want to disconnect one object from another, first select the object. Then double-click its in port to break the thread to a preceding object, or double click its out port to break the thread to a subsequent object. Alternatively, you can select the object and click either the in port or the out port once. Then click the other end of the thread to break it.

You can also release an object from a Text thread by selecting it, then choosing Type > Threaded Text > Release Selection. Or, if you want to remove the threading from an object while leaving text in place, select it and choose Type > Threaded Text > Remove Threading.

WRAPPING TEXT AROUND OBJECTS

Illustrator CS handles text wrapping a little differently from previous versions. Text wrapping is now an object attribute and is set specifically for each object that will have text wrapped around it (known as a *wrap object*). First, make sure that the object you want to wrap text around is above the text you want to wrap around it in the Layers palette. Then select the wrap object and choose Object > Text Wrap > Make Text Wrap. The Text Wrap Options dialog box will appear. Here, you'll choose the amount of offset and also have the option to choose Invert Wrap (which reverses the side of the object that text wraps around). You can also wrap text around a group of objects. In order to add a new object to the text wrapped group, just drag its icon in the Layers palette into the group. To release an object from text wrapping, select it and choose Object > Text Wrap > Release Text Wrap. To change the options for an existing wrap object, select it and choose Object > Text Wrap > Text Wrap Options. (For more information on text wrapping, see the *User Guide*.)

CHARACTER AND PARAGRAPH STYLES

As in previous versions, Illustrator's Character and Paragraph palettes (Window > Type > Character and Window > Type > Paragraph) let you format text by changing one attribute at a time. Illustrator CS takes formatting to the next level by introducing Character and Paragraph styles. Now you can apply multiple attributes to text simply by applying the appropriate style.

You can access the new Character Styles and Paragraph Styles palettes via Window > Type > Character Styles, or Window > Type > Paragraph Styles. New styles

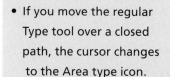

Legacy text

Illustrator's new text engine makes a lot of new type features possible. But it also means that text is handled very differently from previous versions, so *legacy text* (text created in earlier versions of Illustrator) needs to be updated before it can be edited in Illustrator CS. When you open a file containing legacy text, a dialog box warns you that it contains text that needs to be updated. The dialog box gives you the choice of updating the text then and there by clicking "Update," or waiting till later by clicking "OK." Text that hasn't been updated can be viewed, moved, and printed, but it can't be edited. When selected, legacy text is displayed with an X through its bounding box. When text is updated, you may see the following types of changes:

- Changes to leading, tracking, and kerning
- In Area type: words overflowing, shifting between lines or to the next linked object

You can choose to update all legacy text at any time by choosing Type > Legacy Text > Update All Legacy Text. Update specific legacy text by clicking it with the Type tool. You'll also have the option to preserve legacy text on a layer below the updated text for comparison.

can either be created from scratch or based on existing styles. To create a new style with a default name (that can be changed later if you like), click the Create New Style button in either the Character Styles or the Paragraph Styles palette. If you want to name your new style from the get-go, choose New Character Style from the Character Styles palette menu, or New Paragraph Style from the Paragraph Styles palette menu. Type a name for your new style in the dialog box that appears, click OK, and your new style will appear in the Character Styles or Paragraph Styles palette.

To create a new style based on an existing one, select the existing style in the Character Styles or Paragraph Styles palette. Then choose Duplicate Character Style or Duplicate Paragraph Style from the palette menu. Your new "cloned" style will appear in the palette.

To change the attributes of a new or existing style, select its name in the Character Styles or Paragraph Styles palette, and choose Character Style Options or Paragraph Style Options from the palette menu. The Options dialog box will let you set all your desired attributes for the style—everything from basic characteristics, such as font, size, and color, to OpenType features.

To apply a style to text, just select the text you want to format, click the name of the style in the Character Styles or Paragraph Styles palette, and *voila!*—your formatting is applied to the selected text. (This won't work if the type has *overrides*—extra formatting—applied, in which case you may need to remove the override by clicking a second time. For more information on overrides and other elements of using Character and Paragraph Styles, see the *User Guide*.)

TAKING ADVANTAGE OF OPENTYPE

As mentioned previously, underneath Illustrator CS's hood lies a powerful new text engine. And one of the main reasons Adobe revamped the way Illustrator handles text was to allow users to take full advantage of the sophisticated features of OpenType fonts. (To underscore the point, Illustrator CS ships with a bundle of free OpenType fonts, so you can put them to work immediately.) One great benefit of OpenType fonts is that they're platform-independent, so they can move easily between Mac and Windows.

When you use any OpenType font, Illustrator CS will automatically set standard ligatures as you type (see example at right). You can set options for other OpenType features via the OpenType palette, which is nested by default with the Character and Paragraph palettes, and accessible via Window > Type > OpenType. The OpenType palette includes two pop-up menus that let you control the style and positioning of numerals, and buttons that let you choose whether or not to use standard ligatures (for letter pairs such as fi, fl, ff, ffi, and ffl), optional ligatures (for letter pairs such as ct and st), swashes (characters with exaggerated flourishes), titling characters (for use in uppercase titles), stylistic alternates (alternative versions of a common character), superscripted ordinals, and fractions.

If you'd like more information on what the various commands in the OpenType palette do, we've included a helpful guide by Sandee Cohen on the *Wow! CD* (OpenType_Guide.pdf). These pages, taken from Cohen's *InDesign CS Visual QuickStart Guide*, give you a primer in how to work with OpenType fonts.

THE GLYPHS PALETTE

Illustrator's new Glyphs palette gives you quick access to a wide variety of special characters, including any ligatures, ornaments, swashes, and fractions included in that OpenType font. Choose Window > Type > Glyphs to display the palette. With the Type tool, click to place the insertion point where you want the special character to appear, and then double-click the character you want in the Glyphs palette to insert it in the text. You'll find many specialty characters (like ✳ or ❧) that once required separate fonts, sitting there in your Glyphs palette. See the *User Guide* for more information on the Glyphs palette.

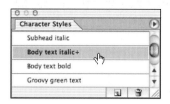

Character Styles palette

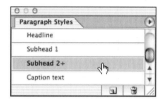

Paragraph Styles palette

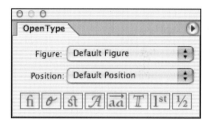

OpenType palette

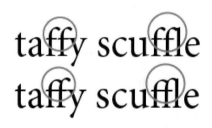

OpenType fonts automatically set standard ligatures as you type (unless you turn this feature off in the OpenType palette). In the example above, the type on the top row is set using the standard version of Adobe's Minion font. The bottom row is set using Minion Pro, one of the OpenType fonts included with Illustrator CS. Minion Pro supplies the ligatures for "ff" and "ffl" (visible in the bottom row), which give the type a more sophisticated look

Glyphs palette

Lorem ipsum dolor sit amet, consectetuer adipiscing elit. Sed at nibh. Nam ultrices erat nec pede. Vivamus est ante, aliquet vel, fermentum et, nonummy eget, ante. Morbi metus nisl, placerat ut, accumsan id, aliquet vel, nulla. Aenean scelerisque dapibus nunc. Proin augue. Vestibulum dictum. Morbi eget urna. Phasellus id augue. Nulla congue imperdiet dolor. Lorem ipsum dolor sit amet, consectetuer adipiscing elit. Sed at nibh.

Text composed using Single-line Composer

Lorem ipsum dolor sit amet, consectetuer adipiscing elit. Sed at nibh. Nam ultrices erat nec pede. Vivamus est ante, aliquet vel, fermentum et, nonummy eget, ante. Morbi metus nisl, placerat ut, accumsan id, aliquet vel, nulla. Aenean scelerisque dapibus nunc. Proin augue. Vestibulum dictum. Morbi eget urna. Phasellus id augue. Nulla congue imperdiet dolor. Lorem ipsum dolor sit amet, consectetuer adipiscing elit. Sed at nibh.

The same text composed using Every-line Composer, which automatically creates less ragged-looking text blocks with more uniform line lengths

Multinational font support

Illustrator supports multinational fonts, including Chinese, Japanese, and Korean. Check the Show Asian Options box in the Type & Auto Tracing area of Preferences to reveal Asian text options in the Character palette (if necessary, click on the double arrows on the Palette tab to fully expand it). To utilize multinational font capabilities you must have the proper fonts and language support activated on your system. Even then, some multinational options won't work with fonts that don't support the appropriate languages, including most fonts intended primarily for English and Western European languages.

THE EVERY-LINE COMPOSER

Illustrator CS offers two composition methods for determining where line breaks occur in blocks of text: the old Single-line Composer and the new Every-line Composer.

The Single-line Composer applies hyphenation and justification settings to one line of text at a time, as Illustrator did by default in previous versions. But this can result in uneven, ragged-looking blocks of text, so the new Every-line Composer thinks ahead by automatically determining the best combination of line breaks across the entire run of text. The result is even-looking text blocks with minimal hyphenation and consistent line lengths and spacing, without having to fine-tune line breaks by hand. However, if you're into micromanaging your text and you want manual control over every line break, you still have the option to choose the old Single-line Composer.

To choose between composition methods, select the text to be composed and choose Adobe Every-line Composer or Adobe Single-line Composer from the Paragraph palette menu.

MORE TYPE FUNCTIONS (TYPE & WINDOW MENUS)

• **Find Font:** If you try to open a file and don't have the correct fonts loaded, Illustrator warns you, lists the missing fonts, and asks if you still want to open the file. You do need the correct fonts to print properly; so if you don't have the missing fonts, choose Find Font to locate and replace them with ones you do have.

Find Font's dialog box displays the fonts used in the document in the top list; an asterisk indicates a missing font. The font type is represented by a symbol to the right of the font name. You can choose to replace fonts with ones on your system or used in the document. To display only the font types you want to use as replacements, uncheck those you don't want to include in the list. To replace a font used in the document, select it from the top list and choose a replacement font from the bottom list. You can individually replace each occurrence of the font by clicking Change and then Find. Otherwise, simply click Change All to replace all occurrences.

Note: *When you select a font in the top list, it becomes selected in the document.*

The Find Font dialog box

- **Type Orientation** lets you change orientation from horizontal to vertical, or vice versa, by choosing Type > Type Orientation > Horizontal or Vertical.

- **Change Case:** You can change the case of text selected with the Type tool via the new Type > Change Case submenu, which offers four choices: UPPERCASE, lowercase, Title Case, and Sentence case.

- **Fit Headline** is a quick way to open up the letter spacing of a headline across a specific distance. First, create the headline within an area, not along a path. Next, set the type in the size you wish to use. Select the headline by highlighting it, then choose Type > Fit Headline, and the type will spread out to fill the area you've indicated. This works with both the Horizontal and Vertical Type tools.

- **Show Hidden Characters** reveals soft and hard returns, word spaces, and an oddly-shaped infinity symbol indicating the end of text flow. Toggle it on and off by choosing Type > Show Hidden Characters.

CONVERTING TYPE TO OUTLINES

You can use the Appearance palette to apply multiple strokes to editable type (see the *Transparency & Appearances* chapter for details about working with multiple strokes or fills). You can also reliably mask with live, editable type! So although there are fewer and fewer reasons to convert your type to outlines, there are still some times when converting type to outlines is your best option (see "Why convert type to outlines?" following). As long as you've created type with fonts you have installed on your system (and can print) and you've finished experimenting with your type elements (e.g.,

If you don't have the fonts...

Missing fonts? You can still open, edit, and save the file, because Illustrator remembers the fonts you were using. However, the text will not flow accurately and the file won't print correctly until you load or replace the missing fonts. Type objects that use missing fonts will be highlighted when Highlight Substituted Fonts is checked in the Type area of Document Setup.

Choose text carefully!

Having access to dozens of fonts doesn't necessarily make you a type expert, any more than having a handful of pens makes you an artist. Experiment all you want, but if you need professional typographic results, consult a professional. I did. Barbara Sudick designed this book.

To set what the Eyedropper picks up and the Paint Bucket applies, double-click either tool to open the Eyedropper/Paint Bucket Options dialog box.

Eyedropper text

To restyle part of a text string or block, pick up a new sample with the Eyedropper tool, hold down the Option (Mac)/Alt (Win) key to select the Paint Bucket tool and drag the cursor (as you would with the Type tool) over the text to be restyled. —*David Nelson*

Reflow text as in page layout

Resize a text block by its bounding box handles (see the *Illustrator Basics* chapter) and the text will reflow. —*Sandee Cohen*

The appearance of stroked text

To add strokes to type without distorting the characters, use the Appearance palette to "Add New Stroke," move this new stroke *below* the original, and set the new color and weight.

adjusting size, leading, or kerning/tracking), you have the option to convert your live type to Illustrator objects. Your type will no longer be editable as type, but instead will be constructed of standard Illustrator Bézier curves that may include compound paths to form the "holes" in objects (such as the transparent center of an **O** or **P**). As with all Illustrator paths, you can use the Direct Selection tool to select and edit the objects To convert type to outlines, select all blocks of type you wish to outline (it doesn't matter if non-type objects are selected as well) and choose Type>Create Outlines. To fill the "holes" in letters with color, select the compound path and choose Object>Compound Path>Release (see the *Drawing & Coloring* chapter for more about compound paths). **Note:** *Outlining type is not recommended for small font sizes—see the Tip "Don't outline small type."*

Why convert type to outlines?

Here are several cases where this option may be useful:

- **So you can graphically transform or distort the individual curves and anchor points of letters or words.** Everything from minor stretching of a word to extreme distortion is possible. See the lower right **M** on the facing page, and Galleries later in this chapter. (Warp Effects and Envelopes can sometimes be used for these purposes, too; see the *Live Effects & Graphic Styles* chapter.)

- **So you can maintain your letter and word spacing when exporting your type to another application.** Many programs that allow you to import Illustrator type as "live" editable text don't support the translation of your custom kerning and word spacing. Convert text to outlines before exporting Illustrator type in these instances to maintain custom word and letter spacing.

- **So you don't have to supply the font to your client or service bureau.** Converting type can be especially useful when you need to use foreign language fonts, when your image will be printed while you're not around, or when you don't have permission to embed all of your fonts. If your service bureau doesn't have its own license for a font, in most cases your own license for the font won't allow you to give it to them. So converting the type to outlines may be necessary at that point. (See the Model United Nations logo at lower right and lessons and Galleries later in this chapter.)

USING THE APPEARANCE PALETTE WITH TYPE

When you work with type, you work with the letter characters or with the container that holds the characters—or with both. Understanding the difference between characters and their container, the "type object," will help you access and edit the right one when you style type. To help understand the difference, you'll need to watch the Appearance palette as you work.

Characters

You work directly with the letter characters when you click with the Type tool and enter text. In the Appearance palette, you'll see a blank Stroke and a black Fill listed underneath the Characters line in the palette. You can apply a color or pattern to the characters' fill and stroke. To edit a characters' fill and stroke, drag across the text with the Type tool or double-click Characters in the Appearance palette.

There are some things you *can't* do when working with the characters (although you can with their containers). You can't move the stroke under the fill or the fill above the stroke in the Appearance palette. You can't apply an Effect to characters' fill or stroke. And you can't apply a gradient fill to the characters, or add multiple fills or strokes directly to the characters.

Type Object

All text is contained in a Point, Area, or Path type object. You work with the object when you select the text with the Selection tool and move it on your page.

Transporting foreign or unusual fonts (artwork by Kathleen Tinkel)

Filling with patterns or gradients

Masking with type (artwork by Min Wang for Adobe Systems)   *Transforming outlines (artwork by Javier Romero Design Group)*

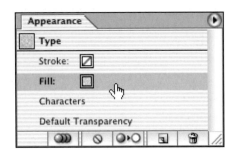

The Appearance palette showing the Spiral pattern filling the type object and the resulting type object filled with the Spiral pattern

The Appearance palette showing the Spiral pattern filling the type character and the resulting type character filled with the Spiral pattern

BRYCE CANYON
Navajo Loop (Sunset Point)
1.3 miles (2.2 km) / 521 ft (159 m)
Moderate Hike: 1 to 2 hours
Attractions: Thors Hammer,
Two Bridges, Wall Street

See Gordon's "Floating Type" lesson in the Transparency & Appearances chapter to learn how to create transparent backgrounds for your area type objects

You can think of the type object as a group whose members are the letter characters. There are things you can do to this group that you couldn't do when working directly with the letter characters.

For example, you can add another fill (choose Add New Fill from the Appearance palette pop-up menu). Notice that the Appearance palette changes—now there is another listing of Fill and Stroke, but this time they are positioned above the Characters line in the palette. The fill and stroke you worked with at the character level still exist. You can reveal them by double-clicking Character in the palette. Doing so, however, brings you back to character editing; re-select the type object with the Selection tool to return to editing the type object rather than its characters.

When you add a new fill or stroke to the type object, its color or effects interact with the color of the characters. You can predict the visual results of changes to the type object and characters by knowing that all the fills and strokes applied to type are painted, with those listed at the top of the palette painted on top of those listed below (including the stroke and fill you see listed when you double-click Characters in the palette). So if you add a new fill and apply red to it, the type now appears red (the red fill of the type object is stacked above the black fill of the characters).

To experiment with how this works, create two type objects in a large font size (72 pt, for example). Next, edit at the character level by dragging through one of the objects with the Type tool, and then in the Appearance palette applying the Spiral pattern to the default black fill. (The Spiral pattern in the Swatches palette ships with Illustrator.) Notice the red spiral appears surrounded by white inside the letter characters.

To edit at the type object level instead, select the other type object with the Selection tool. Add a new fill (choose Add New Fill from the Appearance palette menu) and apply the same Spiral pattern. When the type object fills with the spiral, the red spiral lines appear surrounded by black. This is because Illustrator paints the spiral pattern on top of the black of the characters.

Knowing the difference between a type object and its characters rewards you in this experiment. And it will help you understand later why bad things seem to happen to good type (like the black surrounding the red spirals) so that you can make good things happen to type. Reading and working through the lessons and galleries that follow will help you master the difference between characters and their type object.

EXPORTING ILLUSTRATOR TYPE

While the new Illustrator CS Type engine opens the door to new levels of typographic control and flexibility, sending your typography out into the world may seem anything but controlled or flexible. Type objects in files that you export to legacy versions of Illustrator (version 10 and before) or as EPS files will either be broken into groups of point or path type objects, or converted to outlines. Your only control is to select File > Document Setup > Type and choose Preserve Text Editability or Preserve Text Appearance from the Export menu.

As the illustration at right shows, choosing Preserve Text Editability breaks the word "typography" into a group of eight separate Point type objects. Choosing Preserve Text Appearance, by contrast, will convert all type to outlines. In either case, your type will be severely limited for others who need to use it in older versions of Illustrator.

You should test bringing Illustrator CS type into other applications before proceeding during a critical project or urgent deadline. While you may not need to edit the type in another program, you should ensure that it imports correctly and looks as it did in Illustrator CS.

Penciling in changes

With all of the changes to the way that Illustrator controls type, one editing function is missing: You can no longer reshape Path type with the Pencil tool. Instead, use the Direct Selection tool to select points on the path and adjust their handles. Also, you can manipulate points on a path using the Anchor Point tools (click and hold the mouse down on the Pen tool in the Tool palette to find the Anchor Point tools).

Typography
Typography
Typography

The original Illustrator CS point type object at the top; in the middle, the same type object exported using Preserve Text Editability; at the bottom, the type object exported using Preserve Text Appearance

Custom Text Paths

Trickling Type with Variations of Type Style

Overview: *Prepare and Place text; create a set of evenly-spaced paths; copy and paste text into appropriate path lines; adjust text baseline paths and placement of text on the paths.*

1

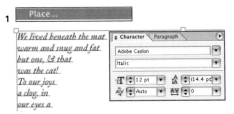

Placed text creates a new rectangle which contains the type; choose a font and size while the text is still selected

2

Option-drag /Alt-drag to create a second path below the first; use Object > Transform > Transform Again (or ⌘-D / Ctrl-D) to repeat this step

3

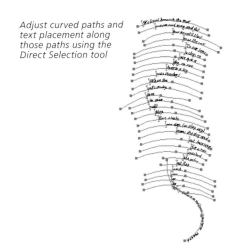

Grab the I-beam to move the text along the path

Adjust curved paths and text placement along those paths using the Direct Selection tool

Laurie Szujewska placed type on curved Bézier paths to emulate the shaped lines of Lewis Carroll's original hand-lettered poem from *Alice's Adventures Underground* (an early version of *Alice in Wonderland*).

1 Preparing your type. Use a word processor to proofread and spell-check your text. In Illustrator, choose File > Place and select your text document; this creates a rectangle containing your text. Choose a typeface and size.

2 Creating your baselines and placing your type. Next to your type, draw a curved path with the Pen tool (see "Zen Lessons" on the *Wow! CD* folder for Pen help). With the Path Type tool, click on your Bézier path and type a few characters. To determine the spacing between lines, switch to the Selection tool, grab the path, hold the Option/Alt key and drag the selected path downward, until the second path is spaced correctly (release the mouse button while still holding down the key). To duplicate the path and the spacing between paths, press ⌘-D/ Ctrl-D (Object > Transform > Transform Again), repeating until you've created the desired number of text paths.

Switch to the Type tool, select the text you want for the top path and Copy. Now click on the top path and Paste. Repeat with the remaining lines.

3 Adjusting the type. With all text placed, use the Direct Selection tool to adjust the curves. If you wish to see all of the text paths at once (whether selected or not), switch to Outline View. To move the starting point for lines of text, click on the path with the Selection tool and drag the I-beam along the path. For downward curving text, Szujewska's adjusted the path, then individually selected the last words, progressively reducing them in size.

We lived beneath the mat
warm and snug and fat
but one, & that
was the cat!
To our joys
a clog, in
our eyes a
fog, on our
hearts a log,
was the dog!
When the
cat's away,
then
the mice
will
play.
But, alas!
one day, (so they say)
came the dog and
cat, hunting
for a rat,
crushed
the mice
all flat,
each
one
as
he
sat underneath the mat, warm, & snug and fat... Think of that!

Szujewska / Adobe Systems, Inc. / adapted from Lewis Carroll's Alice's Adventures Underground

Stretching Type

Fitting Type by Converting to Outline

Overview: *Enter type onto individual lines of point type objects; transform type into outlines; custom justify type by Lassoing or Direct-selecting partial paths and stretching the horizontal strokes of the letterforms using the Arrow keys.*

Though there are more ways than ever to modify your type characters while keeping the text "live" for future editing, there are still some adjustments that require you to "outline" your type characters.

To create this beautiful *Ketubah* (traditional Hebrew wedding certificate), Ari M. Weinstein had to observe strict design guidelines, since the *Ketubah* needed to serve the dual role of legal document and work of art. The guidelines required the text to be fully justified and enclosed within a decorative border. Traditionally, in order to justify Hebrew text, calligraphers elongated the horizontal strokes of individual letterforms, instead of using paragraph justification (which would result in non-uniform word and letter spacing). To replicate this method, Weinstein needed to outline the type, so he could stretch individual horizontal strokes.

1 Placing the text. Having chosen a calligraphic-style Hebrew font, Weinstein entered his text line by line on unconnected Point type paths in order to avoid automatic

Weinstein began by pulling out a set of vertical guides from the rulers. He then entered the body text line by line to avoid unattractive line breaks and hyphenation

text wrap. This allowed him to maintain control over word placement from one line to the next. He inserted two lines below the main text for witness signatures.

2 Converting the text to outlines. Since converting type to outlines is permanent, make sure that you carefully proof and spell-check your text first. After proofing his text, Weinstein selected each single line of text and chose Type > Create Outlines (⌘-Shift-O/Ctrl-Shift-O) to convert each line of characters to outlines. Converting each line separately automatically groups the converted characters together.

3 Stretching a letter's horizontal strokes. Weinstein was now able to replicate the traditional scribal method of crafting the length of each line by stretching the horizontal strokes on the letterforms. In order to stretch a horizontal stroke, Weinstein used the Direct Selection and the Lasso tools to select the left side of a letter's outline. With these portions of the letterform selected, he then stretched them in 1 pt increments using the left Arrow key. He adjusted the spacing between entire words and individual characters by using the Group Selection tool and similarly moving them using the Arrow keys. Weinstein was able to justify the text block perfectly, using the ruler guides to the left and right of the main body text.

4 Finalizing the *Ketubah*. Weinstein was required by tradition to omit one leg of the letter *Kuf* in a word near the end of the text (the eighth word from the right on the last line of the main text). This letter segment was to be drawn by hand on the wedding day in front of the rabbi. The vertical stroke of the letter was selected and deleted. Weinstein brought his calligraphy tools along to the wedding to officially complete the *Ketubah* as part of the prenuptial proceedings. The dove at the top of the *Ketubah* encloses the bride's and groom's initials, hand drawn by Weinstein.

2

One by one, the individual lines of copy were Direct-selected and converted to outline. Each resulting set of paths was automatically grouped for easier selection later

3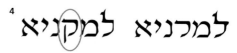

Direct-selecting the path segments of the cross-strokes and stretching them with the Arrow keys

4

After Direct-selecting the vertical cross-stroke of the letter Kuf, Weinstein deleted it

PlanTea

l l l l   P P

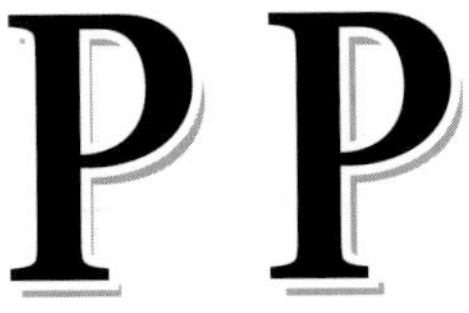

John Burns

Lettering artist John Burns developed this logo for PlanTea, an organic fertilizer for plants that is brewed in water, like tea. He began by typing the name and then converted the letters to outlines (Type > Create Outlines). After drawing a leaf and placing it on the stem of each letter **a**, he selected and copied the artwork, pasted it in back (Edit > Paste in Back) to form the drop shadows, and offset them down and to the right. Burns then filled the copied letterforms with 40% black. To prevent the drop shadows from touching the black letterforms (creating a more stylized look), he selected the black artwork and again pasted it behind (but in front of the drop shadows) and then applied a white fill and thick white stroke to the pasted letterforms. The stages of his process, here applied to the **l**, are shown above left. Finally, Burns used the Direct Selection tool to reshape some of the drop shadow shapes, adjusting the thickness of some of the shadow letter strokes and hiding slivers of shadows that stuck out a little behind the black letters (the **P** directly above shows the shadow before and after reshaping).

HORNALL ANDERSON DESIGN WORKS

Hornall Anderson Design Works / John Hornall (Art Director)

Designers at Hornall Anderson Design Works set the name "Yves" for this healthy, vegetarian line of foods in Gill Sans and then modified the letterforms to fit the logo design. First, they placed the text along a curve and then converted the font characters to outlines (Type > Create Outlines). To create the shadows on the left side of the name's characters, designers used the Scissors tool to cut the character paths, the Direct Selection tool to move cut pieces, and the Pen tool to connect points and close objects. Another way to accomplish a similar effect is to Copy the original letterforms and Paste in Back twice. Give the top copy a white Fill and a thick white Stroke; while still selected, choose Object > Path > Outline Path and set the new outline stroke to a small width.

Move the bottom copy of the letterforms to the left. Then select the two copies and choose the Minus Front command from the Pathfinder palette. Lastly, delete extraneous objects and use the Scissors and Direct Selection tools to reshape the remaining objects.

Masking Letters

Masking Images with Letter Forms

Overview: *Create a large letter on top of a placed TIF image; convert the letter to outlines; select all and make the letter form into a clipping mask for the placed image.*

THREINEN-PENDARVIS

Placing the TIF image; creating Point Type letter

Converting the letter "S" to outlines

Selecting both the letter form and the image beneath; making a clipping mask

Selecting an object using the Layers palette, then moving it with the Direct Selection tool

This "**S** is for Surfing" was created by Cher Threinen-Pendarvis for an alphabet poster. Although you can mask with "live" type, Threinen-Pendarvis converted her type to outlines. For additional lessons on masking, see the Gallery opposite and the *Advanced Techniques* chapter.

1 Positioning elements and converting a large letter to outlines. Place a TIF image into your Illustrator file by using File > Place. Using the Type tool, click on top of your image to create a Point Type object and type one letter. Choose a typeface with enough weight and a point size large enough for the bottom image to show through the letter form itself. Select the letter with a Selection tool and choose Type > Create Outlines.

2 Creating the clipping mask and adjusting the image position. The topmost object in a selection becomes the mask when you make a clipping mask. If your letter isn't the top object, select it, Cut, then Edit > Paste in Front. To create the mask, select the outlined letter and the images to be masked and choose Object > Clipping Mask > Make; the mask and masked objects will be grouped. To adjust the position of an object or the mask, select it from the Layers palette or with the Direct Selection tool, then use the Direct Selection tool to move it. Threinen-Pendarvis ended by applying Effect > Stylize > Drop Shadow (default settings) to a filled copy of the **S** below the mask group, above a TIF background created in Procreate's Painter.

NEWMAN

Gary Newman

Artist Gary Newman combined a compound
path and masking to create this title illustration. First, Newman typed the word "Careers"
and converted the text to outlines (Type >
Create Outlines). Next, he made a single compound path by choosing Object > Compound
Path > Make. Newman masked a copy of his
background artwork with this compound path.
With the compound object on top and all
elements selected, he chose Object > Clipping
Mask > Make. He then selected the masked
background objects and used Filter > Colors >
Adjust Colors, increasing the black percentage. Newman added a drop shadow by layering a black-filled copy of the type behind
the background-filled type. He set the words
"Changing" and "at mid-life" in black type,

and added drop shadows behind them;
drop shadows can also be made using the
Transparency palette to adjust Blending
Modes and Opacity (for help with Blending
Modes and Opacity, see the *Transparency &
Appearances* chapter).

Book Cover Design

Illustrator as a Stand-alone Layout Tool

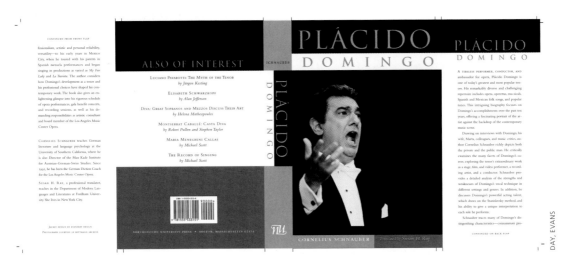

Overview: *Set your document size; place guides and crop marks; place EPS files and make Area type for columns and Point type for graphic typography; visually track type to fit.*

Page layout programs such as InDesign and QuarkXPress are essential for producing multipage, complex documents. However, Rob Day and Virginia Evans often use Illustrator for single-page projects such as book jackets.

Setting up the Artboard and layout specs

1 Setting up your page. Choose File > Document Setup to set up the Artboard for your design. Click on landscape or portrait page orientation and enter your Artboard size, making sure it's large enough for crop and/or registration marks (the "Size" parameter will automatically switch to "Custom"). Choose View > Show Rulers and "re-zero" your ruler origin to the upper left corner of where your page will begin (see the *Basics* chapter for more on repositioning the ruler origin), and use View > Outline/Preview to toggle between Outline and Preview modes. Although you can generate uniform grids with Preferences > Guides & Grid, for columns of varying sizes, Day and Evans numerically created two sets of rectangles: one for bleeds, one for trims. With the Rectangle tool, click to make a box sized for a trim area (see the *Basics* chapter for Rectangle tool help), then immediately Option-click/Alt-click on the center of the trim area box to numerically specify a box .125" larger in each dimension in order to create a bleed area box. Day and Evans made trim and bleed boxes for the front, back, flaps, and spine. To place an overall trim mark, select the boxes that define the entire trim area and choose Filter > Create > Crop Marks.

2 Customizing your guides. Select your trim and bleed boxes (not the crop marks) and create Guides by choosing View > Guides > Make Guides.

3 Placing and refining the elements. Choose File>Place to select an EPS image to import into your layout. Create rectangles or other objects which will define the area for columns of text. Click on the path of one of these objects with the Area Type tool. Once the text cursor is placed, you can type directly or paste text (see "Custom Text Paths" in this chapter). Area Type is used in this layout for columns of type on the flaps. Alternately, click with the Type tool to create Point type, which is used to place lines of type for titles and headlines, and other individual type elements. To track type visually to fit a space, select a text object and use Option/Alt-←/→. For help with rotating or scaling objects (this applies to text objects as well), see the *Zen* chapter and the *Zen Lessons* on the *Wow! CD*.

Creating "Crop Marks" versus "Crop Area"

Every time you choose Filter > Create > Crop Marks, you'll make a set of visible (selectable) Illustrator crop marks that indicate the bounding area of your current selection. Use Object > Crop Area > Make to create *one* set of *non*-selectable crop marks that are visible in Illustrator, but invisibly mark the crop area when placed into programs such as Photoshop (see "Software Relay" lesson in the *Illustrator & Other Programs* chapter). You can specify the area with a selected rectangle, or if nothing is selected, the crop area will be sized to the Artboard. To remove a "crop area," choose Object > Crop Area > Release, or, since there can be only one Crop Area per file, make a new selection and choose Object > Crop Area > Make.

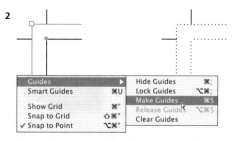

Converting trim and bleed boxes into Guides

All of the elements placed into the layout

Close-ups of an Area Type object

Close-ups of Point Type objects

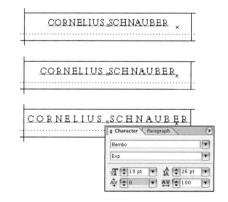
Tracking a line of Point Type with Arrow keys

Brushed Type

Applying Brushes to Letterforms

Overview: *Create centerlines for font characters; customize art brushes and apply brushes to the centerlines and outlines of the letterforms to simulate hand-rendered lettering.*

For a map title that looked artistic, Steven Gordon blended the traditional artistry of pencil and brush with the classicism of serif font characters. Because Illustrator applies brushes as strokes, not fills, Gordon drew centerlines for the font characters before painting the centerlines with natural-looking customized brushes.

1

Original characters from Garamond font, filled with gray

Letterform centerlines hand drawn with the Pencil tool on a layer above the font characters

Font characters with a radial gradient replacing the original gray fill on a layer below gray-stroked copy of font characters

1 Creating letter centerlines and outlines. To re-create Gordon's painted lettering, begin by typing text in a serif font (Gordon chose Garamond Bold Condensed Italic and 112 pt from the Character palette.) Select the text and give it a 20% black Fill so you can see the letterforms while drawing the centerlines later. Copy the layer with the text by dragging the layer onto the Create New Layer icon at the bottom of the palette. To create the font outline, select the text on the copied layer and convert the characters to outlines (Type > Create Outlines), then change their Fill to None and Stroke to gray. Now create a new layer (click the Create New Layer icon in the Layers palette) and drag this layer between the other two. On this new layer, draw centerlines for each font character with the Pen or Pencil tool. The paths don't have to be smooth or centered inside the letterforms because you will paint them with an irregularly shaped brush in the next step. Finally, change the gray fill of the bottom layer letters to another color or to a gradient (as Gordon did).

2

Top, the default Splash brush; below, the edited brush with color fills

2 Creating and applying custom brushes and effects. Gordon looked to Illustrator's brushes to give the letter centerlines the color and spontaneity of traditional brushwork. He opened the Artistic_Paintbrush brush palette (Window > Brush Libraries > Artistic_Paintbrush) and selected the Splash brush. To customize a brush, first drag the brush from the palette to the canvas. Select each brush object with the Direct Selection tool and replace the gray with a color. Next, drag the brush artwork into the Brushes palette and select New Art Brush from the New Brush dialog box. In the Art Brush Options dialog box, further customize the brush by changing Width to 50%, enabling the Proportional brush setting, and clicking OK. (You won't see the change in width displayed in the dialog box's preview.) Make several brush variations by copying the brush and then editing brush Direction, Width and other parameters. Now individualize your letterforms by selecting the first centerline and clicking on a brush from the Brushes palette. Try several of the brushes you created to find the best "fit." Continue applying brushes to the remaining centerlines.

Experimenting by applying different brushes to centerlines to lend individuality to the letter

On top, the Dry Ink brush; left, the customized brush applied to the font outline; right, the Roughen Effect applied to the brushed outline

To create the look of loose pencil tracings for the character outlines on the top layer, Gordon edited the Dry Ink brush from the Artistic_PaintBrush library palette, changing its Width to 10% in the Art Brush Options dialog box. He completed the look by selecting each character outline and applying the Roughen Effect (Size=1%, Distort=10%, Smooth). (See the *Transparency & Appearances,* and *Graphic Styles & Effects* chapter to learn more about applying Effects and using the Appearance palette.)

Artwork on three layers, from bottom layer (left) to top layer (right)

3 Finishing touches. Gordon selected all the centerlines and offset them up and left while moving the font outlines down and right from the original font characters on the bottom layer, suggesting a loose style. He also simulated the appearance of hand-rendering by adjusting the transparency and blending modes of the brushed letterforms: Gordon selected the centerline objects, and in the Transparency palette, chose Multiply mode and reduced transparency to 75%. This caused the colors of brushed centerline paths to darken where they overlapped, mimicking the effect of overlapping transparent inks.

3

Left, the horizontal and vertical centerlines of the letter "t" with Normal blending mode and 100% opacity; right, strokes placed to form letter "t" and with Multiply blending mode and 70% opacity

Finished lettering on three layers, shown in composite view

?!ABCDEFGHIJKLMNOPQRSTUVWXYZ1234567890

MÜLLER-LANCÉ

Joachim Müller-Lancé

The original characters of Joachim Müller-Lancé's Flood typeface were drawn with a worn felt marker during a type seminar hosted by Sumner Stone. Two years later Müller-Lancé rediscovered the drawings when Adobe asked him for new font ideas. Realizing that the original character traces were not of font quality, he redrew all of the characters using Illustrator's Pen and Pencil tools. He composed many of the characters as separate, black-filled objects, which he moved around while also adjusting width, slant, and scale until he got the look he wanted. He used the Merge command from the Pathfinder palette to join the overlapping objects of each character into a single shape. He also drew the holes and streaks as white-filled objects above the black-filled objects and used Minus Front (also from the Pathfinder palette) to knock out the holes and streaks in the characters. Then Müller-Lancé copied the artwork for each character and pasted it directly into the appropriate character slot in Fontographer, where he completed the font.

T H E MATRIX

GIRVIN

Tim Girvin /
Tim Girvin Strategic Branding & Design

Designer Tim Girvin began the logo for this futuristic film by setting the title in Times New Roman and converting the type outlines to paths (Type > Create Outlines), He drew objects with the Rectangle and other tools that he used with the Divide command from the Pathfinder palette to break the letterforms into pieces. After modifying some of their shapes with the Direct Selection tool, Girvin repositioned the pieces to form the asymmetrical letterforms of the logo.

BARTLETT

Jennifer Bartlett /
Tim Girvin Strategic Branding & Design

Jennifer Bartlett set this logo using a proprietary Girvin font. To keep the letters of the tagline upright but parallel to the wave of the background banner, Bartlett selected individual characters by dragging with the Text tool and adjusted their vertical positions by entering positive values (to move characters up) or negative values (to move characters down) in the Character palette's Baseline Shift field, accessed by choosing Window > Type > Character and choosing Show Options from the Character palette's pop-up menu.

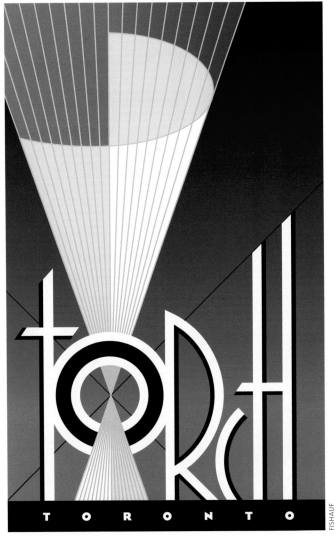

FISHAUF

Louis Fishauf / Reactor Art + Design

Asked to create the visual identity for a proposed news cafe and media tower, designer Louis Fishauf drew the letters for the name with the Pen tool, first assigning a thick stroke to the paths and then outlining the strokes (Object > Path > Outline Stroke). He moved points in the letter tips using the Direct Selection tool, angling the tips parallel to the black lines behind the name. To convey perspective, Fishauf pasted copies of the letters **t** and **H** behind the name, filled them with black, and manually offset each of these shadows to the left or right. For the letters **R** and **c**, Fishauf drew the shadows with the Pen tool, keeping the curves parallel to the white letterforms in front.

ZIMBABWE

Traditional Pot

Dance

Thumb Piano

Wire Car ...vroom vroom

Ellen Papciak-Rose intheStudio @ gomet.co.za

PAPCIAK-ROSE

Ellen Papciak-Rose / In The Studio

Ellen Papciak-Rose created the title "Zimbabwe" using geometric objects she drew with the Rectangle, Ellipse, and other tools. She composited the objects and used Minus Front and other commands from the Pathfinder palette to knock out parts of the objects, forming the title letterforms. Papciak-Rose then painted the strokes of the objects with two custom-built variations of a Charcoal-Rough

brush found in the Artistic_ChalkCharcoalPencil library (Window > Brush Libraries > Artistic_ChalkCharcoalPencil). In the four panels of the poster, Papciak-Rose painted outlines of characters from the Sand font with the two custom-built rough charcoal brushes.

ICE HOUSE PRESS (AKSELSEN)

Bjørn Akselsen / Ice House Press

For this logo for Private Chef, a gourmet food and catering company, designer Bjørn Akselsen avoided the orderly appearance of calligraphic and script fonts by using Illustrator to distort letterforms. First Akselsen drew the letterforms with traditional brush and ink, then scanned the artwork and placed it in Illustrator, where he traced the letterforms. Next he reshaped their outlines and interiors with the Direct Selection tool to emphasize contrast in the strokes and applied three Distort filters from the top section of the Filter menu (Pucker & Bloat, Roughen, and Tweak) to further distort the letter shapes and enhance their individuality. Finally, Akselsen used the Pencil tool to smooth out rough edges.

Pattie Belle Hastings / Ice House Press
(Sharon Steuer illustration and production)

In redesigning the logos for The Traveling Radio Show, Pattie Belle Hastings wanted to convey activity in the title type treatment. Starting with characters from TheSans typeface, Hastings created the title in one line (as it appears on the business cards and brochures) and then outlined the characters (Type > Create Outlines). Zooming in on the characters, she pulled down four guidelines from the horizontal ruler (View > Show Rulers), so she could use them to align the letters. She then selected individual type characters and positioned each vertically, visually aligning it to one of the guidelines. The characters were also individually colored, and then horizontally positioned by Shift-selecting letters, and nudging them

ICE HOUSE PRESS (HASTINGS) / STEUER (ILLUSTRATION / PRODUCTION)

with the left and right Arrow keys. For a sticker design (shown above), the title was split into two lines and enlarged.

JONEN

Frank Jonen

Frank Jonen started the typeface, Book of Days, as an experiment in drawing a handwritten typeface by customizing some of the brushes that ship with Illustrator. He first sketched the letterforms on paper, then inserted the sketches into his Wacom tablet and opened Illustrator. Jonen selected the Paintbrush tool, and from the Brushes palette, selected the 6 pt Flat brush. He drew some freeform circles and flourishes, testing the look and feel of the brush. To adjust the brush settings, Jonen double-clicked the Stroke attribute in the Appearance palette (which is the same as selecting Options of Selected Object from the Brushes palette menu) and adjusted settings for Angle, Roundness and Diameter. Once he was satis-

fied with the brush's roundness and slope, Jonen traced the letterforms by drawing over them with the Wacom stylus. When he finished drawing the letters, he fine-tuned the brush for some paths by double-clicking their Stroke attribute in the Appearance palette and edited values in the Stroke Options (Calligraphic Brush) dialog box. Jonen completed the font by saving it as an EPS file and then importing the EPS into FontLab using the ScanFont plug-in.

Crunching Type

Transforming Type with Warps & Envelopes

Overview: *Create and color a title using Appearances; use a warp effect to bow type; create an outline shape to "crunch" type; give the crunched type a dynamic, curved perspective effect using an envelope warp.*

HAMANN

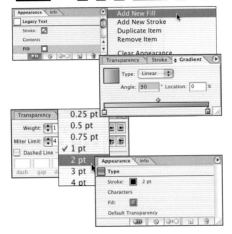

Using Add New Fill in the Appearance palette menu to add a gradient fill to the type

Warps and Envelopes are your superheroes for transforming headline type into any form you wish. No more need to convert type to outlines and laboriously move each anchor point by hand. Using Envelopes, it's literally as easy as drawing an outline and commanding the type to conform. With Warps and Envelopes, the type remains editable no matter how much you "crunch" it. Warps and Envelopes are always on hand to help rescue you from those looming deadlines!

1 Creating and coloring the E-Men title. To create the E-MEN cover title, use 72 point Arial Black font. To add a gradient fill to your type, select the type and choose Add New Fill from the Appearance palette menu. See the *Transparency & Appearances* chapter for more on the Appearance palette.

2 Using a Warp effect to make the E-Men bow. There are 15 standard Warp shapes that can be turned into styles. For "E-MEN," Hamann applied Effect > Warp > Arc Lower. With Preview enabled, he used the Bend slider to bow the bottom of the letters (to 23%), then clicked OK.

Effect > Warp works in many instances, but it didn't warp his gradient-fill along with the type. After applying Undo, Hamann chose Object > Envelope Distort > Envelope Options, enabled Distort Linear Gradients, and applied Object > Envelope Distort > Make with Warp, with the Arc Lower option at 23%.

3 Using a path to "crunch" type. To create the "CRUNCH!" Hamann again used the Appearance palette, this time to color "Crunch!" with a subtle gradient fill and a strong red stroke. Then, starting with a rectangle, he applied Object > Path > Add Anchor points twice, and then moved the rectangle's anchor points to form a dynamic jagged path. He then placed the path over the type, and with both the path and type selected he chose Object > Envelope Distort > Make with Top Object.

4 Using Envelope Distort > Make with Warp to create a curved perspective effect. To create a curved perspective effect, use Envelope Distort > Make with Warp to warp the "crunched" type. Because you can't nest one envelope inside another, first select your "crunched" type and choose Object > Envelope Distort > Expand. With your expanded type selected, choose Object > Envelope Distort > Make with Warp. Choose Arc in the Style pop-up menu of the Warp Options dialog box, and adjust the sliders until you find the desired curved perspective look.

5 Adjusting and adding a stroke to the type. To complete the "CRUNCH!" type, Hamann used Object > Envelope Distort > Edit Contents to adjust the type. Using the Appearance palette, he added (in order) a yellow gradient fill, a 5 point black stroke, and a 10 point red stroke to the envelope enclosing the type to get the desired final effect.

With Effect > Warp > Arc Lower, the gradient fill remains horizontal

Using Object > Warp > Make with Warp (with Distort Linear Gradients enabled in the Envelope Options dialog box), the gradient bends also

The type and path before and after applying Object > Envelope Distort > Make with Top

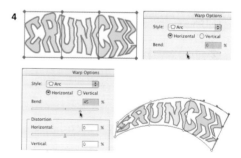

The released type; with Warp sliders set to 0 showing the starting envelope shape; the final Warp option settings; the resultant envelope

The final strokes and the finished type

Offset Fills

Covering a Pattern with an Offset Fill

Overview: *Create a pattern using Scribble effect; apply the pattern to letter characters; add a new fill to the text object; choke the new fill by applying a negative Offset effect; use Roughen to warp type edges.*

1

Top, black rectangle; Below, with Scribble applied to fill

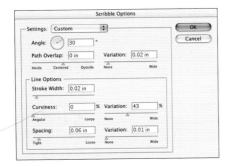

Scribble Options dialog box

Top, Scribble effect expanded to a path; Below, Thick Pencil brush applied to scribble pattern path

Filling lettering with patterns is a simple way of turning familiar fonts into fresh designs. Sometimes, though, you want a pattern to fill only part of each letter character. Finding a way to block patterns from the center of letter strokes was a challenge that Sandee Cohen, AKA VectorBabe, solved in creating this logo.

1 Creating and expanding a pattern, applying a brush, saving the pattern as a swatch. Breaking the edges of type is the key to making font lettering look aged. Illustrator's Scribble effect is a perfect tool for replacing the solid fill of letter characters with an irregular pattern. Cohen started by drawing a rectangle and filling it with black. With the rectangle selected, she chose Effect > Stylize > Scribble. In the Scribble Options dialog box, Cohen customized the default values until she was satisfied with the loose drawing style the effect produced.

You can further customize the scribbled object by turning it into a path and applying a brush to it. To do this, make sure the scribble rectangle is selected and then choose Object > Expand Appearance. This converts the Scribble effect in the rectangle into a path. Cohen applied the Thick Pencil brush (one of the brushes that ships with Illustrator) to the expanded scribbled path.

In order to use the scribble object with the type you'll create, convert your brushed scribble object into a pattern swatch by dragging it to the Swatches palette.

2 Creating the type and filling it with the scribble pattern. Once your pattern is made, you're ready to create your text. First, open the Appearance palette—this will help you see whether you're editing the characters or their type object as you perform the following steps. Select the Type tool from the Toolbox, click on the Artboard, and type your text (Cohen used 72 pt Caslon). Select the characters by dragging through the text with the Type tool; the text will have a black fill. Then select the Fill attribute in the Appearance palette and select your scribble pattern from the Swatches palette.

3 **Adding a new fill, applying the Offset effect and using the Roughen effect.** Cohen needed a way of covering up the scribble pattern in the centers of the letters. Using the Offset effect, she created a fill that covered part of the lettering underneath. To do this, first select the type object by clicking on it with the Selection tool. Now, create a new fill by choosing Add New Fill from the Appearance palette menu. The new fill, by default, will be colored black and will completely cover the pattern that filled the letters. With the new fill selected, choose Effect > Path > Offset Path and, from the pop-up Offset Path dialog box, enter a negative value in the Offset field. Be sure that the Preview box is checked so you can gauge the visual effect of the number you enter in the Offset field. (Cohen used -1 pt for Offset.)

Complete the aging of your type by applying Roughen to the type object's fill to warp its edges. Select the type object with the Selection tool and choose Effect > Distort & Transform > Roughen. Because Cohen used a font with thin character strokes and serifs, she entered a small value for Size (0.4 pt), and selected Absolute, to be sure that the edges were not overly distorted.

A Pattern of Change

Pattern swatches are global. If you edit or create a pattern, simply drag the artwork with the Option (Mac) or Alt (Windows) key depressed and drop it on the swatch in the Swatches palette. The pattern filling your type will automatically change to the new pattern.

2

Top, the type with default black fill; Below, the black fill replaced by the pattern

3

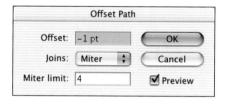

Offset Path effect applied to the new fill (shown here filled with gray instead of black)

Offset Path dialog box

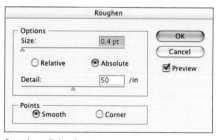

Roughen effect applied to the new fill (shown here in gray)

Roughen dialog box

Enlargement of two letters

Antiquing Type

Applying Scribble in an Opacity Mask

Advanced Technique

Overview: *Create a type object; copy the object then style the text with the Roughen effect; create an Opacity Mask and paste the type object; apply the Scribble effect to the opacity mask; return to Outline mode.*

When you want to recreate a hand-rendered or historical look but don't want to stray from the fonts you're already using in a project, consider using Illustrator's effects menu and an opacity mask. For this book title, Steven Gordon made an opacity mask that allowed him to chip away the edges of lettering when applying the Scribble effect, turning contemporary type into antiqued letters.

1

Left, the original type object with letter characters filled with black; Right, the type object filled with a custom gradient

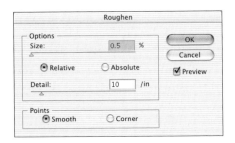

The Roughen dialog box

Every type is unique

Your settings for one type object will look different applied to another type object. Experiment!

1 Creating text, adding a new Fill, and applying the Roughen effect. Gordon began by typing his text and dragging with the Type tool to select letters in order to apply two different fonts (Zapfino for the **Z** and Optima for the other letters). Before further styling his type, Gordon clicked on the Selection tool and then choose Edit > Copy. (You'll need a copy of the type object for the opacity mask you'll make in the next step.)

Now Gordon was ready to start styling his type. First, he made sure the type object was still selected and then opened the Appearance palette and chose Add New Fill from the palette menu. Gordon clicked on the new Fill attribute in the palette and applied a gradient to it. (For information on creating or editing gradients, refer to the *Blends, Gradients & Mesh* chapter.)

The Roughen effect changes the smooth edges of objects to jagged or bumpy edges, which gives a hand-drawn appearance. To roughen your type object, make sure the Fill attribute is *not* selected (you can deselect it by clicking in an empty area of the Appearance palette) so the effect will be applied to the whole object. Then choose

Effect > Distort & Transform > Roughen. In the Roughen dialog box, adjust the Size, Detail, and Points controls. (Gordon chose Size=0.5, Detail=10, and Points=Smooth for his type object.)

2 Copying the type object, creating an opacity mask, pasting the object and applying Scribble. You can antique your roughened type by making it look chipped or scratched. To do this, select your type object, open the Transparency palette, and, from the palette menu, choose Make Opacity Mask. Next, click on the opacity mask thumbnail (the rightmost of the two thumbnails in the palette) and select Invert Mask. Lastly, paste the type you copied in the first step (use Paste in Front instead of Paste so this copy will overlay the original you copied).

Changes you make in the opacity mask will affect the transparency of the original type object—black artwork in the mask will punch holes in the original type. With the copy you just pasted still selected, choose Effect > Stylize > Scribble. In the Scribble dialog box, choose one of the ready made settings from the Settings menu, or customize the effect using the dialog box's controls. Gordon started with the Sharp setting and then changed several of its values. With the dialog box's Preview enabled, he moved the Path Overlap slider to 0.2" to thin some of the chips in the edges. He also changed the Angle from the default, 30°, to 15°, so the chips aligned better with the angles in the type characters.

3 Editing the type. Once you've finished with the Scribble effect, click the artwork thumbnail (the leftmost thumbnail) in the Transparency palette. If you need to edit the type—in order to change the text or modify kerning, for example—you'll have to do it in *both* the original type object and in the copy in the opacity mask.

For some edits you make to the type, like scaling or rotating, you only need to work with the type object. The opacity mask will be changed simultaneously with the type object.

2

Choosing the Opacity Mask in the Transparency palette

Customizing the options in the Scribble dialog

3

Selecting the artwork mode (as opposed to Opacity mask mode) in the Transparency palette

Getting your Fill

To ensure that the effects you will apply later in the opacity mask cut opaque holes in the artwork, make sure that the characters are filled with black. (Double-click *Characters* in the Appearance palette and check the Fill attribute.) If you then select the type object with the Selection tool and paint the object (rather than its characters) by adding a new fill in the Appearance palette, the copied type object will not adversely affect the opacity mask.

GORDON / CARTAGRAM, LLC

Steven Gordon / Cartagram, LLC

To create this label design, Steven Gordon simulated a sunburst using the Flare tool in an opacity mask. He started by drawing a rectangle and filling it with a three-color gradient. He then selected the Type tool and typed "Zion" (he left the type object black so, when used later as a mask, the artwork would remain opaque). Next, Gordon clicked on the Selection tool and copied the type object. He opened the Transparency palette and chose Make Opacity Mask from the palette menu. To select the opacity mask and begin working in the mask, Gordon clicked on the mask thumbnail (the right thumbnail) and then clicked on Invert Mask (he left the Clip option enabled). Next,

he chose Edit > Paste in Front to paste the type object into the mask. To make the sunburst, Gordon chose the Flare tool from the Rectangle tool pop-up menu. He positioned the cursor between the **o** and **n** letters and clicked and dragged the flare to extend it outward. To fine-tune the look of the flare, he double-clicked the Flare tool icon and, in the Flare Tool Options dialog box, he adjusted the controls for Diameter, Opacity, Direction, and other options. To return to working with the non-mask artwork, Gordon clicked on the artwork thumbnail (the left thumbnail) in the Transparency palette. He finished the label by applying a dark brown color to the selected type object.

Blends, Gradients & Mesh

7

220 Introduction

220 Blends

223 Gradients

225 Gallery: Rick Barry / DeskTop Design Studio

226 Examining Blends: *Learning When to Use Gradients or Blends*

228 Shades of Blends: *Creating Architectural Linear Shading*

229–233 Galleries: Janet Good, Gary Ferster, Linda Eckstein, Peter Cassell, Steven Stankiewicz

234 Unlocking Realism: *Creating Metallic Reflections with Blends*

236–237 Galleries: Jared Schneidman, Andrea Kelley

238 Unified Gradients: *Redirecting Fills with the Gradient Tool*

239–243 Galleries: Filip Yip, Hugh Whyte, Caryl Gorska, Tim Webb

244 Rolling Mesh: *Converting Gradients to Mesh and Editing*

246 Advanced Technique: Mastering Mesh: *Painting with Areas of Color Using Mesh*

249–251 Galleries: Ma Zhi Liang, Yukio Miyamoto

Blends, Gradients & Mesh

"W" Blend tool *"G" Gradient tool*

The speed of the blend

To control the speed of the blend, create the blend and set the number of blend steps. This creates the blend spine, which is editable just like any other Illustrator path. Using the Convert Anchor Point tool, pull out control handles from the anchor point at each end of the blend spine. By extending or shortening these control handles along the spine, the speed of the blend is controlled. This is very similar to how blend speeds are controlled in a gradient mesh.
—*Derek Mah*

Recolor after expanding blends

If you've expanded a blend, you can use *filters* to recolor blended objects. Direct-select and recolor the fill for the start and/or end objects, then select the entire blend and choose Filter > Colors > Blend Front to Back. Your objects' fill colors will reblend using the new start and end colors (this won't affect strokes or compound paths). Also try Blend Horizontally or Vertically, Adjust Colors, and Saturate.
Note: *This doesn't work if your blend includes gradients.*

BLENDS

Think of blends as a way to "morph" one object's shape and/or color into another. You can create blends between multiple objects, and even gradients or compound paths such as letters (see the *Drawing & Coloring* chapter for more on compound paths). Blends are *live*, which means you can edit the key objects' shape, color, size, location, or rotation, and the resulting *in-between* objects will automatically update. You can also distribute a blend along a custom path (see details later in this chapter).
Note: *Complex blends require a lot of RAM when drawing to the screen, especially gradient-to-gradient blends.*

The simplest way to create a blend is to select the objects you wish to blend and choose Object > Blend > Make. The number of steps you'll have in between each object is based on either the default options for the tool, or the last settings of the Blend Options (discussed in the following section). Adjust settings for a selected blend by selecting the blend, then double-clicking the Blend tool (or via Objects > Blend > Blend Options).

A more reliable method of creating smooth blends between two individual paths is to *point map* using the Blend tool. (Keep in mind that a smooth blend will only occur between two individual paths—as opposed to compound paths or groups—that have the same number of selected points.) First, select the two objects that you want to blend (with the Group Selection tool), then use the Blend tool to *point map* by clicking first on a selected point on the first object, and then on the correlating selected point on the second object.

When a blend first appears, it's selected and grouped. If you Undo immediately, the blend will be deleted, but your source objects remain selected so you can blend again. To modify a key object, Direct-select the key object first, then use any editing tool (including the Pencil, Smooth, and Erase tools) to make your changes.

Blend Options

To specify Blend Options as you blend, use the Blend tool (see the *point map* directions in the previous section) and press the Option/Alt key as you click the second point. To adjust options on a completed blend, select it and double-click the Blend tool (or Object > Blend > Blend Options). Opening Blend Options without any blend selected sets the default for creating blends *in this work session*; these Options reset each time you restart.

- **Specified Steps** specifies the number of steps between each pair of key objects. Using fewer steps results in clearly distinguishable objects, while a larger number of steps results in an almost airbrushed effect.

- **Specified Distance** places a specified distance between the objects of the blend.

- **Smooth Color** allows Illustrator to automatically calculate the ideal number of steps between key objects in a blend, in order to achieve the smoothest color transition. If objects are the same color, or are gradients or patterns, the calculation will equally distribute the objects within the area of the blend, based on their size.

- **Orientation** determines whether the individual blend objects rotate as they follow the path's curves. **Align to Path** (the default, first icon) allows blend objects to rotate as they follow the path. **Align to Page** (the second icon) prevents objects from rotating as they're distributed along the path's curve (objects stay "upright" as they blend along the curve).

Blends along a Path

There are two ways to make blends follow a curved path. The first way is to Direct-select the *spine* of a blend (the path automatically created by the blend) and then use the Add/Delete Anchor Point tools, or any of the following tools, to curve or edit the path: the Direct Selection,

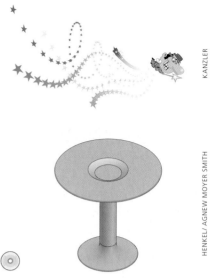

KANZLER

HENKEL/ AGNEW MOYER SMITH

John Kanzler created the fairy (top) with multi-object blends and a replaced spine; Rick Henkel used gradient-to-gradient blends for the pedestal of his table (see his explanation in "Henkel-Flared Effect.ai," on the Wow! CD *for full details)*

To blend or not to blend...

In addition to blending between individual paths, or groups of objects, you can also blend between symbols (see the *Brushes & Symbols* chapter for more on symbols), or between Point type objects (see the *Type* chapter for more on Point type objects). Some of the objects that you *can't* include in a blend are meshes, raster images, and type objects that aren't Point type. One last tip: When blending between objects containing brushes, effects, and other complex appearances, the effect options are blended, which can help you create interesting animations (see the *Web & Animation* chapter for more on how to export animations).—*Teri Petit*

STEUER (blend consultant: Eric Hess)

*Groups of objects blended into each other (pumpkins into pumpkins, shadows into shadows) using the Align to Path orientation, Specified Distance, and the "spines" edited into **S** curves (for more about blends see "SteuerSharon-Pumpkin Blend.ai" on the* Wow! *CD)*

Reverse Front to Back

To reverse the order of a blend with only two key objects, Direct-select one of the key objects and choose Object > Arrange, or for any blend choose Object > Blend > Reverse Front to Back.

Lasso, Convert Anchor Point, Pencil, Smooth, or even the Erase tool. As you edit the spine of the blend, the blend objects will automatically be redrawn to align to the edited spine.

The second way is to replace the spine with a customized path: Select both the customized path and the blend, and choose Object > Blend > Replace Spine. This command moves the blend to its new spine.

It's a bit tricky, but you can also blend between multiple objects. Create your first set of objects and Group them (⌘-G/Ctrl-G). Next, select this group. Then hold down Option/Alt and drag off a copy (making sure that you release your mouse button before releasing the keyboard—see "A Finger Dance" in the *Zen of Illustrator* chapter for help). Select both sets of grouped objects, and click on the first group with the Blend tool. Then hold Option/Alt as you click on the second group to specify the number of steps. As long as you maintain the same number of points, you'll get a predictable blending between the groups. Once the objects are blended, you can rotate and scale them, and use the Direct Selection tool to edit the objects or the spine. (See "SteuerSharon-Pumpkin Blend.ai" on the *Wow! CD.*)

Reversing, Releasing, and Expanding Blends

Once you've created and selected a blend, you can do any of the following:

- **Reverse** the order of objects on the spine by choosing Object > Blend > Reverse Spine.

- **Release** a blend (Object > Blend > Release) if you wish to remove the blended objects between key objects and maintain the spine of the blend (be forewarned—you may lose grouping information!).

- **Expand** a blend to turn it into a group of separate, editable objects. Choose Object > Expand.

GRADIENTS

Gradients are color transitions. To open the Gradient palette: double-click the Gradient tool icon on the Toolbox, or choose Window > Gradient. Gradients can be either radial (circular from the center) or linear.

To apply a gradient to an object, select the object and click on a gradient swatch in the Swatches palette. To view only gradient swatches, click on the gradient icon at the bottom of the Swatches palette.

To start adjusting or creating a new gradient, click on the gradient preview in the Gradient palette. Only after clicking on the preview will you see the color stops and midpoints. Make your own gradients by adding and/or adjusting the stops (pointers representing colors) along the lower edge of the gradient preview, and adjust the midpoint between the color stops by sliding the diamond shapes along the top of the preview.

You can adjust the length, direction, and centerpoint location of a selected gradient. In addition, you can apply a gradient to multiple selected objects across a unified blend by clicking and dragging with the Gradient tool (see the "Unified Gradients" lesson later in this chapter, and for a lesson incorporating radial gradients, see Laurie Grace's "Distort Filter Flora" lesson in the *Drawing & Coloring* chapter). *Hint: A special feature of the Gradient palette is, even if it's docked with other palettes, you can expand it both taller and wider so you can get a better view of the Gradient bar.*

To create the illusion of a gradient within a stroke, convert the stroke to a filled object (Object > Path > Outline Stroke). You can use this method to create a "trap" for gradients (for more about this technique of trapping gradients, see the Christopher Burke Gallery in the *Drawing & Coloring* chapter).

To turn a gradient into a grouped, masked blend, use Object > Expand (see the *Advanced Techniques* chapter for more on masks and masked blends).

To insert objects into a blend

Direct-select a key object and Option/Alt-drag to insert a new key object (the blend will reflow) that you can Direct-select and edit. You can also insert new objects by dragging them into the blend in the Layers palette.

Reset gradients to defaults

After you select an object that has an altered gradient angle (or highlight), new objects you draw will have the same altered angle. To "re-zero" gradient angles, Deselect All and fill with None by pressing the "/" key. When you next choose a gradient, angles will have the default setting. Or, for linear gradients, you can type a zero in the Angle field.

Adding color to your gradient

- Drag a swatch from the Color or Swatches palette to the gradient slider until you see a vertical line indicating where the new color stop will be added.
- If the Fill is a solid color, you can drag color from the Fill icon at the bottom of the Toolbox.
- Hold down the Option/Alt key to drag a copy of a color stop.
- Option/Alt-drag one stop over another to *swap* their colors.
- Click the lower edge of a gradient to add a new stop.

MIYAMOTO

PAIDRICK

PAIDRICK

The amazing work with mesh only starts in this chapter—don't miss the additional mesh artwork in the Advanced Techniques *chapter— including this work by Yukio Miyamoto (cat) and Ann Paidrick (olives and tomatoes) !*

GRADIENT MESH

If you see an amazing photorealistic image created in Illustrator, chances are it was created using gradient mesh. A *mesh object* is an object on which multiple colors can flow in different directions, with smooth transitions between specially defined *mesh points*. You can apply a gradient mesh to a solid or gradient-filled object (but you can't use compound paths to create mesh objects). Once transformed, the object will always be a mesh object, so be certain that you work with a copy of the original if it's difficult to re-create.

Transform solid filled objects into gradient mesh objects either by choosing Object > Create Gradient Mesh (so you can specify details on the mesh construction) or by clicking on the object with the Mesh tool. To transform a gradient-filled object, select Object > Expand and enable the Gradient Mesh option.

Use the Mesh tool to add mesh lines and mesh points to the mesh. Select individual points, or groups of points, within the mesh using the Direct Selection tool or the Mesh tool in order to move, color, or delete them. For details on working with gradient meshes (including a warning tip about printing mesh objects), see Galleries and lessons later in this chapter, and see the *Advanced Techniques* chapter as well. **Hint:** *Instead of applying a mesh to a complex path, try to first create the mesh from a simpler path outline, then mask the mesh with the more complex path.*

Expanding

Items such as gradients, meshes, blends, and patterns are complex and can't be used to define other complex art unless the art is Expanded first using Object > Expand. Once expanded, you can use the objects within the art to define a brush, pattern, or blend.

Get back your (mesh) shape!

When you convert a path to a mesh, it's no longer a path, but a mesh object. To extract an editable path from a mesh, select the mesh object, choose Object > Path > Offset Path, enter 0, and press OK. If there are too many points in your new path, try using Object > Path > Simplify (for more on Simplify see "Map Techniques" in the *Brushes* chapter). —*Pierre Louveaux*

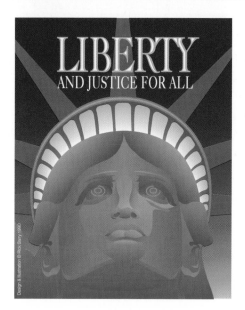

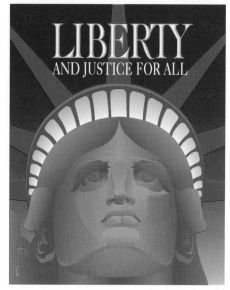

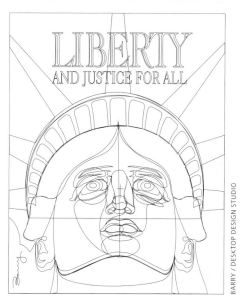

BARRY / DESKTOP DESIGN STUDIO

Rick Barry / DeskTop Design Studio

To demonstrate the difference between blends and gradients, Rick Barry took an image he created in Illustrator (upper left Preview mode, lower left Outline mode), selected the blends (by clicking twice with the Group Selection tool on one of the blend objects) and deleted them. The objects used to create the blends remained, and Barry filled these objects with custom gradients and then adjusted the rate and range of the gradients with the Gradient tool (upper right Preview mode, lower right Outline mode).

Examining Blends

Learning When to Use Gradients or Blends

Overview: *Examine your objects; for linear or circular fills, create basic gradients; for contouring fills into complex objects, create blends.*

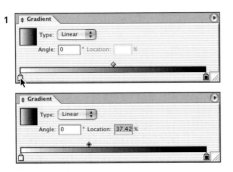

Adjusting the placement of colors, and then rate of color transition in the Gradient palette

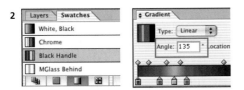

Selecting a gradient from the Swatches palette and setting the gradient Angle

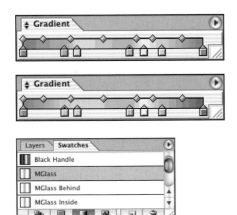

One gradient duplicated and altered for application to different related objects

You need to take a number of factors into consideration when you're deciding whether to create color transitions with blends or gradients. Steve Hart's magnifying glass, created for *Time* magazine, is a clear-cut example that demonstrates when to use gradients or blends.

1 Designing gradients. Select an object you'd like to fill with a linear gradient. Open the Gradient palette. Click on the gradient icon at the bottom of the Swatches palette. Choose Name from the Swatches pop-up menu and click on the "White, Black" gradient. This minimal gradient has two colors: white (at the left) and black (at the right). Click on the left gradient slider to display its position on the scale from 0–100% (in this case 0%). Move the slider to the right to increase the percentage displayed in the scale, and increase the black area of the gradient. Click on the bottom edge of the scale to add additional pointers. Click on a slider to access its numeric position, or to change its color or tint. Between every two pointers is a diamond icon indicating the midpoint of the color transition (from 0–100% between each color pair). Grab and drag a diamond to adjust the color transition rate, or type a new position into the percent field.

2 Storing and applying gradients and making adjustments. To store a new gradient you've made within a selected object, hold Option or Alt and click the New Swatch icon and name your gradient. Hart filled his magnifying glass handle with a gradient set at a 135° angle (in the Gradient palette). He created slightly different variants for gradients representing the metal rings around the outside, along the inside, and inside behind the glass. To create variants of a current gradient, make color adjustments first, then Option-click/Alt-click the New Swatch icon to name your new gradient. Although you can experiment with changing the angle of a gradient, be forewarned that continued adjustments to a gradient in the Gradient palette will not update the gradient stored in the Swatches palette! (See the intro to this chapter.)

3 Using blends for irregular or contoured transitions.

A blend is often best for domed, kidney-shaped or contoured objects, such as shadows (for Gradient Mesh, see later in this chapter). Scale and copy one object to create another and set each to the desired color. With the Blend tool, click an anchor point on one, then Option-click/Alt-click a related point on the other. The default blend setting, "Smooth Color," often means many steps; however, the more similar the colors, the fewer steps you'll actually need. You can manually choose "Specified Steps" from the pop-up and experiment with fewer steps. Hart specified 20 steps for the glow in the glass, 22 for the handle knob and 12 for the shadow. To re-specify the steps of a selected blend, double-click the Blend tool (you may have to uncheck and recheck Preview to see the update). To blend selected objects using previous settings, click with the Blend tool without holding the Option/Alt key.

With the Blend tool, clicking first on a selected point of one path, then Option/Alt-clicking on a selected point of the other to open Blend Options; choosing Specified Steps from the pop-up and entering 20; the blended objects

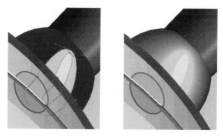

Selected paths before and after a 22-step blend

Before and after a 12-step blend to create a shadow

The final image as it appeared in Time

Automatically updating colors

Changing a spot or global color definition (see the *Drawing & Coloring* chapter) automatically updates blends and gradients containing that color. Blends between tints of the same spot color (or a spot color and white) update when changes are made to that color, even if the blend isn't "live."—Agnew Moyer Smith

Shades of Blends

Creating Architectural Linear Shading

Overview: *Create an architectural form using rectangles; copy and paste one rectangle in front; delete the top and bottom paths and blend between the two sides.*

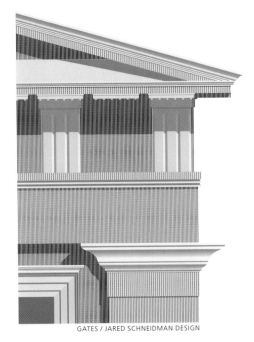

GATES / JARED SCHNEIDMAN DESIGN

1

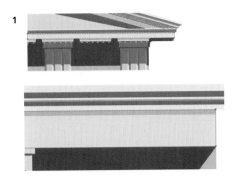

A selected rectangle copied and pasted in front in full view, and in close-up

2

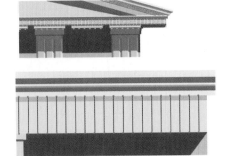

The top and bottom deleted with the sides selected

The full blend and a close-up detail

Without much difficulty, Illustrator can help simulate the traditional artistic conventions for rendering architectural details. Jared Schneidman Design developed a simple, but exacting, method to apply vertical line shading.

1 Creating an architectural structure. After establishing the overall form, color and tonality of your illustration, select and copy one rectangle. Choose Edit > Paste in Front to place the copy on top, then set the fill to None and the stroke to .1 pt Black. Choose Window > Info to note the line's width in points (to change your ruler units, see Tip, "Changing measurement units," in the *Illustrator Basics* chapter). Calculate the width of the rectangle, divided by the spacing you'd like between lines. Subtract 2 (for the sides you have) to find the proper number of steps for this blend.

2 Deleting the top and bottom and blending the sides. Deselect the copy, Shift-Direct-select the top and bottom paths and delete, leaving the sides selected. With the Blend tool, click on the top point of each side and specify the number of steps you determined above.

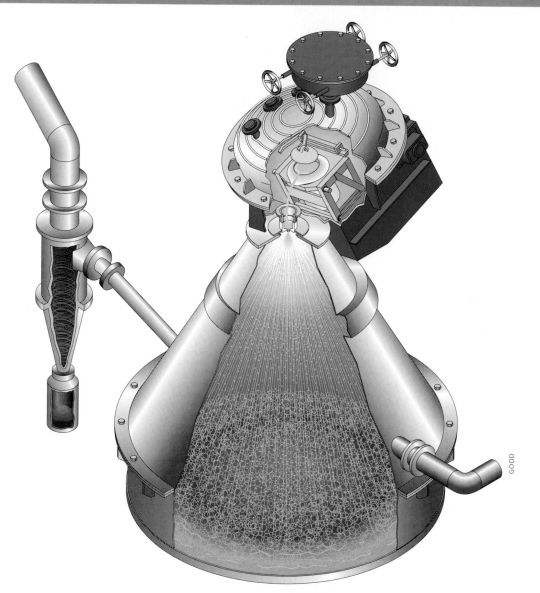

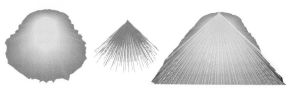

Janet Good / Industrial Illustrators

Illustrator Janet Good's image of the white-hot glow of molten metal spraying inside a chamber of liquid nitrogen is based on a drawing by Crucible Research. For the fiery glow at the top of the chamber, she first drew yellow and orange objects and then blended them. (By making the edge of the orange object jagged, she created a blend that appears to have rays.) On a layer above the blend, Good drew several pairs of yellow and white lines, blending the pairs to form a fan of glowing light rays.

FERSTER

Gary Ferster

For his client Langeveld Bulb, Gary Ferster used blends to create the in-between layers in this flower bulb. He began by styling the outer peel with a .5 pt stroke in a dark brown custom color and filled the object with a lighter brown custom color. He then created the inner layer, filled it with white and gave it a .5 pt white stroke. Selecting both objects, Ferster specified a six-step blend that simultaneously "morphed" each progressive layer into the next while lightening the layers towards white. Blends were also used to create the leafy greens, yellow innards and all the other soft transitions between colors.

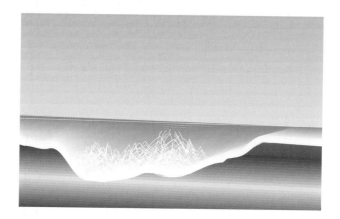

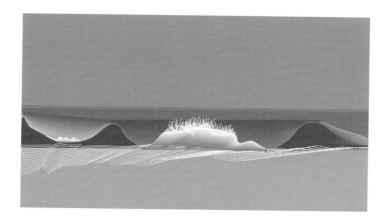

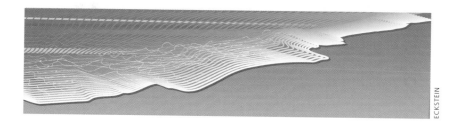

ECKSTEIN

Linda Eckstein

Linda Eckstein used blends in Illustrator to create these beautiful seascapes. In addition to controlling the regularity of blends to depict the ocean, Eckstein needed to control the irregularity of the blends as well. On the bottom layer of her image are blends that establish both the general composition and the broad color schemes. On top of these tonal-filled object blends are irregularly shaped linear blends that form the waves and surf. Using the Direct Selection tool, she isolated individual points and groups of points to stretch and distort the waves.

CASSELL

Peter Cassell

Using the Blend tool is a great way to save time; it lets Illustrator automatically create the intermediate paths between two paths. In this adoption announcement for Morgan Katia Hurt, Peter Cassell drew the two outermost lines of longitude for the globe using the Pen tool. With the two paths selected, he chose the Blend tool and clicked on the end-points of the two paths (to blend properly, be sure to pick two points that have the same relative position on their respective paths). He set the number of intermediate paths by double-clicking the Blend tool, choosing Specified Steps from the Spacing pop-up menu, and keying in **4** in the Spacing field. To create the bulging effect of a sphere, Cassell wanted to spread out the intermediate paths. To do this, he selected the blend, chose Object > Expand and then Object > Ungroup. After selecting the four intermediate paths, Cassell double-clicked the Scale tool and in the Scale dialog box, entered **125** in the Horizontal field, while keeping the Vertical field at **100**. He spread the two inner paths farther apart by applying horizontal scaling again.

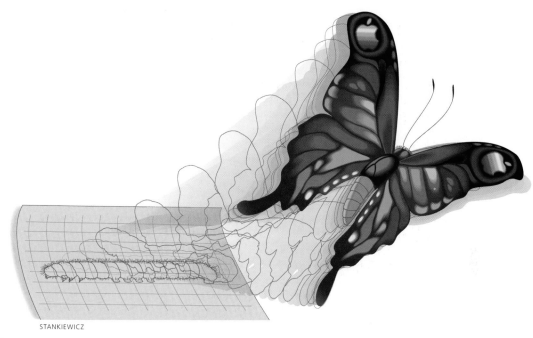

STANKIEWICZ

Steven Stankiewicz

Steven Stankiewicz uses a technique he calls "blends to blends" to smooth one colorful blend with another in his illustrations. To create a butterfly wing, he first drew the wing shape and its spots with the Pen tool and then colored each object. For the wing blend, he copied the wing object, pasted it in front, and scaled it smaller with the Scale tool. After selecting the original and the copy, he used the Blend tool to click on an anchor point on the original wing and Option-click on the corresponding point of the copied (smaller) wing. From the pop-up Blend Options dialog box, Stankiewicz chose the Smooth Color option. Then he performed the same steps to create blends for each of the wing spots. Stankiewicz decided to smooth the color transition

between each wing spot blend and the wing blend behind it. To accomplish this, he chose the Direct Selection tool and selected the outermost object in one of the wing spot blends; then he Shift-selected the innermost object of the wing blend behind it. With both objects selected, Stankiewicz clicked points on both objects that were in roughly the same position on each object. As a result, a new blend was created that smoothly bridged the blend of a wing spot with the blend of the wing behind it.

Unlocking Realism

Creating Metallic Reflections with Blends

Overview: *Form the basic shapes of objects; create tonal boundaries for future blends that follow the contours of the objects; copy, scale, recolor and adjust the anchor points of tonal boundaries; blend highlights and shadows.*

1

Designing the basic objects and choosing a base tone (Note: Gray strokes added to distinguish objects)

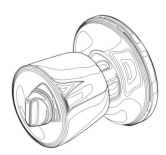

Creating tonal boundaries for future blends by following the contours of the objects

Achieving photorealism with Illustrator may appear prohibitively complex and intimidating, but with a few simple rules-of-thumb, some careful planning and the eye of an artist, it can be done. Brad Neal, of Thomas • Bradley Illustration & Design, demonstrates with this image that you don't need an airbrush to achieve metallic reflectivity, spectacular highlights or warm shadows.

1 Preparing a detailed sketch that incorporates a strong light source, and setting up your palette.
Before you actually start your illustration, create a sketch that establishes the direction of your light source. Then, in Illustrator, set up your color palette (see the *Drawing & Coloring* chapter). Choose one color as a "base tone," the initial tint from which all blends will be built, and fill the entire object with that value. After you create the basic outlines of your illustration, work in Outline mode to create separate paths—following the contours of your objects—for each of your major color transitions. After completing the initial line drawing of the lock set, Neal visually, and then physically, "mapped" out the areas that

would contain the shading. He added a few highlights and reflections in the later stages of the project, but the majority of blends were mapped out in advance.

2 Using your color transition paths to create blends.
Next, use the contouring paths you've created to map out your tonal boundaries. Choose one of the objects and fill it with the same color and tonal value as its underlying shape. In the Neal locks, this initial color is always the same color and value selected for the base color. Then, copy the object and Paste in Front (Edit > Paste in Front). Next, fill this copy with a highlight or shadow value, scale it down and manipulate it into the correct position to form the highlight or shadow area. You can accomplish this step by one of two methods: by scaling the object using the Scale tool, or by selecting and pulling in individual anchor points with the Direct Selection tool. In order to ensure smooth blends without ripples or irregular transitions, the anchor points of the inner and outer objects must be as closely aligned as possible and should contain the same number of points. To then complete this highlight or shadow, use the Blend tool to *point map* (see the intro to this chapter for details). The blend in Figure 2 required eight in-between steps. If your blend isn't smooth enough, then use the Direct Selection tool to select anchor points on the key objects and adjust their position or Bézier handles until the blend smooths.

3 Blending in smaller increments. Some blend situations may require more than two objects to achieve the desired look. For instance, to control the rate at which the tone changes or the way an object transforms throughout the blended area, you may wish to add an intermediate object and blend in two stages, instead of one.

4 Using blends to soften hard transitions. Always use blends when making tonal transitions, even when you need a stark contrast shadow or highlight. A close look at Neal's shadow reveals a very short but distinct blend.

2

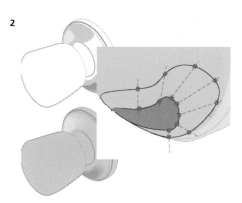

Pasting in Front a scaled down and adjusted copy with the same number of aligned points

3

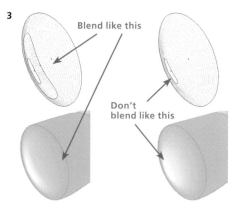

Adding an in-between contour to help control the rate and shape of blends; blending with too few contours flattens the image

4

Long, close-up, and Outline close-up views of highlight and shadow transitions

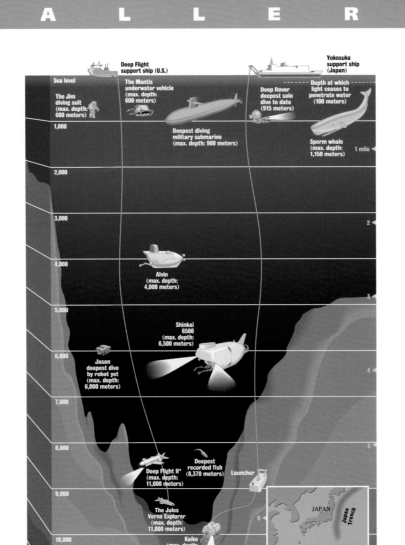

Sea level
The Jim
diving suit
(max. depth:
600 meters)

Deep Flight
support ship (U.S.)

The Mantis
underwater vehicle
(max. depth:
600 meters)

Yokosuka
support ship
(Japan)

Deep Rover
deepest solo
dive to date
(915 meters)

Depth at which
light ceases to
penetrate water
(100 meters)

1,000

Deepest diving
military submarine
(max. depth: 900 meters)

Sperm whale
(max. depth:
1,150 meters)

1 mile

2,000

3,000   2

4,000

Alvin
(max. depth:
4,000 meters)

3

5,000

Shinkai
6500
(max. depth:
6,500 meters)

6,000

Jason
deepest dive
by robot yet
(max. depth:
6,000 meters)

4

7,000

8,000

Deep Flight II*
(max. depth:
11,000 meters)

Deepest
recorded fish
(8,370 meters)

Launcher

5

9,000

The Jules
Verne Explorer
(max. depth:
11,000 meters)

JAPAN

Japan Trench

10,000

Kaiko
(max. depth:
11,000 meters)

6

PACIFIC
OCEAN

Mariana Trench

Challenger Deep

THE
PHILIPPINES

Challenger
Deep

11,000 meters

7 miles

SCHNEIDMAN

Jared Schneidman / JSD

Illustrator blends helped Jared Schneidman convey the murky depth and bright exploring lights in this *Newsweek* infographic about deep trenches in the Pacific Ocean. Schneidman created the subdued highlights and shadows of the subterranean trench using blended objects.

For the searchlights emanating from the explorer vehicles, Schneidman first made cone objects filled with a pale yellow. He then made companion objects using the dark colors of the ocean and trench. Finally, he made blends between each cone and its companion object.

KELLEY

Andrea Kelley

To illustrate this North Face camping equipment, designer Andrea Kelley carefully analyzed fabric folds, stitched seams, and the play of light and shadow. She began the sleeping bag by drawing the outline of the bag, creating a blend object and masking it with a copy of the sleeping bag outline. She drew each stitched seam as a solid line, and the fabric folds around the seams as jagged, filled shapes. Over the sleeping bag, Kelley drew light-gray-filled objects for the fabric highlights between the seams. Kelley created the tent by first drawing its outline, and then creating a multiple-object blend, which she masked with the tent outline. Kelley created additional masked blends to define other shapes that make up the tent. For the front flap, Kelley created a blend object and masked it with an oval, and then drew light and dark triangles on top of it to show wrinkles in the fabric.

Unified Gradients

Redirecting Fills with the Gradient Tool

Overview: *Fill objects with gradients; use the Gradient tool to adjust fill length, direction, center location and unify fills across multiple objects.*

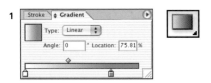

The Gradient palette, and the Gradient tool (This tool has the same name and icon as the one in Photoshop, but is completely different.)

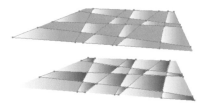

Filling the first group with the cyan gradient, then the other group with the purple gradient

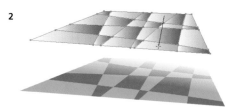

Clicking and dragging with the Gradient tool to unify the gradient fill across multiple objects, and to establish the gradient's rate and direction

How long can a gradient be?

Click and drag the Gradient tool anywhere in your image window; you don't need to stay within the objects themselves. Also, see the Elberg-Comet Gradient Lesson.ai by Eve Elberg, on the *Wow! CD*.

The Gradient tool allows you to customize the length and direction of gradient fills, and to stretch gradients across multiple objects. For this *Medical Economics* magazine illustration, Dave Joly used the Gradient tool to customize each gradient and unify the checkerboard floor.

1 Filling objects with the same gradient. Select multiple objects and fill them with the same gradient by clicking on a gradient fill in the Swatches palette. Keep your objects selected.

2 Unifying gradients with the Gradient tool. Using the Gradient tool from the Toolbox, click and drag from the point you want the gradient to begin to where you want it to end. Hold down the Shift key if you want to constrain the angle of the gradient. To relocate a radial gradient's center, just click with the Gradient tool. Experiment until you get the desired effect. To create his checkerboard, Joly used the Knife tool to segment the floor, grouped every other tile together and filled these with a cyan-to-white gradient fill. He then duplicated the gradient, changed the start color to purple and applied this purple gradient to the remaining tiles. With all tiles selected, he again applied the Gradient tool.

Filip Yip

Filip Yip prefers the simplicity of linear and radial gradients to the photo-realism of blends in creating the stylized look of many of his illustrations. The images above began as pencil sketches that Yip scanned, placed in Illustrator as templates and then traced over to create compositional elements. For the spoonful of vegetables, Yip developed gradients that share similar colors but differ in the number and location of intermediate colors and midpoints along the slider in the Gradient palette. The lobster is more stylized, conveying shadows with color-to-gray gradients. Both illustrations contrast the soft gradient effects with crisp highlights and shadows in strong, solid-filled colors.

Chapter 7 *Blends, Gradients & Mesh* **239**

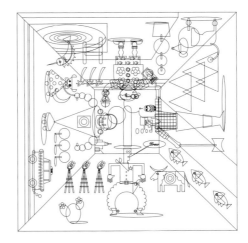

Hugh Whyte / Lehner & Whyte

In this image designed for a promotional poster, Hugh Whyte used gradients and the Gradient tool to create a colorful, cut-out look that is both flat and volumetric. The Outline view at right reveals that Whyte constructed the image entirely of gradients, with no blends.

GORSKA

Caryl Gorska

Caryl Gorska created "Bountiful Harvest" as a package design for Nunes Farms' dried fruits, nuts and chocolates. She used the Gradient tool to customize her radial blends (made of process colors). A scan of parchment paper, saved as an EPS file, is Placed on the bottom layer (see the *Layers* chapter).

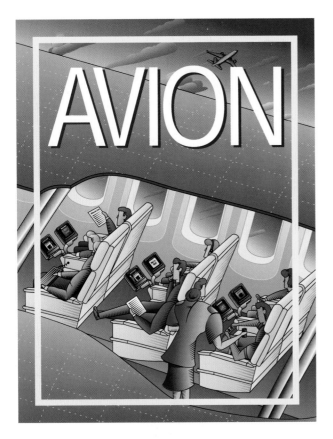

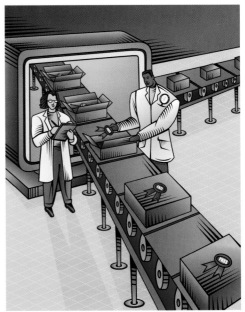

WEBB

Tim Webb

In these two magazine illustrations, Avion (for *Avion* magazine) and Quality Control (for *Field Force Automation* magazine), Tim Webb created a small palette of gradients and varied the gradient angle of the fill to achieve a wide range of color. With an object selected, he clicked and dragged with the Gradient tool from the beginning point to the endpoint of the area in which he wanted to place the gradient. Webb varied the angle and distance of the gradient to create specific fill colors. The sky, clouds, and windows in Avion are all filled with the same gradient. In Quality Control, the floor and yellow shadows share the same gradient. Using a small palette of gradients allowed Webb to quickly change the color of an object and maintain subtleties of color throughout his illustrations.

Tim Webb

Tim Webb used just a few features of Illustrator to create his Victory Climb and Road lessons illustrations. The crisp woodcut appearance is a result of bold line work layered above gradient fills. Webb began by drawing the image with the Pen tool. Webb then created his color palette by importing colors from a swatch library into the Swatches palette. He then double-clicked the Gradient tool icon to open the Gradient palette and created gradients by dragging colors from the Swatches palette onto the stops of the Gradient palette. (For more detail on creating a gradient, see the gradients section of the introduction to this chapter).

After he created and saved the gradients in the Swatches palette, Webb drew closed paths and filled them with either a linear or a radial gradient, varying the direction and length of the gradient in order to give volume to the image. The woodcut appearance was created by blending between two triangular shapes on a curved path. Webb created custom art brushes to make the small rocks and the raindrops.

Rolling Mesh

Converting Gradients to Mesh and Editing

Overview: *Draw shapes and fill with linear gradients; expand gradient-filled objects into gradient meshes; use various tools to edit mesh points and colors.*

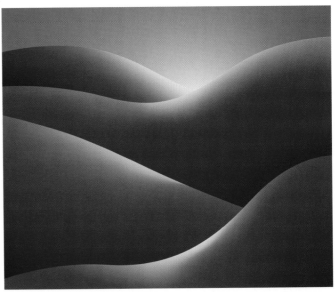

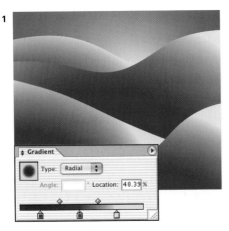

The hills shown filled with radial gradients—although there is some sense of light, it isn't possible to make the radial gradient follow the contours of the hills

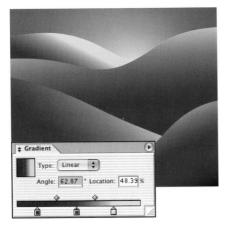

The hills shown filled with linear gradients, which are easier to edit than radial gradients when converted to gradient meshes

For many images, gradients can be useful for showing the gradual change of light to shadow (if you need to learn more about creating and applying gradient fills, first see "Unified Gradients" earlier in this chapter). For these rolling hills, artist Sharon Steuer expanded linear gradients into gradient mesh objects so she could better control the curves and contours of the color transitions.

1 Drawing shapes and then filling them with linear gradients. Begin your illustration by creating closed objects with any of the drawing tools. After completing the objects, select each object with the Selection tool and Fill it with a linear gradient fill. For each linear gradient, adjust the angle and length of the gradient transition with the Gradient tool until you can best approximate the desired lighting effect. Steuer created four hill-shaped objects with the Pen tool, filled them with the same linear gradient, then customized each with the Gradient tool. **Note:** *Although in some objects radial gradients might look better before you convert them, linear gradients create gradient mesh objects that are much easier to edit!*

2 Expanding linear gradients into gradient meshes. To create a more natural lighting of the hills, Steuer converted the linear gradients into mesh objects so the color transitions could follow the contours of the hills. To accomplish this, select all the gradient-filled objects that you wish to convert and choose Object >Expand. In the Expand dialog box, make sure Fill is checked and specify Expand Gradient to Gradient Mesh. Then click OK. Illustrator converts each linear gradient into a rectangle rotated to the angle matching the linear gradient's angle; each mesh rectangle is masked by the original object (see the *Advanced Techniques* chapter for help with masks).

3 Editing meshes. You can use several tools to edit gradient mesh objects (use the Object >Lock/Unlock All toggle to isolate objects as you work). The Mesh tool combines the functionality of the Direct Selection tool with the ability to add mesh lines. With the Mesh tool, click *exactly on* a mesh anchor point to select or move that point or its direction handles. Or, click *anywhere* within a mesh, except on an anchor point, to add a new mesh point and gridline. You can also use the Add Anchor Point tool (click and hold to choose it from the Pen tool pop-up) to add a point without a gridline. To delete a selected anchor point, press the Delete key; if that point is a mesh point, the gridlines will be deleted as well.

Select points within the mesh using either the Mesh tool or the Lasso tool, using the Direct Selection tool to move multiple selected points. Move individual anchor points and adjust direction handles with the Mesh tool in order to reshape your gradient mesh gridlines. In this way, the color and tonal transitions of the gradient will match the contour of the mesh object. Recolor selected areas of the mesh by selecting points, then choosing a new color.

If you click in the area *between* mesh points with the Paint bucket tool (from the Eyedropper tool pop-up) you'll add the Fill color to the four nearest mesh points.

By using these tools and editing techniques, Steuer was able to create hills with color and light variations that suggest the subtlety of natural light upon organic forms.

2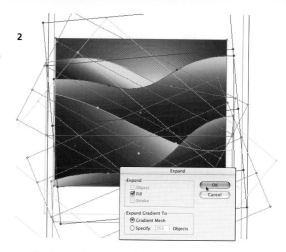

After Expanding the gradients into gradient mesh objects

3

Using the Mesh tool to add a mesh line, then moving the mesh point with the Direct Selection tool

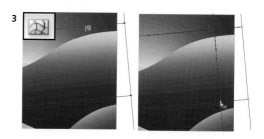

Using the Add Anchor Point tool, using the Lasso to select a point, moving selected point (or points) with the Direct Selection tool

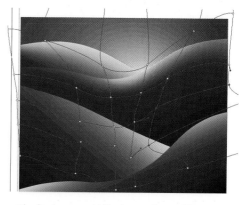

The final rearmost hill, shown after making mesh adjustments

Mastering Mesh

Painting with Areas of Color Using Mesh

Advanced Technique

Overview: *Create simple objects to make into gradient mesh; edit and color mesh objects; create compound-path masks for copies of mesh; make a mesh with no grid to reshape.*

TORRES

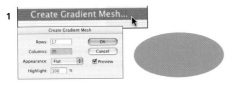

The original oval; choosing Object > Create Gradient Mesh; setting the Mesh options

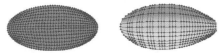

The mesh created; after selecting points and deleting to create a pattern in the mesh

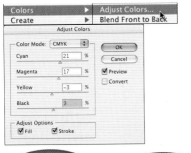

Recoloring selected rows and columns using the Color palette and the Adjust Colors filter

With a background in painting, sculpture and 3D imaging, Ivan Torres knew that the Gradient-mesh tool would allow him to paint in a powerfully unique way. In creating this fish illustration, he demonstrates how, unlike *any* other medium, the mesh allows him to *move a stroke of color* without changing the relationship between colors.

1 Creating the fish's body. Create a solid-filled oval; while it's selected, choose Object > Create Gradient Mesh. Set fairly high numbers for rows and columns; for his fish (shown above at about 30% actual size) Torres set 17 rows, 35 columns. Set Flat for Appearance, 100% Highlight and click OK. Next, to make the base for the fish's stripes, you'll need to create an irregular pattern within the mesh. With the Direct Selection tool, select anchor points and delete—the connected rows and columns will be deleted along with the points. Torres deleted 8 columns and 10 rows. Marquee horizontal anchor points with the Direct-selection tool. For even more selection control, try working in Outline mode, disable Use Area Select in Preferences > General, or select points using the Lasso tool. With horizontal rows of points selected (make sure you are now in Preview mode), mix or choose new colors in the Colors palette (use View > Hide/Show Edges to hide/show selection edges). Torres horizontally selected sections of the mesh, changing colors to create a sense of volume. For more subtle color transitions, select an area and choose Filter > Colors > Adjust Colors to adjust the color cast of your selection. Carefully Direct-select points and reposition them to form the fish body.

2 Making the fish's tail and fins. Create several colored rectangles and ovals. Again, convert each object to a gradient mesh, but assign a *low* value for columns. Direct-select sections of each object and use the Adjust Color Filter to create gradual changes in tone (use ⌘-Option-E (Mac)/Ctrl-Alt-E (Win) to reopen the last-used filter). Direct-select points on the objects and adjust them to form tail and fin shapes. Move each object into a separate layer for easy editing (see the *Layers* chapter for help).

3 Creating the fish's eye and lips. Create three circles: one small, one medium and one large. Convert the medium-size circle to a gradient mesh this time by clicking on the circle with the Gradient-mesh tool. Add additional rows or columns by clicking again with the tool; delete by Direct-selecting points, rows or columns and deleting. Torres ended up with unevenly spaced rows and columns (five of each), which he colored to achieve a wet, reflective-looking surface. When you are pleased with the glossy part of the eye, combine all the circles and adjust the outlines of some to be less perfect.

To create the fish's mouth, begin with a rectangle on a layer above the fish. Convert the rectangle to a gradient mesh using Object > Create Gradient Mesh, and enter different low values for rows and columns, maintaining Flat for Appearance. Select areas of the object and use the Eyedropper to load colors from the fish to create smooth color transitions between the mouth and the body. Move this object into position and reshape it to form a mouth.

4 Creating shadows for the fish. Duplicate the layer containing the fish's body by dragging that layer to the New Layer icon in the Layers palette. On a layer above this one,

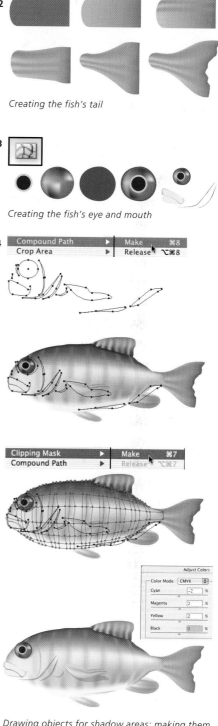

Creating the fish's tail

Creating the fish's eye and mouth

Drawing objects for shadow areas; making them into a compound path; masking a copy of the fish with the compound path; using Filter > Colors > Adjust Colors to darken a copy of the fish; the final fish shown with completed shadows

An oval

After applying a mesh with values of 1, deleting the original oval anchor points (in orange)

The remaining points moved and colored

use the Pen tool to draw a contour defining each shadow as a closed object. Select all the shadow objects and choose Object > Compound Path > Make to unite them into one compound object. Use these shadow objects as a mask for the copy of the fish body. Select both the compound path and the copy of the fish body (in the Layers palette, Option-Shift-click/Alt-Shift-click the shadow and fish copy layers to select all objects on those layers) and choose Object > Clipping Mask > Make. To simulate shadow colors, select the masked copy of the fish and use the Adjust Colors filter to darken the area and reduce the contrast. Torres created a shadow that contrasted the cyan color cast of the fish by decreasing cyan and increasing yellow and magenta—each in increments of 2 to 5%. After applying the filter, with selection edges hidden ⌘-H (Mac)/Ctrl-H (Win), he reapplied the filter using ⌘-E (Mac)/Ctrl-E (Win), until he was satisfied.

5 Creating the border "bone" shape. Create an oval; while it's selected, choose Object > Create Gradient Mesh, assigning 1 for rows and columns and "Flat". Using the Delete Anchor Point tool, delete the four original points of the oval, leaving only the mesh points. Reposition the remaining points to create an arcing effect, and assign colors to each point. Next, use the Reflect tool to flip a copy of this object horizontally. With the copy selected, choose Filter > Colors > Invert Colors. Lastly, use the Shear tool to adjust the copied image to touch the original border object (see *Zen* chapter for Reflect and Shear help).

After reshaping is complete, a copy is created, reflected and sheared, and colors are inverted

Adding to the mesh

To add new rows and columns to your mesh, click on the mesh object with the Mesh (U) tool. To add a new mesh row, click on a column mesh line. To add a new mesh column, click on a row.

Printing gradient mesh objects

Gradient mesh objects rely on PostScript Level 3 (PS3) to print. Gradient mesh objects printed to older printers will convert to a 150-pixel-per-inch JPEG! If you can't print to a PS3 printer, you may wish to use Illustrator's Rasterize or Export commands. ***Hint:*** *Also see the Tip "Grouping masks" in the* Advanced Techniques *chapter.*

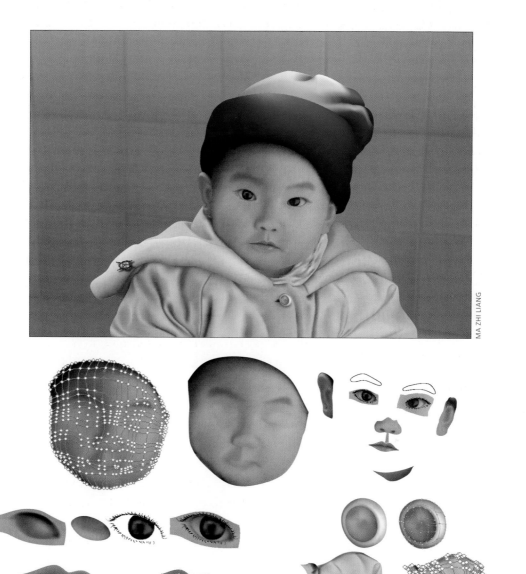

MA ZHI LIANG

Ma Zhi Liang

Ma Zhi Liang is an artist from China who painstakingly rendered this illustration from a photograph using Gradient Mesh. This portrait of his niece is a lovely example of how mesh can be used to show light, texture, and detail. The face is comprised of one mesh that makes up the "mask" of the face. Layered above the "mask" are other mesh objects that create the details of the facial features, such as the nose, eyes, and lips. Shown above are the mesh points that create the shadows and highlights in the fabric, lips, and button.

MIYAMOTO

Yukio Miyamoto

Yukio Miyamoto combined gradients, gradient mesh, and basic fills to render this photorealistic illustration of a motorcycle for his book, *The Adobe Illustrator Super Guide* (published in Japan). The in-process version above provides an insider's view into his methods for creating the finished piece at right. Miyamoto began by placing a photo as a template. He then traced over the photo using the Pen tool, creating solid black objects. He then systematically began to fill the individual objects with color, gradients, and gradient mesh, using the Eye-

dropper tool to pick up color from the photo for his objects, mesh points, and gradients. Miyamoto also combined masking techniques with gradient mesh in the wheels (see the *Advanced Techniques* chapter for more).

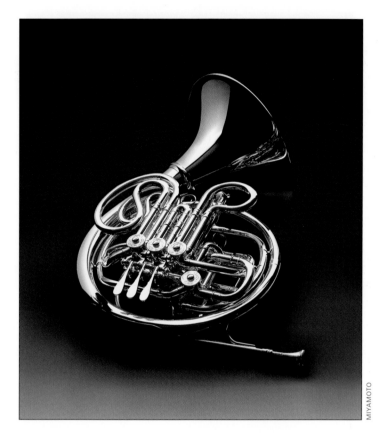

MIYAMOTO

Yukio Miyamoto

As with his motorcycle (opposite), Yukio Miyamoto began this illustration of a Yamaha French horn by tracing over a photo with the Pen tool, then filling the objects with solid fills. In layers above the basic tracing, Miyamoto drew the reflections and details of the tubular structure and filled them with linear gradients. He used the Mesh tool to define several reflections within the horn, with the most obvious on the horn's bell. He then created other areas of reflection with clusters of solid and gradient-filled objects (as on the bell and the valves). Miyamoto made the background out of a large, rectangular, gradient mesh. Within this mesh,

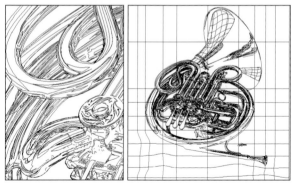

he created the horn's shadow. The magnificent level of detail is evident even when the image is viewed in Outline mode (a detail is shown directly above left; the full image in Outline is above right).

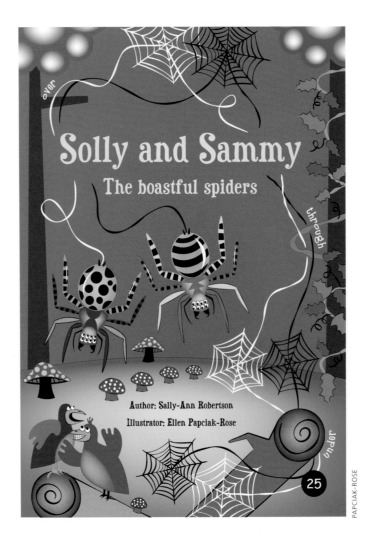

PAPCIAK-ROSE

Ellen Papciak-Rose

In this children's book cover illustration (Heine-mann Publishing), Ellen Papciak-Rose applied the Mesh tool to create glowing areas of color. Papciak-Rose began her illustration by draw-ing and coloring one of each object (such as a leaf, mushroom, spider, or tree). She then made one or more of each object and used the Scale (on the rounded mushrooms), Rotate (on the snail shells), and Reflect (on the tree and triangular-shaped mushrooms) tools to create variations. Papciak-Rose selected each object and chose the Mesh tool, clicked on the center anchor point of the object, and then, still using the Mesh tool, clicked on the desired contrast-ing color in the Swatches palette to create the center of the glow.

Transparency & Appearances

8

254 Introduction

254 Basic Transparency

263 Appearances

264 The Finer Points of Appearances

266 Transparency 101: *Assigning Opacity to Default Brushes*

268 Advanced Technique: Transparent Color: *Customizing Transparent Brushes & Layers*

272 Basic Transparency: *Blending Modes, Opacity & Isolate Blending*

274 Basic Highlights: *Making Highlights with Transparent Blends*

275–277 Galleries: Nancy Stahl, Tiffany Larsen, Louis Fishauf

278 Basic Appearances: *Making and Applying Appearances*

280 Floating Type: *Type Objects with Transparency & Effects*

282 Advanced Technique: Tinting a Scan: *Using Transparency Effects & Simplify Path*

284 Advanced Technique: It's a Knockout!: *See-through Objects with a Knockout Group*

286 Advanced Technique: Opacity Masks 101: *Applying Glows and Using Opacity Masks*

288–290 Galleries: Peter Cassell, Adam Z Lein

Transparency & Appearances

Illustrator's sophisticated use of transparency is woven throughout the application—you use transparency not only whenever you apply an opacity percentage, a blending mode, or an opacity mask from the Transparency palette, but also whenever you apply certain kinds of effects (such as shadows, feathers, and glows) or styles that include those features. Although it's easy to apply transparent effects to your artwork, it's important that you understand how transparency works, because this will help you later when you export or print.

Illustrator CS gives you helpful new tools to increase your control over how you print and output artwork that includes transparency, and allows you to save your transparency flattening settings as time-saving *presets*. There are now no less than four handy ways to control flattening settings: through the new Flattener Preview palette (Window > Flattener Preview), the Flatten Transparency dialog box (Object > Flatten Transparency), the Advanced options in Illustrator's new comprehensive Print dialog box, or the Transparency Flattener Presets dialog box (Edit > Transparency Flattener Presets). Once you've specified your flattening settings using any of these methods, you can save them as presets.

If the concepts of Transparency, Flattening, Appearances, Targeting, or Opacity Masks are new to you, it's very important that you take the time to master the lessons in this chapter. Although this is not an advanced techniques chapter, we do assume that by now you have a basic knowledge of fills, strokes, and especially layers. If you're unable to keep up with this chapter, please see the *Drawing & Coloring* and *Layers* chapters first.

BASIC TRANSPARENCY

Although the Artboard may look white, Illustrator treats it as transparent. To visually distinguish the transparent areas from the non-transparent ones, choose View >

Show Transparency Grid. To set the size and colors of the transparency grid, select File > Document Setup > Transparency. You can check Simulate Colored Paper if you'll be printing on a colored stock (click on the top swatch to open the color picker to select a "paper" color). Both Transparency Grid and paper color are non-printing attributes and are only visible in on-screen preview.

The term *transparency* refers to any changes in blending modes and opacity. Some masks or effects, such as Feather or Drop Shadow, use these settings as well. As a result, when you apply these masks or effects, you're relying on Illustrator's transparency features. To apply transparency to an object or group, make a selection or click on the target indicator in the Layers palette, then adjust the opacity slider in the Transparency palette. (Objects and groups are automatically targeted when you select them; if you want to apply transparency at the layer level, target the layer explicitly.) Completely opaque is equal to 100% opacity and 0% is completely see-through, or invisible. Be careful how you apply transparency; it's easy to get confused—correctly targeting and applying transparency is very important (see the "Basic Transparency" lesson in this chapter).

Blending modes control how the colors of objects, groups, or layers interact with one another. Blending modes are color mode–specific and yield different results in RGB and CMYK. As in Photoshop, the blending modes show no effect when they're over the *transparent* Artboard. To see the effect of blending modes, you need to add a color-filled or white element behind your art.

Opacity Masks

Opacity masks allow the dark and light areas in one object to be used as a mask for other objects. Black within the mask indicates areas of the masked artwork that will be completely transparent. White within the mask represents areas of the masked artwork that will be fully opaque and visible. Grays allow a range of transparency. (This works exactly like Photoshop *layer masks*).

Need more transparency?
Look for more lessons and Galleries involving transparency in the *Live Effects & Graphic Styles* and *Advanced Techniques* chapters.

Editing Opacity Masks

- **Disable**—Shift-click the mask thumbnail to turn it off. A red **X** will appear over the preview.
- **Enable**—Shift-click to reapply the mask.
- **Mask View**—Option-click (Mac)/Alt-click (Win) the mask thumbnail to toggle between viewing and editing the masking objects on the Artboard, or the mask grayscale values.
- **Release Opacity Mask (palette menu)**—releases the masking effect.
- **Toggle between working on artwork or Opacity Mask**—click the appropriate icon to control what you are editing.
- **Link or unlink the Opacity Mask to artwork**—click between the mask and artwork to toggle the link/unlink option.

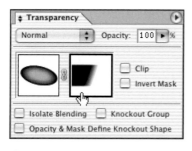

The Transparency palette with all options shown (choose Show Options from the Transparency palette menu)

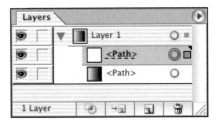

Opacity masks are indicated by a dashed line in the Layers palette

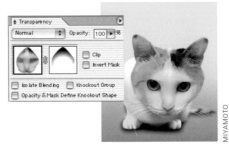

This cat by Yukio Miyamoto relies heavily on opacity masks (for details, see the *Advanced Techniques chapter*).

The easiest way to create an opacity mask is to first create the artwork you want masked. Next, place the object, group, or raster image you want to use as the mask above it. Select the artwork and the masking element, and choose Make Opacity Mask from the Transparency palette pop-up menu. Illustrator automatically makes the topmost object or group the opacity mask.

You may want to start with an empty mask and draw into it—in effect, painting your objects into visibility. To create an empty mask, start by targeting a single object, group, or layer. Since the default behavior of new opacity masks is clipping (with a black background), you'll need to turn off the "New Opacity Masks Are Clipping" option in the Transparency palette menu or your targeted artwork will completely disappear when you first create the empty mask. Next, choose Show Thumbnails from the Transparency palette menu, and double-click in the right thumbnail area. This creates an empty mask and puts you in mask editing mode; the Layers palette changes to show the opacity mask. Use your drawing and editing tools to create your mask. (For instance, if you create an object filled with a gradient, you'll see your artwork through the dark areas of the gradient.) While the opacity mask thumbnail is selected, you won't be able to edit anything else in your document. Choose to work on your artwork or your opacity mask by clicking on the appropriate thumbnail (the artwork thumbnail is on the left; the opacity mask is on the right).

A few hints can help you with opacity masks. First, the masking objects may display in color, but behind the scenes they're being converted to grayscale. In addition, if you select Invert Mask, you'll reverse the effect of dark and light values on the opacity—dark areas of the mask will be more opaque and light areas will be more transparent. To identify which elements have an opacity mask, look for the dashed underline in the Layers palette next to the object or group with the mask.

The link icon in the Transparency palette indicates that the position of the opacity mask stays associated with the position of the object, group, or layer it is masking. Unlinking allows you to move the artwork without moving the mask. The content of the mask can be selected and edited just like any other object. You can transform or apply a blending mode and/or an opacity percentage to each individual object within the mask.

Option-click (Mac) or Alt-click (Win) on an opacity mask thumbnail in the Transparency palette to hide the document's contents and display only the masking element in its grayscale values. Shift-click the opacity mask thumbnail to disable the opacity mask.

Knockout Controls

Choose Show Options from the pop-up menu of the Transparency palette to display the checkboxes that control how transparency is applied to groups and multiple objects.

With a group or layer targeted, check the Knockout Group option to keep individual objects of the group or layer from applying their transparency settings to each other where they overlap. This is particularly useful for blends containing one or more transparent objects. For this reason, Illustrator automatically turns on the Knockout Group option on all newly created blends.

Check Isolate Blending for a targeted group or layer so the transparency settings of the objects inside the group only affect their interaction with other objects *inside* the group (see the "Basic Transparency" lesson later in this chapter).

The final checkbox, Opacity & Mask Define Knockout Shape, is used in very specific situations to limit the knockout of a color to the area defined by the opacity and the mask. To see any effect, you must use this option on a transparent object inside a knockout group.

This option is most useful on raster images and feathered edges. It's automatically turned on inside the appearance of Drop Shadow, Blur, Feather, and Photoshop effects. If it weren't, putting objects with these effects in knockout groups would produce unwanted results: the

Transparency is cumulative

The total effect of transparency is determined by the object, group, sublayers, and container layer. **Note:** *There isn't any way to clear all effects for the multiple levels. You have to target each level and click the Clear Appearance icon (see the "Appearances" section later in this chapter).*

Knockout Group checkbox

In addition to being checked or unchecked, the Knockout Group checkbox has a third or neutral state that is indicated by a dash (in the Mac version) or grayed checkmark (in the Windows version). Illustrator automatically sets all newly created groups and layers to this neutral state so that simply grouping objects will not cause their transparency to change. The neutral state prevents the new group from overriding the knockout setting of the enclosing group. (See "It's a Knockout!" later in this chapter.)

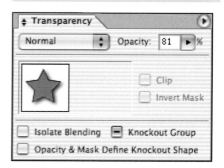

The Transparency palette with the Knockout checkbox in its third, or neutral, state (indicated by a dash in the Mac version shown here), as described in the Tip above

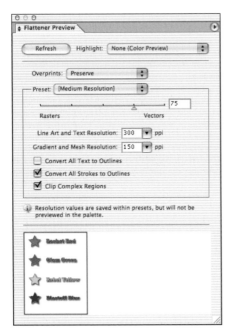

The Flattener Preview palette with all options showing (choose Show Options from the palette menu), including the Flattening Preset settings in the center of the palette. Click the Refresh button at the top of the palette, and the current document will be displayed in the preview area at the bottom of the screen. The section "Using the Flattener Preview palette," later in this chapter, explains how to use this preview to highlight areas of your art that will be affected by flattening

entire rectangular bounding box of Drop Shadows, Blurs, and Photoshop effects would knock out, as would the unfeathered outline of Feathered objects.

The art of flattening

PostScript printing devices and file formats such as EPS can only reproduce transparent artwork in "flattened" form. Illustrator's flattening process is applied temporarily if you print, and permanently if you save in a format that doesn't support transparency natively. Flattening occurs when areas of transparent overlap are converted into opaque pieces that look the same. Some of your objects may be split into many separate objects, while others may be rasterized.

As previously mentioned, Illustrator CS provides convenient new tools that give you increased control over exactly how your art is flattened. Illustrator's new Flattener Preview palette (Window > Flattener Preview) lets you see how flattening will affect your art, by means of a preview built right into the palette. The Flatten Transparency dialog box (Object > Flatten Transparency) and the Advanced section of the Print dialog box also let you choose transparency and flattening settings. And the Transparency Flattener Presets dialog box (Edit > Transparency Flattener Presets) gives you quick access to your presets (discussed in the "Working with flattener presets" section following this one), allowing you to edit existing custom presets and create new ones.

Here are the flattening options you can adjust:

- **Name** lets you name settings to be saved as a preset.
- **Raster/Vector Balance** lets you control the degree to which your artwork is rasterized (discussed in greater detail in the "Setting Raster/Vector Balance" section a little further on in this chapter).
- **Line Art and Text Resolution** sets the resolution for vector objects that will be rasterized when flattening.
- **Gradient and Mesh Resolution** lets you set the resolution for gradient and mesh objects that will be rasterized in the course of flattening.

- **Convert All Text to Outlines** keeps the width of text consistent during flattening by converting all type objects to outlines and discarding glyph information.
- **Convert All Strokes to Outlines** ensures that the width of text stays consistent during flattening by converting all strokes to simple filled paths.
- **Clip Complex Regions** reduces stitching artifacts by making sure that the boundaries between vector artwork and rasterized artwork fall along object paths.
- **Preserve Alpha Transparency** (Flatten Transparency dialog box only) preserves the alpha transparency of objects being flattened.
- **Preserve Overprints and Spot Colors** (Flatten Transparency dialog box only) preserves spot colors and overprinting for objects that aren't involved in transparency.

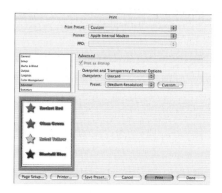

The Advanced section of the Print dialog box (choose File > Print, then select Advanced in the menu just above the preview)

To access these settings in the Flattener Preview palette, open the palette and choose Show Options from the palette menu. In the Flatten Transparency dialog box, you can access them by selecting any existing preset as a starting point and then making changes in the dialog. In the Advanced section of the Print dialog box, choose any existing Preset from the Presets menu and click the Custom button to change the settings. See the *User Guide* for more details about Illustrator's flattening options.

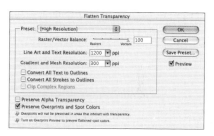

The Flatten Transparency dialog box (Object > Flatten Transparency)

Working with Flattener Presets

Once you've adjusted any of the settings above, you can save the results as a preset, so you won't have to create them from scratch the next time you want to apply the same flattening settings (or create a slight variation).

Illustrator comes with three default presets to get you started: High Resolution (for final press output and high-quality proofs such as color separations), Medium Resolution (for desktop proofs and print-demand-documents to be printed on PostScript color printers), and Low Resolution (for quick proofs to be printed on black-and-white desktop printers). You can't edit these default presets, but you can use them as a starting point, making changes and saving them as your own custom presets.

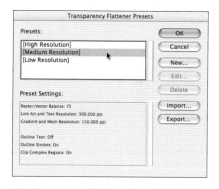

The Transparency Flattener Presets dialog box (Edit > Transparency Flattener Presets)

The Transparency Flattener Preset Options (New) dialog box that results when you click the New button in the Transparency Flattener Presets dialog box (above)

Click the Custom button in the Advanced section of the Print dialog box to display the Custom Transparency Flattener Options dialog box, where you can create a new custom preset

Overprint Preview

Previewing overprints on your screen has never been easier. Choose View > Overprint Preview to see how your overprints will look when they print. Overprint Preview also provides the best spot color simulations, although editing your file in Overprint Preview mode is slightly slower than in regular Preview mode.

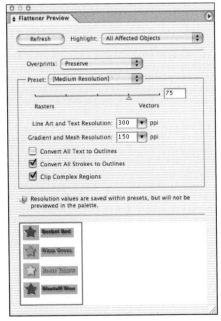

The Flattener Preview palette showing artwork highlighted in red in its preview area, after we chose All Affected Objects from the Highlight menu

You can create and save your own custom flattening presets in any of the four following ways:

- **Using the Flattener Preview palette:** Select an existing preset from the Preset menu. Make your changes to its settings in the palette (choose Show Options from the palette menu if they aren't visible), and then choose Save Transparency Flattener Preset from the palette menu. Give your new preset a name and click OK. (If the existing preset you chose isn't one of the predefined default presets, you can also choose to apply your changes as an edit to that preset by choosing Redefine Preset.)

- **Using the Object > Flatten Transparency dialog box:** Choose an existing preset from the Presets dropdown menu, adjust the settings in the box and click Save Preset to name and save your new settings.

- **Using the Edit > Transparency Flattener Presets dialog box:** Click the New button to create and name a new Preset; click the Edit button to make changes to an existing (non-default) preset.

- **Using the Advanced section of the Print dialog box:** Under the Overprint and Transparency Flattener Options heading, click the Custom button next to the Preset dropdown menu to create a custom preset. Click the Save Preset button at the bottom of the Print dialog box to name and save your new preset.

To apply flattening presets when you're ready to print or export, choose an existing preset (or create a new custom preset) in the Advanced section of the Print dialog box. (For more on flattening presets, see the *User Guide*.)

Using the Flattener Preview palette

The Flattener Preview palette lets you highlight areas of your artwork that will be affected when you flatten it, so you can see the effect of various settings and adjust them accordingly.

To begin, choose a preview mode from the palette menu: either Quick Preview (which gives you the fastest preview, but excludes the All Rasterized Regions option in the Highlight menu) or Detailed Preview (which enables All Rasterized Regions). Then choose an option from the Overprint menu: Preserve, to retain overprinting; Simulate, to imitate the appearance of printing to separations; or Discard, to prevent any Overprint Fill or Overprint Stroke settings that have been set in the Attributes palette from appearing on the composite.

Now you're ready to choose a flattening preset from the Preset menu (or create a new one), as described earlier in the "Working with flattener presets" section. When you've done that, click the Refresh button at the top of the palette, which will update the display in the palette's preview area according to the settings you've chosen. At this point, you can use the palette's Highlight menu to highlight areas that will be affected by the flattening process. You can choose from a variety of options—from All Affected Objects to specifics such as Outlined Strokes or Outlined Text. You'll see the areas in question flagged out in red in the preview. See the *User Guide* for more details about the various Highlight Options, and other aspects of using the Flattener Preview palette.

Setting Raster/Vector Balance

The Raster/Vector Balance setting, one of the flattening settings mentioned in "The Art of Flattening" earlier in this chapter, determines how much art is rasterized and how much remains vector. In case you're unfamiliar with the terms, raster art is made up of pixels, while vectors are discrete objects. These days, most programs contain aspects of both vectors and rasters, but Photoshop is primarily raster and Illustrator primarily vector.

By default, Illustrator's Raster/Vector Balance setting is 100—which results in the greatest possible amount of art remaining in vector form. At the highest setting, the file contains the most vector objects and may produce longer print times. As you move the slider to the left, toward zero, Illustrator tries to convert vectors (like pure Illustrator files) to rasters (like Photoshop files). At a setting of zero, Illustrator converts *all* art to rasters.

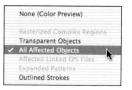

The Flattener Preview palette's Highlight menu

Not all versions of PDF support transparency, so it's important to pay attention to the version of PDF you're using. Illustrator CS, like Illustrator 10, uses PDF 1.4 as its native format and is compatible with Adobe Acrobat 5. But Illustrator CS can also save in the new PDF 1.5 format, which is compatible with Acrobat 6, and can take advantage of Acrobat 6's new PDF layers features. (See the *Illustrator Basics* chapter for more info on PDF formats and saving for Acrobat 6, including Illustrator's new PDF presets). There are also two older formats you might encounter. PDF 1.3 is compatible with Acrobat 4 and does not support transparency. PDF 1.2 is the basis for Quartz, the rendering engine of Mac OS X, which uses Apple's own extensions to implement a limited form of transparency.

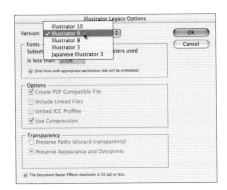

The Illustrator Legacy Options dialog box, showing the legacy versions to which you can export files (File > Export, then choose Illustrator Legacy from the Format menu and click Export)

Usually you get the best results using the all-vector setting of 100, but if this takes too long to print, try the all-raster setting of 0. In some cases, when transparent effects are very complex, this might be the best choice. Generally, the in-between settings create awful results.

Because objects are always flattened to a white background, you might see color shifts after you flatten your artwork. To preview the way your artwork would look if flattened, you can turn on Simulate Paper (Document Setup > Transparency) or Overprint Preview (in the View menu), and you can use the new Flattener Preview palette to highlight the areas that would be affected.

The last word on transparency

When working with transparency, it is extremely important to know when your files will become flattened. When you print a file, the artwork gets flattened, but your file isn't permanently affected (because the flattening only happens to a temporary *copy* of the file during the printing process). Also, know that there are two kinds of EPS files you can make from Illustrator—Adobe Illustrator 9 (AI9) and newer, and Adobe Illustrator 8 (AI8) and older—and there's a big difference. (Illustrator CS allows you to export to a variety of Illustrator Legacy formats, including AI8, AI9 and AI10.) When you export an EPS to AI9 or a newer format (or you Save as EPS in Illustrator CS), two versions of your file actually get saved in the EPS—a flattened version *and* a native unflattened version. This allows you to print the file to a PostScript device (or import it into another application such as QuarkXPress). It also allows you to reopen the file in the current version of Illustrator in unflattened form so you can make edits to the file. However, exporting as AI8 EPS (or earlier versions) only saves the flattened version of the file. This means that if you reopen the exported AI8 EPS file in a later version of Illustrator, you'll see that all your art is flattened. Reopening a flattened AI8 EPS file in Illustrator results in a loss of spot colors and layer information, and some of your objects may be broken apart or rasterized.

In addition, all text and strokes will have been converted to outlines (they become separate objects and will no longer be editable in the same way). Furthermore, if you export as AI9 or AI10, you'll lose any Illustrator CS-specific features (they'll be expanded and lose their editability). So, it's *really* important to save in Illustrator CS EPS format if you need EPS. If you have to export to an earlier Illustrator EPS format, be sure to also save a copy of your file in native Illustrator CS format. See the *User Guide* for more about exporting to Illustrator Legacy EPS formats.

APPEARANCES

Within an appearance are a collection of strokes, fills, effects, and transparency settings. An appearance can be applied to any path, object (including text), group, sublayer, or layer. The specific appearance attributes of a selection are shown in the Appearance palette. Attributes within the appearance are added to the palette in the order they are applied. Changing the order of the attributes will change the appearance. An object and its enclosing groups and layers can all have their own appearances.

To apply an appearance, make a selection or click on a target indicator (Layers palette). Then add transparency, effects, multiple fills, and/or multiple strokes (see the "Adding Fills and Strokes" section). When a group, sublayer, or layer is targeted, strokes and fills will be applied to the individual objects within the selection, but any effects or transparency settings will be applied to the *target* (see Tip "Selecting vs. targeting" in the *Layers* chapter). Drag the target indicator (in the Layers palette) from one layer to another to move an appearance or Option-drag (Mac) or Alt-drag (Win) the indicator to copy the appearance. To re-use an appearance, save it as a style in the Graphic Styles palette.

Appearance palette

When an item is selected or targeted, the Appearance palette displays all the attributes associated with the current

If you can't see an appearance

If you're trying to alter an appearance but nothing seems to be changing on the screen, make sure that:
- your objects are selected
- you're in Preview mode

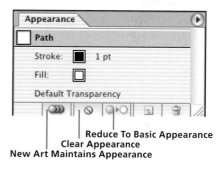

Reduce To Basic Appearance
Clear Appearance
New Art Maintains Appearance

Appearance palette indicators

The appearance indicators for Paint, Effects, and Transparency only show up in the Appearance palette on layers or groups that contain elements with these attributes.

Layers appearance icons

An object has a basic appearance as long as it does not contain multiple Fills or Strokes, transparency, effects, or brush strokes. It is indicated by an open circle in the Layers palette.

More complex appearances are indicated by a gradient-filled icon in the Layers palette.

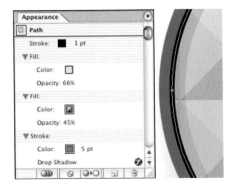

An example of multiple Strokes and Fills, including a 1 pt black stroke, a solid fill at 66% Opacity, a pattern fill at 45% Opacity, a 5 pt green stroke, and a Drop Shadow effect (see the *Live Effects & Graphic Styles* chapter for more about live effects)

Move or copy appearances

In the Layers palette, drag the Appearance icon circle from one object, group, or layer to another to *move* the appearance. To *copy* the appearance, hold Option (Mac) or Alt (Win) as you drag the icon.

Target all elements

When a group or layer is targeted, you can double-click the Contents line in the Appearance palette to target all the individual elements inside the group or layer.

—*Pierre Louveaux*

selection. If there isn't a selection, the palette will display the attributes for the next object drawn. When the current target is an object, the Appearance palette always lists at least one fill, one stroke, and the object-level transparency. When the target is a group or layer, no Fill or Stroke is shown unless one has been applied (see "Adding Fills & Strokes" following). "Default Transparency" means 100% opacity, Normal blending mode, Isolate Blending off, and Knockout Group off or neutral.

A basic appearance isn't always a white fill and a black stroke (as suggested by the icon). An appearance is defined as a *Basic Appearance* when it includes one fill and one stroke (with either set to None); the stroke is above the fill; there are no brushes or live effects; opacity is 100%; and blending mode is Normal (the defaults).

If the current selection has more than the *basic* attributes you can choose what attributes the next object will have. The first icon at the bottom of the palette is New Art Maintains Appearance (when disabled) and New Art Has Basic Appearance (when selected). For example, if your last object had a drop shadow but you don't want the next object to inherit this attribute, click on the icon and the new object will only inherit the basic attributes.

Click on the Clear Appearance icon to reduce appearance attributes to no fill, no stroke, with 100% opacity. Click on the Reduce to Basic Appearance icon to reduce the artwork's appearance to a single stroke and fill along with the default transparency. To delete an attribute, drag it to the Trash, or click it and then click the Trash. **Note:** *Keep in mind that Reduce to Basic Appearance removes all brush strokes and live effects!*

THE FINER POINTS OF APPEARANCES
Adding fills & strokes

It's not until you start adding multiple fills and strokes to an appearance that you completely understand how useful the Appearance palette is. See lessons and Galleries later in this chapter for some great examples of why you would want to use multiple strokes and/or fills.

The Appearance palette has a stacking order similar to that of the Layers palette. Items at the top of the palette are at the top of the stacking order. You can click on items in the palette list to select them, and you can rearrange them by dragging them up and down.

Select Add New Fill or Add New Stroke from the palette pop-up menu to add these attributes to an appearance. You can also add effects and transparency attributes to each fill or stroke by first clicking on the desired fill or stroke line in the palette.

There are several ways to duplicate or delete a fill, stroke, or effect. You can select the attribute in the palette list and drag it to one of the icons at the bottom of the palette. You can also select the attribute and click the appropriate icon at the bottom of the palette. Finally, you can choose the appropriate item from the pop-up menu.

Multiple fills & strokes

Create multiple line effects by adding multiple strokes to a path. Select a path, group, or layer and choose Add New Stroke from the Appearance palette pop-up menu. A new stroke is added to the Appearance. In order to see the additional stroke on the path, you must give it different attributes from the initial stroke. Target one stroke (in the Appearance palette) and adjust the color, point size, shape, and/or transparency settings. (See Teri Pettit's tutorial "Pathfinder_Strokes.ai" on the *Wow! CD* for details on how to use pathfinder effects to construct specialty strokes.)

To create multiple fills, target an object, group, or layer and choose Add New Fill. As with multiple strokes, before you can see the effect of the added fill, it needs a different appearance. To vary the results of additional fills, apply an effect or different transparency settings.

If you're having trouble seeing the results of your multiple strokes, start with a wider stroke on the bottom (see the example opposite). To vary the results, try applying dashed lines and/or different end caps. For fills, try patterns or gradients with transparency.

GORDON

For a step-by-step lesson applying multiple Strokes, Fills, and brush strokes to "outlined" type, see Steven Gordon's "Brushed Type" lesson in the Type chapter

Expandable text shapes

Want to make a text button? Type a word, then select the text object. Choose Add New Fill (in the Appearance palette menu) and drag this new fill below the Characters line. Click on the Fill line, apply the desired fill color, and then choose a shape from the Effect > Convert to Shape submenu. Set the Relative Extra Width and Extra Height to how far you want the button to extend around the text, and click OK. Each time you edit the text, the button will automatically resize itself.

Transparency 101

Assigning Opacity to Default Brushes

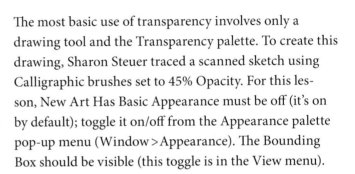

STEUER

Overview: *Prepare an image for tracing in Illustrator; set Paintbrush preferences; set up the Brush and the level of Transparency; draw, using Layers to save your work in stages.*

1

A scanned sketch, saved as a grayscale TIFF file

The TIFF in Layer 1; converting Layer 1 to a template layer

2

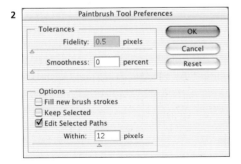

Set the Paintbrush Tool Preferences to prevent new brush strokes from filling and to prevent redraw of marks already made

The most basic use of transparency involves only a drawing tool and the Transparency palette. To create this drawing, Sharon Steuer traced a scanned sketch using Calligraphic brushes set to 45% Opacity. For this lesson, New Art Has Basic Appearance must be off (it's on by default); toggle it on/off from the Appearance palette pop-up menu (Window > Appearance). The Bounding Box should be visible (this toggle is in the View menu).

1 Preparing an image for tracing in Illustrator. Scan a photograph or drawing you want to trace. Save the image in TIFF format. Open it in Illustrator (File > Open). Your scanned image will be contained within Layer 1. In order to be able to draw in great detail without having to resize your brushes, enlarge the image. Click on it with the Selection tool, then Shift-drag a corner to enlarge (Shift-Option-drag/Shift-Alt-drag to enlarge from the image's center). To convert Layer 1 to a template layer in order to prevent your template image from exporting or printing, double-click on Layer 1 in the Layers palette, select the Template option, type in a dimming factor other than the default 50% (if desired), and click OK. (For more about templates and layers, see the *Layers* chapter.)

2 Setting Paintbrush preferences. You'll need to set the Paintbrush Tool Preferences so you can freely make overlapping marks. Double-click on the Paintbrush tool, then uncheck the Options "Fill new brush strokes" (so your marks will be stroked and not filled) and "Keep Selected" (so new marks won't redraw the last drawn mark). With the "Keep Selected" option disabled, you can still redraw a mark by selecting it first with a selection tool, then drawing a corrected mark within the distance specified in the Within field of the Paintbrush Tool Preferences dialog box. To create accurate marks, Steuer set the Fidelity to .5 pixels and the Smoothness to 0%. If you want Illustrator to smooth your marks, experiment with higher settings.

3 Setting up the Brush and the level of Transparency.
Create a new layer by clicking the New Layer icon in the Layers palette. With the Paintbrush tool selected, open the Brushes palette. The first six default brushes are Calligraphic brushes. Click on one to choose it. Using the Color palette, choose a Stroke color. Next, in the Transparency palette, move the Opacity slider to approximately 50%. To change the opacity of future brush strokes at any point, move the Opacity slider to a new setting.

4 Drawing, and using Layers to save your work in stages. Start drawing. Notice that the opacity you chose will apply after you complete each stroke. Feel free to switch to any of the other Calligraphic brushes; Illustrator will maintain your transparency and color settings. Once you have a group of marks you're satisfied with, make a new layer and begin working into it. Working this way will allow you to easily return to the last stage you were pleased with. Hide and show any layer by clicking on the icon in the leftmost column next to the layer name in the Layers palette. Delete any layer by dragging its name to the Trash icon at the bottom of the palette.

Although your drawing should look as though it were painted with ink washes, real ink was never this flexible or editable. See the next lesson for a more advanced variation of this technique involving Custom brushes, changes in Transparency, and Layers. For more about working with brushes, see the *Brushes & Symbols* chapter.

3

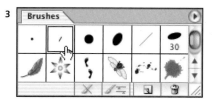

Open the Brushes palette (Window menu) and choose a Calligraphic Brush

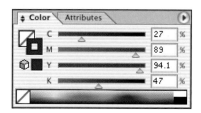

Open the Color palette (Window menu), then set the Fill to None and choose a Stroke color

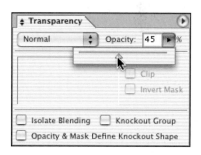

Open the Transparency palette (Window menu), then preset the opacity of future brush strokes by adjusting the Opacity slider

4

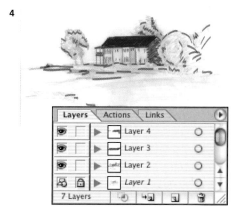

Use the Layers palette to organize groups of brush strokes and save stages of the illustration; you can hide or show layers by clicking on the visibility icon in the left column

Transparent Color
Customizing Transparent Brushes & Layers

Advanced Technique

Overview: *Create custom Calligraphic brushes, setting Paintbrush Tool Preferences and Opacity; create sublayers for categories of objects and for grouping of similar marks; use layers to separate different types of marks and to easily choose brush styles; experiment with blending modes; add finishing touches and a Clipping Mask to crop the image.*

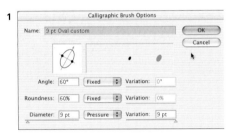

1

Customize the settings for each new Calligraphic brush using the Brush Options window

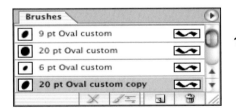

Four custom Calligraphic brushes in List view (from the Brushes palette pop-up)

Preset the opacity for future objects by moving the Opacity slider in the Transparency palette to the desired percentage

Illustrator's Calligraphic brushes are among Sharon Steuer's favorite digital tools. For the painting above, she customized Calligraphic brushes, varying the Opacity and colors to achieve a watercolor-like look. For this lesson, the New Art Has Basic Appearance feature must be off (it's on by default); toggle it on/off in the Appearance palette pop-up menu (Window > Appearance).

1 Create custom Calligraphic brushes and set the Paintbrush Tool Preferences and Opacity. You'll first customize a few brushes so you can better control the size of the marks you make. If you have a pressure-sensitive tablet, you can customize brushes so they respond to your touch. To make the first brush, start a new file, then open the Brushes palette (Window > Brushes), click the New Brush icon at the bottom of the palette, select New Calligraphic Brush, and click OK. In the Calligraphic Brush Options window, experiment with various settings, then click OK and make a stroke to test the brush. To try other settings, double-click the desired brush in the Brushes palette. For her first custom brush, Steuer chose a Pressure setting for Diameter (9 pt with a 9 pt Variation), set the Angle to 60° and the Roundness to 60% with both Fixed, and clicked OK. For greater stroke variation, try choosing a Pressure or Random setting for each option (pressure settings are unavailable or don't work unless you have a graphics tablet installed). To create each of the brush variations, drag the first custom brush over the New Brush icon and adjust the settings.

Once you have created your initial brushes, set the Paintbrush Tool Preferences so you can freely create overlapping marks: Double-click the Paintbrush tool, and uncheck the "Fill new brush strokes" and "Keep Selected" options. (For more on Paintbrush Tool Preferences, see step 2 of the previous lesson.) In order to draw with the maximum amount of detail, Steuer also set the Fidelity to .5 pixels and the Smoothness to 0%.

To paint in transparent color, after you've chosen a Calligraphic brush and a color, open the Transparency palette (Window > Transparency). To set Transparency, click and hold the triangle to the right of the Opacity field to reveal the Opacity slider, which you can adjust.

2 Creating sublayers for categories of objects, then sublayers for each grouping of similar marks. Create sublayers for the major categories of objects within your composition. Whenever you intend to draw a group of marks within a broader grouping (such as Steuer's thicker stalks within the vase), create a sublayer for those (use the New Layer or New Sublayer icons at the bottom of the Layers palette). It's helpful to create nested sublayers because, although you can expand any layer to view the <Path> for each separate object, expanding a layer that contains many objects can slow Illustrator down. It's also helpful to name the layers that contain sublayers so you can identify which layers you can easily expand or collapse. Although she didn't name all of her layers, Steuer named the sublayers that contained further sublayers (flowers and vase). To rename a layer, double-click

2

The New Sublayer and New Layer icons found at the bottom of the Layers palette

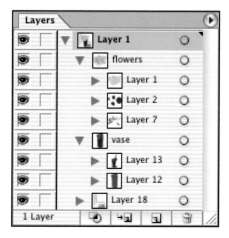

An early stage of the image showing organizational sublayers nested within a master layer (top Layer 1). Steuer custom-named sublayers that contained additional sublayers so she could identify which ones she could easily expand without slowing down Illustrator

3

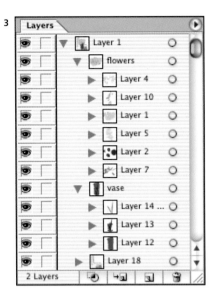

Steuer used Illustrator's built-in layer location and style duplicating features to easily create new sublayers in the desired locations and with the desired styling

4

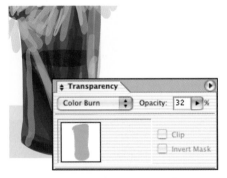

Above, Steuer chose the Screen blending mode with Opacity set to 55% to achieve a brightening effect on the stem objects. Below, she chose the Color Burn blending mode with Opacity set to 32% on a duplicate copy of the vase shape layer to achieve a glassy effect

the layer in the Layers palette. By holding down Option for Mac or Alt for Windows as you click the New Layer or New Sublayer icon, you can name a new layer as you create it. Drag layers to the trash if you no longer need their contents. Steuer created and trashed many sublayers as she worked, which resulted in some out-of-sequence sublayer names.

3 **Using the layers to separate different types of marks and to easily choose the right brush style.** One of the wonderful aspects of working with Illustrator is that your last selected object determines the styling and "stacking order" for the next object you draw. For instance, say you select a petal, then deselect it by clicking outside of the image itself (or ⌘-Shift-A for Mac /Ctrl-Shift-A for Win), the next mark you make will match the styling of the last selected object and will be placed at the top of the same layer. If you want the new object to be placed directly above an existing one, click on the existing one in the Layers palette before drawing the new one. If objects on top obstruct your ability to click on the object you want to select, then first select the problem objects and lock them with Object >Lock >Selection (⌘-2 /Ctrl-2). Or expand the layer to find the object in the Layers palette and then select it by clicking to the right of the targeting circle for that <Path>.

4 **Experimenting with changing the blending modes of your marks.** In addition to setting the Opacity, you can also adjust the blending mode for selected objects by choosing from the pop-up menu in the upper left corner of the Transparency palette. For example, after creating a batch of stems on one layer within the vase, Steuer wanted to make them appear brighter, so she changed the mode from Normal to Screen. To adjust the blending mode for all objects within a layer or sublayer, click to the right of that layer's targeting circle (on the far right side of the layer name) to select all the objects within that layer, and then experiment with different blending modes. To

enhance the effect, you can duplicate the sublayer (by dragging the sublayer to the New Layer icon). If this makes the effect too strong, you can reduce the opacity of the upper sublayer. To enhance the glass vase, Steuer duplicated the sublayer containing the vase shape (by dragging the sublayer to the New Layer icon), and moved the duplicate on top of the other vase objects by dragging its name up in the Layers palette. In the Transparency palette, she chose the Color Burn blending mode for the duplicate vase sublayer, and reduced the Opacity to 32%. Be aware that custom blending modes are retained from the last selected object in the same way as the brush style, color, and opacity are retained. You can manually reset your blending mode to Normal, or any other mode, before or after you create the next object.

5 Finishing touches, and perhaps a Clipping Mask to crop the image. For finishing touches, you can work into your layers, adding details. Steuer continued to add sublayers above and below others to add the final details to her still life, and to add a signature.

To neatly trim your illustration, create a Clipping Mask that crops out everything outside the mask. To apply a Clipping Mask across multiple layers, all your objects and sublayers must be contained within one layer (which we'll call the master layer) and the topmost path within your master layer will become your mask. If you haven't been working within a single layer, you'll need to create a master layer. To do this, first select all the layers you want masked by ⌘-clicking each layer for Mac /Ctrl-clicking for Win (you can Shift-click to select contiguous layers) and choose Collect in New Layer from the palette pop-up menu. This converts your layers into sublayers within a new master layer. To make a topmost masking object, first click on the master layer's name to highlight it, then use the Pen tool or Rectangle tool to create a path that will define your mask. With your master layer still highlighted, click the Make Clipping Mask icon at the bottom of the Layers palette.

5

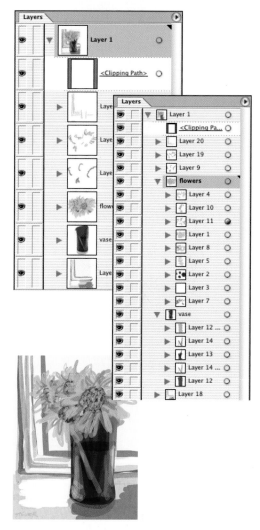

Before and after the finishing touches and cropping, and the final Layers palette shown collapsed (left, with enlarged icons) and expanded (right)

Chapter 8 *Transparency & Appearances*   **271**

Basic Transparency

Blending Modes, Opacity & Isolate Blending

Overview: *Arrange elements; selectively apply blending modes to objects using Layers, Appearance and Transparency palettes; modify layer opacity; assign a blending mode to objects; group objects and isolate blending.*

1

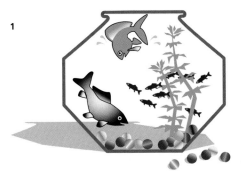

Elements of the final illustration before transparency effects

2

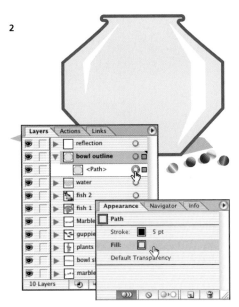

Use the Layers palette to target a path, and the Appearance palette to select the Fill attribute

Once you have mastered selecting and targeting in Illustrator, you can create cool effects using basic transparency. In this illustration, Diane Hinze Kanzler incorporated three aspects of the Transparency palette: opacity, blending modes, and Isolate Blending.

1 Arrange elements of the final illustration on layers.
The logical placement of groups and objects in layers will be helpful as you apply transparency effects to an illustration. In this illustration, for example, all parts of one fish are on one layer, the marbles in the bowl are on a separate layer from the marbles outside of the bowl, etc. (see the *Layers* chapter for help with organizing layers).

2 Selectively apply a blending mode to an object.
Kanzler wanted the gray fill of her bowl to have a slight deepening color effect on the objects in the layers below. First, she selected the bowl and gave it a fill of light gray and a stroke of dark gray. Next, she targeted the bowl path in the Layers palette. In order to correctly apply a blending mode to the fill of the bowl, Kanzler selected Fill in the Appearance palette by clicking once on the Fill attribute. She chose Multiply from the list of blending modes in the Transparency palette. The light gray fill of the bowl has a blending mode applied to it, but the dark gray stroke of the bowl remains opaque, as intended.

To apply a blending mode to one of the paths in the water layer, Kanzler used the same targeting method. First, she targeted the larger water path (not the splash drops) and selected Fill in the Appearance palette. Then Kanzler chose Multiply as a blending mode in the Transparency palette.

3 Using the Opacity slider. For the reflection effect on the bowl, Kanzler simply reduced the opacity of the white objects. She targeted the "reflection" layer, and in the Transparency palette used the Opacity slider to reduce the opacity of the reflection objects to the desired amount. In this instance, the Appearance palette wasn't even used, as the effect was applied to the entire layer.

4 Isolate the blending. In order to prevent a blending mode from affecting objects beneath a certain point, the blending effect must be *isolated*. With Kanzler's illustration, she wanted the aquatic leaves and stems to be transparent with each other as they overlap, and those plants to show the fish behind them. But she also wanted to prevent the plants from interacting with the bowl shadow which is beneath the plants on a lower layer.

So that the individual paths in the plant group would interact with each other and with the fish, she first *selected* the plant paths by Option (Mac)/Alt (Win)-clicking on the plant <Group>. Then Kanzler chose the Hard Light blending mode in the Transparency palette. If she had *targeted* the plant layer instead, the blending mode would have applied to the plant group as a *whole,* and the overlapping leaves would not blend with each other. To prevent the bowl shadow from showing through the plants, Kanzler selected the plant group and rearmost fishes group and chose Object > Group, which placed all into one new group. She *targeted* that group in the Layers palette, and then selected the Isolate Blending checkbox in the Transparency palette, which maintained the blending mode within the group, but prevented the group from being transparent to layers below.

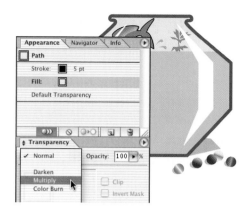

Docking the Transparency palette under the Appearance palette to keep both conveniently available

3

The Opacity slider in the Transparency palette was used to reduce opacity of the reflection highlight shapes

4

Apply a blending mode to multiple objects individually by selecting rather than targeting before applying the blending mode

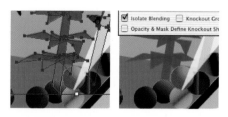

Use the Layers palette to target a group of objects that have been assigned a blending mode, then enable Isolate Blending (in the Transparency palette) to prevent that blending mode from affecting objects outside the group

Basic Highlights

Making Highlights with Transparent Blends

Overview: *Create your basic objects and a light-colored highlight shape; use blends to make the highlights; scale the highlights to fit.*

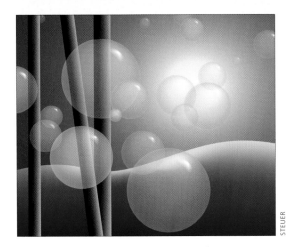

The original objects (locked in the layers palette) shown with the basic highlight shape

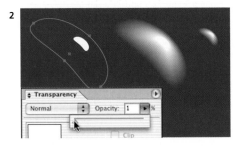

The highlight objects before blending (the outer object is set to 0% Opaque in the Transparency palette); after blending in 22 steps; the blend shown at actual size

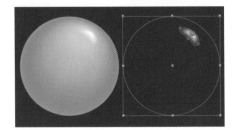

The final blend in place and shown in a "registration" circle for easy scaling on other bubbles

Using transparency, highlights are now as simple as creating a blend in the correct highlight shape. For help creating smooth contoured blends, see "Unlocking Realism" in the *Blends, Gradients & Mesh* chapter.

1 Creating your basic objects and determining your basic highlight shape and color. Artist Sharon Steuer created this "Bubbles" image using overlaying transparent radial gradients (to see how she created the hill, see "Rolling Mesh" in the *Blends, Gradients & Mesh* chapter). She modified an oval with the Direct-selection tool to create her basic highlight shape. After creating your main objects, make a light-colored highlight object on top. Use the Layers palette to lock everything except the highlighted object (see the *Layers* chapter for help).

2 Creating the highlight. Select the highlight shape and Copy, choose Edit > Paste in Back, then Object > Lock. Now, select and shrink the front copy (for scaling help see the *Zen* chapter). Choose Object > Unlock All, then set the Opacity of this selected outer object to 0% in the Transparency palette. Select both objects, then with the Blend tool, click on one anchor point of the outer object, then Option/Alt-click on the corresponding anchor point of the inner object and specify the number of blend steps (Steuer chose 22 steps). Steuer scaled copies of her highlight blend (with a "registration circle") for each bubble.

Nancy Stahl

Nancy Stahl created a soft, airbrushed look throughout her illustration for *The Illustrator 9 Wow! Book* cover by using opaque-to-transparent blends, as described in the "Basic Highlights" lesson opposite. Shown bottom left are the steps Stahl used in creating the hat band: the first two figures in the first diagram show her custom Pattern Brush and that brush applied to a path (see the *Brushes & Symbols* chapter for help with brushes), third down shows the opaque-to-transparent blends on top of the brushed path, next are the brush and blends masked, at bottom is that masked group on the hat colors, with the brushed path set to a Multiply mode with a 65% Opacity (Transparency palette). At bottom right is the gondolier with and without the opaque-to-transparent blends.

LARSEN

Tiffany Larsen

In this Illustration about Mardi Gras nightlife, artist Tiffany Larsen combined a posterized look with layers of subtle transparency to create depth and atmosphere. Larsen typically uses two colors in her illustrations. The primary color, of multiple shades, creates texture. The secondary color (red) is used as a highlight, and is limited to one or two shades and simple blocks of color. Here, Larsen also introduced a third color (turquoise) within the transparent smoke swirls. She applied varying opacities of 10%-30% using the opacity slider in the Transparency palette, all with the Blending mode set to Normal. The complex layering of transparent smoke over the solid blocks of color heightens the energy of the composition.

FISHAUF

Louis Fishauf

Louis Fishauf created the holiday glow that radiates from his mischievous Santa by using Illustrator's Gaussian Blur effect, the Transparency palette, and one of a set of custom art brushes. Fishauf created the background by drawing a large circle with a purple radial gradient and applied a 25 pixel radius Gaussian Blur. He selected the Star tool and drew a shape. He then selected Blur > Gaussian from the Effect menu, setting the Opacity to 25%. To create the illusion that the orbiting streak fades into the distance behind Santa, and to add a sense of depth to the entire image, Fishauf applied an art brush he created with short tapered ends to a 0.36 pt white stroke. He then integrated the streak into the image by giving it an opacity of 34% with the Lighten mode. As

for St. Nick, Fishauf constructed the globe-like body, legs, arms, head, and hat from gradient-filled objects. He then made copies of these and pasted them behind the original set of objects, applying to each a white Fill and white Stroke ranging from 5 points to 7.26 points. A Gaussian Blur was applied to these objects, along with a uniform opacity of 68%. The gift box, computer, and Christmas tree each received individual glows. Fishauf added even more visual interest by adding a Drop Shadow to Santa's face and beard. Santa's list was created from a set of white Strokes, behind which Fishauf pasted a white-filled shape with an Opacity set to 50%, and a second copy of the shape with a gradient fill set to Lighten mode for a subtle modeled effect.

Basic Appearances

Making and Applying Appearances

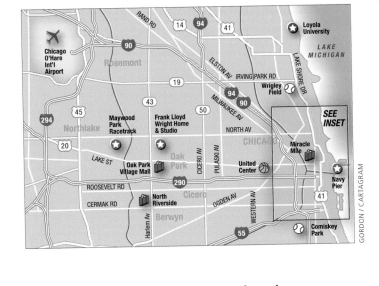

GORDON / CARTAGRAM

Overview: *Create appearance attributes for an object; build a three-stroke appearance, save it as a style, and then draw paths and apply the style; target a layer with a drop shadow effect, create symbols on the layer, then edit layer appearance if needed.*

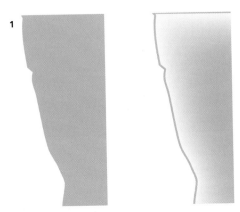

1

On the left, the lake with blue fill and stroke; on the right, the lake with the Inner Glow added to the appearance attribute set

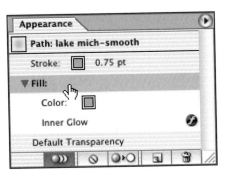

Appearance palette displaying the finished set of attributes (Gordon used the Appearance palette so that he could create a single path for the lake that contained a fill and the coastline stroke above it)

Complexity and simplicity come together when you use Illustrator's Appearance palette to design intricate effects, develop reusable styles and simplify production workflow. In this location map of Chicago, Illinois, cartographer Steven Gordon relied on the Appearance palette to easily build appearances and apply them to objects, groups and layers.

1 Building an appearance for a single object. Gordon developed a set of appearance attributes that applied a coastline, vignette and blue fill to a path symbolizing Lake Michigan. To begin building appearance attributes, open the Appearance palette and other palettes you might need (Color, Swatches, Stroke, and Transparency, for example). Gordon began by drawing the outline of the lake with the Pen tool and giving the path a 0.75 pt dark blue stroke. In the Appearance palette, he clicked on the Fill attribute and chose the same dark blue he had used for the stroke. To give the lake a light-colored vignette, he applied an inner glow to the Fill attribute (Effect > Stylize > Inner Glow). In the Inner Glow dialog box, Gordon set Mode to Normal, Opacity to 100%, Blur to 0.25 inches (for the width of the vignette edge), and enabled the Edge option. He clicked the dialog box's color swatch and chose white for the glow color.

2 Creating a style. Until Illustrator 9, you created a "patterned" line like an interstate highway symbol by overlapping copies of a path, each copy with a different stroke width. Now you can use the Appearance palette to craft a multi-stroked line that you apply to a single path. First, deselect any objects that may still be selected and reset the Appearance palette by clicking the Clear Appearance icon at the bottom of the palette (this eliminates any attributes from the last selected style or object). Next, click the Stroke attribute (it will have the None color icon) and click the Duplicate Selected Item icon twice to make two copies. Now, to make Gordon's interstate symbol, select the top Stroke attribute and give it a dark color and a 0.5 pt width. Select the middle attribute and choose a light color and a 2 pt width. For the bottom attribute, choose a dark color and a 3 pt width. Because you'll use this set of appearance attributes later, save it as a style by dragging the Object icon at the top of the palette to the Styles palette. (Double-click the new style's default name in the palette and rename it in the dialog box if you want.)

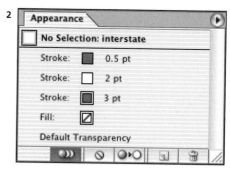

Appearance palette for Gordon's interstate highway symbol

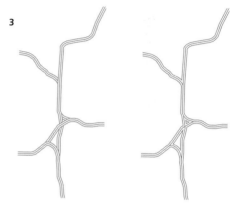

3 Assigning a style to a group. Draw the paths you want to paint with the new style you created above. Then choose Select All and Group. To get the three levels of strokes to merge when paths on the map cross one another, click on Group in the Appearance palette and then apply the interstate style you just saved.

On the left, the interstates with the Style applied to the individual paths; on the right, the interstate paths were grouped before the Style was applied

4 Assigning appearance attributes to an entire layer. By targeting a layer, you can create a uniform look for all the objects you draw or place on that layer. Create a layer for the symbols and click the layer's target icon in the Layers palette. Then select Effect > Stylize > Drop Shadow. Each symbol you draw or paste on that layer will be automatically painted with the drop shadow. Later, you can modify the drop shadows by clicking the layer's targeting icon and then double-clicking the Drop Shadow attribute in the Appearance palette and changing values in the pop-up Drop Shadow dialog box.

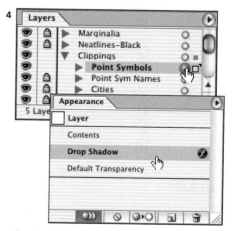

Top, targeting the layer in the Layers palette; bottom, the Appearance palette showing the Drop Shadow attribute (double-click the attribute to edit Drop Shadow values)

Floating Type

Type Objects with Transparency & Effects

Overview: *Create an area type object, key in text; add a new fill attribute in the Appearance palette; convert the fill to a shape; change transparency and add an Effect.*

Using the Convert to Shape effect, you can create an area type object with transparency and effects that will save you from making and manipulating two objects (a type object and a rectangle with transparency and effects below it). For a virtual guide to Bryce Canyon National Park, Steven Gordon created a transparent area type object with a hard-edged drop shadow that provided information for each of the Park's most popular hiking trails.

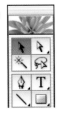

Left, the Selection tool selected; right, the Type tool selected

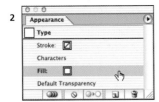

The type object after clicking with the Selection tool (the background photograph has been hidden in this view)

1 Making the area type object. Start by selecting the Type tool, dragging it to create an area type object, and then keying in your text. When you have finished typing, click on the Selection tool (the solid arrow icon) in the toolbox. This deselects the text characters while selecting the type object, preparing the object (rather than the characters) for editing in the next step.

2 Creating a new fill and converting to a shape. Open the Appearance palette and select Add New Fill from the palette menu. Drag the new Fill attribute below Characters in the palette. The Fill attribute will be automatically deselected when you move it in the palette so you'll need to click on it again to select it. Next, apply a light color to it (Gordon chose white from the Swatches palette). Now choose Effect > Convert to Shape > Rectangle. In the Shape Options dialog box, control the size of the rectangle around your type object by modifying the two Relative options (Extra Width and Extra Height). To make the

The Appearance palette after selecting the fill attribute and applying white to it

shape wrap more tightly around his area type object, Gordon keyed in 0 inches for the Extra Width and Extra Height options.

The Shape Options dialog box with the Relative options edited

3 Adjusting transparency and adding a drop shadow effect. Gordon designed each trail information box to incorporate transparency and a drop shadow, so its text would float above, but not obscure, the background photograph. To adjust the transparency of the shape you converted in the previous step, first ensure that the type object's Fill or Rectangle attribute is selected in the Appearance palette. (If either attribute is not selected, then the transparency changes you're about to make will also affect the text characters.) Open the Transparency palette and adjust the transparency slider or key in a value (Gordon chose 65% for transparency).

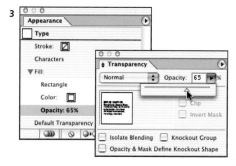

Left, the Appearance palette with the transparency attribute selected; right, the Transparency palette

Instead of creating a soft drop shadow, Gordon opted to make a hard-edged shadow. To create this shadow, make sure the Fill attribute is still selected in the Appearance palette. Choose Effect > Stylize > Drop Shadow and in the Drop Shadow dialog box set Color to black, Blur to 0, and then adjust the X Offset and Y Offset sliders so the shadow is positioned as far down and to the right as you wish.

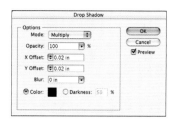

The Drop Shadow dialog box

4 Editing the area type object. As you continue working, you may decide to resize the type object you originally created when you dragged with the Type tool. (This is different than editing the Shape Options dialog values to change the size of the transparent rectangle around the type object, as you did previously). To resize the object, click on the Direct Selection tool and then click on the edge of the type object you want to drag in or out. Because the transparent drop shadow shape was formed using the Convert to Shape effect, it is "live" and will automatically resize as you resize the type object.

Similarly, if you edit the text by adding or deleting words, the type object will resize, causing your transparent drop shadow shape to resize automatically.

The Direct Selection cursor when it nears the edge of an area type object

Getting an edge

It can be hard to click the edge of a type object that has a drop shadow. To easily find the edge, choose View > Outline. Now the selectable edge will display as a black line.

Tinting a Scan

Using Transparency Effects & Simplify Path

Advanced Technique

Overview: *Place an EPS image and its clipping path; tint the image using the clipping path, blending modes and Opacity; reduce a path's anchor points using Simplify; use Isolate Blending to prevent double shadows.*

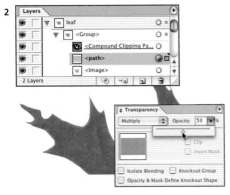

The grayscale leaf scan; the outline selection converted to a path in Photoshop and designated as a clipping path (the small hole in the leaf has been included in the path, making it a compound clipping path in Illustrator)

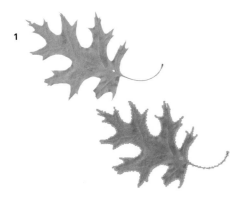

Drawing the russet-colored rectangle into the compound clipping path group; targeting the rectangle path and specifying a Multiply blending mode and opacity of 50%

Diane Hinze Kanzler enhanced her original salamander illustration using transparency effects and Simplify to make her image more unique and naturalistic.

1 Scanning and placing an image and its clipping path. If you don't have access to Photoshop, place a grayscale image with a simple outline shape and manually create your own clipping path (see the *Advanced Techniques* chapter for help). To add a bit of nature to her illustration, Kanzler scanned a real oak leaf in grayscale mode in Photoshop. To create a clipping path for the leaf, she used Photoshop's Magic Wand tool to select everything except the leaf (using the Shift key to add the hole to her selection) then chose Select > Inverse. To convert the leaf selection into a clipping path, Kanzler chose from the Path pop-up menu (in order): Make Work Path (with .5 Tolerance), Save Path, and Clipping Path (with a 4 Flatness). To preserve the clipping path, she used Save As and chose Photoshop EPS format, then in Illustrator she chose File > Place to place the EPS leaf, disabling the Link option to embed the scan and its clipping path.

2 Tinting the scan. Kanzler used the leaf's clipping path to tint her scan. First, in the Layers palette she located the scan's <Group>, expanded it and clicked the scan <Image>. She then drew a russet-colored rectangle above the scan (bigger than the leaf). She targeted this rectangle in the Layers palette, then set a Multiply blending mode with 50% Opacity in the Transparency palette.

3 Adding a shadow. To create a shadow, Kanzler began by copying her clipping path. She then clicked the New Layer icon, and moved this new layer below the leaf's layer. After moving your new layer below your image, paste your copied outline in proper registration by first turning off Paste Remembers Layers (from the Layers palette pop-up menu), then choose Edit > Paste in Front (⌘-F /Ctrl-F). Kanzler then chose a new fill color for the outline and used Arrow keys to offset its position.

4 Creating a simpler shadow. In order to minimize the overall size of her file, Kanzler wanted to create a simplified shadow for her salamander. In the Layers palette, she selected the salamander outline path by clicking to the right of the target circle. She then made a copy of the selected outline to a layer below by dragging the colored square to the layer below while holding Option /Alt. After choosing a color for the shadow, Kanzler simplified the shape by choosing Object > Path > Simplify, and set the Curve Precision to 82%, thus reducing the path from 655 to 121 path points, while still maintaining the shape's overall look. She then offset the salamander's shadow.

Kanzler selected all the objects in the leaf file, copied, and switched to her salamander illustration. Then with Paste Remembers Layers still on, she pasted. Using the Layers palette, she moved the leaf layers below the salamander layers, and targeted her salamander shadow object. In the Transparency palette, she set a Multiply blending mode for the shadow.

To prevent a "double shadow" effect where shadows overlapped, Kanzler used Isolate Blending. She selected and grouped (Object > Group or ⌘-G /Ctrl-G) the salamander shadow with the leaf group—but *not* the leaf shadow. She *targeted* this *new* group, then clicked Isolate Blending in the Transparency palette.

3

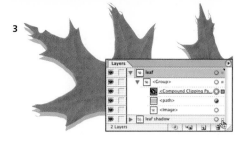

Using a copy of the leaf's clipping path to create an offset shadow on a layer below the leaf scan

4

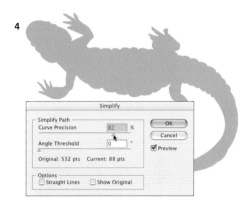

Simplifying the salamander's shadow object path (left: before; right: after Simplify)

Assigning a blending mode to the salamander's shadow in the final, combined illustration

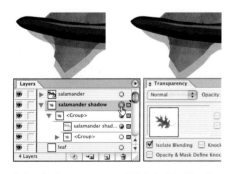

Using the Transparency palette's Isolate Blending feature to prevent an overlapping shadow effect

It's a Knockout!

See-through Objects with a Knockout Group

Advanced Technique

Overview: *Arrange elements in layers; apply a gradient fill and solid stroke to text; modify opacity and use a blending mode; create a Knockout Group; adjust transparency effects.*

1

All elements of the final illustration, before applying blending modes and Knockout Group

A copy of the gradient-filled "Organic" is pasted behind and given a 6 pt stroke of dark blue and a fill of None

2

Detail of the rainbow <Group> after reducing opacity in the Transparency palette

For this sign, Diane Hinze Kanzler used Illustrator's Knockout Group feature to allow wood grain to show through text while blocking out other elements.

You may already be familiar with the concept of knockout from darkroom or film prepress work. A knockout film is typically used to "punch a hole" in an illustration or photograph, thus revealing images, text, or even the paper color below.

The Knockout Group feature in Illustrator (found in the Transparency palette) works according to the same principle as prepress knockout film, yet it is much more powerful because it also allows transparency effects to be applied with the knockout. The real trick to controlled use of the Knockout Group feature is the proper use of the Layers palette to correctly select or target objects.

1 Arrange elements of the final illustration on layers, convert text to outlines, and apply a gradient fill. It is important, particularly when you're planning to use a Knockout Group, that all of your illustration's elements be placed on layers in a logical fashion (see "Organizing Layers" in the *Layers* chapter) and grouped (Object > Group or ⌘-G/Ctrl-G) when appropriate. This will make selecting or targeting groups much easier.

Create some text using a font bold enough to fill with a gradient, and convert the text to outlines using Type > Create Outlines (converted text is automatically grouped). Next, select the group and click on a Gradient-fill swatch to apply the fill to each letter of the text.

To add a stroke to her text without distorting it, Kanzler selected "Organic," copied it, deselected the text, created a new layer below the filled text layer and chose Edit > Paste in Back with the Paste Remembers Layers toggle off (see the Layers palette pop-up). She gave that copy a fill of None and a thick stroke of dark blue.

With a blending mode applied to the gradient-filled "Organic," all lower layers show through, and can be affected by the blending mode (also shown enlarged)

2 Apply transparency effects to chosen objects.

Kanzler wanted her rainbow to be transparent, so she targeted the layer of her rainbow group and set the Opacity slider to 75% in the Transparency palette. She also wanted the wood grain of the background to show through "Organic" while still being affected by the gradient fill. In order to do this Kanzler targeted the gradient-filled text group in the Layers palette, then chose a blending mode of Hard Light in the Transparency palette. At this point, all the objects below the gradient-filled "Organic" showed through, including the thick strokes from the copy of "Organic."

3
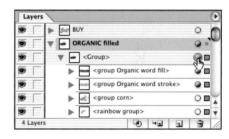

Option-Shift-click /Alt-Shift-click on layers to select objects within multiple layers. Object > Group will move all selected objects into a new <Group> on the topmost selected layer.

3 Grouping objects and creating a Knockout Group.

Kanzler controlled which objects showed through the topmost "Organic" with the Knockout Group feature. First, she Option-Shift-clicked (Alt-Shift-click for Win) each of the layers containing objects she wanted to select, including the layers containing the filled "Organic" text, the stroked "Organic" text, the corn, and the rainbow, and Grouped (Object > Group, or ⌘-G/Ctrl-G). Next, she targeted the group (in its new position in the Layers palette), and clicked on the Knockout Group box in the Transparency palette until a ✓ appeared (you may have to click more than once to get the ✓). With a Knockout Group applied, each object knocks out all the objects below it within the group. In this case all objects within Kanzler's group were knocked out by the shape of her topmost object. This allowed the wood grain (which was not part of the Knockout Group) to show through and be affected by the blending mode of the filled "Organic" text.

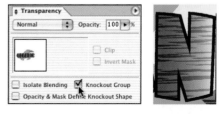

Target the new group, now composed of all objects to be included in the Knockout Group

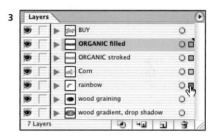

Knockout Group applied to targeted group; the topmost object's shape "punches a hole" through the rest of the objects in the group and reveal lower objects not included in the group

Opacity Masks 101

Applying Glows and Using Opacity Masks

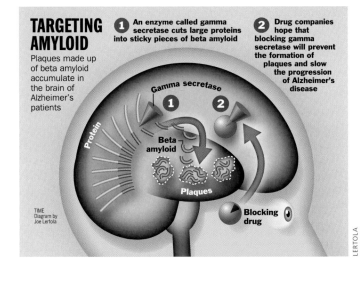

Advanced Technique

Overview: *Scan sketched artwork, place it as a template, and draw objects; apply Inner Glow; blend one object into another using an Opacity Mask.*

1

Pencil sketch layout of the illustration

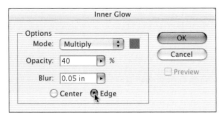

2

Top, head before and after applying Inner Glow; bottom, the Inner Glow dialog box

Blending complex shapes and achieving contoured glows and shadows can be daunting tasks—unless you know how to use Illustrator's Transparency palette and Effect menu. Joe Lertola makes the most of glows and opacity masks in this *TIME* magazine illustration, enjoying the convenience of applying raster effects in Illustrator.

1 Sketching and scanning, then drawing. Draw the objects to which you want to add a glow. Lertola placed a scan of a rough pencil layout in Illustrator as a tracing template (File > Place, and check the Template box) and drew the brain, lobes, arrows, and other elements.

2 Creating Inner Glows. Heighten the visual drama of the objects you've drawn by applying glows, shadows, and other effects from the Effect menu. For example, Lertola selected the outline of the head and choose Effect > Stylize > Inner Glow. In the pop-up dialog box, he selected Multiply for Mode, entered 40% for Opacity, and set the Blur. Next, he clicked the color icon to bring up the Color Picker dialog box and chose a dark color. To start the Inner Glow color at the edge so it fades inward to the object's center, Lertola selected Edge. (To create the glow with a color chosen in the Color Picker dialog box at the center of an object—and fading outward to the edges—

you would select Center.)

Similarly, you can add a drop shadow to a selected path by choosing Drop Shadow from the Effect > Stylize menu and specifying Opacity, Offset, and Blur in the Drop Shadow dialog box.

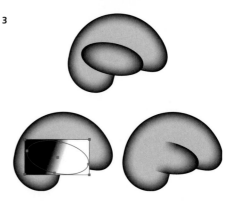

3 Applying an opacity mask. Making an object appear to blend into another object may seem difficult. Using an opacity mask, you can perform this trick easily. First, make sure the object that will be blended into another is in front (in Lertola's illustration, the lobe was moved in front of the brain by dragging it in the Layers palette).

To make an opacity mask, draw a rectangle (or other shape) in front of the object you want to fade. Fill with a black-to-white gradient, placing the black where you want to fully hide the top object and the white where you want that object fully revealed. (See the *Blends, Gradients & Mesh* chapter for more about gradients.) Next, select both the rectangle and the object to be masked (Shift-click the outlines of both objects to select them). Make sure the Transparency palette is open (display the palette by selecting Window > Transparency), and choose Make Opacity Mask from the palette's pop-up menu.

Once you've made the opacity mask, the object and its mask are linked together (moving the object will move the mask with it). To edit the object's path, click on the artwork thumbnail in the Transparency palette and use any of the path editing tools; to edit the mask, click on the mask thumbnail. Edit the gradient using the Gradient palette or the Gradient tool.

Top, brain with overlying lobe; bottom left, lobe and opacity masking object (black-to-white gradient fill) selected; bottom right, lobe following Make Opacity Mask

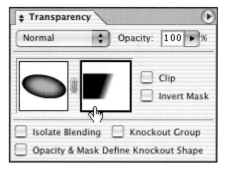

Entering mask-editing mode by clicking on the mask thumbnail in the Transparency palette

Why can't I draw now?

You may be in mask-editing mode and not know it if:

- You draw an object, deselect it, and it seems to disappear
- You fill an object with a color, but the color doesn't display

If you are in mask-editing mode, the Layers palette tab will read Layers (Opacity Mask). To exit mask-editing mode, click on the artwork thumbnail in the Transparency palette.

Opacity Masks—source materials

You do not have to limit yourself to a single vector object when making an opacity mask. Any artwork will do. Experiment with placed images, gradient meshes, and even objects that contain opacity masks of their own. Remember that it's the grayscale luminosity of the masking artwork that determines the opacity of the masked artwork, not its color or vector structure.

CASSELL

Peter Cassell / 1185 Design

As a kind of artwork not normally associated with Illustrator's hard-edged vector tools, Peter Cassell's fluffy cumulus clouds comprised one of the packaging illustrations created for Adobe Illustrator 9 (see Cassell's cityscape Gallery opposite). Cassell began by placing a photographic image on a template layer in Illustrator. Next, he created a gradient mesh with the maximum number of rows and columns (50). To color the clouds, he first chose View > Outline (so he could see the cloud image on a layer below the mesh). Next, he selected the Direct-selection tool, clicked on a mesh point, selected the Eyedropper tool, and then clicked in the cloud image to sample its color. He repeated this process to color the rest of the mesh to match the cloud image. To reshape parts of the grid to follow the contours of the clouds, Cassell clicked mesh points with the Mesh tool and dragged them. Where he

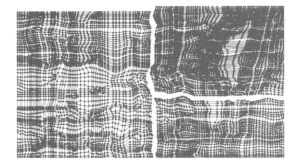

needed more detail, Cassell added rows and columns to the mesh by clicking on a mesh line or in an empty space in the mesh with the Mesh tool. As the composition became unwieldy with detail, Cassell selected overlapping sections of the mesh and copied and pasted each section into a separate file. Once he finished with a section, Cassell copied and pasted it into the final, composite file. He was careful not to adjust mesh points where sections overlapped, so he could maintain a seamless appearance where the separate sections he had worked on overlapped.

CASSELL

Peter Cassell / 1185 Design

Peter Cassell's European cityscape, commissioned for the Adobe Illustrator 9 packaging illustration, was built with mists he created using a gradient mesh as an opacity mask. After drawing the rough shapes of reflections in the water, Cassell drew a rectangle on a layer above the water and filled the rectangle with white. He copied the rectangle, pasted it in front, filled it with black, and then selected Object > Create Gradient Mesh to turn it into an 18 x 15 mesh. He edited the mesh by selecting mesh points with the Direct-selection tool and filling the points with gray values varying from

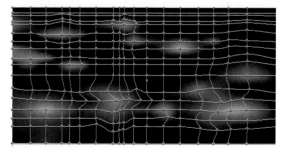

30% to 50% black. To shape a mist, he selected and moved mesh points. To mask the white rectangle with the gradient mesh above it, Cassell selected the mesh and the rectangle and chose Make Opacity Mask from the Transparency palette's pop-up menu.

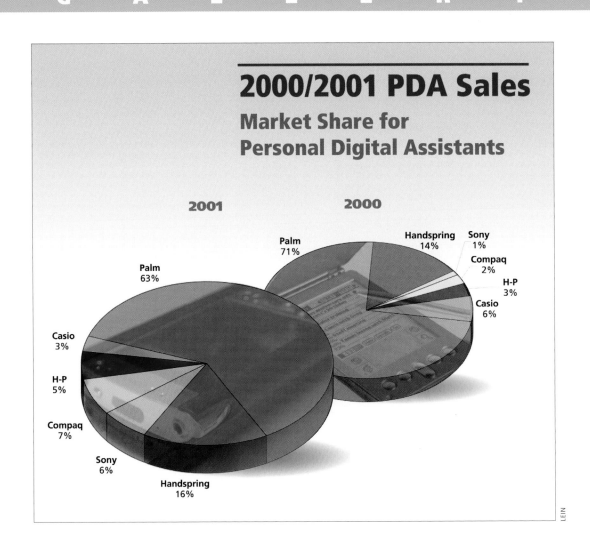

2000/2001 PDA Sales

Market Share for Personal Digital Assistants

2001

2000

Palm 71%

Palm 63%

Handspring 14%

Sony 1%

Compaq 2%

H-P 3%

Casio 6%

Casio 3%

H-P 5%

Compaq 7%

Sony 6%

Handspring 16%

LEIN

Adam Z Lein

Adam Z Lein began this pie chart in Microsoft Excel by selecting data and using Excel's Chart Wizard to turn the data into a chart tilted in a perspective view. Lein used the Acrobat 5 PDF maker to create a PDF of the graph. When he opened the PDF in Illustrator, the graph retained all of the shapes as vector objects and the type as outlines. Lein then placed a photographic image on a layer below the pie chart artwork and used the Transparency palette to

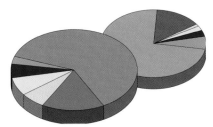

set the blending mode to Luminosity and the transparency to 30%. To fit the image within the pie chart, Lein created a clipping mask from the circle and edge of the pie chart. (See the *Advanced Techniques* chapter for more about clipping masks.)

Live Effects & Graphic Styles

9

292 Introduction

292 Effects vs. Filters

293 Raster effects

293 3D Effects

298 Scribble Effect

298 Warps and Enveloping

300 Effect Pathfinders

301 Effect > Pathfinder > Hard Mix and Soft Mix

302 Graphic Styles in Illustrator

303 Gallery: Steven Gordon / Cartagram

304 Scratchboard Art: *Using Multiple Strokes, Effects, and Styles*

306 Embossing Effects: *Building 3D Appearances*

308 Blurring The Lines: *Photorealism with Blends and Effects*

311 Gallery: Ted Alspach

312 Warps & Envelopes: *Using Warping and Enveloping Effects*

316 Quick & Easy 3D: *Simple 3D techniques*

318 3D Effects: *Extruding, Revolving, and Rotating Paths*

321–325 Galleries: Robert Sharif, Trina Wai, Mordy Golding, Tom Patterson, Joe Lertola

326 Scribble Basics: *Applying Scribble Effects to Artwork*

328 Gallery: Todd Macadangdang/Adobe

Live Effects & Graphic Styles

See Joe Lertola's "Opacity Masks 101" lesson in the Transparency & Appearances *chapter*

The palette formerly known as...

The Graphic Styles palette is the same palette that was simply called the Styles palette in previous versions of Illustrator. The word *Graphic* has been added to its name to distinguish it from Illustrator's new Paragraph and Character Styles palettes (discussed in the *Type* chapter).

Transform effects!

This one is a gem! Any transformation can be applied as an *effect* (Effect > Distort & Transform > Transform). Know exactly how much you've rotated, sheared, or scaled an object and you can completely undo or adjust it.

Some effects don't scale

You must fully select a group to scale effects applied to the group. Layer effects don't scale with objects; so if you need to scale layer effects, target the layer and Expand Appearance.

The effects that Illustrator offers us get better with each release. Illustrator 9 brought us live effects, Illustrator 10 brought us warps and envelopes, and now Illustrator CS expands this repertoire to include the 3D and Scribble effects. This chapter will bring you up to speed on Illustrator's various effects and will also acquaint you with the Graphic Styles palette.

EFFECTS VS. FILTERS

Illustrator provides a variety of methods for altering or enhancing paths and fills. The *Drawing & Coloring* chapter introduces you to some basic methods, from manual adjustments to Pathfinder filters. This chapter focuses on effects. Effects are similar to filters, with one exception—*effects* are live, whereas filters permanently change your artwork. Effects alter the look of your work without permanently changing the base art—and therefore they can be edited or removed at any time. When an effect is applied to an object, group, or layer, it will display as an attribute in the Appearance palette. The effect's position in the palette indicates which element it will modify.

The Effect menu is divided into two sections. The effects in the upper section (in the 3D through Warp submenus) can be applied to either CMYK or RGB artwork. Those in the lower section (in the Artistic through Video submenus) can be applied only when your document is in RGB color mode (with the exceptions of the Blur effects, the Pixelate effects, and the Unsharp Mask).

Although none of the effects let you save or export presets of settings that you like from within their dialog boxes, you *can* save any set of effect attributes that you like as a Graphic Style. To save your set of effects as a Graphic Style, just drag the set of appearance attributes from the Appearance palette to the Graphic Styles palette (for more about Graphic Styles, see the final section of this chapter introduction: "Graphic Styles in Illustrator").

RASTER EFFECTS

Illustrator's default resolution for the Document Raster Effects Settings (Effect >Document Raster Effects Settings) is deliberately set low, because it allows effects to preview faster while you're editing the artwork. But when you get ready to print, you'll want to re-execute your effects at a higher resolution setting. If you don't change those settings for your effect, your effect will print at that default 72 ppi (pixel per inch) setting—even if your file is printed at a much higher resolution! To re-execute your effect, double-click it in the Appearance palette and change the resolution there (see Tip "Applying effects"). After printing or flattening, you'll probably want to restore the lower resolution if you intend to continue editing objects with effects on them, because working with a high Document Raster Effects resolution can be slow.

There's an important distinction between the raster effects that originated in Photoshop and were then added to Illustrator (the ones in the bottom part of Illustrator's Effect menu, such as Gaussian Blur), and the raster effects that were developed specifically for Illustrator such as Feather, Glow and Drop Shadow. The Photoshop effects specify their options in pixels, whereas the native Illustrator effects specify their distances in ruler units. So if you apply a Gaussian Blur at 3 pixels, it looks much more blurry when the resolution is 72 ppi than when it is 600 ppi. On the other hand, if you have a drop shadow with a blur of 3 pt, it automatically adjusts to the resolution, and just covers more pixels at a higher resolution. For this reason, if you have Photoshop effects applied and you change the Document Raster Effects resolution, you may need to adjust the specific effect options, such as blur distance, as well. (This process should be familiar to anyone who has changed the resolution of a Photoshop document that already had Layer effects in it.)

3D EFFECTS

Illustrator CS breaks new ground by offering the power to transform any two-dimensional (2D) shape, including

Applying effects

Once an effect has been applied to an object, double-click the effect in the Appearance palette to change the values. If you re-select the effect from the Effect menu, you'll apply a second instance of the effect to the object, not change it. (In the case of 3D, you'll want to avoid applying two 3D effects to a single object. Understanding what you can do in the various 3D dialog boxes will help you avoid that; see the Tip "3D—Three dialogs" later in this chapter.)

Why duplicate items?

Why are there duplicate items in both the Filter and Effect menus? Adobe kept duplicates in the Filter menu because they save you a step (namely, the Expand Appearance step) when you don't want them live.

Flare—tool or effect?

The Flare tool turns up in some of the lessons and Galleries in this chapter. That's because although the Flare tool isn't technically an effect, it behaves like one—you can select and re-edit your Flare tool work using the Flare Tool Options dialog box (double-click the Flare tool to open it).

GORDON

Extruding an object using the Effect >3D > Extrude & Bevel dialog box—the two-dimensional object on the left was extruded to create the three-dimensional house image (and also rotated to change its angle).

2D or not 2D...?

Although Illustrator's 3D effect does a terrific job of rendering objects that look fully three-dimensional, you should bear in mind that Illustrator's 3D objects are only *truly* three-dimensional while you're working with them in a 3D effect dialog box. As soon as you're done tweaking your object and you click OK to close the dialog box, the object's three-dimensional qualities are "frozen"—almost as if Illustrator had taken a snapshot of the object—until the next time you edit it in a 3D dialog box again. On the page, it's technically an impressive 2D rendering of a 3D object that can only be worked with in two-dimensional ways. But because the effect is live, you can work with the object in 3D again any time you want, just by selecting the object and choosing the effect you want to work with from the Effect > 3D submenu.

type, into a shape that looks three-dimensional (3D). As you're working in Illustrator's 3D effect dialog boxes, you can change your 3D shape's perspective, rotate it, and add lighting and surface attributes. And because you're working with a live effect, you can edit the source object at any time and observe the resultant change in the 3D shape immediately. You can also rotate a 2D shape in 3D space and change its perspective. Another exciting feature of the 3D Effect is the ability to map artwork, in the form of a symbol, onto any of your 3D shape's surfaces.

To begin, think of Illustrator's horizontal ruler as the X axis and the vertical ruler as the Y axis. Now imagine a third dimension that extends back into space, perpendicular to the flat surface of your monitor. This is the Z axis. There are two ways to create a 3D shape using 3D effects. The first method is by extruding a 2D object back into space along the Z axis, and the second is by revolving a 2D object around its Y axis, up to 360 degrees.

Once you apply a 3D effect to an object, it'll be listed in the Appearance palette. As with other appearance attributes, you can edit the effect, change the position of the effect in the palette's stacking order, and duplicate or delete the effect. You can also save the 3D effect as a reusable graphic style (see "Graphic Styles in Illustrator," later in this chapter).

Extruding an object

To extrude a 2D object, begin by creating an open or closed path. Your path can contain a stroke, a fill or both. If your shape contains a fill, it's best to begin with a solid color. (See the Tip "Solid advice on 3D colors.") With your path selected, choose Extrude & Bevel from the Effect > 3D submenu. The top half of the 3D Extrude & Bevel Options dialog box contains rotation and perspective options that we'll examine a bit later, but for the moment we'll concentrate on the lower portion of the dialog box. Choose the depth to which you'd like your 2D object extruded by entering a point size in the Extrude Depth field or by dragging the popup slider. Choosing to add a cap to your object will give it a solid appearance, while choosing to turn the cap option off will result in a hollowed-out looking object.

You also have the option to add a beveled edge to your extruded object. Illustrator offers you ten different styles of bevels to choose from, and a dialog box in which to enter the height of the bevel. You can choose between a bevel that will be added to the original object (Bevel Extent Out), or subtracted from the original shape (Bevel Extent In). These options result in objects that appear radically different from each other.

Remember that because you're working with a Live Effect, any changes you make to the original 2D source shape will immediately update the 3D object. The original shapes of the vector paths will be highlighted when you select the 3D shape and you can easily edit them just as you would any other path. You can always edit the settings you've entered for a particular 3D effect by double-clicking it in the Appearance palette. The appropriate dialog box will reopen and you can adjust any settings that you've previously entered.

Revolving an object

You can also create a 3D object from a 2D path (either open or closed) by revolving it around its Y (vertical) axis. Solid strokes work just as well as filled objects. Once you've selected your path, choose Effect > 3D > Revolve. In the 3D Revolve Options dialog box, you can set the number of degrees you wish to revolve the object by entering a value from 1 to 360 in the Angle text field, or by dragging the slider. An object that is revolved 360 degrees will appear solid. An object revolved less than 360 degrees will appear to have a wedge carved out of it. You can also choose to offset the rotation from the object's edge. This will result in a 3D shape that appears to be carved out in the center. And finally, as with extruded shapes, because the 3D options you've chosen are live effects, any changes you make to your original source object will immediately change the look of the 3D shape you've revolved.

HAMANN

Revolving an object using the Effect > 3D > Revolve dialog box—the two-dimensional shape on the left was revolved to create the three-dimensional object on the right (for more on the Revolve effect, see the "3D Effects" lesson later in this chapter)

Solid advice on 3D colors
You'll get best results by choosing solid fill colors for objects you'll be working with in 3D. Gradients and pattern fills don't produce reliable results.

3D—Three dialogs
There are three different dialog boxes for the 3D effect, and some of the features overlap. So before you apply 3D effects to an object, you'll want to first decide which single 3D effect will accomplish all of your goals. If all you need to do is rotate or change the perspective of an object, use the Rotate dialog box. If you want to map a symbol to the object, you'll need to use either Revolve or Extrude & Bevel. If you still need to rotate the object after that, you can do so from within the Revolve and Extrude & Bevel dialog boxes.
—*Brenda Sutherland*

You can rotate objects in three dimensions by using the Effect >3D >Rotate dialog box (or the upper halves of the Revolve and the Extrude & Bevel dialog boxes). The star on the left was rotated in 3D to create the star on the right.

HAMANN

Another example of rotating an object in three dimensions

3D effect—pass it on

Although in this book we generally recommend working with the New Art Has Basic Appearance setting turned off, you might want to turn it on when working with 3D effects. Otherwise, any new paths that you create subsequent to applying 3D effects to an object will also have the same appearance set, unless you first clear the appearance set from the palette, or click on the default fill and stroke icon in the Tools palette. On the other hand, if you *want* your next object to have the same 3D effects as the one you just created, leave New Art Has Basic Appearance turned off.

Rotating an object in 3D space

The Rotate dialog box can be accessed directly by choosing Effects >3D >Rotate. It can be used to rotate both 2D and 3D shapes. It also appears in the upper half of both the Extrude & Bevel and the Revolve Options boxes. The 3D Rotate Options dialog box contains a cube representing the planes that your shape can be rotated through. You can choose a preset angle of rotation from the Position menu, or enter values between -180 and 180 in the X, Y and Z text fields. If you'd like to manually rotate your object around one of its three axes, simply click on the edge of one of the faces of the white cube and drag. The edges of each plane are highlighted in a corresponding color that tells you which of the object's three planes you're rotating it through. Red represents the object's X axis, a green highlight represents the object's Y axis, and blue edges represent the object's Z axis. The object's rotation is constrained within the plane of that particular axis. Remember, to constrain the rotation you must be dragging an edge of the cube. Notice the numbers changing in the corresponding text field as you drag. If you wish to rotate your object relative to all three axes at once, click directly on a surface of the cube and drag, or click in the black area behind the cube and drag. Values in all three text fields will change.

Changing the perspective of an object

You can change the visible perspective of your object by entering a number between 0 and 160 in the perspective text field, or by dragging the slider. A smaller value simulates the look of a telephoto camera lens, while a larger value will simulate a wide-angle camera lens, with more of an "exploded" perspective.

Applying surface shading to 3D objects

Illustrator allows you a variety of choices in the kind of shading you apply to your 3D object. These range from dull and unshaded matte surfaces to glossy and highlighted surfaces that look like plastic. And because you can also choose how you light your object, the possible variations are limitless.

The surface shading option appears as part of both the 3D Extrude & Bevel and the 3D Revolve Option dialog boxes. Choosing Wireframe as your shading option will result in a transparent object whose contours are overlaid with a set of outlines describing the object's geometry. The next choice is No Shading, which will result in a flat-looking shape with no discernible surfaces. Choosing the Diffused Shading option results in your object having a soft light cast on its surfaces, while choosing the Plastic Shading option will make your object appear molded out of shiny reflective plastic.

If you choose either the Diffused Shading or Plastic Shading options, you can further refine the look of your object by adjusting the direction and intensity of the light source illuminating your object. By clicking the More Options button, the dialog box will enlarge and you'll be able to make changes to the Light Intensity, Ambient Light level, Highlight Intensity, Highlight Size and number of Blend Steps. You can also choose a custom color to light your object.

Mapping art onto an object

One of the most exciting aspects of the 3D Effect is the ability to map artwork onto any of the surfaces of your 2D or 3D shape (as with the label on the wine bottle shown above). Whenever you have the Extrude & Bevel, Revolve, or Rotate Options dialog boxes open, you can simply click on the Map Art button and choose one of the available symbols from the menu. You can specify which of your object's surfaces the artwork will map onto by clicking on the left and right Arrow keys. The selected surface will appear in the window and you can either scale the art by dragging the handles on the bounding box or make the art expand to cover the entire surface by clicking the Scale to Fit button. Note that as you click through the different surfaces, the selected surface will be highlighted in your document window.

GOLDING

Mordy Golding used the Map Art feature to wrap the label art (above left) around the bottle (shown in detail, above right)—to create the bottle he used the 3D Revolve effect with a custom Surface Shading (for more about this art see the Mordy Golding Gallery later in this chapter)

Mapping—don't get lost!

Here are some tips to help you avoid getting confused about what surface you're mapping symbols to:

- Remember that you need to choose a surface in the dialog box. Select by clicking the Arrow keys to view each surface.
- When clicking through the various surfaces, it's sometimes easier to identify the surface you want by the red highlight on the object itself than by the flattened proxy in the mapping dialog box.
- Even the red highlight can fool you. If the symbol isn't mapping to a selected surface, it may be because it's being mapped to the *inside* of the surface.
- If the object has a stroke, this will add more surfaces.

—*Brenda Sutherland*

The Scribble effect can be applied to the stroke, the fill, or both the stroke and the fill of an object

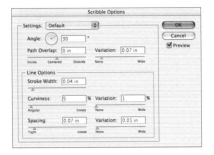

The Scribble Options dialog box

GORDON / CARTAGRAM, LLC

COHEN

For more lessons with Scribble, see Steven Gordon's "Antiquing Type" and Sandee Cohen's "Offset Fills" lessons in the Type chapter

Crosshatching using Scribble

You don't have to duplicate a shape to create a crosshatch effect using Scribble. Instead, after applying Scribble to the object's fill (and with your object selected), choose Add New Fill from the Appearance palette menu. Then choose Effect > Stylize > Scribble, and for the Angle setting, add 90° to the angle. —*Mike Schwabauer*

SCRIBBLE EFFECT

The new Effect > Stylize > Scribble effect lets you quickly create a variety of looks for your artwork, from a loose, *scribbly*, hand-drawn look to a tight crosshatch. The Scribble effect can be applied to the fill and/or stroke of an object depending on what you have targeted in the Appearance palette when you apply it.

The Scribble Options dialog box (shown at left) is divided into three sections. The Settings menu contains a fixed number of Scribble presets. Use the Angle slider to control the overall direction of the Scribble lines. A setting of 0° causes the Scribble lines to run left to right, 90° makes them run up and down. Use the Path Overlap slider to control how much the scribble stays inside or extends outside of a path boundary. In the Line Options section of the Scribble dialog, use the Stroke Width control to specify how fat or thin you want the scribble line to be. Use the Curviness slider to set how Angular or Loopy the ends of each scribble stroke should be. Use the Spacing slider to specify how tight or loose you want your strokes to be. Use the Variation sliders to further control how each attribute is applied: For a very regular machine-made look, set the slider to None, and for a more freehand and natural look move the slider toward Wide. For more about using the Scribble Options, see the "Scribble Basics" lesson later in this chapter.

But choosing Scribble Options is only the beginning. By combining other effects, or applying brushstrokes to your scribbles, you can create an almost infinite variety of looks. You can then use them as fills or masks, or to transform type; or you can save them as graphic styles to apply to other artwork. See the "Offset Fills" and "Antiquing Type" lessons in the *Type* chapter.

WARPS AND ENVELOPING

Illustrator's warps and envelope tools are robust and very powerful, offering much more than just simple transformations. Warps and envelopes may look similar at first, but there's an important difference between them. Warps are applied as live *effects*—meaning they can be applied to objects, groups, or layers. They're created by choosing from the predefined options in the Warp dialog boxes, and can be saved within a graphic style. Envelopes, on the other hand, are also live, but instead of being effects, they're actual *objects* that contain artwork. You can edit or customize the envelope shape, and the contents inside the envelope will conform to the contour.

Warps

Applying a warp is actually quite simple. Target an object, group, or layer and choose Effect > Warp > Arc. It really doesn't make a difference which warp effect you choose, because you'll be presented with the Warp Options dialog box where you can choose from any of the 15 different warps. While the warp effects are "canned" in the sense that you can't make adjustments to the effects directly, you can control how a warp appears by changing the Bend value, as well as the Horizontal and Vertical Distortion values.

Once a warp is applied, you can edit it by opening the Appearance palette and double-clicking on the warp listed there. Like any other effect, a warp can be applied to just the fill or just the stroke—and if you edit the artwork, the warp updates as well.

Since warps are effects, you can include them as a graphic style, which can then be applied to other artwork. (More on graphic styles later in this chapter.)

Envelopes

While warp effects do a nice job of distorting artwork, there are times when you need more control. That's where Illustrator's envelopes come in.

There are three ways to apply envelopes. The simplest way is to create a shape you want to use as your envelope and make sure it's at the top of the stacking order—above the art you want to place inside the envelope. Then, with the artwork and the shape you created both selected, choose Object > Envelope Distort > Make with Top Object.

"Crunching Type" lesson in the Type chapter

Illustrator will create a special kind of object—an envelope. This envelope is a container in the shape you created, which appears in the Layers palette as <Envelope>. You can edit the path of the envelope as you would any other, and the artwork inside will update to conform to the shape. To edit the contents of the envelope, you need to choose Object > Envelope Distort > Edit Contents. If you then look at the Layers palette, you'll notice that the <Envelope> now has a disclosure triangle that reveals the contents of the envelope—the artwork you placed. You can edit the artwork directly or even drag other paths into the <Envelope> in the Layers palette. When you're finished editing the contents, choose Object > Envelope Distort > Edit Envelope.

There are two other types of envelopes, and they're closely related. Both of them use meshes to provide even more distortion control. One of them is called Make with Warp and it's found in the Object > Envelope Distort submenu. This technique starts off by displaying the Warp dialog. When you choose a warp and press OK, Illustrator converts that warp to an envelope mesh. You can then edit individual mesh points with the Direct Selection tool to distort not only the outer edges of the envelope shape, but also the way art is distorted within the envelope itself. To provide even more control, use the Mesh tool to add more mesh points as desired.

The third way to create an envelope is to start from a rectangular mesh. Select artwork and choose Object > Envelope Distort > Make with Mesh. After you've chosen how many mesh points you want, Illustrator will create an envelope mesh. Use the Direct Selection tool to edit the points and use the Mesh tool to add mesh points.

EFFECT PATHFINDERS

The effects listed in the Effect > Pathfinder menu are effect versions of the Pathfinders described in the *Drawing & Coloring* chapter. To apply a Pathfinder effect, you should either group the objects, making sure that the group is also targeted (see the Tip "Pathfinder Group Alert"), or target the layer with the objects (which applies the effect to *all* objects on that layer). Then, select Effect > Pathfinder and choose an effect. If you don't do one of those two things, and you're applying the effect to a non-group, there may be cases where you won't see a visible result.

Pathfinder Effects vs. Compound Shapes

With live Pathfinder effects, you create a container (group or layer) and then apply one effect (Add, Subtract, Intersect, or Exclude) to the container. But in a compound shape, *each component* independently specifies whether it adds to, subtracts from, intersects with, or excludes from the components below it.

When you're using more than one or two shape modes you'll find it simpler to work with compound shapes. One of the great benefits of compound shapes over Pathfinder effects is that compound shapes behave much more reliably when the objects being combined aren't simple.

Compound shapes can be exported live as Photoshop files (PSD), or copied in Illustrator and pasted into Photoshop as shape layers. Compound shapes can also be used as clipping paths. See the *Drawing and Coloring* chapter for more about Pathfinders and compound shapes.

EFFECT > PATHFINDER > HARD MIX AND SOFT MIX

Hard Mix and Soft Mix change the color of the areas where the objects overlap, in order to simulate transparency (see the Tip at right). Also see "SandeeCs Soft Mix Chart" on the *Wow! CD*, and see the Pathfinder Palette chart in the *Drawing & Coloring* chapter for examples of how Hard Mix and Soft Mix can be used.

Filter versions of these effects are no longer available on the Pathfinder palette. To obtain the equivalent result, apply the effect, then choose Object > Expand Appearance; or use the *Wow!* Pathfinder Filter actions available on the *Wow! CD*. When you expand, or use the action versions of Hard and Soft Mix, the objects get divided just as though you had first applied the Divide command from the Pathfinder palette.

Pathfinder Group Alert

Even if your objects were already grouped, you may still get the following warning when you apply a Pathfinder Effect:

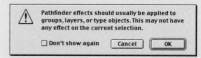

This happens if you Direct-select the objects and miss some of their points, causing the objects to get targeted.

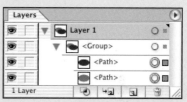

To fix this, target the group

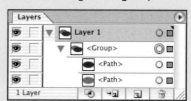

the objects are in, then apply the Pathfinder effect. To avoid the problem and ensure that the group gets selected, hold down Option (Mac) /Alt (Win) to switch from the Direct Selection tool to the Group Selection tool while selecting your grouped objects.

Hard/Soft Mix & Transparency

You can obtain the same color effect as the Hard Mix Effect by setting the Transparency Blend Mode to Darken and Opacity to 100%. There is no Transparency equivalent for Soft Mix.

GRAPHIC STYLES IN ILLUSTRATOR

If you want to apply an appearance more than once, whether it's a simple stroke and fill or a complex combination of effects, save it as a graphic style in the Graphic Styles palette. A *graphic style* is simply a combination of one or more appearance attributes that can be applied to objects (including text objects), groups, and layers. See the previous chapter for more about appearances.

To save a set of appearance attributes as a graphic style, in the Appearance palette (with or without an object selected) select the desired appearance attributes, and then either click the New Graphic Style icon on the bottom of the Graphic Styles palette or drag the appearance thumbnail from the Appearance palette to the Graphic Styles palette. The color mode (color space) is also stored with the Graphic Style.

To apply a graphic style, simply select an object—or target a group or layer—and click on a thumbnail in the Graphic Styles palette. You can also sample a style from another object using the Eyedropper. Alternatively, you can drag a style from the Graphic Styles palette directly onto an object.

To separate a graphic style from an object, click on the Break Link to Graphic Style icon at the bottom of the palette, or select the item from the Graphic Styles palette menu. You might want to do this when you are replacing a graphic style but don't want to change all the objects using the current graphic style to the updated or replaced version (see the Tip "Replacing graphic styles").

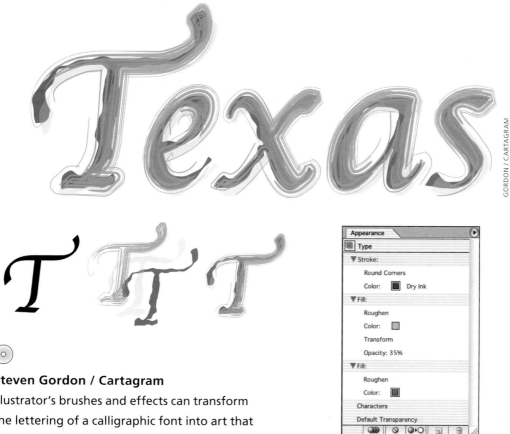

GORDON / CARTAGRAM

Steven Gordon / Cartagram

Illustrator's brushes and effects can transform the lettering of a calligraphic font into art that suggests a more hand-rendered appearance. To begin this map title, Steven Gordon typed "Texas" and then chose a calligraphic font that included swash capital letters (Apple Chancery). He adjusted kerning to fine-tune the spacing between characters. With the text object selected and the Appearance palette open, Gordon selected Add New Fill from the palette's options menu and gave the new fill a purple color. He duplicated the fill by clicking on the Duplicate Selected Item icon at the bottom of the palette, and gave the duplicate a pale blue color. Next, he clicked on a brush in the Brushes palette (Gordon chose the Dry Ink brush that comes with Illustrator's default Brushes palette).

Selecting the stroke in the Appearance palette, he chose a dark blue color. To further customize the title, Gordon selected the pale blue fill in the Appearance palette, offset the fill and distorted the fill's edges using the Transform and Roughen commands from the Effect > Distort and Transform menu. He also made it transparent by moving the slider in the Transparency palette. To finish, Gordon selected the bottom fill and applied the Roughen command from the Effect > Distort and Transform menu. (For a similar technique, see "Brushed Type" in the *Type* chapter and see the *Transparency & Appearances* chapter for more on Appearances.)

Scratchboard Art

Using Multiple Strokes, Effects, and Styles

Overview: *Apply multiple strokes to simple objects; offset strokes; apply effects to strokes; create and apply graphic styles.*

PAPCIAK-ROSE / EEN

The original scratchboard art consists of simple primitive shapes

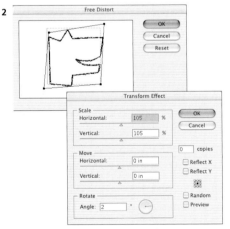

To offset a path's Stroke from its Fill, select the Stroke in the Appearance palette and apply Free Distort and Transform from the Effect >Distort & Transform menu

Artist Ellen Papciak-Rose asked consultant Sandee Cohen if there was a way to simulate scratchboard art in Illustrator. Cohen devised a way to transform Papciak-Rose's artwork using Art Brushes, multiple strokes, and stroke effects, which were then combined and saved as graphic styles. Once a series of effects is saved as a graphic style, you can easily apply that graphic style to multiple objects to create a design theme. Art directors may find this method helpful for unifying and stylizing illustrations created by a number of different artists.

1 Applying Art Brushes and Fills. To create a more natural-looking stroke, Cohen applied Art Brushes to simple objects supplied by Papciak-Rose. Cohen used Charcoal, Fude, Dry Ink, Fire Ash, and Pencil Art Brushes (on the *Wow! CD*). Select a simple object, then click on your choice of Art Brush in the Brushes palette or in a Brush Library. (For more on Art Brushes, see the *Brushes* chapter.) Next, choose basic, solid fills for each object.

2 Offsetting a stroke. To develop a loose, sketchlike look, Cohen offset some of the strokes from their fills. First, highlight a stroke in the Appearance palette and apply either Effect >Distort & Transform >Free Distort or Effect > Distort & Transform > Transform to manually or numerically adjust the position of the stroke so that it separates from the fill. This gives the stroke the appearance of a different shape without permanently changing the path. (You can further reshape the stroke by double-clicking the Transform attribute in the Appearance palette and adjusting the offset of the Stroke attribute.)

3 Adding more strokes to a single path. To add to the sketchlike look, Cohen applied additional strokes to each path. First, she chose a Stroke attribute in the Appearance palette and clicked the Duplicate Selected Item icon at the bottom of the palette. With the new Stroke copy selected, she changed the color, as well as the choice of Art brush. She also double-clicked the stroke's Distort & Transform effect in the Appearance palette and changed the settings to move the Stroke copy's position. Cohen repeated this until she had as many strokes as she liked.

To make a stroke visible only outside its fill, make sure that the object is still selected, and simply drag the stroke below the Fill in the Appearance palette.

4 Working with graphic styles. To automate the styling of future illustrations, Cohen used the Appearance and Graphic Styles palettes to create a library of graphic styles. Whenever you create a set of strokes and fills you like, click the New Graphic Style icon in the Graphic Styles palette to create a new graphic style swatch.

Once Cohen had assembled a palette of graphic style swatches, she could alter the look and feel of the artwork by simply applying a variety of graphic styles to selected paths. Using new colors sent by Papciak-Rose, Cohen's graphic styles from an earlier scratchboard project were re-colored to create the graphic styles used here. The use of graphic styles allows the artist or designer to create a number of overall themes in a graphic style library, and then apply them selectively to illustrations or design elements. This work flow can also be used to keep a cohesive look throughout a project or series.

3

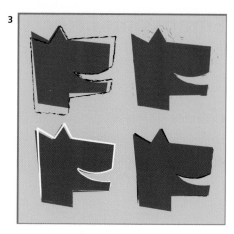

This graphic illustrates the individual strokes that Cohen combined to create the multiple strokes for the face object in the final illustration

4

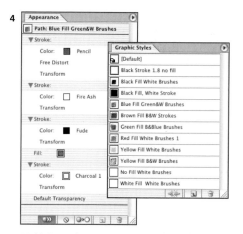

Multiple Strokes applied to an object shown in the Appearance palette; appearance attributes saved in the Graphic Styles palette by clicking the New Graphic Style icon

Applying different graphic styles to objects can give the same artwork several different looks

Embossing Effects

Building 3D Appearances

ALSPACH

Overview: *Apply object-level effects for highlights and shadows; build appearances, save as graphic styles and apply to layers.*

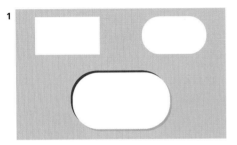

At the top, making the screw slots (on the left, the rectangle and on the right, the rectangle with Round Corners Effect): at the bottom, an enlarged view of the composite appearance

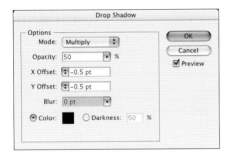

The Drop Shadow options pop-up dialog box; edit the X and Y Offset fields to adjust the position of the shadow and highlight (check the Preview box to see the effect as you work)

Resizing appearances

If you plan to resize an Illustration that contains appearances with stroke values, be sure to apply the appearances to objects, not to layers. Illustrator may fail to re-scale stroke values in layer-targeted appearances.

Ted Alspach, Senior Product Manager for Adobe Illustrator, choose the embossed letters, numbers and lines of a license plate to demonstrate the ease and flexibility of using Illustrator's effects and appearances. In this memorial to French mathematician Pierre Bézier, inventor of the original Bézier curve, Alspach simulated the look of embossing by applying a drop shadow effect and by building a sophisticated graphic style.

1 Applying the drop shadow effect. Start the license plate by drawing the background shape, circles, curves and other linework. While technically not a raised surface, the four screw slots still require highlights and shadows to convey the impression of dimension. To create a slot, draw a rectangle and then Fill with White and Stroke with None. Use the Round Corners Effect (Effect > Stylize > Round Corners) to give the object a more oval shape. To cast the plate's shadow on the edge of the slot, select the slot rectangle and apply the Drop Shadow Effect (Effect > Stylize > Drop Shadow). In the Drop Shadow dialog box, choose black for color, Blur 0, and Offset up and to the left (using negative numbers for "X" and "Y" offsets). Then click OK. Repeat the drop shadow effect to make the highlight, except choose a light color and Offset down and to the right (using positive numbers). To further tweak the drop shadows (modifying their color or width, for example), simply double-click the attribute name "drop shadow" in the Appearance palette (Window > Appearance) and edit the values in the dialog box.

2 Building multiple appearances. Alspach took another approach to embossing by building a sophisticated graphic style in which transparency and multiple offset strokes simulate highlights and shadows.

To make the license plate lettering, type the characters in a sans serif font and convert them to outlines (Type > Create Outlines). Ungroup the characters, select a character and set its Fill to orange. To make the first embossing highlight, select the orange Fill appearance attribute in the Appearance palette (Window > Appearance) and copy it by clicking the Duplicate Selected Item icon at the bottom of the palette. Now, select the lower Fill attribute in the palette, choose white from the Color palette and, in the Transparency palette, set Opacity to 25% and blending mode to Screen. Then, choose Effect > Transform > Distort & Transform to offset it up and to the left by editing the Move fields (negative Horizontal and positive Vertical). Make two more copies of this white Fill attribute by once again clicking the Duplicate Selected Item icon. Offset each copy farther up and to the left by double-clicking the Fill's Transform attribute and editing the Move values in the Transform dialog.

To start the shadows, first duplicate the lowest white Fill. Now select the bottom white Fill and set its color to black, Opacity to 50%, and blending mode to Multiply. Double-click the Fill's Transform attribute and edit the Move values to offset it down and to the right. Copy this shadow and offset it farther down and to the right. When you have finished, the Appearance palette will display six Fill attributes for the object.

3 Creating and applying a graphic style. Alspach turned the appearance set into a graphic style by dragging the Appearance palette's preview icon and dropping it in the Graphic Styles palette. He then applied the graphic style to the layer with the number characters. You can achieve the same embossing look by applying the graphic style to selected character outlines or to a group composed of the character outlines.

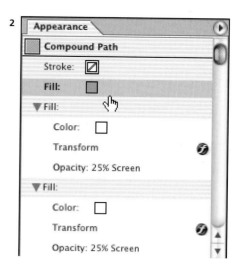

Appearance palette showing the appearance preview icon (top left), and the target of the appearance (Object)

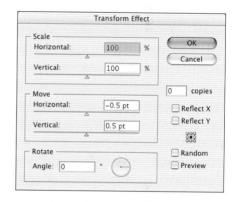

Move values in the Transform Effect dialog box to offset Fill attribute up and left

Close-up view of the embossed letter characters with the multiple highlight and shadow strokes that progressively hide the background artwork

Blurring The Lines

Photorealism with Blends and Effects

Overview: *Trace a placed image; draw objects and fill them with colors sampled from the image; create blends; rasterize objects and apply Gaussian Blur.*

BRASHEAR

1

The original composite photograph (made from separate images in Photoshop) placed on a template layer

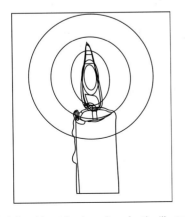

All of the objects Brashear drew for the illustration, displayed in Outline View

Using a technique he calls "Pen and Eyedropper," artist Bruce Brashear reproduces photographs in Illustrator by tracing a placed image and filling objects with colors sampled from the image (see Brashear's Vector Photos in the *Drawing & Coloring* chapter to learn about this technique). In this illustration, Brashear expands his technique by employing blends and Gaussian blurs to capture the subtleties of candlelight and reflections.

1 Placing an image, and drawing and coloring objects.
After beginning a new file, Brashear placed an image of a candle and flame on a template layer (File > Place). He traced the shapes for the candle, wick, flame and halo using the Pen tool. For a complex object like the candle flame or the candle wick, you may need to create several objects or blends to completely illustrate its different colors or shapes (Brashear created 11 objects for his candle flame). To fill your objects with colors from the image on the template layer, select the Eyedropper tool, select an object, and Shift-click in the image to sample its color.

2 Making a halo from blends, rasterizing it, and applying a blur to it. Brashear's soft, round halo behind the flame was created with blends and several effects. To begin a halo, draw at least two objects to blend (Brashear made five objects to serve as transitional color blends in the image's halo). Next, fill each object with a color sampled from the placed image using the Eyedropper tool. Then, select the objects and choose Object > Blend > Make. To set the complexity of the multi-step blend that Illustrator creates, choose Object > Blend > Blend Options (or double-click the Blend tool icon in the Tools palette). In the Blend Options dialog box, click the pop-up menu, select Specified Steps and enter a high enough number to provide a sufficient transition of shapes or colors (the number you choose sets the steps between each pair of objects, not the total steps for the whole multi-step blend). If you need to reshape the halo, click on anchor points with the Direct Selection tool and move the points or their Bézier handles. Finish by drawing a background rectangle and filling it with a color that will contrast with the colors in the halo blend.

While blends can soften the shape and color transitions between objects, you can further soften the appearance of your halo by applying a Gaussian Blur. Because applying a raster effect to a complex blend can tax your computer's processor, consider rasterizing the blend before applying the blur. (Note: because rasterizing artwork will prevent it from being further edited, save a copy of it in case you need it later.) To rasterize, select the black background rectangle and the multi-step blend you created previously and choose Object > Rasterize. In the pop-up Rasterize dialog box, set Resolution to a value that suits the size or medium of your illustration's display or publication; also, set Anti-aliasing to None. Be sure to review the Illustrator Basics chapter for guidance on settings that affect the quality of exported Illustrator files with raster objects and effects.

When you're ready to apply the blur, select the rasterized object and choose Effect > Blur > Gaussian Blur. In the Gaussian Blur dialog box, move the slider to the right or enter a number in the Radius field (Brashear

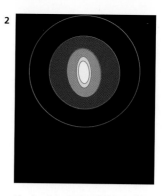

The background and five halo objects (each halo object shown here with magenta stroke for demonstration)

The multistep blend with 12 blend steps between each of the five original component objects

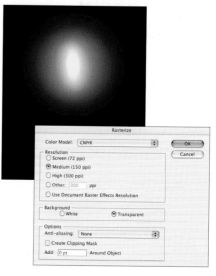

Above, the rasterized object created from the multi-step blend; below, the Object > Rasterize dialog box

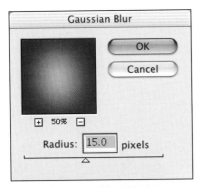

Top, the Gaussian Blur dialog box; bottom, the rasterized object following blurring

3

The original yellow candle flame tip on the left; on the right, the original flame tip and a copy that was scaled smaller and filled with yellow-white

On the left, an elongated copy of the original candle flame tip in front of the yellow and white tips; in the middle, the yellow and white tips are blurred; on the right, the blurred flame tips after being masked

applied a blur with a 20 pixel radius to his halo's blend). If you want to change the blur later, simply select the blurred object and double-click Gaussian Blur in the Appearance palette, and enter another Radius value.

3 Blending, blurring and masking the flame. Brashear observed that the orange tip of the flame in the photographic image was hard-edged along the sides but gradually blurred near the tip. You can achieve this visual effect in Illustrator with a blur and a clipping mask. Start by selecting the object you drew as a triangular flame tip. Then select the Scale tool and click on the bottom-left point of the tip, then click on a point or line on the other side of the tip and drag inward while pressing the Option/Alt key to create a smaller copy of the object. Fill the copy with a yellow-white color. With the copied object still selected, click on the bottom-left point with the Scale tool, click on a point or line opposite it and Option-drag/Alt-drag a new outline that is taller but not wider than the other tip objects. Next, select the first two tip objects and choose Effect>Blur>Gaussian Blur; in the pop-up Gaussian Blur dialog box, set the Radius to 1.0 pixel. To finish, select the blurred tips and the unblurred tip (the second copy you made) and choose Object>Clipping Mask>Make. As a result, the blur is confined to the edges of the clipping mask (but spreads through the empty area at the top of the masking object).

The two faces of Rasterize

When you apply Effect>Blur>Gaussian Blur to a vector object, Illustrator automatically rasterizes the paths "live" (using the parameters found in the Effect> Document Raster Effects Settings dialog). This doesn't happen with the Filter version of the Gaussian Blur, however. You need to convert your vector object to a raster object using Object>Rasterize before you can apply the Gaussian Blur filter. Remember that unless you undo the rasterization, your vector object will be permanently changed to raster—so make a copy first!

Ted Alspach

Ted Alspach used the Flare tool to create an air of mystery in this mock movie poster. The Flare tool simulates a lens flare in a photograph by creating a halo, rays, and rings around an object. Alspach selected the Flare tool (found in the Rectangle tool pop-up menu), clicked and dragged to set the halo size, then click-dragged again to set the distance and direction of the rings, while using the Arrow keys to adjust the number of rings. He colored some elements (such as the type) a light shade of gray to give the flare an illusion of greater brilliance. In addition to the click-drag method, components of the flare can be modified using the Flare Options dialog box. Here, you can adjust the diameter, opacity, and brightness of the flare's center, as well as the fuzziness of the halo, the number of rays, and the flare's crispness.

Taking care of the Flare

The Flare tool is unusual in that it's the only tool that *sometimes* requires a two-step process. When the "Rings" option is checked, you must click-drag to establish the center, and then click or click-drag again to determine the length and direction of the path along which the rings are drawn. If "Rings" is unchecked, drawing a Flare is a one-step process. Many people don't realize the default two-step process and click away onto something else before completing their flare.

Warps & Envelopes

Using Warping and Enveloping Effects

COHEN

Overview: *Group clip art for use with Warp; apply Warp; save Warp effect as a graphic style; apply Envelope using a shaped path; add a shading effect using a mesh.*

Making sure that the flag artwork is grouped. **Note:** *The Appearance palette shows information for the currently targeted (not just selected or highlighted) object in the Layers palette*

The Flag Warp applied to a not-fully-grouped flag artwork. The stripes are grouped, but the stars and the union (blue field) are separate objects

With Preview enabled, experiment with the Warp Options settings

After the tragic events of September 11, 2001, consultant Sandee Cohen wanted to make some flag decorations for her Web site. She used Illustrator's Warping and Enveloping effects to mold copies of a basic rectangular flag into a waving flag and a bow tie.

Warps are the easier of the two methods to understand and use. Simply choose one of the 15 preset shapes from the Warp menu and adjust the shape using the sliders in the Warp Options dialog box.

Envelopes let you use any path, warp preset, or mesh object to shape and mold your artwork into almost any form imaginable. You can further manipulate the shape using the envelope's anchor points.

Although Warps and Envelopes leave original artwork unchanged, only Warps can be saved as graphic styles.

1 Group clip art for use with Warp effects. Cohen started with a standard United States flag from a clip art collection. First, she made sure that the flag artwork was a grouped object by selecting the flag artwork (which also targets it in the Layers palette) and checking its description in the Appearance palette. If the artwork is not a grouped object, then the effects will not be applied to the artwork as a whole, but rather to each of the paths individually (as shown in the sidebar).

2 Make a copy of the flag artwork and apply a Warp effect. Next, Cohen made a duplicate copy of the flag by selecting it and, holding down Option/Alt, dragging it to a position below the original. While the duplicate was still selected, Cohen chose Effect > Warp > Flag to bring up the Warp dialog. She enabled the Preview checkbox in the Warp dialog box so she could preview the effect her settings would have on the artwork. Cohen set the Horizontal Bend slider to –42% to create the first stage of her waving flag effect, and clicked OK to apply the Warp. She then applied a second Warp effect to the flag artwork, to complete her waving flag. With the artwork still selected, she chose Effect > Warp > Arc and, with Preview enabled, set the Horizontal Bend slider to 40%.

Note: *In the Warp dialog box, you have access to the full library of Warp shapes no matter which warp you chose from the Effect > Warp menu. Simply click and drag on the style pop-up menu in the Warp dialog box to access any of the Warp shapes. As long as Preview is enabled, you can then experiment with each Warp shape and settings to see how each will affect your artwork before you apply one.*

To remove a Warp effect, target your artwork. Then, in the Appearance palette, select the Warp and either click on, or drag your selection to, the Trash button.

3 Save your Warp effect as a graphic style. Once you are pleased with a particular Warp effect or effects that you have achieved, you can easily save the effects as a graphic style for application to other artwork. Begin by targeting the artwork that you applied your warp(s) and other effects to in the Layers palette. Then Option-click/Alt-click on the New Graphic Style button at the bottom of the Graphic Styles palette to create and name your new graphic style. If the appearance you save as a graphic style has no fill or strokes, the thumbnail for the graphic style you created will be blank. When this happens, choose either the Small or the Large List View (from the Graphic Styles palette pop-up menu) to view the graphic styles by name. To apply a graphic style, simply target the object, group, or layer, and then click on the graphic style in the Graphic Styles palette.

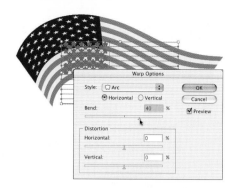

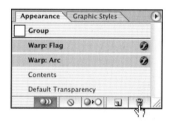
Applying a second Warp effect. Because Warps are live effects, the original flag artwork (seen here as an outline in light blue because the artwork is still selected) remains unchanged

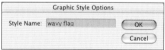
Removing Warp effects from the artwork by highlighting the effects in the Appearance palette, and then clicking on the Trash button to delete them

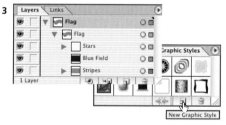
To create a new graphic style, target your artwork, then Option-click/Alt-click the New Graphic Style button, and give your new graphic style a name

Applying a Warp effect graphic style to a grouped object

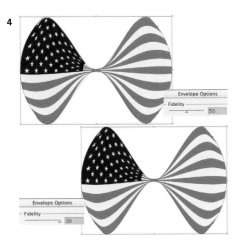

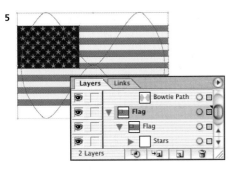

With Envelope Options fidelity set too low, red color in the lower right corner of the upper figure spills outside the bow tie shape. When the fidelity is set to 99% the artwork conforms much more closely to the envelope shape.

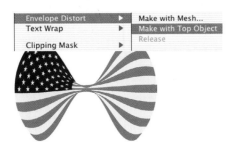

Bow tie path positioned above the flag artwork, and selected, just before making the envelope

Applying the envelope, and the resulting artwork

Using Edit > Paste in Front to create a duplicate positioned directly over the original artwork

4 Use Envelope Options to maximize Envelope fidelity. Envelopes are more versatile in the ways you can shape and manipulate them, but sometimes (especially when the shape you use to create the envelope is kinked or makes sharp changes in direction) the artwork may not conform tightly to the envelope. To minimize this problem, set the Object > Envelope Distort > Envelope Options Fidelity to 99%. Note: Setting Fidelity to 100% creates many more intermediate points along the deformed path, and is usually not necessary.

Cohen used an Envelope to give her flag the shape of a bow tie, and added some shading using a mesh.

5 Apply Envelope using a shaped Path. Cohen added points to a circle and then distorted it into a bow-tie-shaped path. To apply a shaped path of your own, place it above your flag artwork, select both the flag and your shaped path, and choose Object > Envelope Distort > Make with Top Object.

6 Add a shading effect with a mesh. Next, Cohen added a shading effect by using a mesh object on top of her bow tie flag. Begin by creating a duplicate of the bow tie flag (Edit > Copy), then paste it in front of the first one using Edit > Paste in Front to exactly align it over the original. With the duplicate still selected, choose Object > Envelope Distort > Reset with Mesh. In the Reset Envelope Mesh dialog box, make sure that Maintain Envelope Shape and Preview are both enabled. Increase the number of Rows and Columns until you are satisfied with the mesh grid in terms of how you intend to shade it. For her mesh, Cohen used 6 rows and 6 columns. Click OK, and with the mesh artwork still selected, choose Envelope > Distort > Release to free the mesh from the flag. Delete the flag artwork and keep the mesh object. When a mesh object is released from an envelope, it is filled with 20% black. Select the mesh object, then with the Direct-select or Lasso tool, select points on the mesh grid and change their fill to a shadow color. Cohen selected interior grid points and gave them a value of white until she was satisfied with the mesh's shading.

Note: *Multiple contiguous points and large areas in the mesh are most easily selected using the Lasso tool.*

To see the effect of the shading on the original bow tie flag beneath the mesh, Cohen (with the mesh selected) set the Blending Mode in the Transparency palette to Multiply. This applied the Blending mode only to the selected mesh object, and not the whole layer.

Finally, using the same enveloping and mesh techniques described above, Cohen created a center for the bow tie using a copy of some of the stripes and an elongated rounded rectangle path.

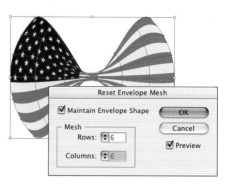

Creating a mesh object using a duplicate of the bow tie flag envelope artwork

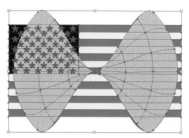

Using Envelope > Distort > Release to free the mesh from the flag artwork

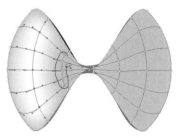

Using the Lasso to select multiple mesh points

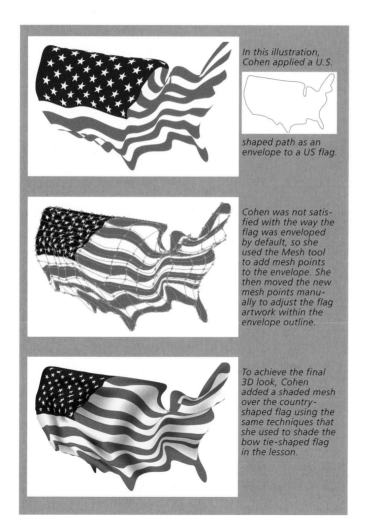

In this illustration, Cohen applied a U.S. shaped path as an envelope to a US flag.

Cohen was not satisfied with the way the flag was enveloped by default, so she used the Mesh tool to add mesh points to the envelope. She then moved the new mesh points manually to adjust the flag artwork within the envelope outline.

To achieve the final 3D look, Cohen added a shaded mesh over the country-shaped flag using the same techniques that she used to shade the bow tie-shaped flag in the lesson.

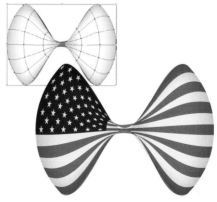

Before and after applying a blending mode of Multiply to the shaded mesh object

Quick & Easy 3D

Simple 3D techniques

Overview: *Draw or modify 2D artwork, prepare artwork for 3D; apply 3D Effect; expand artwork and edit objects to complete visual effects.*

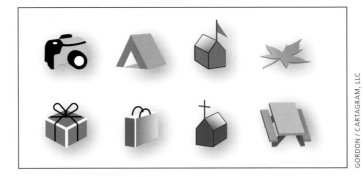

GORDON / CARTAGRAM, LLC

1

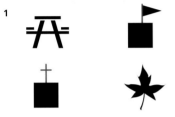

Some of the standard map symbols that Gordon modified for the map symbol set

Left, the original tent artwork objects; center, the white triangle selected; right, the tent after subtracting the white triangle from the black triangle and changing the fill color to green

Steven Gordon was hired to design a set of contemporary map symbols for Digital Wisdom, Inc. that would be sold as a clip-art set of map symbol artwork and Illustrator symbols (www.map-symbol.com). To make this set stand out from other map symbol sets and fonts, Gordon explored Illustrator's new 3D Effect and found that it made it easy to turn the ordinary into the unusual.

1 Drawing artwork, visualizing 3D appearance, and using editing tools to prepare for 3D. Gordon started with some standard map symbol clip-art. For the camping symbol, he modified the tent artwork by removing the bottom horizontal object and applying a light green fill to the remaining triangle. When visualizing how the object would look in 3D, Gordon realized that the white and green triangles would both be rendered as 3D objects; instead he needed the white triangle to form a hole in the green triangle that would become the tent. He selected the white and green triangles and clicked the Subtract from Shape Area icon in the Pathfinder palette to punch a hole in the green triangle.

As you prepare artwork for the 3D Effect, refer to the *Drawing & Coloring* chapter to review techniques for making compound shapes by combining or cutting objects (as Gordon did to make the tent opening), and for making compound paths (which may yield different results than applying a 3D Effect to separate artwork objects). Also, change stroke attributes for caps, joins, and miter limits to round off path intersections in the 3D rendering you'll create in the next step.

2 Apply 3D Effect, modify Position controls to extrude and rotate objects, and create a Style. When you finish creating your artwork, make sure it is selected, and then from the Effect menu, select 3D > Extrude & Bevel. In the 3D Extrude & Bevel Options dialog box, click the Preview checkbox to see what your artwork will look like using the dialog box's default settings.

Artwork in preview mode for several adjustments of the Position cube in the 3D Extrude & Bevel Options dialog box

You can change the artwork's rotation by clicking on the three-dimensional cube in the Position pane of the dialog box and dragging until the artwork moves to an orientation you like. You can also fine-tune the position by keying in values in the X, Y, and Z axes rotation fields.

To change the amount or depth of the extrusion, use the Extrude Depth slider in the Extrude & Bevel pane of the dialog box. To give the tent less depth than the default setting (50 pt), Gordon dragged the slider to extrude by 40 pt. To simulate perspective, drag the Perspective slider to adjust the amount of perspective from none/isometric (0°) to very steep (160°). Gordon used 135° for his artwork. When you are satisfied with your artwork's appearance, click OK to render the object.

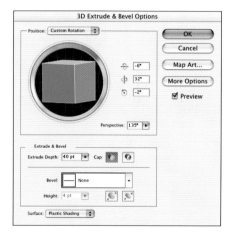

The 3D Extrude & Bevel Options dialog box with the settings Gordon used for the final version of the tent symbol

Gordon converted the 3D appearance he had created for the tent into a reusable style. Refer to the *Live Effects & Graphic Styles* chapter for instructions on creating and modifying styles. You can use a style for other artwork, as way of providing a uniform 3D appearance for several objects, or as a starting point for creating a new 3D appearance for an object.

3 Editing the artwork after using the 3D Effect. After applying the 3D Effect to the tent artwork, Gordon decided to make color and shape changes to the artwork. To edit shapes or change colors of objects in the 3D artwork, you must first expand the appearance by choosing Object > Expand Appearance. (Note: this will remove the "live" editability of the artwork; it's safer to work with a copy of the artwork instead of the original.) Once expanded, ungroup the artwork (Object > Ungroup) and select and edit its paths.

Left, the tent artwork after expanding the 3D artwork (Object > Expand Appearance); right, shapes after filling with different colors

Selecting and modifying one of the shapes to create the interior floor of the tent

Chapter 9 *Live Effects & Graphic Styles*   **317**

3D Effects

Extruding, Revolving, and Rotating Paths

Overview: *Create basic paths working with a custom template layer; extrude, revolve, and rotate paths; map artwork onto shapes.*

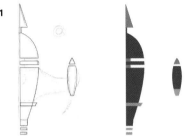

The original pencil drawing, placed as a template, and the vector shapes drawn over them

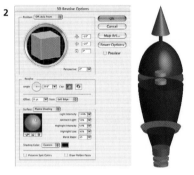

The original group of paths, selected and revolved as a group with the same settings

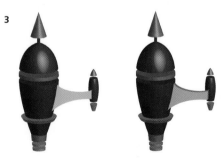

The wing shape drawn to follow the contour of the hull and then extruded and rotated slightly

To complete this illustration, Brad Hamann created a set of basic paths and applied a series of live 3D effects to them. He then added lighting and mapped artwork to the components.

1 Planning ahead. Because he would be rotating his shapes, Hamann needed to draw only one side of the symmetrical space cruiser. Working over a pencil drawing he had scanned in Photoshop and placed on a designated template layer, he drew one closed shape for the hull. He divided it into sections using the Pathfinder tool so he could color each part differently. He filled the paths with solid color and no stroke. When revolved, a filled path with no stroke will present the fill color as its surface color. A stroked shape that is revolved uses the stroke color as its surface color, regardless of fill color.

2 Applying the 3D Revolve effect to a group of shapes and extruding the wings. Hamann chose to revolve the group of shapes that make up the ship's hull all at the same time, because they shared the same left-side vertical rotation line. He also revolved the three shapes making up the rocket-shaped wing end as a group, using the same settings. Once the shapes were revolved, Hamann selected and moved each shape into its proper position within the group, using the Bring to Front command. He deleted the two inner green circles, because they would be invisible within the 3D model anyway.

For the wings Hamann then drew a flat shape for the right wing that followed the contour of the 3D hull and chose Effect > 3D > Extrude & Bevel. He selected an extrusion depth and rotational angle for the wing that would be visually consistent with the hull.

3 Mapping artwork. Hamann decided to map a star pattern, which he had previously saved as a symbol, onto the wing to liven up the look of the spaceship. He was able to return to the 3D Effects settings window by selecting the wing and clicking the Effect setting from the Appearance palette. He then clicked the Map Art button to access the Map Art window, which presented an outline of the first of the six surfaces available on the wing for mapping. Hamann chose his star pattern from the menu of available symbols. He scaled the pattern using the handles on the bounding box and then clicked OK. At this time, he also changed the wing color from green to red. Finally, Hamann selected the wing and the rocket at its end, and reflected and copied the wing to the opposite side of the spacecraft. He made a slight adjustment to the rotational angle of the new wing's Y-axis to account for its new position.

4 Ready for takeoff. Hamann completed his rocket ship by creating a porthole from a circular path to which he applied a 5.5 pt ochre-colored stroke. He then extruded the path and applied a rounded bevel. A blue gradient filled path, and a Gaussian Blur was applied, which completed the porthole.

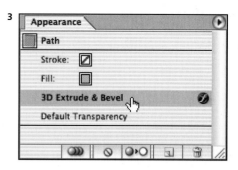

3

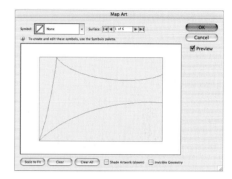

Clicking in the wing's Appearance palette to return to the 3D Effects settings window

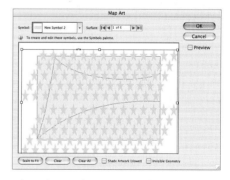

The Map Art window showing the first of the wing's surfaces available to map art onto

After selecting the star pattern from the Symbol menu, the pattern was scaled and positioned onto the wing outline

4

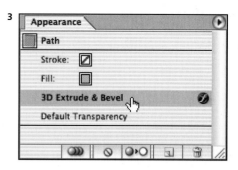

Hamann applied a rounded bevel to a circular path he had extruded to create the porthole

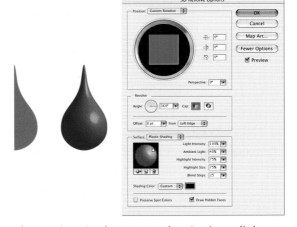

© HALLMARK LICENSING, INC.

Mike Schwabauer / Hallmark Cards

To announce a company blood drive, artist Mike Schwabauer produced this illustration that was emailed as a low-resolution graphic and printed as a sign. For the background flag, Schwabauer started with flat, rectangular flag artwork. He selected the Free Transform tool to rotate and scale the flag. Then he chose Object > Envelope Distort > Make with Warp. In the Warp Options dialog box, he selected Flag from the Style menu. Schwabauer modified the default settings for the Flag style. When he had the look he wanted, he clicked OK. To fade the flag, he drew a rectangle large enough to cover the flag and filled it with a black-to-white gradient. After selecting the rectangle and the flag, he opened the Transparency palette and chose Make Opacity Mask from the palette menu. For the blood drop, Schwabauer drew half of the blood drop shape. Then he chose Effect > 3D > Revolve and customized the settings in the 3D Revolve Options dialog box. After clicking OK, he changed the object's transparency in the Transparency palette to 93% to make the drop look more like a liquid. To complete the blood drop, Schwabauer selected the blood drop object and chose Effect > Stylize > Drop Shadow. In the Drop Shadow dialog box, he set Mode to Multiply, Opacity to 50%, Blur to 0.12 inches, and Offset to -0.5" (X) and 0.2" (Y).

SHARIF

Robert Sharif

Robert Sharif used the power of Illustrator's 3D Extrude & Bevel effect to transform and combine a set of flat shapes into a stunningly realistic rendering of a classic Fender electric guitar. Robert chose Off-Axis-Front as the position for each shape he wanted to extrude, including the red guitar body, the wooden neck/headstock, and a grouped set of shapes containing the fingerboard, frets, and dot-shaped position markers. Because each extrusion shared the same position, the extruded pieces all lined up. Robert varied the value of the extrude depth for each piece, from a deeper extrusion for the body (25 pt), to a shallower extrusion for the white face plate (0.65 pt). Robert also chose to add a variety of bevels to various parts of the guitar, including rounded bevels to the body and neck, and a classic bevel to the control knobs. The three white pickups, the fret board, and other square edged parts were extruded with the Bevel set to None. To create the soft highlights on the guitar body, Robert used the Plastic Shading

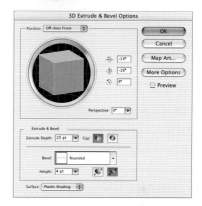

rendering style. The 3D Extrude & Bevel effect was also used to create the screw heads for the tuning pegs, whose shafts were created using 3D Revolve. The tuning peg handles and other parts of the guitar were made using gradient-filled shapes.

WAI

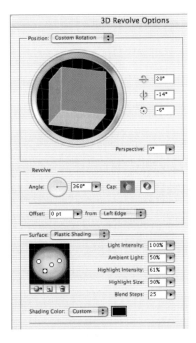

Trina Wai

Trina Wai created her playful panda by taking full advantage of Illustrator CS's 3D Revolve and 3D Extrude and Bevel effects. She started with a series of very simple flat shapes and ended with a truly organic look. Wai began by drawing an open path for one side of the panda's head. Choosing Effect > 3D > Revolve, she rotated the path 360° along its left edge. To create the soft shiny reflections of the panda's fur, Wai specified plastic shading as the surface type and added additional light sources using the New Light button. The bamboo stalk was also revolved from a simple open path, then rotated and grouped with a set of flat leaf shapes. Wai then extruded the main body parts by selecting 3D Extrude and Bevel. Each shape received its own extrusion depth ranging from 150 pt for the legs and body, 37.5 pt for the ears, 30 pt for the nose and 7 pt for the areas

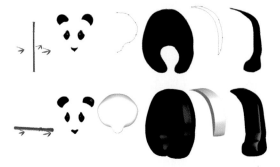

surrounding the eyes. Each shape also received a rounded bevel and plastic shading lit with a single light source. The small eyes were created using a blend between a large black circle and a smaller gray circle.

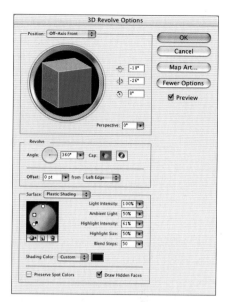

GOLDING / ADOBE SYSTEMS, INC.

Mordy Golding / Adobe Systems, Inc.

To demonstrate the 3D effect of Illustrator CS, Adobe Product Manager Mordy Golding created a wine label and then dragged the label to the Symbols palette (so he could use it next to create the 3D rendering). He drew a half-bottle shape and selected Effect > 3D > Revolve. In the 3D Revolve Options dialog box, Golding clicked the Preview checkbox and then clicked on the Map Art button. From the Map Art dialog box's Symbol menu, he selected the wine label symbol he had created previously. Back in the 3D Revolve Options dialog box, Golding adjusted the preview cube, changing the rotation angles until he was satisfied with the look of the bottle. He finished the effect by adding lights, using the New Light icon in the Surface panel of the dialog box; this created the cascading highlights on the bottle. After creating the cork, using the same technique as he used for the bottle, Golding selected the bottle, moved it above the cork, and changed its opacity to 94% in the Transparency palette.

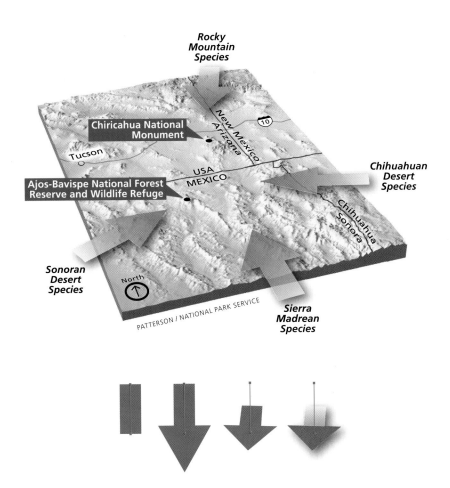

PATTERSON / NATIONAL PARK SERVICE

Tom Patterson / National Park Service

Cartographer Tom Patterson used Illustrator's 3D effect to show species movement across the Sonoran Desert. Patterson drew a straight path with the Pen tool and chose a 20 pt stroke. To turn the path into an arrow, he chose Effect > Stylize > Add Arrowheads. In the Add Arrowheads dialog box, he selected an arrowhead design (11) and specified 25% for Scale. Next, Patterson chose Effect > 3D > Rotate and in the 3D Rotate Options dialog box, he enabled the Preview and dragged the three-dimensional cube in the Position pane to adjust the spatial

orientation of the arrow. When the arrow looked right, he clicked OK. To fill the arrow, Patterson first chose Object > Group to change the arrow from an object to a group. Then he selected Add New Fill from the Appearance palette menu and applied a custom gradient to the new fill. He repeated these steps to create the other three arrows. To finish, Patterson targeted the layer containing the arrows and changed opacity to 80% in the Transparency palette; he also added a drop shadow (Effect > Stylize > Drop Shadow) to the layer.

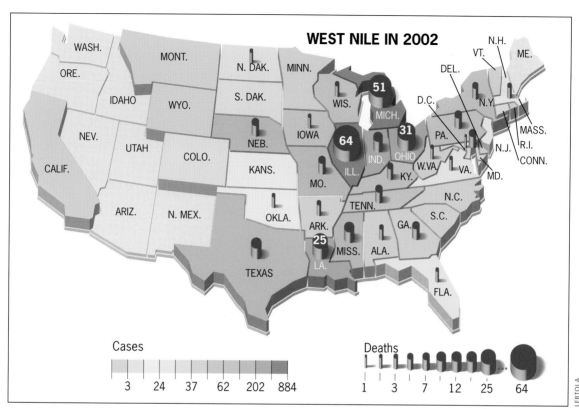

WEST NILE IN 2002

Cases
3 24 37 62 202 884

Deaths
1 3 7 12 25 64

LERTOLA

Joe Lertola / TIME

Joe Lertola of *TIME* Magazine relied on the 3D Effect (Effect > 3D > Extrude & Bevel) to turn an otherwise flat map into an eye-catching 3D thematic map. After drawing all the artwork, Lertola created groups for the gray states and the colored states. To give each group a different height, he applied the 3D Effect to each group, but specified a different Extrude Depth value in the 3D Extrude & Bevel Options dialog box for each group (6 pt for the gray states and 24 pt for the colored states). Lertola completed the effect by adding a second light (he clicked on the New Light icon in the Surface panel) to change the position of the highlight and shadow of each group.

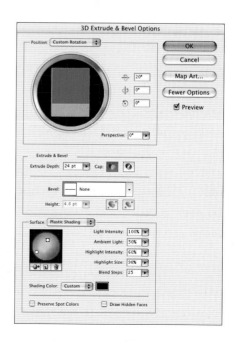

Scribble Basics

Applying Scribble Effects to Artwork

Overview: *Applying default Scribble effect settings; choosing from preset Scribble styles; making custom adjustments to Scribble settings.*

1

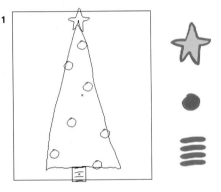

Shown here in Outline mode, Stead created her first tree by drawing with the brush tool

2

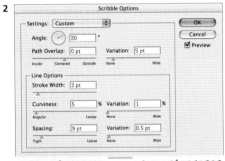

After switching the color scheme for her second tree, Stead selected the red rectangle background, hid the edges, and applied the Custom Scribble option from the Effects menu

Judy Stead's evergreen tree began simply, but with the help of Illustrator's brand new Scribble effect, it evolved into an eye-catching Christmas card. Here, you will learn how to apply the Scribble effect to your artwork, how to make use of the preset Scribble styles, and how to make custom adjustments to the effect in order to add excitement and energy to your art.

1 Creating the base art and the variations. Stead began by using the Brush tool to create a simple, filled shape for the tree. She used a 5 pt round Calligraphic brush to create the star, and applied a red stroke and a yellow fill to the path. The ornament was drawn using the same brush and stroke with a magenta fill added. Stead copied and pasted this shape several times to decorate her tree. She created the base of the tree using a 12 pt oval Calligraphic brush to draw a single horizontal stroke. She then made three copies and grouped them against a white rectangle.

Stead decided that her card would contain three variations of the first tree, so she copied and pasted them into position and gave each one a different color scheme. Beginning with the first variation, she selected the red background rectangle. She chose Effects > Stylize > Scribble, after first hiding the selection edges of her art (⌘-Y) in order to observe the results more clearly. When the Scribble Options menu appeared, Stead clicked Preview. Satisfied with the Default settings, she clicked OK. These settings applied the appearance of a loose, continuous stroke to her solid red rectangle.

2 Using the Scribble presets. For her next variation, Stead first selected the light green tree and chose the Scribble style set entitled Sketch. She decided to leave the Sketch settings as they were and clicked OK. Then she selected the magenta background. After applying the Scribble style set entitled Sharp, she opened up the denseness of the effect's strokes by using the slider to change the Spacing value from 3 pt to 5 pt. The Scribble Options palette also contains sliders to control the thickness of the stroke, the general curviness of the strokes, and the degree of variation or evenness of the effect.

3 Further Scribble settings. For the final variation, Stead selected the green background and chose the Swash settings from the Options palette. Using the circular Angle slider, she changed the preset angle of the strokes from 0 to –30 degrees. Stead then selected all the ornaments on the tree and applied a final Scribble effect using the Dense settings from the Scribble Options palette. Stead was able to go back and readjust all her settings, as needed, by clicking the instance of the effect in each object's Appearance palette. As a final touch, Stead selected the solid red tree and sent it backward (Object > Arrange > Send Backward) so that the green Swash scribble effect would overlay the tree and provide an interesting texture.

2

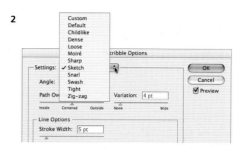

For the light green Christmas tree, Stead chose the Sketch from the Scribble palette's Settings

Stead applied the Scribble palette's Sharp settings to the background, changing spacing setting from 3 pt to 5 pt for a looser appearance

3

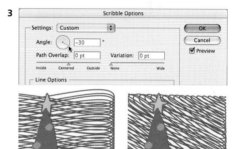

Stead applied Swash from the Scribble palette's Settings to the green background of the final tree art, and changed the angle of the strokes using the Angle slider in the Options palette (which then changed the "Settings" to Custom)

Hiding edges to see the effect

Applying a Scribble effect can generate a complex set of edges that make it difficult to view the artwork underneath. Get into the habit of hiding the edges of your selection before trying out an effect. Use the ⌘-Y keyboard shortcut to toggle the visibility of the edges on and off.

MACADANGDANG

   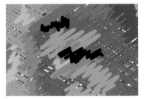

Todd Macadangdang/Adobe Systems, Inc.

Todd Macadangdang used the Scribble effect to turn this photo into an artistic crosshatch sketch. Todd started by adjusting the colors and posterizing the photograph in Photoshop, using adjustment layers. He then placed the image in Illustrator and created filled shapes based on the posterized areas. Starting with the smallest, front-most area, he clicked on the area with the Eyedropper tool to set the Fill color (with Stroke set to None), then traced over it using the Pencil tool. He repeated this process, working his way toward the largest back-most areas; using Object > Arrange > Send Backward as he went along to keep the shapes in the correct visual stacking order. Todd then applied the Scribble effect to each traced area. To give his image a greater sense of depth, he created fatter, looser Scribble strokes (using Settings such as Childlike, Loose, or Snarl) for the front-most areas and used smaller denser strokes (with the Angle setting rotated 90°) for the larger back-most crosshatched areas.

Advanced Techniques

10

330 Introduction

330 Clipping Masks

333 Mask Problem-Solving Strategies

334 Advanced Technique: Colorful Masking:
Fitting Blends into Custom Shapes

336 Advanced Technique: Reflective Masks:
Super-Realistic Reflection

338–341 Galleries: Bradley Neal, David Cater, Gary Ferster, Greg Maxson

342 Advanced Technique: Glowing Starshine:
Blending Custom Colors to Form a Glow

343–347 Galleries: Kenneth Batelman, Alan James Weimer, Marc LaMantia

348 Advanced Technique: Masking Opacity:
Making Transparency Irregular

350 Advanced Technique: Modeling Mesh:
Shaping and Forming Mesh Objects

353–356 Galleries: Javier Romero, Ann Paidrick, Yukio Miyamoto

Advanced Techniques

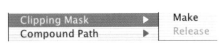

Choose Clipping Mask >Make from the Object menu or use the Make Clipping Mask button on the Layers palette

Choosing Object >Clipping Mask >Make puts all of the masking objects into a group with the masking element at the top of the group

Clicking the Make Clipping Mask button at the bottom of the palette turns the first item below the highlighted group or layer into a clipping path, without creating a new group

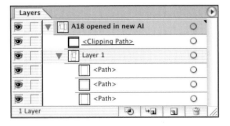

When you open a legacy file with layer-masks, the masked layers become sublayers of the masking layer, because all masking objects must be on the same container layer

This chapter combines techniques found in different chapters of this book. With masking effects in particular, the techniques will be easier to follow if you're comfortable with layers and stacking order (the *Layers* chapter), as well as blends and gradients (the *Blends, Gradients & Mesh* chapter), and are willing to experiment with Pathfinder filters (the *Drawing & Coloring* chapter).

CLIPPING MASKS

There are two kinds of masks in Illustrator: Clipping Masks and Opacity Masks. This chapter will discuss the use of Clipping Masks in a variety of techniques. Opacity Masks are made using the Transparency palette and are discussed in the *Transparency & Appearances* chapter.

Illustrator's Clipping Mask command (left) gathers all the selected objects into a group (moving them onto the same layer as the top object if they aren't already there). It then converts the topmost object in that group into a mask. Portions of the other objects in the clipping group that extend beyond the mask boundaries will be hidden. After you've applied a Clipping Mask, you can easily adjust the contour of the masking object itself, as well as the objects within the mask, using the Lasso or any path-editing tools. Use the Direct Selection tool to edit paths, the Group Selection tool to isolate objects within a group or to select entire objects, or the Selection tool to work with groups of objects.

In order to use multiple objects as a mask, you'll need to first select the objects and convert them to a Compound Path (Object >Compound Path >Make), or a Compound Shape (choose Make Compound Shape from the Pathfinder palette pop-up menu, or use the *Wow! Action* loaded from the Compound Shape Commands group of actions in *Wow! Actions* on the *Wow! CD*). In either case, your multiple objects form one compound object that can then become a single masking object.

Two indicators in the Layers palette can tell you that you have an active Clipping Mask. First, your Clipping Mask path will be underlined and will remain underlined even if you rename it. Second, with an active Clipping Mask, you'll see dotted lines between the clipped items in the Layers palette instead of standard solid lines.

Once you've created the object or Compound object you wish to become your mask, you can convert it into a Clipping Mask using either the Make Clipping Mask button of the Layers palette, or the Object >Clipping Mask > Make command. The Layers palette commands maintain your layers' structure as they mask (recall that the Object menu command gathers all the selected objects into a new group, which can be disconcerting if you've already set up a layer structure). See below for details on both methods.

Masking technique #1: The Layers palette options
To mask unwanted areas of art within a *container* (meaning any group, sublayer, or layer), create an object to use as your mask and make sure it's the topmost item in your container. Next, highlight the container with the object that will become your mask, and click the Make Clipping Mask button on the Layers palette. The result: the topmost object within the selected container becomes the Clipping Mask object (which hides all elements that extend beyond the mask) within that container.

Once you've created a Clipping Mask, you can move objects up or down within the layer or sublayers to change the stacking order. However, if you move items out of the container that has the Clipping Mask, they will no longer be masked (see the *Layers* chapter for more on Layers). Moving the clipping path itself out of the container it was created within releases the mask completely. To release a Clipping Mask without reordering objects or layers, highlight the mask's container in the Layers palette and click the Make/Release Clipping Mask icon.

Before Illustrator 9, if you selected objects on different layers and chose to Make Mask, you'd be creating a "layer-mask" that would hide all objects between the

To insert objects into a Clipping Mask, make certain that Paste Remembers Layers (in the Layers palette menu) is off, then Cut or Copy the objects you wish to insert. Next, select an object within the mask and use Paste in Front or Back to place the copied object into the mask. Alternatively, you can drag the new object into the mask using the Layers palette (see the *Layers* chapter).

Magically move a Clipping Path

Once an object is a Clipping Path, you can move it anywhere *within* its layer or group in the Layers palette and it will still maintain its masking effect!

Figuring out if it's a mask

If you're not sure whether a current selection contains a mask or is being masked, look for:

• The <u>\<Clipping Path\></u> entry in the Layers palette. Even if the entry has been renamed, it will remain underlined if it is a mask. All clipped objects will be in the same layer or group as the mask.

• Object > Clipping Mask > Release being enabled means a mask is affecting your selection.

• An Opacity Mask is indicated with a *dotted* underline.

FABRICS An example of how type can be used as a masking object

selected objects, with the topmost object becoming your mask. If you open one of these files in the current version of Illustrator, you'll see that all your layers are now contained within a new layer called a "master layer."

In order to mask across layers in the current version, you'll have to manually create your own "master layer" into which you'll place everything you want to mask. To do this, first select all the layers that you wish to mask (click on the first layer you want masked, then Shift-click on the bottom layer) and choose Collect in New Layer from the Layers pop-up menu—this places all of your layers within a new "master layer." Although any topmost object can now become your mask (including an entire group or sublayer), it's probably easiest to create or move a masking object in the "master layer" itself. Make sure the element to be used as a mask is at the top of the contents within the master layer; then select the master layer in the Layers palette, and click the palette's Make/Release Clipping Mask button, or choose Make Clipping Mask from the Layers palette pop-up menu. For practice applying a Clipping Mask across multiple layers, see Step 5 in the "Transparent Color" lesson in the *Transparency & Appearances* chapter.

Masking technique #2: The Object menu command
You can also create masks for objects and groups of objects that are independent of layers and sublayers. Use this method when you want to confine the masking effect to a specific object or group of objects that you can easily duplicate and relocate. Since this method modifies your layer structure, don't use it if you need to maintain objects on specific layers.

As before, start by creating a topmost object or compound object that will become your Clipping Mask. Next, select *all* the objects you want to be masked (the topmost object will become the mask). Now, choose Object > Clipping Mask > Make. When you use this method, all the objects, including the new Clipping Path, will move to the layer that contained your topmost

object and will be contained within a new <Group>.
The masking effect will be restricted to only those objects
within the group, and you can easily use the Selection
tool to select the entire clipping group. If you expand
the <Group> in the Layers palette, you'll be able to move
objects up or down within the group to change the stacking order. Expanding the <Group> will allow you to move
objects into or out of the clipping group. This chapter
includes many examples that show how to use this command to create intricate contours by masking complex
groups, such as blends.

MASK PROBLEM-SOLVING STRATEGIES
Using type or type outlines as a mask
You can use editable type as a mask to give the appearance that the type is filled with any image or group of
objects. Select the type and the image or objects with
which you want to fill the text. Make sure the type is
on top, then choose Object > Clipping Mask > Make. To
use separate type characters as a single Clipping Mask,
you have to first make them into a Compound Shape
or Compound Path. You can make a Compound Shape
from either outlined or live (i.e., non-outlined) text. You
can make a Compound Path only from outlined text
(not live text). Once you've made a Compound Path or
Shape of your separate type elements, you can use it as a
mask. (See the Tip "Compound Paths or Shapes?" in the
Drawing & Coloring chapter. And see the *Type* chapter for
examples of masking with text.)

Mask error message
If you've tried to make a Clipping Mask, but you get the
message "selection cannot contain objects within different groups unless the entire group is selected," the objects
you've chosen to mask are part of a subset of a group of
objects. To create a mask with these objects, Cut your
selected objects, then Paste in Front (⌘-F for Mac/Ctrl-
F for Win). Now you'll be able to apply Object > Make
Clipping Mask.

When a mask isn't a mask
Masks used to be the only way to
achieve certain effects. You can
now use gradient mesh objects
to create effects that once had to
be created with masked blends
(see the *Blends, Gradients & Mesh*
chapter). The Pathfinder palette
also provides ways to visually crop
unwanted parts of objects or
groups of objects with the same
styling—but be aware that all
Pathfinders unify the styling of
objects and can delete or alter
strokes. Furthermore, the commands on the bottom row of the
Pathfinder palette permanently
alter the shape of your objects.

Finding masks
Deselecting all objects first and
choosing Select > Object > Clipping
Masks should help you find most
masks, though the command will
not find Clipping Masks that are
inside linked EPS or PDF files.

Memory-intensive masks
Too many masks, or complex
masking paths, may demand too
much RAM and prevent you from
printing. To test whether a specific mask is the problem, select it
and its masked objects, temporarily Hide them (Object > Hide), and
then try to print. Hiding the mask
will free up memory.

Colorful Masking

Fitting Blends into Custom Shapes

Advanced Technique

Overview: *Create a complex blend; mask it with a custom masking object; create a second mask-and-blend combination; make a two-object mask using compound paths.*

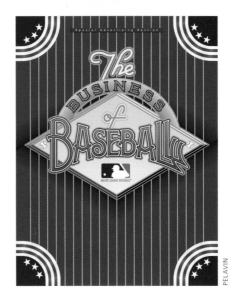

1

The gradient for a pencil body

2

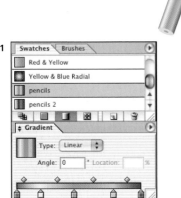

Creating objects and blending them in pairs, then creating an object to use as a mask

Selecting the blends with an overlying object designed as a mask; the blends masked

The best way to learn how to mask is to make some masked blends. With Laurie Grace's pencils, you'll learn how to mask complex blends to fit into custom shapes. And with the patriotic corners of Danny Pelavin's baseball illustration, you'll learn how to mask one blend into two different objects by using compound paths.

1 Creating the basic elements not requiring masking. Create your basic objects. For her pencils, Grace created the long barrel of the pencil with a gradient fill.

2 Creating the first mask-and-blend combination. To prepare a mask for the pencils, create a closed object outlining the shaved wood and pencil tip, and Lock it (Object menu). To ensure that your blend will completely fill the mask, make sure that each created object extends beyond the mask. Then select and blend each pair of adjacent objects (see the *Blends, Gradients & Mesh* chapter). Grace created the slanted outside objects first and the center object last so the blends would build from back to front towards the center. Unlock your pencil-tip object, choose Object > Arrange > Bring to Front, select the blends with the mask object and choose Object > Clipping Mask > Make. Then Object > Group the mask and the blend.

3 Preparing the next masking objects and mask. Select and copy your mask, then select and lock the mask with the masked objects to keep from accidentally selecting any of them as you continue to work. Next, use Paste in Front to paste a copy of your previous mask on top, and make any adjustments necessary to prepare this object as the next mask. Grace cut and reshaped a copy of the full pencil-tip mask until it correctly fit the colored lead at the top. Hide this new mask-to-be (Object > Hide Selection) until you've completed a new set of blends.

Completed objects selected and locked, then a copy of the last mask made into a new mask

4 Creating a new mask that overlays the first. Create and blend new pairs of objects as in Step 2. When your blends are complete, reveal (Object > Show All) your hidden masking object and Bring to Front to place the mask on top of these latest blends. Then select the colored-tip blends with this top object, make a mask as in Step 2 and, as before, Group them together for easy re-selection. Finally, Unlock the first blends (Object > Unlock All), select the entire piece and Group it all together.

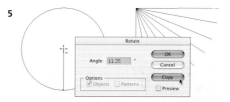

New objects before and after blending, and after being masked

5 Making a mask from a compound path. Create a blend to be masked by two objects. As Pelavin did for his patriotic corners, start with a circle as a template. Turn on View > Smart Guides and use the Pen tool to draw a straight line from the circle's center point to its bottom edge. With the Rotate tool, Option-click/Alt-click on the circle center to specify an 11.25° rotation and click Copy. Then choose Object > Transform > Transform Again seven times to repeat the rotated copy a full quarter of a circle. Recolor every other line and blend from one to the next, as above. Next, create two paths for a mask (Pelavin cut and joined quarters of concentric circles) and choose Object > Compound Path > Make. Place the compound path on top of the blends, select them all and choose Object > Clipping Mask > Make to see your blend show through both paths. Pelavin recolored a copy of the red blend with a range of whites, masked the white blend with a larger arc and placed it behind the reds.

Rotating a copy of a line about a circle's center 11.25°, then applying Transform Again 7 times

Coloring every other line and blending in pairs

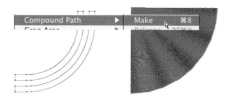

Compounding paths and getting ready to mask

Blends masked by compounds and a final corner (shown here also with a masked white blend)

Reflective Masks

Super-Realistic Reflection

Advanced Technique

Overview: *Move a copy of a blend area; if you're using type, convert it to outlines; shear and adjust it to the right shape; use filters to make an offset; recolor and remask blends; move blend back into position.*

T. NEAL / THOMAS • BRADLEY ILLUSTRATION & DESIGN

A blended area selected and a copy moved off the image area 5" (using Shift-Option/Shift-Alt and Keyboard Increment set to .5" increments); and type converted to outlines

Shearing outlined type, then adjusting and coloring it to fit the blend contour

Creating reflections for an "outline" by copying the outlined type object, then stroking and choosing Object >Path >Outline Stroke and then Unite in the Pathfinder palette

Two techniques in earlier chapters demonstrated how Thomas • Bradley Illustration & Design (T•B I&D) used the Pathfinder palette to generate its basic objects for blending, and how the blends themselves are formed (see "Unlocking Realism" in the *Blends, Gradients & Mesh* chapter). This technique focuses on replicating contouring blends to create reflectivity and surface variation.

1 Replicating an area of your image for placing new details. This process can be used to create color or surface variations, but we'll use the application of type detailing as a demonstration. After you've outlined your image and filled it with contouring blends, choose an area for detailing. With the Shift key down, use Selection and Group Selection tools to select all blends and originating objects for the blends that exist in that area. To move a copy of these blends out of the way, set the Keyboard Increment distance to .5" in Preferences > General. Now hold Shift-Option /Shift-Alt and press the → key to pull a copy of the selected blends 5" to the right (10 times the Keyboard Increment distance). To move this copy further, use Shift → to move the selected blends in 5" increments, or use → alone to nudge in .5" increments. With the Type tool, place a letter or number on top of the moved blend (see the *Type* chapter for help). Click a Selection tool to select the type as an object and choose Type > Create Outlines.

2 Reshaping type to fit your blended contours and creating an offset. Working from templates, references or just your artistic eye, use the Rotate, Scale and

Shear tools with Direct Selection to adjust various anchor points until the type fits the contour. For the type on the race car, T•B I&D sheared the letters (by clicking first in the center of a baseline, grabbing above right, and Shift-dragging to the right). Then they Direct-selected individual points and groups of points, moving them into the visually correct positions.

To create the outlining effect, copy a solid-filled version and set the stroke weight and color. While the object is still selected, choose Object > Path > Outline Stroke, then click on Unite in the Pathfinder palette.

3 Pasting the original back on top, designing new colors for copies of the blends and masking the new blends. First, Paste in Front the original, unstroked type element. Next, select and Lock blends or objects that won't fall within the detail, but that you want to keep for reference. Copy and Paste in Front each of the source (key) objects for new blends and recolor them for your detailing. To recolor a blend, Direct-select each key object you want to recolor and choose a new color—the blend will automatically update! As necessary, recolor each pair of key objects using the same procedure (bear in mind, blending between Spot colors results in Process in-between colors). T•B I&D recolored the car blends for the red **3**, then added a tear-shaped blend for more detail. Select and copy the original **3**, use Paste in Front, press the Shift key and click to add the new grouped blends to the selection, then choose Object > Clipping Mask > Make. Group and Hide these finished masked objects and repeat the recoloring of copied blends, masked by a top object for any additional highlights and shadows. Choose Object > Show All when these masks are complete, group all the masks together and use the Arrow keys to snap this group of reflective details into position. T•B I&D created one more version of the **3** for a dark offset. For areas requiring more reflections, they constructed even more masks upon masks, as well as occasionally applying compound-masks (see previous lesson "Colorful Masking").

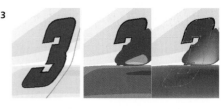

3

Re-creating blends in new colors and preparing to mask them with a copy of the 3 on top

With the red, reflective blends masked, creating a darker, offset 3

The dark 3 and the entire group of objects complete, before and after being moved back into position with Arrow keys

Other elements require more stages of blending (see "Colorful Masking" in this chapter for compounding multiple objects, like type elements, to apply as a single mask)

BRADLEY NEAL / THOMAS • BRADLEY ILLUSTRATION & DESIGN

Bradley Neal

Bradley Neal combined an attention to detail with Illustrator's wide range of drawing and rendering tools to create this photo-realistic image of a Ford Taurus stock car. Beginning with a contour shape filled with a flat color, Neal overlaid a series of custom blends to replicate the subtle modeling of the car's surface. Neal simulated the grill work at the front of the car by overlaying a series of four dashed stroked paths. The racing logos on the side of the car were drawn by hand, grouped, and positioned using the Shear tool. The Taurus, Valvoline, and Goodyear logos were fitted to the contour of the body with the help of the Envelope Distort tool. To achieve the realistic look of the front right wheel, Neal created customs blends with outer edges that blended smoothly into the flat color of the underlying shapes. Neal created a drop shadow for the car using a carefully controlled blend. This blend had an inner path that contained a solid black fill that blended to white as it approached the outer edge.

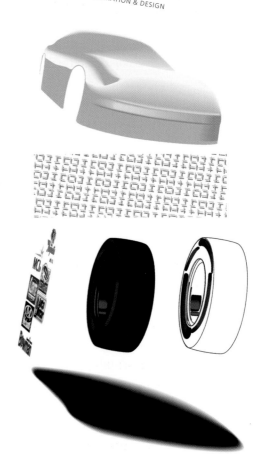

CATER(©INMOTION 2003)

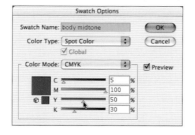

David Cater

David Cater created this Mini Cooper image for reproduction on T-shirts, posters, and note cards. Knowing that different clients would want the car in a variety of colors, he started by creating two spot color swatches for the mid and shadow tones of the car. He then used those two spot colors (global process colors would also work) to create the handful of gradients he used to fill each of the approximately 1,500 shapes he used to create the car.

Because he was careful to color only the body panels using gradients created from those two colors, he was later able to easily change the color of the car by simply double-clicking on each of the two color swatches and using the CMYK sliders to redefine the colors. Although he could have used blends more extensively (he only used a few for the cowlings along the front and side of the car), Cater found it faster and easier to use simple gradient-filled shapes.

FERSTER

FERSTER

Gary Ferster

In creating a product illustration, Gary Ferster strives to combine realism with a dramatically appealing view of the product. For the Jeep and the sneaker, Ferster began by scanning photographs of the products and placing these grayscale TIFFs on template layers (see "Digitizing a Logo" in the *Layers* chapter). On layers above the templates, he drew the objects' out-lines with the Pen tool and then drew the base objects that would be used to create blends, created his blends, and then masked the blends with copies of the outlines. For each sneaker lace, Ferster created several dark-colored blends overlaying a light background. Then he masked each of the blends and background with the lace outlines.

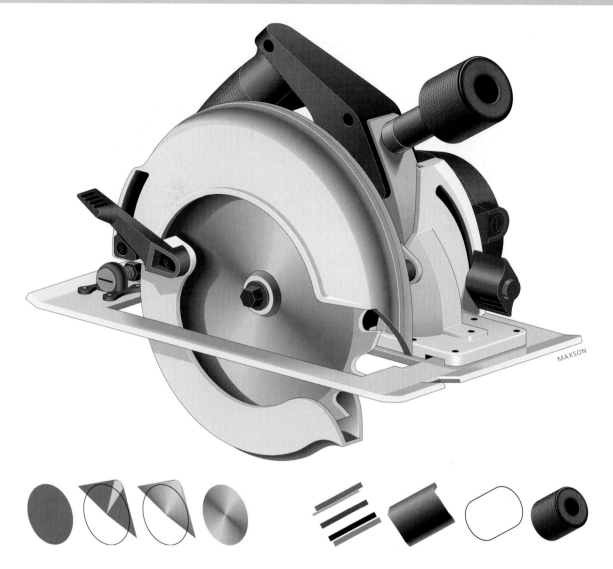

Greg Maxson / Precision Graphics

Illustrating the metal surfaces of this circular saw required Greg Maxson to create overlapping blends. For the blade, Maxson began with an ellipse filled with a dark gray. Next, he created two blending objects, one filled with the same dark gray as the ellipse and the other (on top) filled with a light gray. Maxson blended these to create the highlight and shadow. He used the Reflect tool to create a copy of the blend for the bottom half of the blade. He copied the dark gray ellipse and used the ellipse to mask both blends. For the round grip, Maxson created five blend objects, and blended between them to form the grip's surface. He masked these blends with an object built by connecting ellipse shapes (the cylinder and the circular face at the end of the cylinder) to form the grip.

Glowing Starshine

Blending Custom Colors to Form a Glow

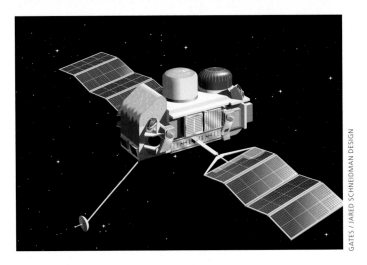

GATES / JARED SCHNEIDMAN DESIGN

Advanced Technique

Overview: *Create a custom color for the background and the basic object; scale a copy of the object; make object adjustments and blend a glow.*

1

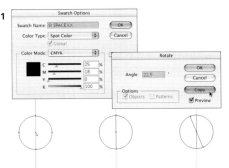

The background spot color; dragging a guide to the center of a circle, drawing a center line and rotating a copy of the line

After pressing ⌘/Ctrl-D six times, making guides and adding anchor points at guide intersections

2

After Shift-Option/Shift-Alt scaling the circle smaller and changing the center to 0% tint; Direct-selecting and moving top, bottom and side points outward

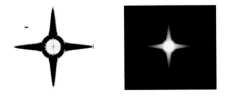

Before and after a 12-step blend

Illumination is the key to creating a realistic nighttime sky. This variation on a technique by Guilbert Gates and Jared Schneidman Design (JSD) will help you create glowing lights, not just stars, simply and directly.

1 Creating a custom color and the basic object. Create a background rectangle filled with a dark, spot color. JSD's background was 25% C, 18% M and 100% K. In Outline mode, make a circle, then drag a guide from the ruler until it "snaps" to the circle's center (the arrow turns hollow). With the Pen tool, click on an edge of the circle where the guide intersects, hold Shift and click on the other edge. Select this line, double-click the Rotate tool, specify 22.5° and click Copy. Press ⌘/Ctrl-D to repeat the rotate/copy six times, then select only the lines and choose ⌘/Ctrl-5 to make the lines into guides. Use the Add Anchor Point tool to add eight points, one on each side of the circle's original points at guide intersections.

2 Creating the glow. With the circle selected, use the Scale tool to make a smaller copy of the circle (hold Shift and Option/Alt keys), then in the Color palette specify a 0% tint fill. Direct-select the top point of the bigger circle and Shift-drag it outward; do the same to the bottom and side points. With the Blend tool, click on corresponding selected points from each circle and specify 12 steps.

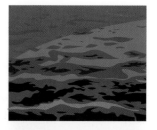

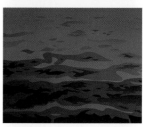

BATELMAN

Kenneth Batelman

Batelman drew his small stars using dashed line patterns applied to marks made with the Pencil tool. To simulate a variety of star sizes, spacing, and values, he created a number of different dashed strokes using the Strokes palette. All of his dashes begin with a 0 value for the "dash" field, and then have varied values for the gap (between from 20 to 90 points). He chose the rounded options for both the Cap and Join, and then set Stroke values ranging from .85 to 2.5 points. Using these settings, Batelman's "dashes" actually appear as a range of small dots that vary in spacing and size. Choosing warm gray colors for the strokes, he applied different dash patterns to marks drawn with the Pencil tool (dashes are shown directly above right: applied to lines, in the Stroke palette, and applied to a mark made with the Pencil tool). To create each of the larger star

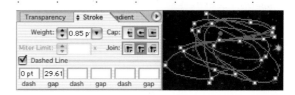

"bursts" shown in three stages, Batelman used the Ellipse tool to create a circle, and then the Star tool to place a star on top. Circle and star were each filled with radial gradients that start with a lighter color at the center, and end with a color matching the background sky. To create less "perfect" bursts, he stretches the star's endpoints using the Direct Selection tool. From a distance, Batelman's spectacular water looks photographic, but viewed up close it's simply constructed of irregular flat objects, interwoven with gradients and blends (see the *Blends, Gradients & Mesh* chapter). The Water details show before (top right) and after (directly below) gradients and blends are applied .

Chapter 10 *Advanced Techniques*   **343**

WEIMER

Alan James Weimer

Alan James Weimer achieved the detailed symmetry in the above design using Illustrator's Rotate and Polar Grid tools. After selecting the Polar Grid tool, he clicked where he wanted to position the grid. Within the dialog box, Weimer entered the width and height of the circle, as well as the number of concentric and radial dividers. (The Polar Grid tool can also be clicked and dragged to create the grid. Use the Arrow keys on the keyboard to adjust the concentric circles and dividers.) The grid was then made into a guide (View > Guides > Make Guides). Alan created the individual elements of the design, such as the pink flower petal,

by drawing half of the petal with the Pen tool and creating a copy for the other side using the Reflect tool. Next, Weimer positioned the petal on one of the guides, selected the Rotate tool, and Option-clicked (Alt-click for Win) the cursor once on the centerpoint of the circle. In the dialog box, he entered "360 / 8" (in order to have Illustrator calculate 360°÷8, the total number of petals he wanted), and clicked Copy. He then pressed ⌘-D (Ctrl-D for Win) to continue copying and rotating six more petals around the circle.

WEIMER

Alan James Weimer

To make the two medallions for a horizontal "tile" (right), Alan Weimer used the circle-and-guides technique described on the opposite page. After arranging the medallions and other elements to form the tile, he Option-dragged / Alt-dragged the tile to the right to form the first row. To create the repeating pattern, Weimer diagonally Option-dragged /Alt-dragged copies of the first tile row onto a grid of guidelines to form rows above and below the first row. To "crop" the design, he drew a rectangle on the same layer as the tiled design,

and, at the bottom of the Layers palette, clicked the Make / Release Clipping Mask icon. On a layer above the mask he added a border composed of blended, stroked rectangles.

LAMANTIA

Marc LaMantia

Marc LaMantia scanned a photograph into Photoshop and saved it in PSD format. He then opened a new Illustrator document and chose File > Place, and selected Place as Template (see "Digitizing a Logo" in the *Layers* chapter). On layers above the template, LaMantia then began to meticulously trace the details of the photograph using the Pen tool. To create the posterized appearance, he began by initially tracing shapes with less detail. On additional layers, as he worked he increased the amount

of detail with each subsequent pass of tracing. To soften some areas, such as the wall adjacent to the door and the creases in the coats, he applied a Feather Effect by selecting Effect > Stylize > Feather with a 2 pt feather radius. LaMantia used varying opacities to make the reflections in the store window. To create a look of concrete and stone, he applied a Pointilize effect (Effect > Pixelate > Pointilize). (For more about effects, see the *Live Effects & Graphic Styles* chapter.)

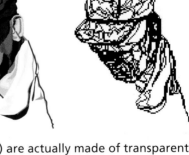

Marc LaMantia

Marc LaMantia scanned one of his photographs to create this illustration of a subway exit, in which he used the techniques described on the opposite page. In this piece, LaMantia depicts the beauty of a single moment of an ordinary day in New York City. Transparency effects were used throughout the entire illustration (see the *Transparency & Appearances* chapter). Many of the shadow areas (such as within the steps) are actually made of transparent pink, red, and magenta shapes, layered above black. Rarely is a color used at full opacity. The layering of numerous transparent layers (all in Normal mode) brings enormous depth and interest to the posterized style. When viewing the image in Outline mode (above right), the level of detail becomes apparent.

Masking Opacity

Making Transparency Irregular

Advanced Technique

Overview: *Draw an object outline and convert it to gradient mesh; duplicate the mesh and convert it to grayscale; make a copy of the grayscale mesh; rasterize, "reverse" and blur it; add it to the grayscale mesh and create an opacity mask.*

1

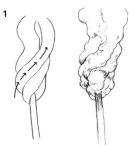

Original sketches of the movement of the flame

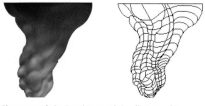

Flame mesh in Preview and Outline modes

Rasterization resolution

If you're using live Effects and the screen redraw is too slow, set the Resolution in Effect > Rasterize > Raster Effects Settings to Screen (72 ppi). But don't forget to reset this to the correct output (typically twice the line screen), and adjust each Effect setting, before saving for print! —*Ivan Torres*

TORRES

Ivan Torres found that Illustrator's gradient mesh and opacity mask provided the perfect solutions for creating the light-and-dark, opaque-and-translucent character of a match flame, while allowing him to do all of his work within Illustrator rather than moving artwork between Illustrator and a bitmap program like Adobe Photoshop.

1 Drawing the gradient mesh. Torres began his flame by placing a scan of a sketch into Illustrator to use as a tracing template. He drew a filled outline of the flame and converted it to a gradient mesh (Object > Create Gradient Mesh). See the *Blends, Gradients & Mesh* chapter to find out more about creating and editing gradient meshes. Torres edited the mesh to color the flame.

2 Making an opacity mask and modifying its opacity.

As Torres observed, a flame can contain transparent and opaque parts. To achieve irregular transparency, you can build and apply a customized opacity mask. First, select the gradient mesh object you made, Copy, and then Paste in Front. Next, convert the color mesh to grayscale by selecting Filter > Colors > Convert To Grayscale. Now use the Direct Selection tool to click on intersection points in the grayscale mesh and change their gray values in the Color palette. (The darker the point's gray value, the more transparent the object will be when the mesh is made into an opacity mask and applied to the object.)

3 Adding a blurred outline, then completing the opacity mask.

Torres added a blurred outline to the grayscale mesh, so that when applied later as an opacity mask it would soften the edge of the flame. To create a blurred edge, begin by duplicating the grayscale mesh (Copy, then Paste in Front). In the Object menu, select Rasterize, and in the Rasterize dialog box, click to enable Create Clipping Mask. Next, release the mask you just made (Object > Clipping Mask > Release) and Ungroup; select the square (which is the rasterized grayscale copy) and delete it. This leaves the mask object, an exact duplicate of the flame outline. Give this mask object a black stroke.

Next, create a "reverse" version of the mask using drawing tools or the Pathfinder functions (see the *Drawing & Coloring* chapter for more on creating and modifying paths). Fill this reverse object with black, and blur the object by selecting Effect > Blur > Gaussian Blur and assigning a blur radius that is wide enough to create the look you want.

To finish constructing the opacity mask, select the blurred object and the grayscale gradient mesh you created earlier and group them (Object > Group).

4 Applying the mask.

Select the mask artwork and the original color gradient mesh and choose Make Opacity Mask from the Transparency palette's pop-up menu.

2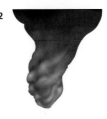

At the left, color mesh converted to grayscale; at the right, the edited version of the grayscale mesh made by changing the gray values of individual mesh intersection points

3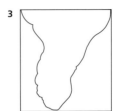

In Outline View, the rasterized grayscale gradient mesh (with the mask outline and the raster rectangle) on the left; on the right, the "reverse" object Torres created by cutting the top line with the Scissors tool, deleting the top segment, and then joining the remaining segments

The filled "reverse" object of the rasterized mask on the left, and the same object on the right after blurring

4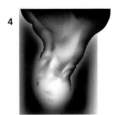

On the left, the composite artwork of the opacity mask (the grayscale gradient mesh and the blurred "reverse" object); on the right, the opacity mask applied to the flame

Modeling Mesh
Shaping and Forming Mesh Objects

Advanced Technique

Overview: *Create an outline for smoke; create a simple rectangular mesh; bend the mesh using the Rotate and Direct Selection tools; align the mesh to your outline; add columns to lend a 3D effect; color your mesh; use the Screen Blend mode to make the smoke transparent.*

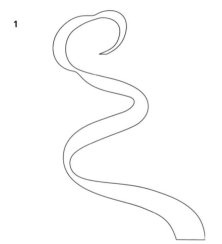

Create an outline of the desired final smoke form

Smoke outline locked on a layer, with the starting mesh above

Ivan Torres molded a mesh as though it were a piece of clay to form the smoke in his art piece "Meshsmith." One of the highlights of this lesson is Torres's use of the Rotate tool to bend *portions* of a mesh (as opposed to using it to rotate *whole* objects).

1 Setting up your artwork. Start by using the Pen or Pencil tool to create an outline of a smoke form. Lock the smoke outline in a layer, then place a rectangle at the base of the smoke. Convert the rectangle to a mesh, using the Object > Create Gradient Mesh command, with 1 column and 3 rows. Keep your starting mesh simple, it is easier to add rows as needed later.

2 Making the rough bends. Make your first big bend using the Rotate tool. Start by Direct-selecting all but the bottom two points of the mesh. Next with the Rotate tool click on the inside of the first curve of the smoke outline to place the center for rotation, and then grab the top of your mesh rectangle and drag it around the center of rotation to form the first curve (see images at right).

At each bend or pinch in the smoke, you will need a row in order to make the next bend. If an existing row of your mesh is nearby, Direct-select it and move it over the bend or pinch. To add a row, click with the Mesh tool on the edge of the mesh outline, at the bend or pinch. Once you have placed or added a mesh row at a bend or pinch, leave those points out of the next selection as you work your way up the smoke. Repeat this step until you reach the top of your smoke outline.

3 Aligning and straightening the mesh rows. Once you have the mesh roughly aligned, zoom in at each pinch and bend where you placed a mesh row and make it straight and perpendicular to the curve. Straightening out the mesh rows is essential for your final smoke to look correct and work smoothly.

4 Aligning the mesh curves with the smoke. With the Direct Selection tool, start at the bottom and click a section of the mesh curve. Adjust the direction handles so they align with the smoke outline. You may have to go back and forth between the next and previous sections of the curves in order to properly adjust the sides of the mesh to fit the smoke outline.

5 Adding columns to lend a 3D effect. The final 3D form of the mesh will be defined by where the highlight and shadow colors are placed on the mesh. If you were to draw evenly spaced columns around the actual smoke and photograph it, the columns in the photograph would appear to be closer together near the edges of the smoke outline and farther apart in the middle of column. To create this

2

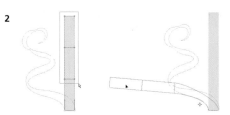

Selecting top portion of mesh. After clicking on inside of the first curve to set the rotation point (blue crosshair in lower right), clicking the top of the rectangle, and dragging to left and down

Working up the smoke, rotating the mesh at each major bend; placing mesh rows at pinches and using the Direct Selection tool to adjust

3

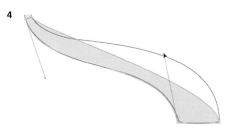

Aligning the rows with the pinches in the outline, making them straight and perpendicular to the sides of the curve

4

Starting from the bottom, using the Bézier handles to align the curves of the mesh to the outline of the smoke

5

Adding columns to the smoke mesh using the Gradient tool and spacing them closer at the edges to create a rounded 3D look

The completed smoke mesh

Creating a highlight at a mesh point

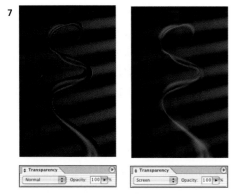

The smoke before and after setting the Blend Mode to Screen on the Transparency palette

3D effect, use the Mesh tool to add a first column by clicking on the center of the bottom edge of the smoke. Next, add two more columns close to each outside edge of the smoke. Then, place two columns between the center and the next closest columns on each side—not exactly in between, but closer to the outside edge.

Because of your careful work in steps 3 and 4 above, your new columns will be parallel to—and flow smoothly through—the pinches and bends of your smoke outline.

6 Coloring the mesh. Torres chose a dark blue color for his smoke (if you want to use a different color you will have to adjust the color choices in the steps below). To see where the mesh points are as you work, turn on Smart Guides from the View menu, or ⌘-U/Ctrl-U. In order to make the selection line color interfere less with the mesh color as you work, use a dark shade of blue for the selection line color (choose Dark Blue from the Layer Options Color menu). Also, learn to use the single-key navigation shortcuts to quickly switch between the Mesh (U), Paint bucket (K), and Direct Selection (A) tools.

Start by adding a middle blue value to the whole mesh. Next, from the Color palette pop-up menu, choose HSB, and then use the Brightness ("B") slider to create lighter highlight or darker shadow tints of your starting color. At the center of where highlight or shadow areas should be, use the Paint bucket to apply your highlight or shadow color. If there is no mesh point there, use the Mesh tool to add one. Because the point where you click with the Mesh tool remains selected, you can easily adjust the fill color using the HSB sliders. For final tweaking of the highlights and shadows, use the Direct Selection tool or Lasso tool to select areas, and then make adjustments using the HSB sliders.

7 Making the smoke transparent. Select your smoke and on the Transparency palette, experiment with various combinations of the Screen Blend mode and Opacity settings until you get the desired effect.

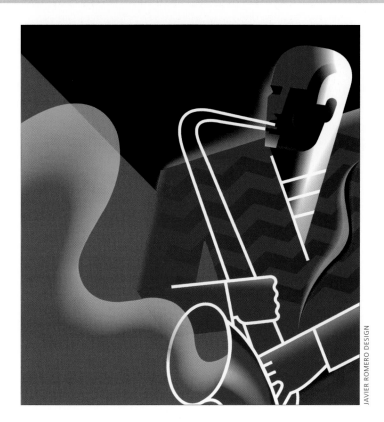

JAVIER ROMERO DESIGN

Javier Romero / Javier Romero Design Group

Throughout this illustration for the *Illustrator 10 Wow! Book* cover, Javier Romero adjusted the opacity and blending modes of his objects to soften the transitions and overlaps, and to create a glowing look. To create the wavy lines in the shirt he filled several wavy shapes with a black to white linear gradient. He then used the Gradient tool to adjust the angle of the gradient uniformly across all the shapes (see the "Unified Gradients" lesson in the *Blends, Gradients & Mesh* chapter for help with this). Romero then applied a 30% Opacity and a Multiply Blending Mode to the wavy shapes. To confine the waves to the shirt, Romero masked the waves by transforming a copy of the shirt

path into a clipping mask (see earlier in this chapter for help with clipping masks). To make these lines slightly lighter on the sax player's left shoulder, he made a duplicate of the wavy lines, adjusted the Opacity to 25% and masked that set with a narrow shape defining the left shoulder. To create the swirl of sound coming from the horn, Romero created a blend from a light yellow object set to 50% Opacity, to a dark red object set at 100% (directly above, right). Another of the blends forms the orange glow on the shoulder; the top orange object is set to Lighten 66%, and the dark object below is set to Multiply at 18% (shown in Normal mode at 100% Opacity, top right).

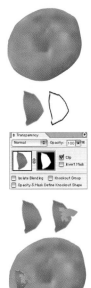

PAIDRICK (©EBY/PAIDRICK DESIGNS, INC. 2002)

Ann Paidrick

With an original photograph as a reference, Ann Paidrick recreated these ripe and juicy tomatoes using a complex combination of gradient mesh, blends, gradients, masking techniques, and symbols. For the tomato slices, Paidrick used the Pen tool to draw basic shapes. She then filled them with a base color and turned each into a mesh (Object > Create Gradient Mesh). Paidrick used the Direct Selection tool to select and place rows and columns into the desired position, and to select points to color using the Color palette. To create the darker seeded areas of the tomato (above right), Paidrick filled a new object with a linear gradient. To create a smooth transition from this darker area to the tomato mesh, she created an opacity mask. To do so, she copied that object and pasted two copies in front (⌘-F/ Ctrl-F). She filled the bottom copy with black and the top with white. With the top white object selected, she double-clicked on the Scale

tool in the Tools palette and decreased its size slightly. She selected both the black and white objects and chose Object > Blend > Make (see the *Blends, Gradients & Mesh* chapter). Paidrick then selected the blend objects, along with the linear gradient, and chose Make Opacity Mask from the Transparency palette, and selected Clip. The blended object became both a clipping mask and an opacity mask, blending the dark area into the underlying background. The plate is made with three layers of mesh objects. The top and bottom mesh objects form the whites of the plate. The middle object forms the inner rim shadow, which Paidrick created by applying the opacity masking technique described above, to a red-hued mesh. Paidrick also applied opacity masks to the objects that make up the tomato shadows, and varied the opacities and blending modes. She applied the small highlights with symbols (see the *Brushes & Symbols* chapter).

PAIDRICK (©EBY/PAIDRICK DESIGNS, INC. 2002)

Ann Paidrick

Using techniques similar to those described on the previous page, Ann Paidrick created this delicious-looking bowl of olives. The olives and pimentos were created with gradient mesh objects. Paidrick applied an opacity mask to make the hole where the pimento sits. She highlighted the olives with objects blended from black to white. Within the Transparency palette, she then adjusted the opacities, set the Blending Mode to Screen, and selected Knockout Group to reveal the color of the olive below. Paidrick used a combination of mesh objects with opacity masks throughout the many individual shapes that make up the glass bowl (details above right). The outside rim is filled with a radial gradient and layered with solid filled shapes and mesh shapes. The

outside rim handle was created with three gradient mesh shapes layered above a solid filled shape (shown above). The ribs of the bowl are linear gradients with solid filled highlights, and the larger ribs are mesh shapes with an opacity mask below. Lastly, Paidrick made the background out of a large square gradient mesh and created the illusion of the surface reflections by carefully coloring mesh points.

MIYAMOTO

Yukio Miyamoto

Using a photograph of his cat, Chinta, as a template, Yukio Miyamoto created a realistic rendering using gradients and gradient mesh. With the Pen tool, he traced over the template. Before coloring his shapes, he double-clicked on the Eyedropper to open the Options dialog box, and disabled the Appearance checkbox. This allowed him to sample color with the Eyedropper from the placed image with a click, rather than having to continually Shift-click. He filled the objects that would be the mesh shapes with a base color sampled from the photograph using the Eyedropper. Then he used the Mesh tool and created the mesh points within the shape. Toggling between the Eyedropper and the Direct Selection tool (using the ⌘/Ctrl key), he clicked on the image and picked up color for his mesh points.

Miyamoto also sampled colors from the image for his objects and gradients. The head is made of four main shapes sculpted with gradient mesh: the overall head shape, the white area of the face, and the ears. To transition these gradient mesh shapes into one another, Miyamoto applied an opacity mask to each of the gradient mesh objects. The body was created using the same method. Details, such as the whiskers and bits of fur, were drawn with a 1 pt round brush. To soften many of the objects, he applied Effect > Stylize > Feather. The nose, eyes, and shadow beneath the cat are gradient-filled objects with a Feather effect. To give a furry appearance to the outline of the cat, Miyamoto applied a Feather effect to a filled shape matching the contour of the cat.

Web & Animation

11

358 Introduction

358 Working in RGB in Illustrator

358 A few thoughts on RGB and CMYK color

359 Assigning URL'S and Slicing

361 Release to Layers

362 Export File Formats

364 SVG

365 Data-Driven Graphics

367 Gallery: Ivan Torres

368 Off in a Flash: *Making Artwork for a Flash Animation*

371 Gallery: Kevan Atteberry

372 Layering Frames: *Turning Layered Artwork into Keyframes*

374 Webward Ho!: *Designing a Web Page in Illustrator*

377 Gallery: Steven Gordon / Cartagram

378 Advanced Technique (Illustrator with Photoshop):
Making Waves: *Transforming and Blending for Animation*

Web & Animation

Because Illustrator allows you to mix colors in CMYK, RGB, or HSB color modes, be aware of which color palette is displayed when you're creating colors. If your file is in RGB, you should switch the color palette to RGB or Web safe RGB. If you're doing print work, you would normally work in CMYK, but you may need to work in RGB in order to apply some of the Photoshop filters. If you intend to use your artwork for both print and the Web, your best bet is to work first in CMYK (with its narrower color gamut) and then create the final Web output by exporting to an RGB format and adjusting colors to approximate the original CMYK colors.

Choosing color models from the Color palette's pop-up menu. You can also cycle through color models by Shift-clicking on the Color Spectrum. Selecting a different color model to mix colors does not change the color mode of the file

If you need Photoshop...

Don't forget to look at the *Illustrator & Other Programs* chapter for details about working with Illustrator and Photoshop.

This chapter focuses on how you can use Illustrator to prepare artwork for on-screen display. Although everything in this chapter relies heavily on Illustrator, some of the techniques also involve working with other applications (see the *Illustrator & Other Programs* chapter).

The actual assembly of animations and Web graphics in this chapter was produced using a number of other programs, including Macromedia's Director; Adobe's Premiere, After Effects, and GoLive; Yves Piguet's GIF Builder; Thorsten Lemke's GraphicConverter; and Bare Bones Software's BBEdit.

Web designers will find that Illustrator supports a wealth of file formats, and a streamlined work flow for creating Web graphics. Save for Web in the File menu makes it easy to optimize graphics for the Web, by letting you visually compare examples of different quality settings and file compression options side by side, in a multi-view dialog box. And Pixel Preview allows you to view precise antialiasing right in Illustrator.

WORKING IN RGB IN ILLUSTRATOR

To create artwork in RGB, first start with a new RGB file (File > New and Color Mode > RGB Color in the dialog box). Choose a Web safe RGB palette of colors if you want to create colors that are never dithered when viewed on 8-bit monitors. This is a great opportunity to take advantage of Illustrator's new Templates feature. If you base your new file on any of the Web templates that ship with Illustrator, you'll be in RGB color mode by default.

A FEW THOUGHTS ON RGB AND CMYK COLOR

• **You should work in the RGB color mode (space) if you're creating graphics for on-screen display.** If you're designing for the Web, it's particularly important to keep file sizes to a minimum, and the final files must be in RGB (see "The Web Swatches library" below).

- Don't convert the same artwork repeatedly between RGB and CMYK. Converting RGB to CMYK forces one range of colors (a gamut) into a smaller range of colors. This process involves either clipping or compressing certain colors, and can make the colors in your file appear muddy or muted. If you absolutely need both CMYK and RGB versions of your artwork, maintain two versions of your art—one in RGB and one in CMYK. To experiment with clipping or compressing colors between gamuts, see the *User Guide* on choosing the appropriate rendering intent in the Color Settings dialog box.

- **If you're going to use your artwork for both print and on-screen viewing, create in CMYK and then export the art to RGB.** With the CMYK color space's smaller color gamut, and with the control available to produce predictable color for print, it makes sense to create artwork in CMYK *before* exporting it to RGB for display on a monitor. RGB has a wider gamut, so it won't clip or compress the colors of your CMYK document.

The Web Swatches library

Illustrator includes a non-editable Web safe swatches library. Its 216 RGB colors are common to both Mac and Windows platforms, and are the most reliable colors for creating Web artwork when you don't know the color depth or platform your audience will be using. To access this library, choose Open Swatch Library > Web from the Swatches palette menu, or choose Window > Swatch Libraries > Web. To create a smaller custom library from the Web safe library, simply drag the desired color swatches to the Swatches palette for storage and save the file. (Remember to clear the Swatches palette before you build your custom library—see "Setting up your palettes" in the *How To Use This Book* section.)

ASSIGNING URL'S AND SLICING

Illustrator's Attributes palette lets you create an image map area and assign a URL (Uniform Resource Locator)

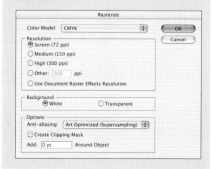

Save as GIF if your art has large areas of solid color and/or is made up of "vector" graphics (such as Illustrator objects). Export as a JPEG if your art includes "raster" images (photos) with a wide range of colors or grays, or if your image contains gradients or gradient meshes. If your art includes a high-contrast photo or has both large areas of solid colors and images, experiment with different optimizations in File > Save for Web to see which looks best at the smallest file size.

Batch optimizations

You can combine File > Save for Web with the Actions palette to batch optimize GIF files that share a custom palette. Make a new file, then copy into it the group of Illustrator files that need to share a palette. Use Save for Web to find the optimum combination of colors and palette size, then choose Save Color Table from the bottom pop-up menu. Close this file, and open one of the individual Illustrator files. Start recording a new Action, then choose Save for Web, load the color table, and save the file. Now you can run this custom action to automatically process the rest of your GIF files.
—*Cynthia Baron*

to any object, group, or layer in your artwork. Creating image maps is an essential tool for Web designers because it allows them to create links to other Web pages by defining clickable parts of the artwork. Illustrator creates a separate HTML (HyperText Markup Language) file containing the URL information, which can be imported into an HTML editor such as Adobe GoLive, Macromedia Dreamweaver, or BareBones Software's BBEdit.

To assign a URL to a selection, open the Attributes palette (Window > Attributes), select the type of image map from the Image Map pop-up, and type the URL into the URL text field (see the Gulf Shores Web page Gallery in this chapter for more on making image maps). If you need to verify whether your URL is correct, simply click the Browser button in the Attributes palette. This will launch your default Web browser and automatically open the link. You can export the file by using Save for Web and choosing Save as Type: HTML and Images (*.html).

Illustrator also provides another way for you to assign URLs or links to objects—by using Web slices. Web slicing is a way to divide a large image into several smaller pieces that are displayed in HTML as a table. This allows you to optimize individual parts of your artwork in different formats (e.g., GIF, JPEG, SVG), and helps the files download faster to a Web browser. To assign a URL to a Web slice, apply a slice to an object by selecting the object and choosing Object > Slice > Make, and then with the object still selected, choose Object > Slice > Slice Options. In the URL field, enter the correct link information. You can also get to the Slice Options dialog box by double-clicking on a slice with the Slice Select tool in the Save for Web dialog box.

When you apply a slice to an object, group, or layer using the Object menu, you've actually assigned a slice as an "attribute." This means that if you update your artwork, your slice will update automatically. So, once you make a slice, you never have to re-create it.

If you want to create a slice whose position remains unchanged when you update the artwork from which the slice was originally generated, choose Object > Slice > Create from Selection, or draw the slice using Illustrator's Slice tool. (In ImageReady, this kind of slice is called a *user slice.*) Slices applied as attributes are exported as *layer-based slices* when you choose File > Export > Photoshop (*.PSD) and you select the Write Slices option. If you edit the exported layers in Photoshop or ImageReady, the corresponding slices will reshape themselves just as they would have done in Illustrator. This PSD export option only works on slices attached to elements that are not contained inside any groups or sublayers. All other slices are exported as user slices.

RELEASE TO LAYERS

Illustrator gives you the ability to take multiple objects or blended objects and distribute each onto its own layer. For example, having the objects on separate layers makes it easier to develop animations. ("Macromedia Flash (SWF) export," in this chapter, explains how to move Illustrator art into Flash for animation work.) Highlight a layer, group, live blend or symbol set in the Layers palette by clicking on it—if you merely select or target the artwork, this won't work. Next, choose Release to Layers (Sequence) from the palette menu. Each new layer is created within the current layer or group and consists of a single object. To perform an additive effect, choose Release to Layers (Build). Instead of containing a single object, each new layer is generated with one more object. You end up with the same number of layers, but what appears on those layers is very different.

When releasing objects to separate layers, keep in mind that their stacking order in the Layers palette can affect the final animation. With scatter brush art, it's sometimes hard to predict the order in which the individual objects will be released to the layers: stacking order is dependent on the direction of the path. You can reverse the direction of a path by clicking on an end anchor point with the Pen tool. You can reverse blends by choosing Object > Blend > Reverse Front to Back.

Save for Web

Save for Web provides many options for optimizing Web graphics:

- **Tools:** A limited set of tools lets you zoom, pan, select slices, and sample colors in the artwork.
- **Views:** Multiple views are available for you to compare compression settings against the final image quality.
- **Settings:** Preset compression settings are easily accessed from the Settings pop-up menu. If you are new to Web graphics, start with one of these settings. You'll notice that as you select different presets, the options for the specific file type are updated under the Settings grouping. Save your own settings by choosing Save Settings from the pop-up menu to the right of the Settings menu.
- **Color Table:** The color table updates the number of colors in the image for GIF and PNG-8 file formats. You can lock colors or shift to a Web safe color by clicking on the icons at the bottom of the palette.
- **Image Size:** To change the dimensions of the final optimized file, but not the original artwork, click on the Image Size tab and enter a new size.
- **Browser button:** To preview the optimized image in a browser, click on the browser button at the bottom of the dialog box.

Which GIF options are for you?

- **Color Table:** 8-bit images have a maximum of 256 colors. The Perceptual table is more sensitive to colors that can be differentiated with the human eye. Selective gives more emphasis to the integrity of the colors and is the default setting.

- **Colors:** You can have up to 256 colors in a color table. However, the image might not need that many. Select a smaller number of colors when you optimize by adjusting the number of colors in the color table. The fewer colors, the smaller the file.

- **Dither:** Blends colors in a limited color palette. Diffusion dither is usually best. Vary the amount of dither to reduce banding of solid-color areas by adjusting the Dither slider. Leave it off for clean-edged vector graphics.

- **Transparency:** Choose this for non-rectangular artwork that you want to put over multicolored backgrounds. To reduce edge artifacts, choose a color to blend with the transparent edges from the Matte pop-up.

- **Interlacing:** Allows viewers to see a low resolution version of the image as it downloads, which continues to build until the image is at full resolution. A non-interlaced image draws one line at a time.

EXPORT FILE FORMATS

Save for Web

An important feature for Web designers is the ability to export optimized files from the Save for Web dialog box. GIF and JPEG are the Web's two most common image formats (see the Tip "GIF or JPEG?" in this chapter). The GIF format's compression works well with vector-based images or files that have large areas of solid color. GIF files support transparency; JPEGs don't.

JPEG provides a variable level of compression and works best for images with gradients or photos that have continuous tones. Although JPEG is a "lossy" format (when you optimize the file size you lose image detail), this trade-off still tends to result in good-quality images, making JPEG a particularly useful format for Web designers. It can also be a useful alternative to a PDF file. For example, a JPEG file can be used to transfer a layout for client approval. JPEGs are much smaller than PDFs while sacrificing very little image detail, and smaller files transfer more easily (and sometimes more reliably) via the Internet. Other JPEG options include progressive and optimized. A progressive JPEG is similar to an interlaced GIF—it first appears blurry, then builds up with increasing clarity until the image is fully displayed.

Note: *If Progressive is checked, checking Optimized will not make the file any smaller.*

To save a version of your artwork for use on the Web, choose File > Save for Web and adjust the various optimization settings (see the Tip "Save for Web" in this chapter). If you've defined slices in your file, use the Slice Select tool to click on and select the slice you want to optimize, then select a file type from the Optimized file format pop-up. If you want to compare the compression of two or more settings, click on one of the other views, either 2-Up or 4-Up. The final file format, size, download time, and specifics about the compression are listed under each preview panel. Finally, if you want to export your artwork now, click the Save button to specify how you want your files saved. If you have slices, you can choose to export the images and the HTML as well. If you opened Save for Web only to define the optimization settings for your slices, you can press the Done button and Illustrator will take you back to your file, while remembering all the settings you just applied. See the *User Guide* for a complete description of format options.

Note: *PNG, SWF, and SVG are available file formats in the Save for Web dialog box, but these formats may require browser plug-ins in order to be viewed on the Web.*

Macromedia Flash (SWF) export

Although many multimedia artists and designers use Illustrator with Macromedia Flash to create Web pages and animations, there is no completely foolproof method for bringing artwork from one program to the other. Illustrator now comes with a Flash export module, but as of this writing it has some significant problems, ranging from poor rendering quality to the creation of extra frames and symbols. Be aware that it may also break your artwork into many separate objects. If you have very simple artwork, you can try copying and pasting art from Illustrator to Flash, or try using Illustrator's Flash Export dialog box (File > Export, then choose Macromedia Flash from the Format menu). Here are some strategies for maximizing the quality and usefulness of your Illustrator files in Flash:

- **Use Illustrator symbols for repeating objects.** Illustrator lets you convert both raster and vector artwork into *symbols* that you can *place* multiple times, instead of using multiple copies of the original art. Each time you place an instance of a symbol, you are creating a *link* to the symbol stored in the palette, rather than duplicating the artwork. This reduces the size of your Illustrator file and of any SWF files you export from Illustrator.

- **Use flat colors rather than blends, gradients, or gradient mesh objects.** You'll make smaller SWF files if you use Flash to add your gradient colors. If you must use

SVG and alpha channels

Illustrator CS ships standard with (and installs by default) the SVG 3.0 browser plug-in. If you're creating SVG graphics, make sure that whoever is viewing them also downloads the free SVG 3.0 viewer that's available from the www.adobe.com/svg Web page.

Transparency and Web colors

Even if you've been working in RGB mode with Web safe colors, if you've used Illustrator's transparency in your file, you will end up with out-of-gamut shades when the artwork is rasterized or flattened. Files with extensive transparency use should be saved as JPEG, not as GIF, to avoid excessive dithering.

Web safe RGB

The Web Safe RGB Color palette will not display the Out of Gamut warning for CMYK colors, but the RGB color palette will.

LiveMotion 2 support

LiveMotion 2 can read native Illustrator files (version 10 or higher) and even understands Illustrator's native transparency. To use Illustrator art in LiveMotion 2, simply save the file as an Illustrator file. Make sure the Create PDF Compatible File option is checked when you save.

gradients or gradient mesh objects, recognize that you'll be creating bitmapped images that will result in larger file sizes.

- **If you import or create rasterized art for the Internet,** rasterize at 72 ppi, not the default, to keep file sizes small.

- **To export a file's layers or paths selectively,** hide the ones you don't want before exporting.

- **If the object you want to export to Flash contains a dashed stroke,** expand it using the Tip "Outlining Dashed Strokes" in the *Drawing & Coloring* chapter. Or you can use your operating system's clipboard to copy the stroke from Illustrator and paste it into Flash. To preserve the dash and gap pattern of the Illustrator object, choose Preferences > File Handling & Clipboard and then select PDF for the Copy As option. If you don't do this, the dash and gap pattern will be converted to the default pattern in Flash.

- **Choosing Export AI Layers to SWF Files turns each Illustrator layer into a separate Flash file.** This is the preferred method of exporting Illustrator elements for animation.

SVG

Illustrator supports the export of Scalable Vector Graphics (SVG). SVG is an emerging standard for a Web graphic format that contains a combination of elements such as vectors, gradients, type, raster effects, and JavaScript events, all based on the popular XML standard. SVG is also a text-based format, which means it can be easily edited even after the file has been uploaded to a Web server. We'll talk more about this later when we discuss data-driven graphics. SVG is potentially a very exciting file format, because it combines very small file sizes with crisp artwork that, like Illustrator vector art, can be zoomed into and scaled up or down with no loss of quality. As with Flash, in order for exported SVG files to be viewed in a browser, a special viewer (plug-in) is required. The SVG plug-in is automatically installed in your browser when you install Illustrator.

The SVG format supports JavaScript interactivity as well as static image display. To add a JavaScript event to your artwork you must know JavaScript! Open the SVG Interactivity palette (Window > SVG Interactivity); then, with an object selected, choose an event from the pop-up menu, and type a JavaScript command in the JavaScript text field.

DATA-DRIVEN GRAPHICS

With Illustrator's Variables palette, you can create artwork in Illustrator that can automatically be updated or replaced using a script you write. For example, you can create a template for a news headline where the actual word *headline* is defined as a text variable. With the use of a script you can retrieve a news headline from a database and automatically update the text of your headline with the current news item. The real time saver here is that your template can be used over and over again for each new headline—simply by running the script.

There are four different kinds of variables you can define in Illustrator: text, linked images, graph data, and visibility. When text is defined as a variable, you can apply any attributes to the text and they will stick with the text object (for example: font, color, style information), and the text string will be replaced (as in the headline example we mentioned above). A linked image variable means that one linked image is replaced by another. If scaling or effects have been applied to a linked image, then any image that replaces it will also have the scaling or effects applied to it. (This can be affected by the Placement Options command in the Links palette menu. This command lets you set options for linked objects, such as whether the incoming art remembers transformations such as scaling, or whether it's placed according

Pixel preview
Choose View > Pixel Preview and zoom in to 200% or more to display a rasterized preview of your vector artwork.

No more SVG export?
Illustrator now lets you save as SVG directly from the Save and Save As dialog box. If you check the Preserve Illustrator Editing Capabilities option, a native version of the AI file will be included in the SVG file, allowing for complete editability in Illustrator.

Go, Go Dynamic!
You can take dynamic graphics a step further if you're using Adobe GoLive 6.0 or higher, which understands Illustrator's variable content. Simply save your file in SVG format and import it into GoLive as an Illustrator Smart Object. The variables you defined in Illustrator can then be changed in GoLive.

CSS Layers
Illustrator allows you to export CSS (Cascading Style Sheets) layers. Newer browsers take advantage of DHTML, which allows you to overlap artwork layers. Top level layers can be converted to CSS layers on export from the Save for Web dialog box, and you can specify what layers to export from the Layers tab there.

What is Graphics Server?

Adobe Graphics Server is an image server product that allows you to automatically generate graphic content for the Web in real time. It uses complex scripts to take Illustrator templates and update them with a database as a user browses a Web site.

Exploiting data sets

Illustrator's variables are all based on the XML standard. You can import and export variable libraries with ease via the Variables palette menu. For a detailed description of how Illustrator's XML variables are defined, see the XML Grammar guide PDF on the Adobe Illustrator CS application CD.

Variables and objects

The following variables can be applied to the following objects:
- Visibility: any layer, group, or object
- Text String: any text object
- Graph Data: any graph object
- Linked File: any linked file object

to other characteristics, such as proportions, file dimensions, or how it fills the bounding box. See the *User Guide* for more about Placement Options.)

Graph variables allow you to design a graph using Illustrator's graph tools and link the graph to a database; when data changes, the graph is automatically updated. The final variable type is visibility, which allows you to show or hide artwork. You define whether artwork is visible or not simply by showing or hiding the layer or sublayer for that artwork in the Layers palette.

To define a variable, open the Variables palette (Window > Variables). Type some text on the Artboard and click on the Make Text Dynamic button on the Variables palette. (The same button changes to Make Graph Dynamic or Make Linked File Dynamic depending on your selection.) Use the same technique to define other kinds of variables. For visibility variables, use the Make Visibility Dynamic button.

You can also store multiple data sets in Illustrator—which almost makes Illustrator itself into a database. Once you've defined your variables, click on the Capture Data Set button (or choose Capture Data Set from the Variables palette menu). You can then change the data of your variables, capture another data set, and repeat. At that point, you can use the Previous Data Set and Next Data Set icons to step between data sets and see the data update on your screen. This is a great technique for seeing how multiple versions of data will look when you design your template. Or, on the other hand, if you have multiple versions of a design or layout to present to a client, you could assign the same variable to equivalent attributes in each version of the layout design.

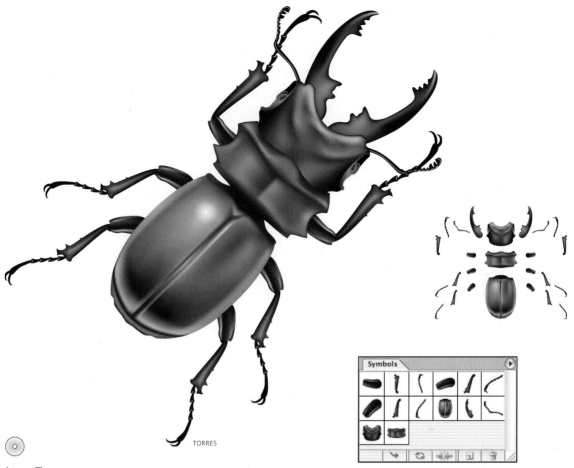

TORRES

Ivan Torres

Symbols can dramatically reduce file size, especially in art destined for the Web. Artist Ivan Torres began this beetle by first creating individual body parts, many of which were complex gradient meshes. (To learn more about creating and editing gradient meshes, see the *Blends, Gradients & Mesh* chapter.) Then he converted the parts into symbols by dragging and dropping each onto the Symbols palette. To assemble the beetle from body part symbols, Torres dragged the parts from the Symbols palette and dropped them on the artboard, creating instances of the symbols.

To create the body parts with mirrored twins on opposite sides of the beetle body, he used the Reflect tool, chose Vertical and clicked Copy. When he had completed the illustration, Torres chose File > Export and selected Macromedia SWF format. In the pop-up dialog box, he picked Export As: AI File to SWF File. After opening Macromedia Flash (SWF), Torres imported the Illustrator Flash file (File > Import) and then used Flash's tools to manipulate the body part symbols to create an interactive animation.

Off in a Flash

Making Artwork for a Flash Animation

Overview: *Sketch character artwork; create brushes and blend objects for moving parts in the animation; export the artwork as a static Macromedia SWF file and a SWF animation; preview animations in Illustrator.*

1

Character parts sketched with a custom calligraphic brush (see the Brushes chapter for help with brushes)

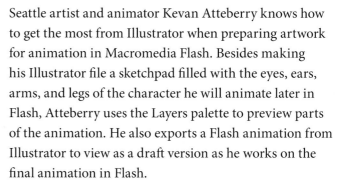

Symbols palette displayed in Large List View

Seattle artist and animator Kevan Atteberry knows how to get the most from Illustrator when preparing artwork for animation in Macromedia Flash. Besides making his Illustrator file a sketchpad filled with the eyes, ears, arms, and legs of the character he will animate later in Flash, Atteberry uses the Layers palette to preview parts of the animation. He also exports a Flash animation from Illustrator to view as a draft version as he works on the final animation in Flash.

1 Sketching characters, drawing body parts. Atteberry began with a custom calligraphic brush, sketching a series of facial expressions and figure poses, honing the visual character of a lemur until he was satisfied with the characterization and ready to construct the lemur's body parts. Once you're done drawing your character's parts, you can keep your artwork as Illustrator objects or turn the artwork into symbol instances. It takes fewer steps to convert your artwork to symbol instances in Illustrator than to bring your artwork into Flash and make symbols there. Also, if you plan to export a Flash movie from Illustrator, turning your character parts into symbol instances results in a smaller and faster-loading Flash file.

To make symbol instances, select the artwork for each part body you drew and Shift-drag it into the Symbols palette. After you release the mouse button, Illustrator adds the artwork as a symbol in the Symbols palette and replaces the selected artwork with an instance of the symbol that was just made. (See the *Brushes, & Symbols* chapter for more on symbols and instances).

2 Making brushes, creating blends for objects, expanding blends, and creating symbols. For any part you animate, you will need to create a sequence of parts— for example, a leg that moves from straight to bent. Atteberry created art brushes for the lemur's moving parts, so he could paint each part in the motion sequence with the brush. (This saved the effort of creating separate art for each part in the sequence.) First, draw a straight version of the part. When you have the look you want, drag-and-drop it on the open Brushes palette. In the New Brush dialog box, choose New Art Brush.

Next, you'll create artwork for the two extremes in the motion sequence. Draw the straight part, and a few inches away draw the bent part. Select both paths and apply the art brush to both. Now, to make other parts in the movement sequence, make sure both paths are selected and choose Object > Blend > Make; then choose Object > Blend > Blend Options and key in the number of steps in the Spacing: Specified Steps field. Consider using a small number of blend steps—Atteberry uses three or four—so that if used as frames in a Flash animation, your SWF file will have a smaller number of frames and a smaller file size. Finally, expand the blend (Object > Blend > Expand) and ungroup it so you have separate objects to use in constructing poses for the motion sequence.

3 Exporting an SWF animation. Once your artwork is complete, you can export the file as a draft or final animation that you can view in a browser or in the Flash player. To prepare your file for animation, first add as many

2

Two of the brushes Atteberry created for the moving parts

The straight and bent lemur legs representing the extremes of a motion sequence that Atteberry used to create a Blend

A blend using three steps created between the straight and bent lemur legs

AI instances to Flash symbols

If you make symbols in Illustrator and want to import them into Flash, be sure to make instances of your symbols first. When you export an SWF file from Illustrator, the Symbols palette is not exported with the SWF file. Flash will recognize Illustrator's instances in the SWF file, however, and add them as symbols to its own Library.

Exporting an SWF file

Illustrator's three Export As options for exporting an SWF file produce files you can import into the Macromedia Flash application.

Previewing a motion sequence using Illustrator's Layers palette as a crude film projector

layers as frames needed to show the motion sequence. Treating each layer as an animation frame, assemble the artwork for a particular pose or step in the motion sequence on each layer. Move from layer to layer, creating renditions of the character on each layer until the character has performed all of the poses or movements you want to preview. When you have completed all the layers, select File > Export. From the Format pop-up, select Macromedia Flash (SWF) and in the Format Options dialog box, choose Export As: AI Layers to SWF Frames. If your animation will use a lot of frames, or will include complex motion sequences that require many intermediate poses or steps, create the final animation in Flash instead of in Illustrator. Flash's tweening commands automatically create many of the intermediate poses you would otherwise assemble manually in Illustrator.

There is another animation technique you can use to preview motion—from within Illustrator itself. Atteberry constructed a draft version of part of the animation to preview the look of objects and of the motion sequence. To do this, you can construct a preview by first following the steps described above for positioning poses on successive layers. After you've filled all your layers with artwork, select Palette Options from the Layers palette menu. Click on the Show Layers Only checkbox to enable this option and key in 100 pixels in the Other field. To preview the animation, position the cursor over a Layers palette scrolling arrow and press the mouse button to cause the layer thumbnails to scroll like frames in a projector.

Pasting into Flash

You can copy Illustrator artwork and paste in Flash. Be careful, though—some Illustrator artwork with complex styles and bitmap effects will not look correct when pasted in Flash.

4 Exporting an SWF file to import into Macromedia Flash. Another use of your artwork is to export it as an SWF file and then import the SWF into Flash to develop the finished animation. To export, choose File > Export and from the Format pop-up, choose Macromedia Flash (SWF). Then, in the Format Options dialog box, choose the Export As option that saves the SWF in the format (single frame file, animation file, or multiple files) that you need.

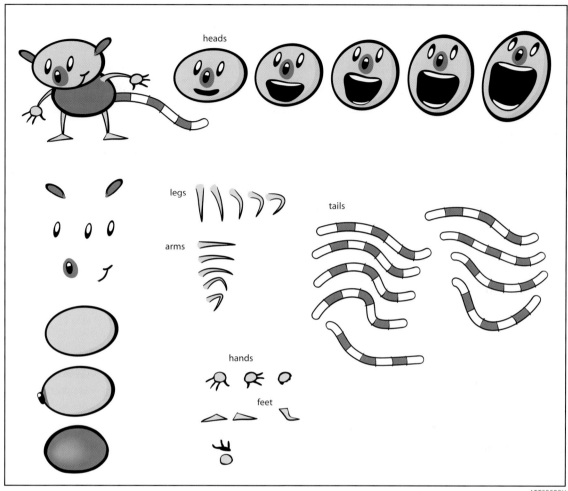

ATTEBERRY

Kevan Atteberry

To assist in constructing his animation "Millard and the Pear," which is described in the previous lesson, artist Kevan Atteberry developed a file of recyclable parts—a cartoon "morgue"—from which he copied parts and pasted them in the file in which he created the animation. To trim the file size of the animation, Atteberry converted the artwork for parts into symbol instances by Shift-dragging them to the Symbols palette. When he needed to edit a symbol,

Atteberry selected the instance and chose Object > Expand. After editing the artwork, Atteberry selected the artwork and Shift-dragged it to the Symbols palette to automatically convert it back into a symbol instance.

Layering Frames

Turning Layered Artwork into Keyframes

Overview: *Draw artwork for print; design animation sequences using artwork; create layers and lay out art and text in positions for animation keyframes; export layers as Shockwave Flash frames.*

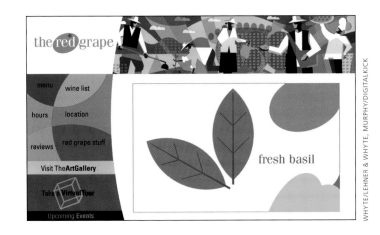

1

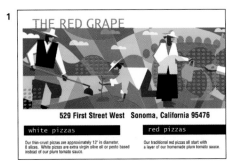

Artwork originally created for The Red Grape's printed restaurant menu

Planning an animation sequence by positioning objects and text at beginning and end of the sequence

After designing the brand identity, menu artwork, and a wall mural in Illustrator for The Red Grape, a Sonoma, California restaurant, Hugh Whyte of Lehner and Whyte faced one more task. He needed to turn his artwork into Flash animations for the restaurant's Web site (www.theredgrape.com). The key to recycling the artwork was to develop a productive workflow between Illustrator and Macromedia Flash that would allow Whyte and Mark Murphy of DigitalKick to work within the software that each designer knew best.

1 Drawing artwork and planning objects and type for keyframes. While his drawings of people and food were originally designed for the printed menus, Whyte returned to the artwork and prepared it for the Web as a Flash animation.

If you are more comfortable designing in Illustrator than in Flash, stay in Illustrator and use the artwork you've already created. Think about how your artwork will move in the animation sequences you plan. Identify the starting and ending locations of each object in an animation sequence. Also note where objects will change direction as they move during the sequence.

2 Arranging artwork on layers. To facilitate their collaboration, Whyte and Murphy devised a workflow in which Whyte created in Illustrator what Murphy would use as keyframes in Flash. You can do the same (even if you will be producing the final animation yourself in Flash) and enjoy the ease of using Illustrator to build the foundation of your animation.

Begin by creating a new file (File >New). In the default layer of the new file, arrange objects and text in the positions you plan for the first frame of the animation. Next, duplicate the default layer by dragging the layer name and dropping it on the Create New Layer icon at the bottom of the Layers palette (see the *Layers* chapter for more on managing layers and the artwork on them). In the new layer, arrange the objects and text for their next positions in the animation sequence. These positions might be the final ones in the animation, or points in the middle of the sequence where something occurs (for example, a text object stops moving). Continue creating new layers, copying and pasting artwork, and positioning the artwork, until you've created as many layers as you'll need to cover the beginning, end, and any important intermediate frames of the animation.

Keep in mind that you don't need to make every frame that will appear in the final animation. That would be unnecessary! Instead, create layers and arrange the text and graphic objects on them for the critical frames (which will be used as "key frames" in Flash). Once exported, the Flash software will generate the in-between frames (or "tweens") to fill in the frames you haven't created, saving time and producing a smaller Flash file size.

3 Exporting the Illustrator layers as Shockwave Flash frames. When Whyte finished building the file, he deleted any artwork or layers that weren't required as Flash frames.

To save the file, choose File>Export and from the Export dialog box, choose Macromedia Flash (SWF) from the Format pop-up. Click Export, and in the Macromedia Flash (SWF) Format Options dialog box choose AI Layers to SWF Frames. Set the other dialog options as you prefer and then click OK.

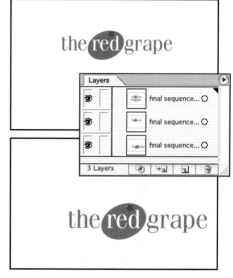

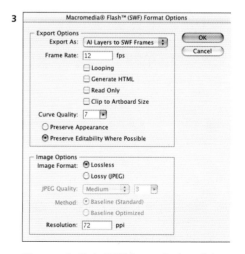

Artwork for the final animation sequence arranged on three layers; the Layers palette showing the layers in the sequential frame order of the animation

Macromedia Flash (SWF) Format Options dialog

Webward Ho!

Designing a Web Page in Illustrator

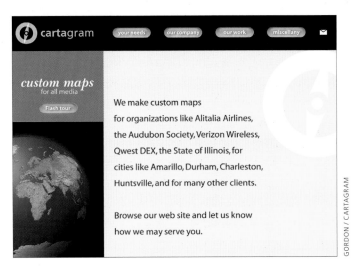

Overview: *Set up a document for Web page design; use layers to structure artwork for pages and frames; save layouts as template images; slice text and artwork and save an HTML file and sliced image files.*

Gordon constructed the Cartagram Web site around a two-frame design; the black rectangle represented the top frame's Web page, used for the logo and main navigation controls; the other colored rectangles served as a design grid for dividing areas of the Web pages that would load in the bottom frame

216 colors, or millions?

The palette of 216 non-dithered, Web safe colors was designed for text and graphics displaying on 8-bit monitors. But how many people are restricted to 8-bit color anymore? Not many. Most computers are now equipped with 24- or 32-bit video boards, rendering Web safe colors unnecessary. So you can choose from millions of colors, not just 216.

If you are comfortable designing and drawing in Illustrator, why go elsewhere to design your Web pages? Steven Gordon uses Illustrator to design and preview Web pages, create comps for client approval, export a layout as a template for use in Adobe GoLive, and slice and optimize artwork before saving it for use on Web pages.

1 Choosing document settings. With Illustrator, you can draw and organize artwork to design a simple Web page or a more complex page with multiple frames. To start your page, create a new document (File > New). In the New Document dialog box, set Units to pixels, specify an Artboard size in pixels equal to that of your intended Web page size, and choose RGB Color for Color Mode. You may want to create a grid (Preferences > Guides & Grid) that will help you align and constrain artwork.

Also, if your artwork will be exported in a bitmap format like GIF or JPEG, consider turning on pixel preview (View > Pixel Preview)—this lets you see the anti-aliasing of your artwork. (See Tip, "Anti-antialiasing," for a technique that helps you reduce the amount of blurring that affects artwork when it is antialiased.)

2 Structuring pages with layers and adding artwork. Let the Layers palette help you organize the layout and content of your Web page. (See "Nested Layers" in the *Layers*

chapter for more on making and manipulating layers.) Gordon created separate layers for the top and bottom frames of his page, and sublayers for multiple pages he designed for the bottom frame. He toggled layer visibility on to preview the layout and content of different pages in the bottom frame of his page design.

Once you've set up the layer structure of your document, you're ready to add content to your page design. As you create text and graphics, and import images, use familiar Illustrator tools and palettes to help make and arrange objects. Gordon relied on the Align palette to easily align and distribute navigation buttons in the top frame and to center or justify colored background rectangles for both frames (using the Align to Artboard option in the Align palette).

3 Saving a Web page design and importing it into GoLive. Once your page design is complete, export it as a GIF or JPEG and import the file into Adobe GoLive as a "tracing image" to help you construct a finished HTML page. If you set up the Artboard to match the dimensions of the Web pages you'll construct in GoLive, you can crop your Illustrator artwork so that it matches those dimensions when exported as a bitmapped image. To do this, either create cropmarks from the Artboard (see the *Type* chapter for instructions on making cropmarks) and then use File>Export, or skip the cropmarks and choose File>Save for Web (which automatically crops artwork to the Artboard).

When you begin working in GoLive, import the image you just exported from Illustrator and use it as a template to guide you in building the page. First, choose Window> Tracing Image; then, in the Tracing Image palette, click the Source checkbox and the Browse icon to select your Illustrator-exported image. Next, adjust the HTML page's frame widths, and create text boxes and other objects in GoLive that match the Illustrator image. Repeat these steps with other exported images when building other pages in GoLive.

2

The layer structure for the Web page design, showing the top and bottom frames, and two sublayers representing separate pages designed to load in the bottom frame

3

The Tracing Image palette in Adobe GoLive5; Gordon clicked the Browse icon to locate the layout image file he had exported previously using Illustrator's Save for Web command

Anti-antialiasing

When artwork is saved as a bitmapped image, straight lines and other objects may be anti-aliased (blurred). To minimize this, first set Keyboard Increment to 0.5 pixels in the Preferences> General dialog box. Then make sure both View>Pixel Preview and View>Snap to Pixel are turned on. Next, draw and position your objects. Finally, turn off View> Snap to Pixel, and nudge aliased objects in 0.5 pixel increments as needed, using the Arrow keys.

—*Mordy Golding*

The numbered slices created after using the Object > Slices > Create from Selection command

In the Save for Web dialog box, a preview of the slices is displayed; Gordon clicked in a slice with the Slice Selection tool to select it and then specified settings related to file format and other image characteristics in the Settings portion of the dialog box

4 Slicing artwork. Instead of using your Illustrator artwork as a template in GoLive, consider using Illustrator's slices to turn text, artwork, and placed images into elements you can use when building your HTML pages. Slices also let you divide a large image or layout into smaller areas that you can save as separate, optimized images. These images will load simultaneously, and usually faster than a single large image in a Web browser.

You can use artwork selections, guides, or the Slice tool to divide your Illustrator design into slices. Gordon's design was divided by colored backgrounds and a masked image. (You can use non-contiguous objects for slicing; Illustrator will add slices to fill in any gaps between objects.) To make the slices, first choose Object > Slice > Clip to Artboard, then select an object and choose Object > Slice > Create from Selection. Repeat these steps until you've created all of the slices you need. If you need to remove a slice, select and delete it; or in the Layers palette drag its name (<Slice>) to the palette's trash icon.

5 Saving slices, and using and previewing the HTML page. When you've finished slicing your artwork, you can save the slices as text and images. Choose File > Save for Web; in the dialog box, click on the Slice Select tool and click one of the slices. Pick the settings that you want to use in saving the selected slice. Gordon set GIF as the file format for the two blocks with solid color fills and text. For the globe image, he chose JPEG as the file format and enabled Optimized to make the file size smaller. After clicking on Save, Gordon entered a file name for the HTML file (which automatically became the root name of each of the sliced image files), and made sure that HTML and Images were selected in the Format pop-up menu. After Illustrator saved the HTML file and the sliced image files, Gordon opened the HTML file in GoLive to add head tags (like meta tags) and then previewed the file in a Web browser.

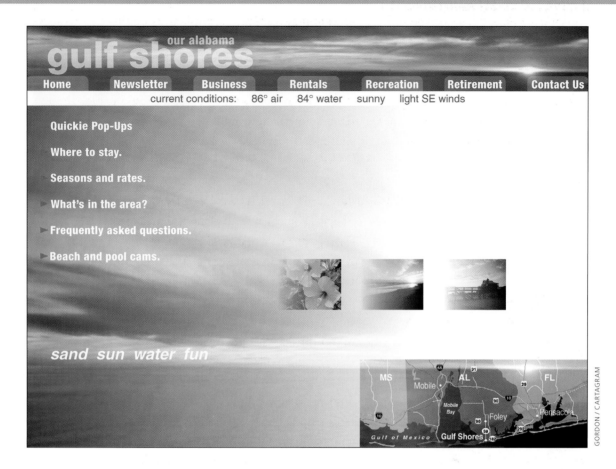

GORDON / CARTAGRAM

Steven Gordon / Cartagram

To build image-mapped buttons at the top of a travel Web page, Steven Gordon first placed a TIFF image in Illustrator to serve as a background image. Next, he drew a button shape with rounded corners and gave it a white Fill and a 25% Opacity using the Transparency palette. He copied the button six times and arranged the buttons in a row above the background image. To space the buttons evenly, Gordon positioned the left and right buttons, selected all buttons, and then clicked the Horizontal Distribute Space icon in the Align palette. To map the buttons to URLs, he selected each button shape and in the

Attributes palette (Window > Attributes) chose Rectangle from the Image Map pop-up menu. He then keyed in the button's URL link in the URL field. In the Save for Web dialog box, Gordon selected JPEG as the output file format, clicked Save, and then chose HTML and Images from the Format pop-up menu. He entered a file name in the Name field and clicked Save.

Making Waves

Transforming and Blending for Animation

Advanced Technique

Illustrator with Photoshop

Overview: *Create "key" frames with transformation tools; blend to create steps; transform your steps; bring the steps into Photoshop.*

1

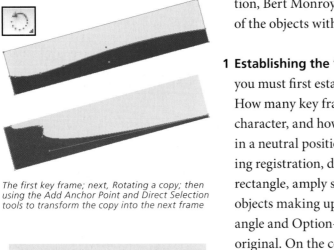

The first key frame; next, Rotating a copy; then using the Add Anchor Point and Direct Selection tools to transform the copy into the next frame

Making certain that the first and last frame have the same number of anchor points in similar alignment for smooth blending (see "Unlocking Realism" in the Blends chapter for more on preparing objects for smooth blending)

Illustrator's transformation tools, used in combination with the Blend tool, are wonderful animation timesavers. Commissioned by Adobe Systems for a special promotion, Bert Monroy used these techniques to prepare many of the objects within a room for animation.

1 Establishing the "key" frames. To create an animation, you must first establish the "key" character positions. How many key frames you'll need will depend on the character, and how it will be animated. Create a character in a neutral position, and if you'll need help maintaining registration, draw an unstroked, unfilled bounding rectangle, amply surrounding the character. Select the objects making up the character and the bounding rectangle and Option-drag/Alt-drag a copy to the side of the original. On the copy of the character (*not* the bounding box), use the transformation tools and Direct Selection editing to create the next extreme position (for more on transformations, see the *Basics* and *Zen* chapters). In Monroy's animation, the characters were: fan, clock second hand, clock pendulum, plant, and the "wave." He first drew the wave in horizontal position using a gray rectangle and a second object for the blue liquid. To create the left-tilted position, he rotated a copy of these two objects, then used the Add Anchor Point and Direct Selection tools to adjust the liquid anchor points manually.

2 Using the Blend tool to generate the in-between steps. Also called "tweening," the secret to smooth animation is to create the correct number of steps between the key frames. For video animations, smooth illusion of motion is achieved with 24 frames per second (fps) of animation; for film it's 30 fps; for on-screen animation it's simply as many frames as is needed for your animation to run smoothly. To make the steps between your first two key frames, select each pair of like objects and blend between them (for help with blends see the *Blends, Gradients & Mesh* chapter); you can only apply a blend reliably between two objects, so you'll have to apply the blend separately for each pair of like objects (including your bounding rectangle), making sure that each pair has the same number of anchor points, and that you select the correlating anchor point in each object when blending. For the wave, Monroy first blended in 12 steps from box to box, and then from liquid to liquid. Since the same number of steps was chosen for each transition, the liquid blends were perfectly registered within the box blends.

3 Transforming blends to extend the animation. Rather than continually starting from scratch, it's often easier to rotate, scale, shear or reflect your blends to extend your animation. Monroy selected the blended boxes and waves, and Reflected them vertically as copies (see the *Zen* chapter, Exercise #9) to create the right-side rocking motion.

4 Pasting into Photoshop. With Illustrator still open, launch Photoshop and create an RGB document larger than your biggest key frame. In Illustrator, copy each character frame and bounding box, and then move to the Photoshop file and paste "As Pixels" to create a new layer with that step. With that object still in memory, also paste "As Paths" for easy re-selection. Monroy used his paths to make selections for applying special effects locally—using Alpha Channels to create effects such as the darkening and bubbles in the liquid. (For more about Photoshop see the *Illustrator & Other Programs* chapter.)

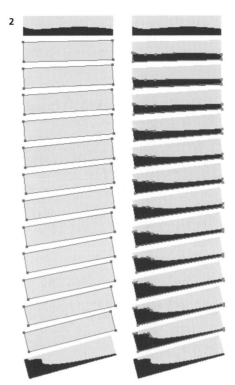

The outer objects after blending (left column), then blending the inner wave (right column)— **Note:** *Selecting the upper right point on the wave gives the smoothest blend*

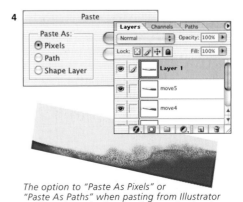

The option to "Paste As Pixels" or "Paste As Paths" when pasting from Illustrator to Photoshop; the frames after pasting into layers; the wave after effects using Alpha Channels

Illustrator & Other Programs

12

382 Introduction

382 Placing Artwork in Illustrator

383 Illustrator & Other Programs

384 Illustrator & Adobe Photoshop

385 Illustrator & Adobe InDesign

385 Illustrator, PDF & Adobe Acrobat

386 Illustrator & Adobe Streamline

386 Illustrator & 3D programs

387 Gallery: Bert Monroy

388 Illustrator with Photoshop: Software Relay: *An Illustrator-Photoshop Workflow*

391 Gallery: Rob Magiera

392 Advanced Technique: Illustrator with Photoshop: Shape Shifting: *Exporting Paths to Shapes in Photoshop*

394-407 Galleries: Judy Stead, Timothy Donaldson, April Greiman, Lance Hidy, David Pounds, Ron Chan, Louis Fishauf, Filip Yip, Chris Spollen, Bryan Christie, Eliot Bergman, Tom Willcockson, Joe Jones

Illustrator & Other Programs

Prevent color shifts

If at all possible, you'll want to avoid color space mismatches and conversions, especially if you use any kind of transparency. If you use color management, choose your settings in Illustrator and then use the same settings in Photoshop and InDesign; and when you exchange PSD files between Illustrator, Photoshop, and InDesign, include the color profiles in the files. —*Pierre Louveaux*

Is EPS obsolete?

If your application (e.g., Illustrator, Photoshop, or InDesign) can place or open the native AI, native PSD, or PDF 1.4 formats, it's better to use those than EPS, because they may preserve transparency, layers, and other features.

Which formats can you link?

Any BMP, EPS, GIF, JPEG, PICT, PCX, PDF, PNG, Photoshop, Pixar, Targa, or TIFF file can be placed linked (rather than embedded).

So you think it's linked?

Applying a filter or flattening transparency of a linked image will automatically embed the image. In addition to increasing the file size, Illustrator will no longer be able to update the link.

This chapter showcases some of the ways you can use Illustrator together with other programs. Although the range of work you can create using Illustrator is virtually limitless, using other programs together with Illustrator increases your creative opportunities, and in many instances can save you significant time in creating your final work. One of this chapter's highlights is the step-by-step technique by renowned artist Rob Magiera for bringing Illustrator images into Photoshop.

We'll begin by discussing how you can place artwork in Illustrator, and then we'll provide a general look at how Illustrator works with other programs. Next we'll examine how Illustrator works with specific programs, including Photoshop, InDesign, Acrobat, Streamline, and other 3D programs. For information about working with Illustrator and other web or animation programs, see the *Web & Animation* chapter.

PLACING ARTWORK IN ILLUSTRATOR

Illustrator can place more than two dozen different types of file formats. The major choice you'll need to make is whether to link or embed the file. When you link a file, you don't actually include the artwork in the Illustrator file; instead a copy of the artwork acts as a placeholder, while the actual image remains separate from the Illustrator file. This can help reduce file size, but keep in mind that linking is supported only for certain formats (see Tip at left). On the other hand, when you embed artwork, you're actually including it in the file. The Links palette keeps track of linked files, but also lists all the raster images used in your document, regardless of whether they were created within Illustrator or embedded via the Place command (see the *Illustrator Basics* chapter for more). For details on how to place artwork (by linking and/or embedding it), see "Importing Artwork," in Chapter 2 of the *User Guide*.

In general, you should embed artwork only when:

- The image is small in file size.
- You're creating web graphics.
- The placed file interacts with other parts of the document via transparency. Embedding will ensure proper flattening and printing.
- You want more than just a placeholder with a preview (e.g., you want editable shapes and transparency).
- Linking isn't supported for the format your artwork is in. In contrast to linked images, embedded image objects can be permanently altered.

And you should link (rather than embed) when:

- Your illustration uses several copies of the same image.
- The image is large in file size.
- You want to be able to edit the placed image using its original application.
- File will be used in Illustrator 88 through version 6.x. Another argument for linking files is that you can make changes to a linked file and resend only the linked file to your service bureau or client. As long as it has exactly the same name, it'll auto-update without further editing of the Illustrator document itself.

ILLUSTRATOR & OTHER PROGRAMS

The first consideration when moving artwork between Illustrator and other programs is to decide which objects in your artwork have to remain as vectors and which can be allowed to become rasterized. Next, is whether you want to move the artwork between two open programs on your desktop (e.g. by using Copy and Paste or Drag and Drop) or if you will be moving your artwork via a file format. Finally, consider whether you want to move only a few objects or the whole file. The details of how to do the above vary depending on the program and are described in the corresponding program sections below.

Depending on the application, when you drag or paste objects between Illustrator and another open program, your objects will either drag or paste as vectors or

Resolution of placed images

Greatly reduce your printing time and ensure optimal image reproduction by properly setting the pixel-per-inch (ppi) resolution of raster images before placing them into Illustrator. The ppi of images should be 1.5 to 2 times the size of the line screen at which the final image will print. For example, if your illustration will be printed in a 150 dpi (dots per inch) line screen, then the resolution of your raster images would typically be 300 ppi. Get print resolution specifications and recommendations from your printer *before* you begin your project!

Open sesame

If you're working in an application that doesn't allow you to save in a format that Illustrator imports (such as EPS or PDF), but does print to PostScript, you may be able to get the vector data by printing to File and then opening the raw PostScript file from within Illustrator.

Faster and smaller "saves"

Turning off the PDF option when you save reduces file size and makes saving faster. However, if you're going to be importing your artwork into certain programs (e.g. InDesign and LiveMotion), be sure to leave PDF compatibility on.

MONROY

See Bert Monroy's Photoshop and Illustrator lesson, "Pattern Brushes" in the Brushes & Symbols *chapter*

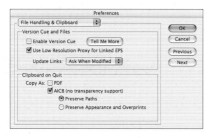

Illustrator File Handling and Clipboard Preferences dialog box. To copy and paste vectors to Photoshop set the clipboard preferences as shown above. (See the User Guide *for more about these options)*

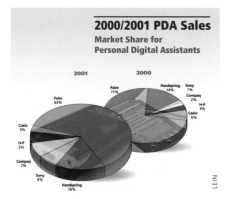

LEIN

See Adam Z Lein's Gallery in the Transparency & Appearances *chapter to find out how he used the Excel Chart Wizard and for this Pie Chart*

as raster objects. In general, any program that supports PostScript drag and drop behavior will accept Illustrator objects via Drag and Drop (or Copy and Paste). For Mac OS only, you need to be sure that the AICB (Adobe Illustrator ClipBoard) is selected in the File Handling & Clipboard panel of the Preferences dialog box at the time you copy the objects between AI and the other application.

When you are dragging and dropping, your Illustrator art will automatically be rasterized at the same physical size, or pixel-per-inch ratio, that you have specified in the raster-based program to which you're dragging the art.

You can Save (via Save, Save As, Save for Web, or Save for Microsoft Office) or Export your Illustrator artwork to many formats, including: EPS, GIF, JPEG, Legacy.ai, PDF, PICT, PNG, Photoshop (PSD) SVG, SWF, and TIFF. Knowing what file formats your other application supports and the type of information (vector, raster, layers, paths) you want to bring from Illustrator into the other program will help you determine which format to use. See the *User Guide* for detailed information about these file formats.

ILLUSTRATOR & ADOBE PHOTOSHOP

As the lessons and galleries in this chapter demonstrate, the creative possibilities for using Illustrator and Photoshop together are limitless.

By default, artwork that you move from Illustrator to Photoshop via the Clipboard (or by using drag and drop) will be rasterized (see figure at left for how to keep vectors as vectors). Moving artwork via a file format can be more straightforward, since Illustrator can open and export Photoshop PSD files. But the rules governing how Illustrator layers get translated into Photoshop layers (and whether or not those layers get rasterized in the process) are complex. How to use these methods to move most types of Illustrator objects (such as simple paths, text, compound paths, and compound shapes) between Illustrator and Photoshop is covered in detail in the corresponding sections of the *User Guide*.

ILLUSTRATOR & ADOBE INDESIGN

When you Copy and Paste artwork from Illustrator into InDesign, the artwork is pasted as either PDF or AICB, depending on which option you specified in the Illustrator File Handling & Clipboard panel of the Preferences dialog box. PDF preserves transparency, while AICB can break your artwork into smaller opaque native InDesign objects that mimic the transparency of your original artwork.

To place Illustrator files in InDesign, you must have saved your Illustrator artwork with the Create PDF Compatible File option enabled. Doing so preserves your gradients, patterns, and transparency (which will allow underlying artwork to show through). But be aware that your artwork is imported as one object, which is not editable using InDesign, and not listed in InDesign's Links palette. For more about moving artwork between Illustrator and InDesign, search the InDesign online help, using the word "Illustrator."

ILLUSTRATOR, PDF & ADOBE ACROBAT

Acrobat's Portable Document Format (PDF) is platform and application independent—this means the format allows easy transfer of files between different operating systems, such as Mac OS, Windows, and even UNIX, as well as between different applications.

Illustrator CS now includes more options for specifying how PDFs are created. These options were previously available only in Acrobat Distiller. You can now save your layered Illustrator CS files as layered Acrobat 6 files. In the Save As dialog box, choose Adobe PDF (pdf), and then in the Adobe PDF Options dialog box, enable the "Create Acrobat Layers From Top-Level Layers" option.

Illustrator and Acrobat share many other features, including Overprint Preview, the transparency grid, and native PDF 1.5 support. To save your file for use in Acrobat, be sure that you enable the Create PDF Compatible File option in the Illustrator Save As dialog box that appears when you Save your Illustrator file.

Illustrator in page layout apps

If you save Illustrator files with the PDF compatibility feature enabled, you'll be able to place .ai files directly into InDesign and Pagemaker. You'll notice that InDesign imports these "native" files through its PDF import option. Though this PDF format, it may not be supported by all programs, most should be able to place your files if you Save or Save As with Acrobat compatibility set to Acrobat 4, 5 or 6. However, the surefire way to ensure that you can place Illustrator files into layout programs that can't see native .ai files is to choose Save As and choose the EPS option.

Using Illustrator with PDF

Illustrator offers particular advantages to those working with Acrobat. If you use Save As, Adobe PDF, you can include the editable Illustrator artwork. You can then use Acrobat to add comments and interactive elements. Then, you can reopen the PDF in Illustrator to make any changes. In Illustrator, you won't see the Acrobat content you added; however, when you resave the document as PDF and later reopen it in Acrobat, your Acrobat content will still be there!
—*Sandee Cohen* (from Adobe Acrobat 5 Master Class: For Interactivity and Digital Documents)

Crop Areas & Acrobat

You can now set the crop area in PDF files in Illustrator. First set the crop area in your Illustrator.ai file (create a rectangle and choose Object > Crop Area) then File > Export it as PDF 1.5. When you open the file in Acrobat 6, the file will be cropped to the crop area you specified in Illustrator. If you want to change the crop area in Acrobat, choose Document > Pages > Crop and enter the new desired crop area. Best of all, you will not lose any art you created in Illustrator that was clipped by the Illustrator specified crop area.
—*Brenda Sutherland*

Antialiased artwork in Acrobat

If your Illustrator artwork looks coarse or jagged in Acrobat 6, it's probably being displayed without antialiasing. To fix this, choose Preferences > Smoothing in Acrobat 6 and enable all the Smooth options. —*Pierre Louveaux*

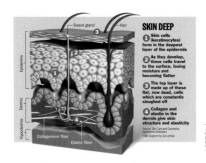

Joe Lertola's Skin Deep image for TIME used Il-lustrator and Lightwave 3D. See his Gallery in the Brushes & Symbols *chapter*

PDF files created by other programs can be edited in Illustrator, but you can only open and save one page at a time, and text that appears to be all in one flow or text box in the PDF may be broken up into multiple text boxes when opened in Illustrator.

ILLUSTRATOR & ADOBE STREAMLINE

A number of artists use Streamline to creatively translate scanned drawings or photos into Illustrator art.

Streamline was designed by Adobe to convert scanned black-and-white or color raster images into editable vector paths and fills that can be brought into Illustrator, Photoshop, and other programs that accept Illustrator vector art. For bitmapped art, Streamline gives you much more control for specifying how the auto tracing is done than Illustrator's Auto Trace tool. You can choose whether to trace the outline of shapes, or create vectors that follow the centerlines of the shapes, or a sophisticated combination (see figure on previous page). For raster images, the basic technique is to posterize the image, and then auto trace the resulting shapes and fill them with the corresponding colors, custom colors, or tints of custom colors.

ILLUSTRATOR & 3D PROGRAMS

In addition to Illustrator's 3D effects (see the *Live Effects & Graphic Styles* chapter) you can also import Illustrator paths into 3D programs to use as outlines and extrusion paths. Once you import a path, you can transform it into a 3D object. Strata's 3D StudioPro and Lightwave 3D are just two of many 3D programs you can use in combination with Illustrator.

© Bert Monroy 1999

MONROY

Bert Monroy
(Photoshop)

Bert Monroy capitalized on layered, resolution-independent artwork that he created in Illustrator and brought into Photoshop to create this image of a neon sign. In the image, Monroy used techniques similar to those detailed in his Rendez-vous Cafe image (see the *Brushes & Symbols* chapter). Monroy's techniques for creating photorealistic images from 2D software are illustrated in his books, *Bert Monroy: Photorealistic Techniques with Photoshop & Illustrator* and *Photoshop Studio with Bert Monroy* (both New Riders Publishing).

Software Relay

An Illustrator-Photoshop Workflow

Illustrator with Photoshop

Overview: *Create paths in Illustrator; build a registration rectangle; organize layers for Photoshop masking; export as a PSD file; copy Illustrator paths and paste in Photoshop for masking.*

MAGIERA

1

Two stages in the construction of the image in Illustrator: left, the shapes as drawn; right, the shapes with fills

Why crop area?

Creating a crop area will automatically set the canvas size of a PSD file you export from Illustrator. Also, by making the crop area the same size as the Artboard, you can easily register the image after you've modified it in Photoshop. Just choose File > Place, select the image file, click Okay, and then drag a corner until it snaps to a corner of the Artboard.

To illustrate mascots for Salt Lake City's 2002 Olympic Winter Games, Utah artist Rob Magiera drew shapes in Illustrator. He then exported the artwork as a Photoshop (PSD) file so he could airbrush highlights and shadows in Photoshop. While working in Photoshop, Magiera sometimes copied an Illustrator object and pasted it in Photoshop to serve as a selection or to modify a Quick Mask. (See the "Shape Shifting" lesson in this chapter to learn another way to move artwork between Illustrator and Photoshop.)

Although Magiera's illustration would be completed in Photoshop, his client needed the original Illustrator artwork for other uses.

1 Placing a sketch in Illustrator, drawing shapes, and making a registration box. Magiera began by scanning pencil sketches and saving them in TIFF format. He created a new Illustrator file with dimensions that were larger than the drawings he would make and then created a crop area the size of the document by choosing Object > Crop Area > Make (this will help when you place the Photoshop image back into Illustrator). Next, he placed the scanned image on a template layer in Illustrator (see the *Layers* chapter for more on templates) and drew the mascot shapes with the Pen and Pencil tools. He filled the shapes with color, leaving the outlines unstroked.

In order to more easily modify rasterized shapes once you get them into Photoshop, make sure you organize your major artwork elements onto separate layers (for help see the "Organizing Layers" lesson in the Layers chapter). (On export to PSD, Illustrator preserves as much of your layer structure as possible without sacrificing appearance.) For objects that overlapped other objects (like the bear's arm or the coyote's leg), Magiera created new layers and moved the overlapping objects onto separate layers so he could easily mask them in Photoshop when he began airbrushing them.

Knowing that he would bring some of the paths he had drawn into Photoshop to help with masking, Magiera devised a way to keep paths registered to other pasted paths and to the raster artwork he would export from Illustrator. You can accomplish this by making a "registration" rectangle in Illustrator that will keep your artwork in the same position relative to the rectangle (and the Photoshop canvas) each time you copy and paste. To make this rectangle, first create a new layer in the Layers palette, and then drag it below your artwork layers. Next, draw a rectangle with no stroke or fill that is the same size as the Artboard. Center the rectangle on the Artboard. With the rectangle matching the size and position of the Artboard, copies of the rectangle will be pasted in Photoshop automatically aligned with the canvas.

Now you're ready to export your Illustrator artwork. Select File > Export, and from the Export dialog box choose Photoshop (PSD) from the Format pop-up.

2 Working with Illustrator paths in Photoshop. After opening the exported PSD file in Photoshop, Magiera

The Illustrator Layers palette organized with separate layers for shapes (shown as selected objects) to be masked in Photoshop

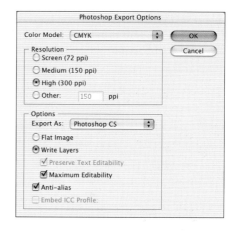

Illustrator's Export: Photoshop Options dialog

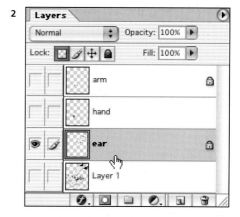

The Photoshop Layers palette showing the layer structure of the Illustrator-exported PSD file

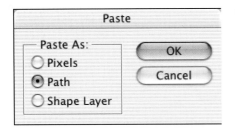

Paste

Paste As:
○ Pixels
◉ Path
○ Shape Layer

OK
Cancel

Photoshop's Paste dialog box for pasting paths

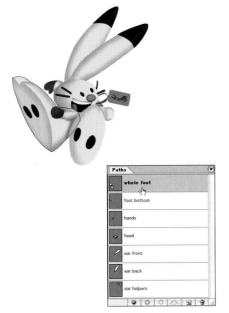

Paths

whole foot

foot bottom

hands

head

ear front

ear back

ear helpers

At top, the bunny figure with the "whole foot" work path selected; bottom, Photoshop's Paths palette showing the selected work path

Masking a shape with a shape

If you mask a raster shape with a pasted Illustrator path in Photoshop, be aware that the mask applies antialiasing to pixels that are already antialiased, resulting in an incorrect appearance. A better way to mask raster shapes in Photoshop is to use the Layers palette's Lock Transparency Pixels option or the Layer > Group with Previous command.

used different masking techniques as he airbrushed highlights and shadows. To mask within a shape, Magiera usually enabled Lock Transparent Pixels for the layer on which the shape was located. If you use the Quick Mask working mode, you can create new masks from objects copied in Illustrator and pasted in Photoshop. To do this, in Illustrator, select both an object *and* the registration rectangle and then choose Edit > Copy. Next, in Photoshop, choose Edit > Paste and in the Paste dialog box, choose Paste as Pixels. Notice that the artwork is in the same position on the Photoshop canvas as it was relative to the registration rectangle in Illustrator. With each pasted path, you can generate a selection and either add to or subtract from your working Quick Mask.

As Magiera worked in Photoshop, he occasionally modified a raster shape and then needed to update the Illustrator path that he originally used to generate the shape. To do this, first make a copy of the Illustrator path and the registration rectangle. Then, in Photoshop, choose Edit > Paste and from the Paste dialog box, choose Paste as Path. Now you can modify the shape's path with Photoshop's drawing tools. When you finish, Shift-select the modified path and the registration rectangle path (click close to an edge of the canvas to select the rectangle) and choose Edit > Copy. Return to Illustrator, select the original registration rectangle, choose Edit > Paste, and drag a corner of the pasted registration rectangle until it snaps to the corresponding corner of the existing registration rectangle. Now you can delete the original path that you are replacing with the modified path.

When Magiera finished airbrushing in Photoshop, he saved the file (which was still in PSD format).

3 Bringing the Photoshop image into Illustrator. For some of the changes to raster shapes he made in Photoshop, Magiera chose to edit the original path in Illustrator. He selected File > Place and imported the image into the Illustrator file, snapping it to the registration rectangle. He edited the paths using the Pen and Pencil tools.

MAGIERA

Rob Magiera

Rob Magiera created these mascots for the 2002 Olympic Winter Games in Salt Lake City, Utah, using many of the same techniques discussed in the previous lesson. After drawing the mascots in Illustrator, he exported a PSD file and airbrushed the rasterized artwork in Photoshop. Then Magiera edited the Illustrator paths to correspond to the changes he had made to some of the shapes in Pho-

toshop. Finally, he saved the Illustrator file (used for silk-screened printed versions of the artwork) and sent Illustrator EPS and PSD files to his client.

Shape Shifting

Exporting Paths to Shapes in Photoshop

**Illustrator with Photoshop
Advanced Technique**

Overview: *Draw paths in Illustrator; convert paths to compound shapes; export in PSD format; apply effects in Photoshop.*

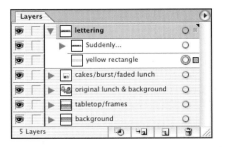

The original Illustrator artwork and the Layers palette shown before the frame, the yellow burst, and the yellow background (behind the type) were turned into compound shapes

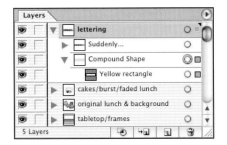

The palette showing objects in a compound shape

Artist Brad Hamann prepared this colorful illustration in Illustrator before exporting it as a PSD file and opening it in Photoshop, where he applied live effects that he could not have created in Illustrator. The key to bringing editable paths into Photoshop is to turn the objects you want to keep as paths into compound shapes. Then, after you export your document as a layered PSD and open it in Photoshop, you will see that your compound shapes have become editable shape layers while the rest of your artwork has been rasterized.

1 Drawing and layering artwork. Hamann used the Pen tool to draw objects and relied on the Blend, Reflect, and Rotate tools to create repeating elements (such as the slanting lines on the side of the milk box). For two of the objects he drew (the yellow burst and the yellow background behind the title), Hamann decided to leave each with a simple fill color in Illustrator and use Photoshop's layer styles and lighting effects to "paint" the objects. Moreover, in order to keep the outer frame looking neat in Photoshop, he had to export it as a single vector object. To do all this, Hamann converted these objects to compound shapes so they would be exported as Photoshop shape layers when he created a PSD file.

Once you've identified the objects you will bring into Photoshop as paths, select each object. From the Pathfinder palette pop-up menu, choose Make Compound Shape. (Choose Release Compound Shape from the Pathfinder palette pop-up menu if you need to turn compound shapes back into regular objects.) Hamann's compound shape frame had two components: a copy of the burst object in Subtract mode, and a rectangular frame. See the *Drawing & Coloring* chapter introduction for details about working with compound shapes and shape modes.

If a compound shape is to remain an editable path when exported from Illustrator, make sure that it is not inside a group or on a sublayer. If it is, move the shape out of all groups and sublayers (see the *Layers* chapter to learn how to move objects using the Layers palette).

2 Exporting a Photoshop (PSD) file. Export your Illustrator file by choosing File > Export, then choose Photoshop (PSD) format and click OK. In the Photoshop Options dialog box, pick a resolution setting that matches the requirements of your printing or display medium and make sure that within the Options section, that all available options are selected.
Note: See the *User Guide* for more details regarding moving artwork between Illustrator and Photoshop.

3 Applying effects to shape layers in Photoshop.
When Hamann opened the exported PSD file in Photoshop, each Illustrator compound shape appeared as a shape layer in Photoshop's Layers palette. To add a layer effect to a shape layer, Hamann double-clicked the shape layer in the Layers palette. He applied Bevel and Emboss effects to his yellow rectangle and starburst shape layers, and even reshaped the shape paths using Photoshop's Direct Selection tool. Finally, he added some Photoshop effects (such as Strokes) to duplicates of some of the shape layers, and applied the Add Noise filter (Gaussian) to a duplicate of the background.

Compound shape to raster
If you turned a stroked object into a compound shape and exported a PSD file, but then found your shape rasterized in Photoshop, don't panic. Either select the object in Illustrator and choose Round Join in the Stroke palette, or remove the object's stroke.

2

A portion of the Options section of the Illustrator File > Export > Photoshop (PSD) dialog box

3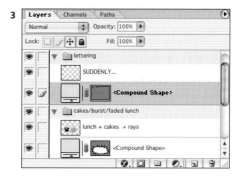

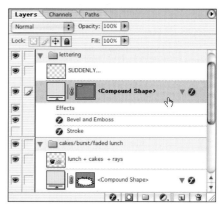

Top shows the Photoshop Layers palette as the PSD is first opened; bottom shows layer effects applied to some of the shape layers

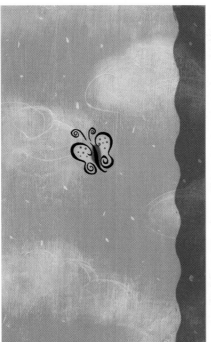 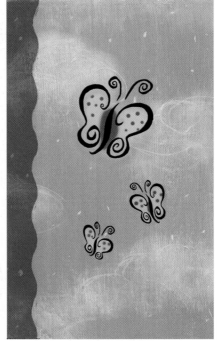

STEAD

Judy Stead
(Photoshop)

Judy Stead combined Photoshop, Illustrator, and traditional painting techniques to design the cover of this Scholastic Book Fairs journal. (Shown above are the back and front covers.) Stead alternated between the three approaches throughout her entire creative process. She first painted the blue clouds on a gesso-textured board with acrylic paint, pastels, and a white pencil (see image inset at right). The image was scanned into Photoshop and the color was adjusted from aqua blue to orange (Image > Adjustments > Hue/Saturation). Stead drew the butterfly in Illustrator, using one of the default Calligraphic brushes and a Wacom drawing tablet, which allowed her to create a line that varied in width (see the *Brushes* chapter). She then exported the file to Photoshop as a PSD file and made several copies of the butterfly, varying rotation, orientation, and size. Stead drew the wavy book spine in Illustrator. In Photoshop, the clouds, spine, and butterflies were combined into a layered Photoshop file. Stead set the blending mode of the cloud layer to Multiply, so the cloud texture was visible through the individual elements. She then added airbrushed detail to the butterfly and continued to adjust the color of the element using Hue/Saturation until she was satisfied with the overall effect.

STEAD

Judy Stead
(Photoshop)

This personal piece, entitled Altered States, began as a scanned marker sketch placed as a template (see the *Layers* chapter). In Illustrator, Judy Stead worked in RGB color mode so she could access the Effect > Artistic filters that are available only for RGB images. Stead traced the template using a Wacom tablet, with a 3 pt round Calligraphic brush (Diameter set to Pressure; Roundness and Angle Fixed). She applied Effect > Artistic > Rough Pastels (choosing a canvas texture and varying the other options) to give a hand-drawn appearance to the lines that make up the facial contour. Next, she blocked in large areas of color with filled shapes drawn with a 3 pt round Calligraphic brush, setting the opacity to Multiply, so the underlying line work was visible. Using the Charcoal Art Brush, Stead added texture to the hair. She then printed the composition (shown above right) onto newsprint drawing paper using an inkjet printer. She colored specific areas of the drawing, such as the hair, with pastels. After scanning the drawing into Photoshop, she applied further enhancements using a variety of Photoshop brushes, adjusting their size, flow, and blending mode. With these brushes, she applied large areas of color to the background, as well as to both sides of the face. On separate layers, using Photoshop brushes with various shapes, textures, opacity, and flow, she added to the drawing until she was satisfied with the end result.

DONALDSON

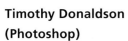

Timothy Donaldson
(Photoshop)

Lettering artist Timothy Donaldson takes delight in the difficulty people have associating his abstract calligraphy, like Ducal (above), with artwork made with Illustrator. Donaldson created every element of the piece using default or custom Illustrator Art brushes. He drew each object on its own layer. Later, when he opened the layered artwork in Photoshop, he selected objects, applied blurs and drop shadows and adjusted transparency. Some of these Photoshop treatments can also be achieved using the Effect menu and the Transparency palette. (See the *Transparency & Appearances* and the *Live Effects & Graphic Styles* chapters for more on the Appearance and Transparency palettes and the Effect menu.)

GREIMAN

April Greiman
(Photoshop)

April Greiman, of April Greiman Made in Space, took advantage of Illustrator's ability to produce resolution-independent vector graphics when creating this large wall mural for the Cafe & Fitness Center at Amgen. Greiman began with source photos and original images. In Photoshop, she combined the images, adjusted the hue, saturation, and opacity and made adjustments with levels and curves. A variety of filters were applied to the images, such as Gaussian Blur, Motion Blur, Ripple, and Noise. Greiman knew that when the image was enlarged, the pixelated effect would enhance the image, just as she wanted. When Greiman was satisfied with the Photoshop image, she saved it as a PSD file. The PSD file was imported into Illustrator and text was added. The text was created on several layers with varying opacities. The size of the Illustrator image was 21 inches x 5 inches, and the final mural measured 36 feet x 11.3 feet. The pixels in the Photoshop image were greatly distorted when enlarged to the final mural size. This desired pixelated effect was combined with crisp text that Illustrator can produce at any magnification. The final image was output from Illustrator and printed directly on vinyl.

Lance Hidy
(Photoshop)

Illustrator Lance Hidy photographed hands holding a book several times until he had a "natural" pose. He scanned the photograph and, in Photoshop, lightened the shadows and other dark tones in the image before printing it. On this print, Hidy drew outlines of the hands directly using a fine-tipped pen. Then he scanned the marked print and placed the resulting TIFF file in Illustrator as a tracing template. He was able to clearly follow the con-

tours and details of the hands as he traced with Illustrator's Pencil tool.

POUNDS

David Pounds
(Photoshop)

David Pounds used to do much of his creative work in Photoshop, but he can now work almost exclusively in Illustrator, due to recent improvements to the program. In this illustration, Pounds used Photoshop to make different versions of the photo in order to accentuate various details. For instance, he created a posterized version (Image > Adjustments > Posterize) to help him see the image as areas of color. He also created a few versions using Levels (Image > Adjustments > Levels) to accentuate specific details of the image. He opened his layered .psd file in Illustrator, then set up layers for tracing the photo with closed paths. Using the Pen tool, he created closed shapes and used the Eyedropper tool, with the Shift key, to pick up color from various layered versions of the photograph in Photoshop (the Eyedropper tool in Illustrator now allows for greater range of color sampling options, much like Photoshop). Whenever he wanted to create another variation of his photo in order to accentuate a missing detail, he created that version in Photoshop (using Levels, for instance). He then chose Select > All, and Copy. Moving back to Illustrator, he created a new layer for this version and used Paste in Front (⌘-F /Ctrl-F), which placed the new version of the photo in perfect alignment with the previous variations of the same-sized Photoshop file.

CHAN

Ron Chan
(Photoshop)

Illustrator Ron Chan began this illustration for the Catellus Web site by employing many of the same Illustrator techniques described in his "Cubist Constructs" lesson (in the *Drawing & Coloring* chapter). After drawing and filling objects with color, Chan brought the artwork into Photoshop, where he selected individual elements and added textures to lend a more organic look the illustration. Similar results can be achieved using Effect menu commands, with transparency and opacity masks (see the *Transparency & Appearances* and *Live Effects & Graphic Styles* chapters for help with effects, the Transparency palette, and opacity masks.)

FISHAUF

Louis Fishauf / Louis Fishauf Design Limited (Photoshop)

For this image about e-commerce, Louis Fishauf brought Illustrator objects into Photoshop, where he created transparency and blurring effects. Fishauf filled the credit card and house front objects with white in Illustrator. Then he pasted them into the Photoshop file and built gradation layer masks to simulate progressive transparency in the objects. Besides using Illustrator-drawn objects as compositional elements in Photoshop, Fishauf also used the objects to create underlying glows (done with Photoshop's layer effects). To see how similar effects can be achieved using transparency, opacity masks, and live effects in Illustrator, see the *Transparency & Appearances* and *Live Effects & Graphic Styles* chapters.

Filip Yip
(Photoshop)

Filip Yip began by drawing Illustrator objects and organizing them on many separate layers (so each object would remain on its own layer when he later exported them to Photoshop). He decided on the overall color scheme, colored the shapes, and added blends. Yip then exported his Illustrator objects into Photoshop in order to add transparency, feathering, and lighting effects. The artwork (shown above right) was exported as a Photoshop PSD file. In Photoshop, Yip was able to easily manipulate the illustrator objects, since they were on separate layers. He enhanced the blends with the

Airbrush tool, adjusted the transparency, and applied the Add Noise filter. Blurring effects (such as Gaussian Blur) were used to highlight details of the image. To further soften the blends, Yip also applied the Fade Brush Tool (Edit > Fade Brush Tool > Fade > Dissolve) in the Dissolve mode.

Chris Spollen
(Photoshop)

Chris Spollen often creates his collage-like illustrations by weaving back and forth between Illustrator and Photoshop. He always starts with thumbnail pencil sketches (below right), which he scans and places as a template in Illustrator (see "Digitizing a Logo" in the *Layers* chapter). He then creates his basic shapes and elements in Illustrator. While some of his illustrations do end up being assembled in Illustrator, this piece, "Hot Rod Rocket," was finalized in Photoshop, with many of the objects becoming "Illustrator/Photoshop hybrids" (such as his white clouds on an angle, which began as simple Illustrator shapes). In order to control his layers in Photoshop, Spollen moved one or more selected Illustrator objects at a time into a single layer in Photoshop using drag-and-drop. Spollen then reworked the shapes in Photoshop using the Paintbrush and Airbrush tools. He also adjusted the opacity. The 3D-looking rocket originated as a scanned toy "rocket gun," while the moon began as a scanned photo. "Hot Rod Rocket" received an Award of Merit in the Society of Illustrator's Show.

SPOLLEN

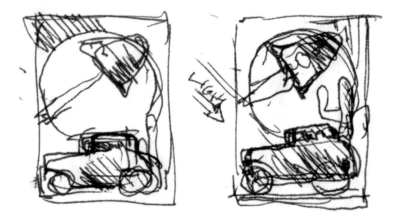

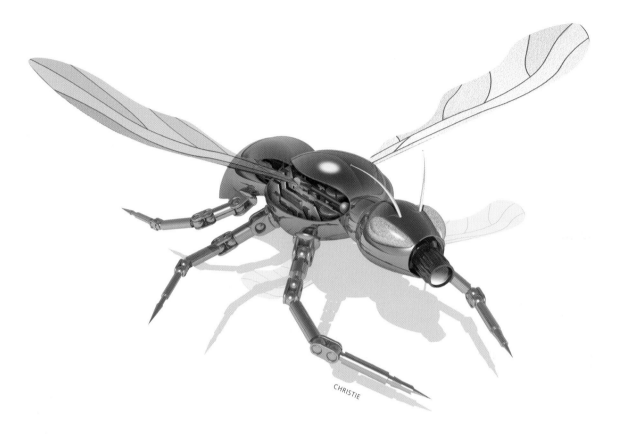

CHRISTIE

Bryan Christie
(Photoshop, MetaTools Infini-D)

Bryan Christie assembled this mechanical bug with Illustrator and later integrated Photoshop and Infini-D, a 3D modeling program. The 3D shapes, such as the leg joints and circuit boards, were first drawn in Illustrator as an outline without detail or color, and then imported into Infini-D and extruded into 3D shapes. To map the color and the details of the circuit boards, Christie drew and colored the circuitry in Illustrator. He then exported the artwork as a PICT and mapped it onto the 3D shapes in Infini-D. Christie created the transparency of the wing by mapping a grayscale image that was origi-

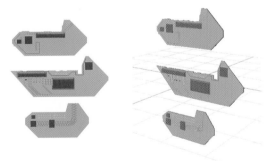

nally drawn in Illustrator onto the wing shape in Infini-D. To complete the mechanical bug, he rendered the artwork in Infini-D, opened it in Photoshop to make minor touchups (such as color correction and compositing separately rendered elements), and finally converted the entire image into CMYK.

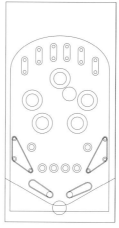

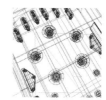

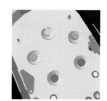

BERGMAN

Eliot Bergman
(Photoshop and Alias Sketch!)

Bergman created this illustration for a trade magazine advertisement with a combination of 2D and 3D programs. He took advantage of the precision possible with Illustrator to draft sections, plans and profiles of objects before importing them into Silicon Graphics Alias Sketch!, a 3D modeling program. He also made color and bump maps in Illustrator, then retouched them in Photoshop. For this illustration, the first step was to draft the layout of the pinball machine in Illustrator. The elements in this design served both as a template for 3D

objects and as a basis for a color map. Bergman used the Gradient tool to create the background, and he used a combination of the Star tool (hidden within the Rectangle tool) and the Filter > Distort > Pucker and Bloat filter to create the starbursts. Bergman imported the artwork into Sketch! where he created 3D objects by extruding and lathing individual items. After rendering a rough preview image, Bergman added the final maps, colors and lights. He brought the finished rendered image into Photoshop for retouching.

Atrium
Hunziker Wing
Wightman Gym
Pool
Coach House
Hunziker Hall
Raubinger Hall
Shea Center for Performing Arts
Hobart Manor

WILLCOCKSON

Tom Willcockson / Mapcraft
(Bryce)

Cartographer Tom Willcockson visited the campus of William Paterson University to acquire photographs, building floor plans and other materials. Then in Illustrator, he built a base map of the campus roads, rivers, vegetation areas, building outlines and other features. After scanning a contour map, Willcockson drew closed contour lines, filling them with gray shades based on elevation. He exported two JPEG images to serve as source images in Bryce: the grayscale contour layer and the base map artwork. In Bryce, Willcockson imported

the contour JPEG and generated a 3D terrain image. Then he imported the base map JPEG and draped it across the terrain. He rendered the image and exported it as a JPEG, which he placed on a template layer in Illustrator. He traced the streets, building footprints and other features in Bryce-rendered perspective view. Willcockson drew the buildings, and then added trees and shrubs as Scatter brush objects from a brush library he had created for other maps. (See the *Brushes* chapter to learn about using scatter brushes for map symbols.)

JONES

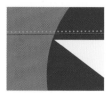  

Joe Jones: Art Works Studio
(Ray Dream Studio, Bryce, Photoshop)

In this World War II tribute entitled "West Field Yardbird," Joe Jones used Illustrator artwork as components in building the 3D model in Ray Dream Studio, and as texture maps to cover the model in Bryce. To start the artwork that would serve as texture maps for the metal panel seams, window masks, rivets and other elements of the model, Jones drew objects on separate layers with the Pen tool. Then Jones brought the artwork into Photoshop where he applied edge treatments and simulated the effects of weathering by painting onto the art. Then he flattened and saved the files. In Bryce, Jones imported and mapped the images onto the modeled plane parts. In all, he filled the scene with nearly 3000 Illustrator objects.

Artists

Erik Adigard, *see* M.A.D.

Adobe Systems, Inc.
345 Park Avenue
San Jose, CA 95110-2704
408-536-6000
see also Laurie Szujewska,
Ted Alspach, Mordy Golding,
Min Wang, Brenda Sutherland,
Julie Meridian, Teri Pettit

Agnew Moyer Smith, Inc.
503 Martindale Street
Pittsburgh, PA 15212
412-322-6333
rhenkel@amsite.com

Bjørn Akselsen, *see* Ice House Press
& Design

Jen Alspach
jen@bezier.com
www.bezier.com

Ted Alspach
Adobe Systems, Incorporated
345 Park Ave., Mailstop W11
San Jose, CA 95110
talspach@adobe.com
www.adobe.com/creative suite

Jack Anderson, *see* Hornall Anderson

Kevan Atteberry
P.O. Box 40188
Bellevue, WA 98015-4188
206-550-6353
kevan@oddisgood.com
www.oddisgood.com

Karen Barranco
323-848-2090
Karen@specialmoderndesign.com
www.specialmoderndesign.com

Rick Barry
DeskTop Design Studio
1631 West 12th Street
Brooklyn, NY 11223
718-232-2484

Jennifer Bartlett
Girvin Strategic Branding &
Design
1601 2nd Ave. The Fifth Floor
Seattle, WA 98101
206-674-7808

Kenneth Batelman
128 Birch Leaf Drive
Milford, PA 18337
888-532-0612
Kenneth@batelman.com
batelman.com

Eliot Bergman
362 West 20th Street
New York, NY 10011

Bruce Brashear
124 Escanyo Drive
South Sanfrancisco, CA 94080
650-588-3388
brucebrashear@attbi.com

Christopher Bucheit/Design Time
P.O. Box 2152
La Crosse, WI 54602
608-796-0885
mail@chrisbucheit.com
www.chrisbucheit.com

Christopher Burke
4408 Chad Court
Ann Arbor, MI 48103-9478
313-996-1316

John Burns
John Burns Lettering & Design
1593 Parkway Drive
Rohnert Park, CA 94928
707 585-7604

Peter Cassell
1185 Design
411 High Street
Palo Alto, CA 94301
650-325-4804
peterc@1185design.com
www.1185design.com

David Cater
510-232-9420
adcater@aol.com

Ron Chan
24 Nelson Ave.
Mill Valley, CA 94941
415-389-6549

K. Daniel Clark
3218 Steiner Street
San Francisco, CA 94123
415-922-7761
www.artdude.com

Sandee Cohen
33 Fifth Avenue, #10B
New York, NY 10003
212-677-7763
sandee@vectorbabe.com
www.vectorbabe.com

Scott Crouse
755 W. Cummings St.
Lake Alfred, FL 33850
863-956-8891

Shayne Davidson
Medical Illustration & Graphics
1301 Granger Ave.
Ann Arbor, MI 48104
734-994-6223 / 734-998-6140
ext133
sdmedill@umich.edu
www.medicalart.net

Rob Day & Virginia Evans
10 State Street, Suite 214
Newburyport, MA 01950
508-465-1386

Timothy Donaldson
Domus Crossheads
Colwich Staffordshire ST180UG
England
01889 88 20 43
e@timothydonaldson.com
www.timothydonaldson.com

Linda Eckstein
201 W. 70th St. #6G
New York, NY 10023
212-721-0821

Eve Elberg
60 Plaza Street East, Suite 6E
Brooklyn, NY 11238
718-398-0950

Mindi Englart
145 Cottage Street
New Haven, CT 06511
203-752-1959

Virginia Evans, *see* Day & Evans

Gary Ferster
756 Marlin Ave., Suite 4
Foster City, CA 94404
650-577-9696
gferster@attbi.com
www.garyferster.com/

Louis Fishauf
47 Lorne Ave.
Kettleby, Ontario
Canada L0G1J0
905-726-1597
fishauf@reactor.ca
www.fishauf.com

Mark Fox
415-258-9663
mfox@blackdogma.com

David Fridberg
Miles Fridberg Molinaroli
4401 Connecticut Ave., NW
Suite 701
Washington, DC 20008
202-966-7700

Guilbert Gates
145 West 12th / Apt 2-5
New York, NY 10011
212-243-7853
see also Jared Schneidman Design

Tim Girvin
Girvin Strategic Branding &
Design
1601 2nd Ave. The Fifth Floor
Seattle, WA 98101
206-674-7808
www.girvin.com

Mordy Golding
Adobe System, Incorporated
345 Park Ave., Mailstop W11
San Jose, CA 95110

Janet Good
Industrial Illustrators, Inc.
P.O. Box 497
Harrison City, PA 15636-0497
800-683-9316
janet@ix3.com
jlgood524@earthlink.net
ix3.com

Steven H. Gordon
Cartagram, LLC
136 Mill Creek Crossing
Madison, AL 35758
256-772-0022
wow@cartagram.com
www.cartagram.com

Caryl Gorska
414 Jackson Street / Suite 401
San Francisco, CA 94111
415-249-0139
see also MAX

Laurie Grace
860-659-0748
lgrace@aol.com

Adele Droblas Greenberg
AD Design & Consulting
202 Sixth Ave. Suite #2a
New York, NY 10013
212-431-9132

April Greiman
620 MoultonAve. No. 211
Los Angeles, CA 90031
323-227-1222
info@madeinspace.la
ww.madeinspace.la

Wendy Grossman
Grossman Illustration
355 West 51st Street
New York, NY 10019
212-262-4497

Brad Hamann
Brad Hamann Illustration &
Design
41 West Market Street
Red Hook, NY 12571
845-758-6186 studio
bhamann@hvc.rr.com
www.darkdesign.com

Steve Hart
TIME / Editorial Art Dept
1271 Sixth Avenue / Rm 2440 D
New York, NY 10020
212-522-3677

Pattie Belle Hastings, see Ice House
Press & Design

Rick Henkel, see Agnew Moyer Smith

Kurt Hess, see Agnew Moyer Smith

Lance Hidy
2 Summer St.
Merrimac, MA 01860
978-346-0075

Kaoru Hollin
kaoruhollin@attbi.com

John Hornall, see Hornall Anderson

Hornall Anderson Design Works
1008 Western Ave., Suite 600
Seattle, WA 98104
206-467-5800
info@hadw.com
www.hadw.com

Ice House Press & Design
Pattie Belle Hastings
Bjørn Akselsen
266 West Rock Ave.
New Haven, CT 06515
203-389-7334

Lisa Jackmore
13603 Bluestone Court
Clifton, VA 20124
703-830-0985
ljackmore@earthlink.net

Jared Schneidman Design
16 Parkway
Katonah, NY 10536
914-232-1499
see also Guilbert Gates

Dave Joly
15 King St.
Putnam, CT 06260
860-928-1042

Frank Jonen
Haupstrasse 15
65510 Idstein
Germany
voice 49-6126 9581 81
fax 49-6126 9581 83
getinfo@frankjonen.com
www.frankjonen.com

Joe Jones
Art Works Studio
802 Poplar St
Denver, CO 80220
303-377-7745
joejones@artworksstudio.com
www.artworksstudio.com

Diane Hinze Kanzler

John Kanzler
424 Adams Road
Greenfield, Ma 01301
413-773-7368
800-210-0711
john@johnkanzler.com
www.johnkanzler.com

Andrea Kelley
Andrea Kelley Design
530 Menlo Oaks Drive
Menlo Park, CA 94025
650-326-1083
andrea@jevans.com

Marc LaMantia
64 Macdougal Street Apt 5
New York, NY 10012
212-677-6907
lamantia2003@yahoo.com

Tiffany Larsen
tiffany@uberpop.com
uberpop.com

Adam Z Lein
3 Woodlands Ave
Elmsford, NY 10523
914-347-1710
adamz@lein.com
www.adamlein.com

Joe Lertola
TIME / Editorial Art Dept
1271 Sixth Avenue / Rm 2442
New York, NY 10020
212-522-3721
www.joelertola.com

Randy Livingston
Bona Fide Design
206 Ernest Street
Washington, IL 61571
309-745-1126

Patrick Lynch
Yale University C/AIM
47 College Street / Suite 224
New Haven, CT 06510
203-737-5033

M.A.D.
Patricia McShane & Erik Adigard
237 San Carlos Ave.
Sausalito, CA 94965
415-331-1023

Ma Zhi Liang
mazhiliangb@online.sh.cn

Todd Macadangdang
348 Arco St.
San Jose, CA 95123
408-536-6373
toddm@adobe.com
toddm@illustratorworld.com

Jacqueline Mahannah
Medical and Biological Illustration
Mahannahj@aol.com

Elizabeth Margolis-Pineo
margolispineo concept, copy &
design
138 Glenwood Avenue
Portland, ME 04103
207-773-8447

Rob Magiera
Noumena Digital
9636 Ruskin Circle
Salt Lake City, UT 84092
801-943-3650

Rob Marquardt
Toast Design
300 First Ave North, Suite 150
Minneapolis, MN 55401
612-330-9863

MAX
246 1st Street / Suite 310
San Francisco, CA 94105
415-543-1333
see also Caryl Gorska

Greg Maxson
116 W. Florida Ave
Urbana, IL 61801
217-337-6069
gmaxti@shout.net
www.portsort.com

Yukio Miyamoto
3-8 Matuba-cyo
Tokorozawa-shi
Saitama-ken 359-0044 Japan
+81-42-998-6631
yukio-m@ppp.bekkoame.ne.jp
www.bekkoame.ne.jp/~yukio-m/
index_e.html

Scott McCollom
808 N. Kaufman St.
Seagoville, TX 75159

Patricia McShane, *see* M.A.D.

Bert Monroy
11 Latham Lane
Berkeley, CA 94708
510-524-9412

Joachim Müller-Lancé
125 A Stillman St.
San Francisco, CA 94108
www.kamedesign.com

Brad Neal
Thomas • Bradley Illustration
& Design
411 Center St. / P.O. Box 249
Gridley, IL 61744
309-747-3266
bradneal@thomas-bradley.com
www.thomasbradley.com

Bradley Neal, Thomas Neal
see Thomas • Bradley Illustration

David Nelson
Mapping Services
721 Grape St.
Denver, CO 80220
303-333-1060

Gary Newman Design
2447 Burnside Rd
Sebastapol, CA 95472
gary@newmango.com
www.newmango.com

Ann Paidrick
5520 Virginia Ave.
St. Louis, MO 63111
314-351-1705
annpaid@attglobal.net
www.ebypaidrick.com

Ellen Papciak-Rose
In The Studio
inthestudio@mac.com
http://homepage.mac.com/
inthe studio

Tom Patterson
National Park Service
Media Development
Harpers Ferry Center
Harpers Ferry, WV 25425-0050
304-535-6020
t.patterson@nps.gov
www.nacis.org/cp/cp28/resources.
html

Daniel Pelavin
90 Varick Street, Suite 3B
New York, NY 10013-1925
212-941-7418

Cher Threinen-Pendarvis
4646 Narragansett Ave.
San Diego, CA 92107
619-226-6050

John Pirman
johnpirman@aol.com
represented by
Gerald & Cullen Rapp
212-889-3337

David S. Pounds
7 Greenmoor
Irvine, CA 92614
949-733-0226
davidpounds@hisnet.org
www.hisnet.org/userpages/
davidpounds

Dorothy Remington
Remington Designs
632 Commercial Street
San Francisco, CA 94111
415-788-3340

Javier Romero
    Javier Romero Design Group
    (JRDG)
    Westport, CT
    203-256-0934
    javierr@jrdg.com

Jared Schneidman Design
    155 Katonah Ave.
    Katonah, NY 10536
    914-232-1499
    jared@jsdinfographics.com
    jsdinfographics.com

Mike Schwabauer
    Hallmark Cards, Inc.
    2501 McGee, Box 419580, MD 142
    Kansas City, MO 64141-6580
    816-545-6948
    mschwa2@hallmark.com

Max Seabaugh, *see* MAX

Robert Sharif
    2791 Lexford Ave.
    San Jose, CA 95124
    rsharif@earthlink.net
    sharifr@adobe.com

Charles Shields
    Shields Design
    415 East Olive Ave.
    Fresno, CA 93728
    209-497-8060

Mitch Shostak Studios
    57 East 11th Street
    New York City, NY 10003
    212 979-7981

Steve Spindler
    Steve Spindler Cartography
    1504 South St.
    Philadelphia, PA 19146
    215-985-2839
    steve@bikemap.com
    www.bikemap.com

Christopher Spollen
    Moonlightpress Studio
    362 Cromwell Ave.
    Staten Island, NY 10305
    718-979-9695
    cjspollen@aol.com
    spollen.com

Nancy Stahl
    470 West End Ave, #86
    New York, NY 10024
    212-362-8779

Steven Stankiewicz
    artfromsteve@aol.com
    www.porfolios.com/
    stevenstankiewicz

Judy Stead
    741 Lake Catherine Drive
    Maitland, FL 32751
    407-310-0051
    judy@judystead.com
    www.judystead.com

Sharon Steuer
    c/o Peachpit Press
    1249 Eighth St.
    Berkeley, CA 94710
    800-283-9444

Barbara Sudick
    California State University
    Dept. of Communication Design
    Chico, CA 95929
    530-898-5028

Laurie Szujewska
    shoe yév skä design
    7045 Toma Lane
    Penngrove, CA 94951
    707 664 9966

Clarke W. Tate
    Tate Studio
    P.O. Box 339 / 301 Woodford St.
    Gridley, IL 61744-0339
    312-453-0694
    clarke@tatestudio.com
    www.tatestudio.com

Thomas•Bradley Illustration
    & Design
    411 Center Street / P.O. Box 249
    Gridley, IL 61744
    309-747-3266

Threinen-Pendarvis *see* Pendarvis

Kathleen Tinkel
    MacPrePress
    12 Burr Road
    Westport, CT 06880
    203-227-2357

Ivan Torres
    12933 Ternberry Ct.
    Tustin, CA 92782
    714-734-4356
    ivanjessica@sbcglobal.net
    ivanjessica2002@yahoo.com
    www.meshsmith.com

Jean-Claude Tremblay
    Illustrator Instructor & Prepress
    Technician
    7180 Des Erables
    Montreal (Quebec)
    H2E2R3

Jean Tuttle
    Jean Tuttle Illustration
    800-816-0460
    jeantuttle@aol.com
    www.jeantuttle.com

Trina Wai
    5027 Silver Reef Dr.
    Fremont, CA 94538

Min Wang, *see* Adobe Systems, Inc.

Timothy Webb
    Tim Webb Illustration
    305 W. Maywood
    Wichita, KS 67217
    316-524-3881
    tim@timwebb.com
    www.timwebb.com

Alan James Weimer
    67 Bliss St.
    Rehoboth, MA 02769-1932
    508-252-9236
    aljames@mindspring.com

Ari M. Weinstein
    ari@ariw.com
    www.ariw.com

Hugh Whyte
    Lehner & Whyte
    8-10 South Fullerton Ave.
    Montclair, NJ 07402
    201-746-1335

Tom Willcockson
    Mapcraft Cartography
    731 Margaret Drive
    Woodstock, IL 60098
    815-337-7137

Filip Yip
    877-463-4547
    filip@yippe.com
    www.yippe.com

Ma Zhiliang, Ma Zhi Liang
    see alphabetized under Ma

Resources

Adobe Systems, Inc.
345 Park Avenue
San Jose, CA 95110-2704
408-536-6000
www.adobe.com

AGFA
prepress, production
Agfa Corp.
100 Challenger Road
Ridgefield Park, NJ 07660
201-440-2500
www.agfa.com

Ambrosia Software, Inc.
SnapzPro,SnapzProX
PO BOX 23140
Rochester, NY 14692
800-231-1816
www.AmbrosiaSW.com

Apple Computer
ColorSync, QuickTime
800-767-2775
www.apple.com

Aridi Computer Graphics
Digital Art
P.O. Box 797702
Dallas, TX 75379
972-404-9171
www.aridi.com

Artlandia, Inc.
Artlandia SymmetryWorks
2015 Barberry Cr.
Champaign, IL 61821-5862
Toll-free: +1 (888) 972-6366
www.artlandia.com

Avenza Systems Inc.
MAPublisher
124 Merton Street Suite 400
Toronto, Ontario
Canada M4S 2Z2
tel: 416-487-5116
fax 416-487-7213
sales: 800-884-2555
www.avenza.com

Bare Bones Software, Inc.
BBEdit
P.O. Box 1048
Bedford, MA 01730
781-778-3100
www.barebones.com

Barney's Mac Software
Border
Barney Hilken
+44 (0) 1204 697223
45, Mason Street
Horwich, Bolton, BL6 5QP, UK
homepage.ntlworld.com/b.hilken

Cartesia Software
Digital Maps
PO Box 757
Lambertville, NJ 08530
800-334-4291 (x3)
www.mapresources.com

CDS Documentation Services
Printer of this book
2661 South Pacific Highway
Medford, OR 97501
541-773-7575

Comnet Co., Ltd.
LogoSpruce FoldUP!3D
Professional design plug-ins
for Illustrator
Sannomiya Grand Building 8F
2-2-21 Isogamidori, Chuo-ku
Kobe 651-0086 Japan
Fax: 1-877-804-2912 (US only)
www.comnet-network.co.jp

Corel Corporation
procreate Painter, Bryce
1600 Carling Ave.
Ottawa, ON Canada K1Z 8R7
1-800-772-6735
www.procreate.com/

CValley, Inc.
FILTERiT4.1 (demo included)
CAD-COMPO (information only)
Xtream Path (information only)
212 Technology Dr. Suite N
Irvine, CA 92618
949-727-9161
www.cvalley.com

Dantz
Retrospect
www.dantz.com

Dynamic Graphics Inc.
Clip art, etc.
6000 N. Forest Pk. Drive
Peoria, IL 61614
800-255-8800
www.dgusa.com

GifBuilder
piguet@ai.epfl.ch

hot door
CADtools, Perspective, MultiPage
101 W. McKnight Way, Suite B
Grass Valley, CA 95949
1-888-236-9540
www.hotdoor.com

Macromedia
FreeHand, Director, Flash MX
600 Townsend Street
San Francisco, CA 94103
800-989-3762
www.macromedia.com

Pantone, Inc.
color matching products
590 Commerce Blvd.
Carlstadt, NJ 07072
866-PANTONE
www.pantone.com

procreate (*see* Corel Corporation)

Strata
Strata3Dplus
567 S. Valley View Dr./Suite 202
St. George, Utah 84770
800-678-7282
www.strata.com

TruMatch, Inc.
Color Matching Software
50 East 72nd, Suite 15B
New York, NY 10021
800-878-9100
www.trumatch.com

Ultimate Symbol
Design Elements, clipart
31 Wilderness Drive
Stony Point, NY 10980
845-942-0003
www.ultimatesymbol.com

Virtual Mirror Corporation
Vector Studio, Retouch Brush Tools
P.O. Box 6727
San Rafael, CA 94903
415-472-3359
www.virtualmirror.com

zenofthepen.org
QuickTime Enhanced Bézier Pen
Tutorials for Illustrator, Photoshop,
InDesign, FreeHand & Fireworks 4+

General Index

2D objects
    extruding, 294–295
    mapping artwork onto, 297
    transforming to 3D, 293–294
"3D—Three dialogs" tip, 293, 295
3D effects, 293–297
    adding columns to create, 351
    applying multiple, 293
    introduction of, xxi, 292
    lessons on, 316–319
    "live" nature of, 294
    and mapping of artwork, 297
    and New Art Has Basic
            Appearance option, 296
    preparing artwork for, 316
    programs for creating, 386
"3D Effects" lesson, 318–319
3D Extrude & Bevel Options dialog
    extrusion settings, 316, 321, 322,
          325
    rotating objects in, 295, 315
    surface shading option, 297
3D modeling programs, 404, 405
3D objects *See also* 3D effects
    applying surface shading to,
        296–297
    choosing fill colors for, 295
    mapping artwork onto, xxi, 297
    revolving, 295, 318–319, 320,
        322, 324
    rotating, 296, 324
3D programs, 382, 386
3D Revolve effect, 318–319, 320,
    322, 323
3D Ribbon effect, 183
3D Rotate effect, 324
3D StudioPro, 386
"9 Lives" cat symbol, 82–85
216-color palette, 30, 359, 374
1185 Design, 288–289, 408
1776 logo, 214–215

A

Acrobat
    antialiased artwork in, 386
    and crop areas, 386
    Distiller, xxiii, 385
    and Illustrator CS versions, xx
    Reader, xxiii, 24
    and transparency, 262
actions, 35–36, 301, 330
Actions palette, 35–36, 37

AD Design & Consulting, 409
Adam Z Lein Gallery, 290
"Add & Expand" lesson, 86–87
Add Anchor Point tool, 10, 43, 245
Add Anchor Points filter, 45, 47
Add New Fill command, 265
Add New Stroke command, 190
Add Pathfinder, 86–87
Add to Shape command, 85
additive colors, 29
Adigard, Erik, 48, 408, 410
Adjust Colors filter, 74–75
Adobe
    Acrobat. *See* Acrobat
    After Effects, 358
    Color Picker, 30, 364
    contact information, 408
    Creative Suite, xx
    Distiller, xxiii, 385
    GoLive. *See* GoLive
    Graphics Server, 366
    Illustrator. *See* Illustrator CS
    ImageReady, 361
    InDesign. *See* InDesign
    LiveMotion, 363
    Photoshop. *See* Photoshop
    PostScript. *See* PostScript
    Premier, 358
    Reader, xxiii, 24
    Streamline, 112, 129, 386
    SVG Viewer, 364
Adobe Illustrator ClipBoard
    See AICB
Adobe Illustrator CS CD, 36, 37, 366
Adobe Illustrator CS Scripting
    Guide, 37
Adobe Illustrator CS User Guide
    See User Guide
Adobe Illustrator Super Guide, The,
    250
Adobe Online, 35
Adobe Systems, 408, 409, 412
    See also Adobe
adoption announcement, 232
After Effects, 358
AGFA, 412
Agfa PostScript Process Color
    Guide, 97
Agnew Moyer Smith, 408
    and automatic updating of colors,
        227
    contact information, 408
    Gallery page, 94

    and "Isometric Systems" lesson,
        92–93
    and "Objective Colors" lesson,
        96–97
.ai file extension, 3
AI files, 3, 24, 386
AICB, 384, 385
Airbrush tool, 402, 403
airplanes, 232, 399, 407
.ait file extension, 3
Akselsen, Bjørn, 210, 408
Alias Sketch!, 405
Alice's Adventures Underground,
    194–195
aligning
    geometric objects, 11
    meshes, 351
    with Optical Margin Alignment
        feature, xxiv
    by snapping to point, 11, 92–93
alpha channels, 363, 379
alphabet poster, 200
Alspach, Jen, 130, 408
Alspach, Ted, 302, 306–307, 311, 408
"Altered States" image, 395
Ambrosia Software, 412
American Express magazine,
    170–173
AMS, 92–93, 96
    See also Agnew Moyer Smith
Anchor Point tools, 193
anchor points. *See also* endpoints
    adding/deleting, 10, 77
    converting, 10
    creating, 7
    dealing with excess, 77
    defined, 6
    selecting, 12–13
    snapping objects to, 9
"Ancient 2000" CD, 105
Anderson, Jack, 408
Andrea Kelley Design, 410
Angle Threshold setting, 77
angles
    for 3D Revolve effect, 295
    for Bézier curves, 8
    constrain, 27, 92, 93, 95
    gradient, 223, 353
    for Miter joins, 75
animation
    exporting, 369–370, 373
    Gallery pages, 367, 371

animation, *continued*
    lessons, 368–370, 372–373,
        378–379
    preparing artwork for, 368–369
    previewing, 368–370, 370
    and Release to Layers command,
        361
    repurposing print artwork for,
        372
    techniques for extending, 379
    timesavers, 378
    tools for working with, 153, 358,
        367, 378
"Anti-antialiasing" tip, 375
antialiasing, 25, 358, 374, 375, 386
"Antiquing Type" lesson, 216–217
appearance attributes, 16, 263–264,
    278–279, 302
Appearance palette, 263–264
    adding strokes to text with, 190
    applying multiple fills/strokes
        with, 189, 265
    designing intricate effects with,
        278
    disabling New Art Has Basic
        Appearance option in,
        xviii
    editing warp effects in, 299
    importance of, 264
    stacking order for, 265
    targeting elements in, 264
    using with type, 191–193
appearances, 263–265
    adding multiple fills/strokes to,
        80, 264–265
    applying, 263, 279
    clearing attributes for, 264
    copying, 264
    creating, 278
    icons for, 263
    lessons on, 278–281
    moving, 264
    reordering attributes for, 263
    resizing, 306
Apple Computer, 412
Apple Display Calibrator, 28
AppleScript, 36
April Greiman Made in Space, 397
architectural drawings, 95, 228
Area type objects, 181–182, 191, 203,
    280–281
Area Type Options dialog box, xxv,
    182
Area Type tool, 203
Aridi Computer Graphics, 412

Arrow keys, 96
    adding/deleting points with, 11
    adjusting Flare tool rings with,
        311
    adjusting Polar Grid tool circles/
        dividers with, 344
    nudging aliased objects with, 375
    offsetting outlines with, 283
    positioning letters with, 210
    positioning reflective masks with,
        337
    sliding objects along axes with, 93
    specifying surfaces for mapping
        with, 297
    stretching path segments with,
        197
    tracking line of Point Type with,
        203
"Art Brush Motions.ai" file, 153
Art Brush Options dialog box, 205
art brushes
    and animations, 153
    applying to closed paths, 133
    artwork for, 121
    creating, 120–121
    creating distortions with, 153
    purpose of, 120–121
    sources of, 133
Art Works Studio, 407, 409
Artboard
    changing background of, 27–28
    and page tiling, 4
    selecting artwork on, 162
    setting up for page design, 202
    transparency of, 254–255
Artistic brush libraries, 133
artistic observation, 78
Artistic_Paintbrush brush palette,
    205
artists, 408–411
    See also specific artists
Artlandia, 412
artwork
    adding brushes to, 132–133
    applying 3D effects to, 316–317
    background, 146–147
    copying and pasting, 383–384
    for creating brushes, 121
    for creating symbols, 123
    distributing to layers, 122
    dragging and dropping, 383–384
    embedding *vs.* linking, 382–383
    expanding, 224
    flattening, 159, 258
    importing from other

        applications, 363
    mapping onto 2D/3D shapes, 297,
        319, 323
    masking, 256
        See also masking; masks
    organizing, 156, 174
    preparing for on-screen display,
        358–359. *See also* Web
        graphics
    previewing before printing, 34, 35
    printing, 4
    scaling, 122
    scanning/digitizing, 164–165
    scattering copies of, 121
    selecting, 162
    tracing, 126
    on *Wow! CD,* xvi
Artwork mode, 7
Asian text options, 188
athlete images, 153
Atteberry, Kevan, 368–371, 408
Attributes palette, 100, 359–361
Auto Add/Delete function, 9–10
Auto Trace tool, 141, 386
auto-tracing program, 112
Avenza Systems, 412
Average function, 14–15, 45
Average-Join function, 47, 85
Average mode, 123
averaging, 46, 47
aviator, 399
Avion **magazine,** 242

B

backups, 23
Bare Bones Software, 358, 360, 412
Barney's Mac Software, 412
Baron, Cynthia, 360
Barranco, Karen, 102, 103, 408
Barry, Rick, 225, 408
Bartlett, Jennifer, 207, 408
baseball illustration, 334–335
"Basic Appearances" lesson, 278–279
"Basic Transparency" lesson,
    272–273
batch optimization, 360
Batelman, Kenneth, 343, 408
BBEdit, 358, 360, 412
bear, 388
beaver lodge logo, 86–87
beetle, 367
Bergman, Eliot, 405, 408

Bert Monroy: Photorealistic Techniques with Photoshop & Illustrator, 387
Bevel joins, 76
beveled edges, 295, 316, 319
Bézier, Pierre, 306
Bézier curves
    creating, with Pen tool, 7, 8
    importance of, 8
    lessons for fine-tuning, 7
    rules regarding, 8
    ways of "hinging," 9
Bézier-editing tools, 9–11
Bianchi USA decal, 81
bike map, 138
birds, 132–133, 197
black-and-white images
    adding color to, 168–169
    color casts in, 29
    placing color under, 161
    sketching/scanning, 168–169
BlackDog, 81
blacks, blackness of, 29
Blend Options dialog box, 221, 233
Blend tool
    and architectural details, 228
    automatically creating intermediate paths with, 232
    and "blends to blends" technique, 233
    and "point map" technique, 220, 235
    specifying Blend Options with, 221
    tweening with, 379
blending modes
    applying selectively, 272–273
    experimenting with, 270–271
    and grayscale scans, 161
    isolating, 273
    purpose of, 255
    and transparency, 255
blends, 220–224
    along paths, 221–222
    for architectural details, 228
    automatically updating colors for, 227
    complexity of, 224
    contouring, 336–337
    contrasted with gradients, 225, 226
    controlling regularity of, 231
    controlling speed of, 220, 235
    creating, 220

creating glow effect with, 229, 342
creating highlights with, 274
creating in-between layers with, 230
creating metallic reflections with, 234–235
deleting, 220
expanding, 222
and file size, 35
Gallery pages, 225, 229–233, 236–237
inserting objects into, 223
isolating, 273
lessons on, 226–228, 234–235, 336–337
masking, 237, 334–335
multi-object, 221
between objects, 221, 222
and photorealism, 234
RAM considerations, 220
recoloring after expanding, 220
releasing, 222
reversing order of, 222
and seascapes, 231
selecting/replacing spine of, 221–222
smoothing, 235
smoothing one with another, 233
softening transitions with, 235
between symbols, 221
when to use, 226–227
"blends to blends" technique, 233
Bloat tool, 76
blood drive sign, 320
Blur effect. *See* Gaussian Blur effect
"Blurring the Lines" lesson, 308–310
"Book Cover Design" lesson, 202–203
book covers, 202–203, 252, 275, 353
Book of Days typeface, 211
Border application, 412
bounding box
    contrasted with Free Transform tool, 19–20
    and Hide Edges, 28
    hiding/showing, 20
    purpose of, 20
    resetting, 20
"Bountiful Harvest" package design, 241
bow tie, 314–315
Brad Hamann Illustration & Design, 409
brain, 286–287
Brashear, Bruce, 112, 308–310, 408

Break Link to Graphic Style icon, 302
breaks, line, 188
Bring Forward command, 162
Bring to Front command, 162
brochure illustration, 95
brochure template, 4
Brush palette, 122
brush strokes. *See also* strokes
    creating, 141–142
    editing, 142
    organizing groups of, 267
    reversing, 144
    using transparency with, 254
Brush tool
    closing path using, 121
    constraining, 121
    creating brush strokes with, 120
    Fidelity/Smoothness options, 12, 121–122
"Brushed Type" lesson, 204–205
brushes, 120–154
    adding to existing artwork, 132–133
    applying to closed paths, 133
    applying to letterforms, 204–205
    assigning opacity to, 267–268
    auto-replacing, 143
    colorization methods for, 122–123
    constraining, 121
    creating, 121, 122, 125, 140–141
    editing, 122
    Gallery pages, 125, 128–131, 136–139, 145
    lessons on, 126–127, 132–135, 140–144
    naming, 121
    painting with, 140–141, 150–151
    setting opacity for, 269
    setting preferences for, 121–122
    setting pressure sensitivity for, 126
    sharing between documents, 144
    types of, 120–121
        See also specific types
    ways of using, 120
    on *Wow! CD*, 120, 304
Brushes palette
    adding brushes to, 122, 141, 144
    altering brush settings in, 133
    creating brushes in, 135, 137
    editing brushes in, 122
    viewing brushes in, 127
Bryce, 406, 407, 412
Bryce Canyon guide, 280–281

"Bubbles" image, 274
Bucheit, Chris, 125, 408
bug, Group command, 162
bug images, 106–107, 404
"Building Brushes" lesson, 140–141
"Building Houses" lesson, 42–47
bunny, 388–390
Burke, Christopher, 100, 408
Burns, John, 198, 408
bus map, 142–144
business card template, xxii, 4
Business Sets, 4
Butt caps, 75
butterflies, 233, 394
buttons, Web page, 377

C

CAD-COMPO, 412
CADtools, 412
café scene, 134, 136
calibration
    hardware, 28
    monitor, 28
    printer, 101
California Statue University, 411
Calligraphic Brush Options dialog
    box, 137
Calligraphic Brush tool, 122–123
    See also calligraphic brushes
calligraphic brushes
    creating "pen-and-ink" drawings
      with, 126–130, 152
    creating watercolor effect with,
      268
    customizing, 120, 127, 133, 137,
      152, 268–269
    and graphics tablets, 122–123, 126
    purpose of, 120
    using multiple, 133, 152
"Calligraphic brushes.ai" file, 152
calligraphic fonts, 303
calligraphy, abstract, 140–141
camping equipment, 237
campus map, 406
candlelight effect, 308–310
cap styles, 75
Capture Data Set button, 366
"Careers" title illustration, 201
cars, 69, 338, 339, 340
Cartagram, 218, 303, 374–376, 377,
    409
Cartesia Software, 412
cartographers, 138, 142, 163, 324
    See also maps

Cascading Style Sheets, 365
Cassell, Peter, 232, 288–289, 408
Catellus Web site, 400
Cater, David, 66, 339, 408
cats, 82–85, 130, 224, 256, 356
CD label template, xxii, 4
CD packaging, 125
CD-ROM drive, 2
CDs
    Adobe Illustrator CS, 36, 37, 366
    Illustrator CS Wow! Book
      See Wow! CD
CDS Documentation Services, 412
CE Software, 55
center point
    relocating, for radial gradient, 238
    rotating around, 52
"Ch02 The Zen of Illustrator" folder,
    xvi
chain links, 134–135
Chalk Scribbler brush, 133
Chan, Ron, 90–91, 400, 408
"Changing measurement units"
    tip, 7
Character palette, 188
character spacing, xxiv
Character Styles palette, xxiv, 180,
    185–186, 187
charcoal brushes, 131, 133, 209
Chart Wizard, Excel, 290
charts, 17, 254, 290, 384
checkerboard pattern, 118, 238
Chicago map, 278–279
Chinese fonts, 188
Christie, Bryan, 404
Christmas tree, 277, 326–327
Cinnabon logo, 207
circle-and-guides technique, 344,
    345
circles
    adding perspective/dynamics to,
      107
    attaching lines to, 84–85
    cutting and joining, 82
    drawing, 108
circular saw, 341
cityscape, 289
Clark, K. Daniel, 408
"Classic Icon" lesson, 48–49
Clean Up command, 34, 77
Clear Appearance icon, 257, 264
Clear Guides command, 27
clip art, 312, 412
Clipping Mask command, 330
clipping masks

advanced techniques, 330–333
blurring edges of, 310
converting objects to, 331
creating/applying, 115, 200, 201,
    271
disabling icon for, 331
finding, 333
identifying, 331, 332
lessons on, 334–337
for multiple layers, 271, 332
clipping paths, 332
clouds, 288, 403
CMY color model, 29
CMYK color
    converting to/from RGB, 29–30,
      359
    meaning of acronym, 28
    and monitor calibration, 28
    and out-of-gamut warning, 32,
      66, 363
    and print output, 29, 358
    and Web output, 358–359
CMYK inks
    contrasted with RGB monitor
      colors, 28
    hiding misrepresentation of, 30
    misregistration of, 100
CMYK percentages, 97
CMYK-to-RGB conversions, 29–30,
    359
Cohen, Sandee
    and 1776 logo, 214–215
    on closing Pencil/Brush tool
      paths, 12
    contact information, 408
    flag decorations, 312–315
    Gallery page, 149
    and InDesign CS Visual
      QuickStart Guide, 187
    and "Intricate Patterns" lesson,
      116
    on joining text boxes, 191
    and "Open-Type_Guide.pdf"
      file, 187
    and "Preparing Art" lesson,
      132–133
    on reflowing text in page layout,
      190
    and simulation of scratchboard
      art, 304–305
    special brushes supplement,
      152–153
    on using Illustrator with PDF, 385
    on using transparency, 254
collages, 403

Color Burn blending mode, 271
Color Guide, Agfa PostScript
    Process, 97
color management, 28, 30
color matching systems, 30–31, 412
color models, 29, 358
    See also color spaces
Color palette
    choosing color models in, 358
    choosing Stroke color in, 267
    purpose of, 65–66
    saving colors mixed in, 66
    Web, 30. *See also* Web-safe color
Color Picker, 30, 364
color printers, 101
color saturation sliders, 98
Color Settings command, 30
color shifts, 29, 382
color spaces
    monitor considerations, 28
    output considerations, 29
    selecting, 29–30
    working in multiple, 29
color swatches. *See* swatches
Color Table option, 361, 362
colored stock, simulating, 255
"Colorful Masking" lesson, 334–335
coloring. *See also* colors
    basic techniques, 64–69
    expanding toolset for, 69–77
    Gallery pages, 98–105
    lessons on, 96–97, 108–110
    with radial gradient, 109
colors, 28–31
    for 3D objects, 295
    additive *vs.* subtractive, 29
    automatically updating, 227
    changing definitions of, 97
    creating custom spot or global,
        96–97
    under grayscale scans, 161
    and monitor calibration, 28
    naming, 97
    organizing, 96, 98
    sampling, 68, 114, 115
    viewing names of, 99
"Colors with Layers" lesson, 168–169
ColorSync, 28, 412
columns
    creating 3D effects with, 351
    creating from non-type objects,
        183
    defining characteristics of, xxiv
    using multiple, in layouts, xxiv
"Comet" Gradient tool exercise, 238

commercial printers, 32, 412
    See also service bureaus
Comnet, 412
compound objects, 49
compound paths, 69–71
    components of, 69
    creating, 69–70
    fills/holes with, 70
    pros and cons of, 71
    vs. compound shapes, 70, 71, 331
compound shapes, 70–71
    converting to single path, 87
    creating, 49, 70–71
    defined, 70
    expanding, 74
    integrating effects into, 71
    pros and cons of, 71
    purpose of, 49
    vs. compound paths, 70, 71, 331
    vs. Pathfinder effects, 301
compression
    JPEG, 362
    lossy, 362
    presets, 361
    SVG, 364
computer. *See also* Macintosh;
        Windows
    chip board illustration, 78–80
    creating traditional line art with,
        164
    system requirements, 2
Computers Freedom & Privacy logo,
        48–49
Constrain Angle
    and architectural drawings, 95
    preferences/settings, 27, 92, 95
    and technical illustrations, 92, 93
Constrain Angle key, 93
constructing-object exercises, 42–47
Construction Guides preferences, 28
Context magazine, 170–173
context-sensitive menus, 6
Convert Anchor Point tool, 9, 10
Convert to Shape effect, 280, 281
converting
    anchor points, 10
    CMYK to/from RGB, 29–30, 359
    compound shapes to path, 87
    gradients to meshes, 244–245
    lines to guides, 176–177
    objects to clipping masks, 331
    paths to meshes, 224
    spot colors to process colors, 97
    type to outlines, 189–191, 197,
        198

copy-and-paste technique, 383–384
copying
    appearances, 264
    artwork, 370, 383–384, 385
    fills/strokes, 17
Corel
    contact information, 412
    Painter, 8, 140–141
corners
    changing shape of, 75–76
    dragging, with Free Transform
        tool, 107
course outline, xvi
CPU, 2
Cracker Jack logo, 164
Create Gradient Mesh command,
        224, 289
Create New Layer icon, 156
Create Outlines command, 198, 199,
        201, 207, 284
Create PDF Compatible File option,
        385
"Creating Simple Object" lesson, 53
Creative Suite, xx
crop areas, 203, 386, 388
crop marks, 116, 203
Crop Pathfinder, 72, 91
cropping
    with clipping masks, 271, 345
    for inset look, 91
    tiled design, 345
crosshatch effect, 298, 328
Crouse, Scott, 408
Crucible Research, 229
"Crunching Type" lesson, 212–213
Crystallize tool, 76
CSS layers, 365
"Cubist Constructs" lesson, 90–91,
        400
cursor
    feedback, 8–9
    and Type tool, 185
curves
    constructing, 83
    creating, with Pen tool, 7, 8
    lessons for fine-tuning, 7
    rules regarding, 8
    ways of "hinging," 9
"Custom Text Paths" lesson, 194–195
customizing
    calligraphic brushes, 120, 127,
        133, 137, 152, 268–269
    gradients, 238
    grids, 27
    guides, 203

customizing, *continued*
    keyboard shortcuts, xvii, 5–6
    radial blends, 241
    tab leaders, xxiv
cut-and-paste technique, 46
cut-out effect, 240
cuts, changing shape of, 114
cutting, using Scissors tool for, 85
"Cutting & Joining" lesson, 82–85, 90
CValley, 412

D

Dantz, 23, 412
dashed lines/strokes, 76, 143
data-driven graphics, 37, 365–366
databases, 366
David Cater Gallery, 339
Davidson, Shayne, 137, 408
Davis, Jack, 141
Day, Rob, 202, 408
Dayton, Linnea, 141
Define Pattern command, 117
Delete Anchor Point tool, 10
deleting
    anchor points, 10, 77
    blends, 220
    layers, 156, 172
    slices, 376
    sublayers, 172
    swatches, 67
    symbols, 148
    warp effects, 313
Density option, 124
Desaturate filter, 75
Design Time, 408
design(s)
    book jacket, 202–203
    companies, 408–411
    cropping, 345
    experimenting with multiple, 103
    graph, 18–19
    mockups, 37
    product packaging, 241
    symmetrical, 344
    Web page, 374–376
DesignTime, 125
DeskTop Design Studio, 225, 408
detailed renderings, 92–93
DHTML, 365
diagrams, technical, 92
Diccolor, 30
Diffused Shading option, 297
digital art, 412
digital maps, 412

digital pens, 12
Digital Wisdom, 316
DigitalKick, 372
"Digitizing a Logo" lesson, 90, 164–165
Dim Images option, 158
Direct Selection tool, 9, 10, 13
direction points, 7
Director, 358, 412
disco clock illustration, 88–89
Distiller, xxiii, 385
"Distort Dynamics" lesson, 106–107
"Distort Filter Flora" lesson, 108–110
Distort filters, 76–77, 108–111
distorting
    letterforms, 210
    raster images, 76
    text, 190, 213
Dither option, 362
"Divide & Color" lesson, 88–89
Divide Pathfinder, 69, 72, 88–89, 113
documents
    changing color mode for, 29
    creating, 2–3
    file extension for, 3
    saving as PDF files, 31–32
dog, 126–127
Domus Crossheads, 408
Donaldson, Timothy, 140–141, 396, 408
"Don't outline small type" tip, 191
door knob, 234–235
dots per inch, 383
"double shadow" effect, 283
dove, 196
dpi, 383
drag-and-drop technique, 383–384
dragonfly, 103
drawing, 64–118. *See also* painting; tracing
    basic techniques, 64–69
    expanding toolset for, 69–77
    Gallery pages, 81, 94–95
    under grayscale scans, 161
    lessons on, 78–80, 82–93
    mechanical objects, 78–80
    troubleshooting, 287
Dreamweaver, 180, 360
Drop Shadow dialog box, 281, 306
drop shadows, 135, 198, 281, 306
Dry Ink brush, 205
Duquesne Incline illustration, 96–97
DVD label template, xxii
dynamic graphics, 365
Dynamic Graphics, Inc., 412

E

e-commerce image, 401
E-MEN cover title, 212–213
eagle decal, 81
Eckstein, Linda, 231, 408
edges
    beveled, 295, 316, 319
    changing shape of two unfilled, 114
    clicking on/viewing, 281
    and CMYK inks, 100
    feathered, 257
    hiding/showing, 22, 28, 327
    jagged, 104
editing
    Bézier curves, 9–11
    brush strokes, 142
    brushes, 122
    envelope effects, 300
    masks, 255, 287
    meshes, 245
    paths, 9–11
    PDF files, 386
    symbols, 371
    type, 217
    warp effects, 299
educational CD-ROM illustrations, 105
Effect menu, 292, 293, 299
effects, 292–328
    3D. *See* 3D effects
    applying, 293
    contrasted with filters, 292
    envelope. *See* envelope effects
    Gallery pages, 303, 311, 321–325, 328
    hiding edges before viewing, 327
    lessons on, 304–310, 312–319, 326–327
    new features, 292
    Pathfinder, 300–301
    raster, 293
    saving attributes for, 292
    scaling, 292
    Scribble. *See* Scribble effect
    transforming lettering with, 303
    warp. *See* warp effects
Elberg, Eve, 19, 238, 408
electric guitar, 321
Ellipse tool, 11, 78, 82
embedded images, 33, 382–383
"Embossing Effects" lesson, 306–307
Encapsulated PostScript
    See EPS format

end cap styles, 75

endpoints. *See also* anchor points
changing end caps for, 75
fixing overlapping, 75
joining, 14–15
sandwiching on top of each other, 14

Englart, Mindi, 408

English language fonts, 188

Envelope Distort tool, 213, 338

envelope effects
applying, 299–300, 314
contrasted with warp effects, 298–299
distort options for, 300
editing, 300
lesson on, 312–315
maximizing fidelity of, 314
and Smart Guides, 300
transforming type with, 212–213
types of, 300

EPS format
and color management, 29
contrasted with other formats, 382
and flattening, 258, 262
importing/exporting, 33, 262–263
Preview feature, 33

Erase tool, 10

European language fonts, 188

Evans, Virginia, 202, 408

Evenson Design Group, 102

Eveready batteries symbol, 82–85

Every-line Composer, xxiv, 188

"Examining Blends" lesson, 226–227

Excel Chart Wizard, 290, 384

Exclude Pathfinder, 72

exercises, xix. *See also* lessons

Expand command, 222, 224

Expand Pathfinder, 86–87

expanding
artwork, 224
blends, 220, 222
compound shapes, 74, 87
gradients, 244–245

Export command, 363

exporting
layered files, 160, 365
type, 193
Web graphics/animation, 362–365, 369–370, 373

extruding objects, 294–295, 321

eye illustration, 139

eye logo, 48–49

Eyedropper/Paint Bucket
options dialog, 68, 190

Eyedropper tool
controlling attributes picked up by, 68
filling objects with, 114, 115
purpose of, 67–68
setting options for, 190
Shift-clicking with, 68, 114
toggling between selection tool and, 114

F

fabric, 237

fairy, 221

Feather effect, 346, 356

feathered edges, 257

Ferster, Gary, 105, 230, 340, 409

Fidelity option, 12, 121–122, 314

Field Force Automation magazine, 242

file formats. *See also* specific formats
and exporting, 362–365
and linking, 382
source of additional information on, 384

file-naming system, 23

files
bringing to front, 26
controlling size of, 35, 37
legacy, 262
naming, 23
optimizing, 360
reverting to earlier version of, 24
saving, 22–23

"Fill Rules.pdf" file, 70

Fill/Stroke icon, 16

fills. *See also* appearances
adding to appearances, 264–265
and compound paths, 70
copying, 17
creating multiple, 265
defined, 64
redirecting, with Gradient tool, 238
setting, 65
swapping attributes for, 65, 85
using tints for, 79
using transparency with, 254

Filter actions, Pathfinder, 301

Filter menu, 293, 299

FILTERiT4.1, 412

filters
for adding anchor points, 45, 47

color modification, 74–75
contrasted with effects, 292
for distorting, 108–110
for Hard Mix/Soft Mix effects, 301
and linked images, 382
setting measurement units for, 7
for trapping, 100

Find Font dialog box, 188–189

finger dances
importance of mastering, 41, 54
for Macintosh, 56, 58, 60
manual dexterity required for, 55
quick reference card, 54
rules for performing, 54–55
and Undo command, 54, 55
and Universal Access conflict, 55
for Windows systems, 57, 59, 61

Fire Ash brush, 133

Fireworks, 412

fish, 147–148, 246–248

Fishauf, Louis, 208, 277, 401, 409

fishbowl, 272–273

flags, 312–315, 320

flame effect, 308–310, 348–349

Flare Options dialog box, 311

Flare tool, 218, 293, 311

Flash
animation, 367, 368–370
copying and pasting artwork into, 370
importing symbols into, 369
and Release to Layers command, 361
using Illustrator files in, 363–364

Flash Export dialog box, 363

Flatten Artwork command, 159

Flatten Transparency command/dialog box, 254, 258, 259

Flattener Preview palette, 34, 36, 254, 258–261

flattening, 258–262
options/settings, 34, 35, 258–259
and PostScript printing devices, 258
presets, 259–261
previewing, 260–261

Flip Horizontal/Vertical option, 21

"Floating Type" lesson, 280–281

Flood typeface, 206

floral application icon, xx

Florence, Ted, 412

flower bulb, 230

flowers, 108–111, 116–117, 268–271

Focoltone, 30, 101

FoldUp!3D, 412
FontLab, 211
Fontographer, 206
fonts. *See also* text; type
    creating, 206
    finding and replacing, 188–189
    getting professional help with, 189
    for hand-rendered look, 216, 303
    highlighting substituted, 189
    for historical look, 216
    licenses for, 191
    multinational, 188
    WYSIWYG menu for, xxv
Ford Taurus, 338
foreign language fonts, 188, 190–191
Fort Santiago illustration, 176
Fox, Mark, 81, 82, 409
fps, 379
fractions, 187
frames
    creating "key," 378
    layering, 372–373
    pasting, 379
    tweening, 379
frames per second, 379
Free Distort filter, 77
Free Transform tool
    adding energy/movement with,
        106–107
    alternatives to, 19, 20
    contrasted with bounding box,
        19–20
    creating perspective with, 107
    distorting objects with, 76
    purpose of, 20
    rotating and scaling objects with,
        320
FreeHand, 412
French horn, 251
Fridberg, David, 409
Friskets, 8
fruit, 241
Full Screen mode, 25
Fund for Animals logo, 86–87

G

Gallery pages, xix
gamut warning, 32, 66, 363
Gary Newman Design, 410
Gates, Guilbert, 150, 228, 342, 409
Gaussian Blur effect, 277, 308,
    309–310
geometric primitives, 11

geometric shapes, 11–12, 78–80
    See also shapes
GIF Builder, 358, 412
GIF format, 360, 362
"GIF or JPEG" tip, 360
gift certificate template, xxii
gingham pattern, 118
Girvin, Tim, 69, 207, 409
Girvin Strategic Branding & Design,
    408, 409
global colors
    for blends/gradients, 227
    changing, 97, 227
    creating, 96–97
    specifying tint percentages, 68
globe, 232
glossary, xvii, 2
glow effect, 229, 277, 286–287, 342,
    353
"Glowing Starshine" lesson, 150, 342
Glyphs palette, xxiv, 180, 187
gnu-zipped format, 364
Golding, Mordy
    on antialiasing, 375
    contact information, 409
    on editing envelopes, 300
    Gallery page, 323
    on warps in Illustrator *vs.*
        Photoshop, 299
    wine bottle, xxi, 297, 323
GoLive
    and Adobe's Creative Suite, xx
    and animation, 358
    and dynamic graphics, 365
    and HTML editing, 360
    and Web graphics, 358
    and Web page layout, 180, 374,
        375
gondolier, 275
Good, Janet, 229, 409
Goodyear logo, 338
Gordon, Steven
    Boston map title, 204–205, 265
    Bryce Canyon virtual guide,
        280–281
    Cartagram Web site, 374–376
    Chicago map, 278–279
    contact information, 409
    Great River Scenic Byway map,
        174
    map symbols, 316–317
    Texas map title, 303
    travel Web page, 377
    Zion National Park label, 218
    Zuni Pueblo book title, 216–217

Gorska, Caryl, 241, 409
Grace, Laurie, 108–111, 166–167,
    334–335, 409
gradient meshes. *See also* meshes
    creating mask effects with, 333
    Gallery pages, 249–251, 354–356
    lessons on, 244–248, 348–349
    and photorealism, 224
    purpose of, 224
Gradient palette, 223, 226–227, 238,
    243
Gradient tool
    adjusting gradient angle with, 353
    creating cut-out effect with, 240
    customizing radial blends with,
        241
    exercise on *Wow! CD*, 238
    opening Gradient palette with,
        223
    redirecting fills with, 238
    unifying gradients with, 100, 238
gradients. *See also* blends
    adding color to, 223
    adjusting, 223, 226–227
    applying to multiple objects, 223
    automatically updating colors
        for, 227
    complexity of, 224
    contrasted with blends, 225, 226
    converting to meshes, 244–245
    creating, 223, 243
    creating illusion of, 223
    customizing, 238
    designing, 226
    expanding, 244–245
    and file size, 35
    Gallery pages, 225, 239–243
    lessons on, 226–227, 238,
        244–248
    linear. *See* linear gradients
    manual trapping of, 100
    naming, 227
    radial. *See* radial gradients
    resetting defaults for, 223
    setting resolution for, 258
    showing change of light to
        shadow with, 244–245
    storing, 226–227
    stretching across multiple objects,
        238
    trapping, 30
    unifying, 100, 238
    varying angle/distance of, 223,
        242
    when to use, 226–227

Graph tools, 17–19
graph variables, 366
graphic design companies, 408–411
graphic styles
    applying, 16–17, 302, 305, 307
    creating library of, 305
    defined, 17, 302
    lessons on, 304–307, 312–315
    "live" nature of, 17
    merging, 302
    replacing, 17, 302
    saving appearance attributes as,
        302
    saving warp effects as, 313
    separating from objects, 302
    simulating embossing with,
        306–307
    updating/replacing, 17
Graphic Styles palette
    and appearance attributes, 302
    creating new graphic styles in,
        305
    and effect attributes, 292
    previous name for, 292
GraphicConverter, 358
graphics. See also artwork; images;
        Web graphics
    data-driven, 37, 365–366
    dynamic, 365
    for on-screen display, 358
Graphics Server, 366
graphics tablet, 126
        See also Wacom tablet
graphs
    changing style of, 17–18
    creating pie charts from, 290
    entering/importing data for, 17
    inserting design elements into,
        18–19
    maintaining "graphness" of, 18
    purpose of, 17
    setting default style for, 17
    ungrouping objects in, 18
    updating with symbols, 20
    using as templates, 19
grasses, 151
Gravity effect, 183
grayscale images, colorizing, 256
grayscale scans, placing color under,
    161
Great River Scenic Byway map, 174
"greeked" type, 180
Greenburg, Adele Droblas, 409
Greenland map, 166–167
Greiman, April, 397, 409

grids
    customizing, 27, 255
    drawing, 12
    hiding/showing, 27
    positioning, 344
    snap-to function for, 27
    splitting objects into, 183
Grossman, Wendy, 409
Grossman Illustration, 409
Group command, 162, 169
Group layers, 160
Group Selection tool, 13
groups
    assigning styles to, 279
    Knockout, 284–285
    organizing objects into, 13, 285
    targeting all elements in, 264
    using transparency with, 254
guidelines, perspective, 105
guides. See also Smart Guides
    and blended objects, 177
    converting lines into, 176–177
    creating, 26–27
    customizing, 203
    locking/unlocking, 27, 177
    setting preferences for, 27
    snap-to property for, 9, 177
guitar, 321
gzipped format, 364

H

Hallmark Cards, 320, 411
halos, 311
Hamann, Brad, 115, 318–319, 392–
    393, 409
hand/eye coordination, 41
hand-rendered effect, 216, 303
Hand tool, 4, 34
handles, 7
hands, 398
handwritten typeface, 211
Happy Meal box, 99
hard drive, 2
Hard Mix Pathfinder, 72, 74, 90–91,
    301
hardware
    calibration, 28
    requirements, 2
Hart, Steve, 226–227, 409
Hastings, Pattie Belle, 210, 409
hatch effects, 124, 298, 328
head tags, 376
Hebrew wedding certificate, 196–197
Heinemann Publishing, 252

Help menu, 35
Henkel, Rick, 93, 94, 96–97, 221, 409
"Henkel-Flared Effect.ai" file, 221
Hess, Eric, 23
Hess, Kurt, 94, 409
Hide command, 162
Hide Edges command, 22
Hide Page Tiling command, 4
Hide/Show Edges command, 28
hiding/showing
    bounding box, 20
    edges, 22, 28, 327
    grids, 27–28
    layers, 156, 158, 167
    masks, 333
    objects, 162
    palettes, 16
    rulers, 26
    text threads, 184
    tiling, 4
Hidy, Lance, 398, 409
Highlight Substituted Fonts option,
    189
highlights, 28, 79–80, 189, 274, 321
highway symbol, 279
Hilken, Barney, 412
hills, rolling, 244–245
holes
    creating simple, 70
    transparent, 118
    using Subtract to cut, 89
holiday card, xxi, 326–327
Hollin, Kaoru, 146–148, 409
Hornall, John, 199, 409
Hornall Anderson Design Works,
    199, 409
hot door, 412
"Hot Rod Rocket" image, 403
houses, 42–47, 266–267
HSB color space, 30
HTML editors/files, 360, 376
human silhouettes, 88–89, 153
HyperText Markup Language, 360
hyphenation, xxv, 188

I

ICC(M) profiles, 28–29
Ice House Press & Design, 210, 408,
    409
iconic images, 48–49
illustrations
    See also graphics; images
    educational, 105
    magazine, 242, 286–287

illustration, *continued*
    product, 78–80, 338–341
    technical, 78–80, 92, 93
Illustrator 9 *Wow!* Book cover, 275, 353
Illustrator CS
    advice for new users of, xviii
    basic techniques for using, 2–37
    course outline, xvi
    flexibility of, 40, 94
    glossary, xvii, 2
    and hand/eye coordination, 41
    integration with other Adobe
        applications, xx,
        xxii–xxiii
    keys to mastering, 40–41
    meaning of "CS" in, xx
    new features, xx–xxvi
    Scripting Guide, 37
    system requirements, 2
    tutorials, 412
    User Guide. See User Guide
    with other programs, 382–386
        See also specific
            programs
    as Web design tool, 374–375
**Illustrator Legacy Options dialog
    box**, 262
IllustratorCS Wow! Course Outline,
    xvi
IllustratorCSWowCD. See Wow! CD
image formats, 32–33, 360, 362
image maps, 359–360, 377
ImageReady, 361
images
    adding perspective to, 176–177
    displaying different aspects of,
        24–25
    file formats for, 32–33, 360, 362
    linked *vs.* embedded, 33, 382–383
    modifying visibility of, 112
    naming, 23
    placing, 112
    saving, 22–23
imagesetters, 32
importing
    artwork, 172, 363
    data for graphs, 17
    to layers/sublayers, 172
    symbols, 369
    variables, 366
in-betweens, 220, 230, 379
in port, 182
In The Studio, 131, 209, 410

InDesign
    and Adobe's Creative Suite, xx
    book about, 187
    and color management, 29
    copying/pasting artwork from
        Illustrator to, 385
    and EPS format, 29
    integration of Illustrator with, xx,
        xxii–xxiii
    online help, 385
    as page layout tool, 180, 202
    tutorials, 412
*InDesign CS Visual QuickStart
    Guide*, 187
Industrial Illustrators, 229, 409
Infini-D, 404
infographics, 236
"Ink Brush Strokes" lesson, 126–127
Ink Brushes library, 139
inks
    contrasted with monitor colors,
        28
    hiding misrepresentation of, 30
    misregistration of, 100
Inner Glow dialog box, 275–277, 286
inset shapes, 91
Intensity option, 124
interlaced GIF, 362
Intersect Pathfinder, 69, 72, 83–84
"Intricate Patterns" lesson, 116–117
Invert Mask command, 217
Isolate Blending option, 273, 283
isometric formulas
    automating, 93
    demonstration on *Wow! CD*, 93
    lesson on, 92–93
    and technical illustrations, 92
"Isometric Systems" lesson, 92–93
"It's a Knockout" lesson, 284–285

J

Jackmore, Lisa, 120, 129, 409
jagged edges, 104
Japanese fonts, 188
Jared Schneidman Design, 228, 236,
    342, 409, 411
JavaScript, 36, 364–365
Javier Romero Design Group, 191,
    353, 411
Jean Tuttle Illustration, 411
Jeep, 340
Jennifer Diamond Foundation logo,
    103
Joe Lertola Gallery, 145

John Burns Lettering & Design, 408
Join function, 14–15, 46–47
joining
    error message, 14
    exercises on, 46, 47
    while averaging, 15, 46–47
Joly, David, 238, 409
Jonen, Frank, 211, 409
Jones, Joe, 407, 409
JPEG format, 360, 362
JRDG, 411. *See also* Javier Romero
    Design Group
JSD, 236, 342
justification settings/controls, xxv,
    188, 196

K

Kanzler, Diane Hinze, 86–87, 272–
    273, 282–285, 409
Kanzler, John, 86–87, 106–107,
    168–169, 221, 409
Kelley, Andrea, 78–80, 237, 410
kerning, 303
Ketubah, 196–197
Keyboard Increment settings, 45,
    92, 375
keyboard shortcuts
    accessing tools with, 5
    customizing, xvii, 5–6
    for Mac *vs.* Windows, xvii
keyframes, 372–373. *See also* frames
Knife tool, 11, 113, 238
Knockout Group feature, 257–258,
    284–285, 355
knockouts
    and compound shapes, 49
    controls for, 257–258
    as film prepress/darkroom
        technique, 284
    Gallery page, 355
    lesson on, 284–285
    purpose of, 284
**Kodak Digital Science Color
    Management**, 28
Korean fonts, 188

L

labels, color, 96–97
LaMantia, Marc, 346–347, 410
Langeveld Bulb, 230
language support, xxv
Larsen, Tiffany, 118, 276, 410
Lasso tool, 12–13, 93, 245

layer-based slices, 361
layer masks, 255
Layer Options dialog box, 156, 157–158
"Layering Frames" lesson, 372–373
layers, 156–177. *See also* sublayers
  adding to Layers palette, 156
  assigning appearance attributes to, 279
  changing, by selecting object, 169
  changing stacking order for, 157
  color-coding of, 157, 168
  coloring black-and-white images with, 168–169
  creating, 156, 167
  deleting, 156, 172
  distributing objects to, 122, 361
  drawing into, 172
  duplicating, 156
  exporting CSS, 365
  exporting to Photoshop, 160
  Gallery pages, 163, 173
  hiding/showing, 156, 158, 167
  importing art into, 172
  lessons on, 164–172, 174–177
  locking/unlocking, 156, 158, 175
  moving objects between, 173
  with names in italics, 158
  naming, 157
  nesting, 174–175
  non-printing, 158
  organizing, 170–172, 284
  and pasted objects, 159
  previewing, 167
  printing, 158
  purpose of, 156
  reordering, 167
  selecting items on, 162
  selecting multiple, 156
  separating symbols onto, 123
  template. *See* Template layers
  troubleshooting, 162
  using transparency with, 254
  for Web page content, 374–375
Layers palette
  adding layers to, 156
  creating clipping masks in, 331–332
  display options for, 175
  making selections in, 162
  moving objects between layers in, 173
  navigating, 156
  organizing, as nested hierarchy, 174–175

organizing groups of brush strokes in, 267
organizing Web page content in, 374–375
performance considerations, 162
pop-up menu, 158–160
previewing animation in, 370
and transportation map, 163
layout programs, 180, 184, 202, 374–375
layouts
  multi-column, xxiv
  reflowing text in, 190
  tools for creating, 180, 184, 202, 374–375
leaves, 150–151
legacy files, 32, 262
legacy text, 186
Lehner & Whyte, 240, 372, 411
Lein, Adam Z, 290, 410
Lemke, Thorsten, 358
lens flare effect, 311
Lertola, Joe, 145, 286–287, 325, 386, 410
lessons, xvi
  Add & Expand, 86–87
  Antiquing Type, 216–217
  Basic Appearances, 278–279
  Basic Transparency, 272–273
  Blurring the Lines, 308–310
  Book Cover Design, 202–203
  Brushed Type, 204–205
  Building Brushes, 140–141
  Building Houses, 42–47
  Classic Icon, 48–49
  Colorful Masking, 334–335
  Colors with Layers, 168–169
  Creating Simple Object, 53
  Crunching Type, 212–213
  Cubist Constructs, 90–91, 400
  Custom Text Paths, 194–195
  Cutting & Joining, 82–85, 90
  Digitizing a Logo, 90, 164–165
  Distort Dynamics, 106–107
  Distort Filter Flora, 108–110
  Divide & Color, 88–89
  Embossing Effects, 306–307
  Examining Blends, 226–227
  Finger Dances, 54–61
  Floating Type, 280–281
  Glowing Starshine, 150, 342
  Ink Brush Strokes, 126–127
  Intricate Patterns, 116–117
  Isometric Systems, 92–93
  It's a Knockout, 284–285

Layering Frames, 372–373
Making Waves, 378–379
Map Techniques, 142–144, 163
Masking Letters, 200
Masking Opacity, 348–349
Mastering Mesh, 246–248
Modeling Mesh, 350–352
Nested Layers, 174–175
Objective Colors, 96–97
Off in a Flash, 368–370
Offset Fills, 214–215
Opacity Masks 101, 286–287
Organic Creation, 150–151
Organizing Layers, 170–172
Preparing Art, 132–133
Quick & Easy 3D, 316–317
Reflective Masks, 336–337
Rolling Mesh, 244–245
Scratchboard Art, 304–305
Scribble Basics, 326–327
Shades of Blends, 228
Shape Shifting, 392–393
Simple Realism, 78–80
Software Relay, 388–390
Stretching Type, 196–197
Symbol Basics, 146–148
Tinting a Scan, 282–283
Tracing Details, 166–167
Transparency 101, 266–267
Transparent Color, 268–271
Unified Gradients, 238
Unlocking Realism, 234–235
Varied Perspective, 176–177
Vector Photos, 112–114
Warps & Envelopes, 312–315
Webward Ho!, 374–376
Zen Rotation, 52
Zen Scaling, 50–51
letterform paths, 140
letterhead template, 4
lettering
  artist, 198
  building brushes for, 140–141
letters. *See also* fonts; text; type
  applying brushes to, 204–205
  converting to outlines, 198
  distorting, 210, 213
  elongating, 196
  embossing, 306–307
  filling with patterns/gradients, 191, 214–215
  masking, 191, 200–201
  stretching, 196, 197
Liang, Ma Zhi, 249, 410
Liberty, Statue of, 225

libraries
    auto-opening, 364
    saving, xxvi, 67
    using objects as, 94
license plate, 306–307
ligatures, 187
Lightwave 3D, 386
line breaks, 188
Line Segment tool, 7
linear gradients. *See also* gradients
    creating stylized look with, 239
    creating woodcut effect with, 243
    expanding to gradient meshes,
        244–245
    filling shapes with, 244, 251
    lesson on, 244–245
lines
    attaching to circles, 84–85
    converting to guides, 176–177
    creating anchor points for, 7
    refining with Pencil tool, 165
    shading, 228
linked image(s)
    applying filters/transparency to,
        382
    and file size, 35, 382
    variables, 365, 366
    vs. embedded, 33, 382–383
"Links are manageable" tip, 31
Links palette, 31, 172
Liquify tools, 76
live effects, 292, 299. *See also* effects
LiveMotion, 363
Livingston, Randy, 410
lobster, 239
Locate Layer command, 175
Locate Object command, 175
Lock command, 161
Lock Guides command, 177
lock illustration, 234–235
locking/unlocking
    guides, 27, 177
    layers, 156, 158, 175
    objects, 161
logos
    adapting for multiple applications,
        102
    constructing, 48–49
    digitizing, 90, 164–165
    trying range of designs for, 103
LogoSpruce, 412
lossy compression, 362
Louis Fishauf Design Limited, 401

Louveaux, Pierre
    on antialiased artwork in Acrobat,
        386
    on expanding compound shapes,
        74
    on extracting path from mesh,
        224
    on outlining dashed strokes, 76
    on preventing color shifts, 382
    on targeting groups/layers, 264
    on using transparency, 254
Lynch, Patrick, 410

M

Ma, Zhiliang, 249, 410
Mac OS X, 19, 262
    See also Macintosh
Mac Software, Barney's, 412
Macadangdang, Todd, 124, 328, 410
Macintosh
    and color management, 28
    finger dances, 56, 58, 60
    and Page Setup button, 4–5
    and PDF format, 19
    rendering engine, 262
    scripting languages, 36
    system requirements, 2
MacPrePress, 411
Macromedia
    contact information, 412
    Director, 358
    Dreamweaver, 180, 360
    Fireworks, 412
    Flash. *See* Flash
    FreeHand, 412
M.A.D., 48, 410
magazine advertisements, 405
magazine illustrations, 242, 286–287
Magiera, Rob, 382, 388–391, 410
magnification percentages, 27
magnifying glass, 226–227
Mah, Derek, 220
Mahannah, Jacqueline, 139, 410
Make Guides command, 177, 203
Make Opacity Mask command, 217,
        218, 256, 289
Make Text Dynamic button, 366
Make Text Wrap command, 185
"Make Time" illustration, 88–89
"Making Waves" lesson, 378–379
"Manual Trapping" tip, 100
map symbols, 316–317, 324
"Map Techniques" lesson, 142–144,
        163

map titles, 204, 303
Mapcraft Cartography, 406, 411
mapping artwork, 297, 319, 323
Mapping Services, 163, 410
maps
    bike, 138
    Chicago, 278–279
    city bus, 142–144
    creating layer structure for,
        174–175
    Great River Scenic Byway, 174
    Greenland, 166–167
    image. *See* image maps
    Sonoran Desert, 324
    sources of, 410, 412
    transportation, 163
    United States, 325
    William Patterson University, 406
MAPublisher, 412
Mardi Gras illustration, 276
Margolis-Pineo, Elizabeth, 410
marks, crop, 116, 203
Marks & Bleed section, Print dialog,
        xxv
Marquardt, Rob, 410
mascots, 388–391
mask-editing mode, 287
masking. *See also* masks
    advanced techniques, 330–333
    blend objects, 237, 334–335
    combining gradient meshes with,
        250
    lessons on, 200, 334–337,
        348–349
    letters, 191, 200–201
    RAM considerations, 333
    raster shapes, 390
"Masking Letters" lesson, 200
"Masking Opacity" lesson, 348–349
masks. *See also* masking
    clipping. *See* clipping masks
    finding, 333
    hiding, 333
    identifying, 332
    inserting objects in, 332
    layer, 255
    opacity. *See* opacity masks
    RAM considerations, 333
    reflective, 336–337
    troubleshooting, 333
    using gradient meshes in place
        of, 333
    using multiple objects as, 330
"Mastering Mesh" lesson, 246–248
Matrix logo, 69, 207

MAX, 410, 411
Maxson, Greg, 341, 410
McCollum, Scott, 410
McDonald's packaging, 99, 176
McShane, Patricia, 48, 410
measurement units, 7, 15, 228
mechanical objects, 78–80, 404
medallions, 345
Medical and Biological Illustration,
410
Medical Economics magazine, 238
Medical Illustration & Graphics, 408
medical illustrations, 137, 145, 408
memory. *See* RAM
menus
    Illustrator CS, 5–6, 6
    restaurant, 372–373
Merge Pathfinder, 72, 206
mermaid, 125
mesh objects, 224. *See also* meshes
mesh points, 224
Mesh tool, 224, 245, 248, 251, 252
meshes. *See also* gradient meshes
    adding columns/rows to, 248
    aligning/straightening, 351
    applying shading effect with,
        314–315
    coloring, 352
    combining masking techniques
        with, 250
    complexity of, 224
    converting gradients to, 244–245
    converting paths to, 224
    creating envelopes from, 300
    editing, 245
    lessons on, 244–248, 350–353
    modeling, 350–352
    painting with, 151
    and photorealism, 224, 249
    printing, 248
    rotating portions of, 350
    setting resolution for, 258
    shading with, 314–315
"Meshsmith" art piece, 350–352
meta tags, 376
metallic reflectivity, 234
metallic surfaces, 341
MetaTools, 404
Microsoft
    Excel, 290, 384
    Office, xxii, xxiii
    Windows. *See* Windows
Miles Fridberg Molinaroli, 409
"Millard and the Pear" animation,
    368–371

Mini Cooper, 66, 339
Minus Back Pathfinder, 70, 72
Minus Front Pathfinder, 206, 209
mist effect, 289
Mitch Shostak Studios, 411
Miter joins, 75–76
Miyamoto, Yukio
    cat, 224, 256
    contact information, 410
    French horn, 251, 356
    Gallery pages, 250–251
    motorcycle, 250
mockups, 37
"Modeling Mesh" lesson, 350–352
modifier keys, 42
monitor
    calibration, 28
    resolution, 2
Monroy, Bert, 134, 136, 378–379,
    387, 410
moon-glow effect, 151
Moonlightpress Studio, 411
Mordy Golding Gallery, 323
morphing, 220, 230
motion effect, 379
motorcycle, 250
mouse, drawing freehand with, 12
movie poster, 311
MS Office, xxii, xxiii
Müller-Lancé, Joachim, 206, 410
multi-column layouts, xxiv
multinational fonts, 188, 190–191
MultiPage, 412
mural, 397
Murphy, Mark, 372

N

Name View, Swatches palette, 99
naming
    brushes, 121
    colors, 97
    files, 23
    gradients, 227
    images, 23
    layers, 157
    patterns, 117
    sublayers, 269–270
    swatches, 97, 98
    views, 24
National Park Service, 324, 410
naturalistic images, 282
    See also photorealism
Navigator palette, 26
Neal, Brad, 234–235, 338, 410

Neal, Thomas, 69, 410
negative space, 89
Nelson, David, 142–143, 163, 167,
    190, 410
neon sign, 387
"Nested Layers" lesson, 174–175
New Art Has Basic Appearance
    option, xviii, 265, 266, 268,
    296
Newman, Gary, 70, 201, 410
newsletter template, xxii
Newsweek infographic, 236
Niagara Falls image, 115
North Face camping equipment, 237
Nunes Farms package design, 241

O

Object Highlighting preferences, 28
"Objective Colors" lesson, 96–97
objects. *See also* shapes
    appearance attributes for, 16
    applying effects to, 293
        See also effects
    applying gradients to, 223, 238
        See also gradients
    applying graphic styles to, 16–17
        See also graphic styles
    assigning URLs to, 359–361
    controlling stacking order of,
        160–162
    creating custom guides from, 27
    creating see-through, 284–285
    creating simple, 53
    deleting stray points from, 10, 77
    deselecting, 56–61
    distorting, 76–77
    distributing to layers, 122, 361
    extruding, 294–295, 321
    filling, 16, 65, 79
    grabbing, 56, 57
    group-selecting, 60, 61
    grouping/ungrouping, 13, 285
    hiding/showing, 162
    highlighting, 274
    inserting in masks, 332
    joining, 46
    linking text, 184
    locking/unlocking, 161
    making compound, 49
    moving, 56–61, 173
    overlapping. *See* overlapping
        objects
    resizing, xxvi, 6

objects, *continued*
   revolving, 295, 318–319, 320, 322, 324
   rotating, 296, 324
   scaling, 20, 21, 22, 50–51
   selecting, 12–14, 160, 161
   snapping to guides/points, 9
   specifying numerical location for, 20
   stroking, 16, 65
   targeting, 161
   tinting, 79
   using as "libraries," 94
   using color labels to find, 97
   wrapping text around, 185
ocean trenches, 236
"Off in a Flash" lesson, 368–370
Office, Microsoft, xxii, xxiii
Offset command, 91
Offset effect, 215
"Offset Fills" lesson, 214–215
Offset Path command, 224
Offset Path dialog box, 215
olives, 224, 355
Olson, Robin AF, 121, 158
Olympic Games mascots, 388–391
opacity masks, 255–257
   creating/applying, 217, 218, 256, 287, 354
   creating monotone image with, 256
   disabling, 257
   editing, 255
   and fills, 217
   identifying, 256
   lessons on, 286–287, 348–349
   purpose of, 255
   source materials for, 287
   tips for working with, 256–257
"Opacity Masks 101" lesson, 286–287
Opacity slider, 269, 273, 285
Open Library command, xxvi, 31
"Open-Type_Guide.pdf" file, 187
OpenType fonts, xxiii–xxiv, 186–187
OpenType palette, xxiv, 180, 187
Optical Kerning feature, xxiv
Optical Margin Alignment feature, xxiv
Optima font, 216
optimizing
   GIF files, 360
   patterns, 117
   slices, 362–363
   Web graphics, 358, 360, 361
"Organic Creation" lesson, 150–151

"Organic" text, 284–285
organizing
   artwork, 156, 174
   brush strokes, 267
   colors, 96, 98
   layers, 170–172, 284
   objects, 13, 285
   sublayers, 170
"Organizing Layers" lesson, 170–172
origin, ruler, 26, 161, 202
Orlando bus map, 142–143
ornaments, 187
out-of-gamut warning, 32, 66, 363
out port, 182, 184
Outline mode, 7–8, 42, 158, 167
Outline Pathfinder, 72
Outline Stroke command, 91, 100, 208
outlines
   converting text/type to, 189–191, 197, 198
   Illustrator CS course, xvi
outlining
   dashed strokes, 76
   paths, 91
   small type, 190, 191
"Outlining Dashed Strokes" tip, 76
overlapping objects
   applying Soft Mix to, 90–91, 283
   creating/positioning, 86–87
   designing images/symbols with, 82–83, 88
   dividing, 88
Overprint Fill option, 100
Overprint Preview mode, 25, 35, 261
overrides, 186

P

package design, 241, 288, 289
page layout programs, 180, 184, 202, 374–375
Page Setup dialog box, 4–5, 34
page tiling, 4
Page tool, 4
PageMaker, 29, 37, 180
Paidrick, Ann, 224, 354–355, 410
Paint Bucket tool, 67–68, 68, 190
paint programs, creating brush strokes in, 140–141
Paintbrush tool, 266–267, 269
Painter, Corel, 8, 140–141, 412
Painter Wow! Book, The, 141
painting
   along paths, 121

   with brushes, 140–141, 150–151
   lesson on, 268–271
   with meshes, 151, 246
   with symbols, 150–151
palettes. *See also* specific palettes
   accessing, 15
   cycling through expanded/ collapsed views of, 16
   hiding/showing, 16
   regrouping, 15
   resizing, 15
   restoring default settings for, 15–16
   setting measurement units for, 7, 15
   setting up, xvii–xviii
   tear-off, 6
panda, 322
Pantone
   Color Specifier, 98
   contact information, 412
   swatch libraries, 30, 67, 101
Papciak-Rose, Ellen, 131, 209, 252, 304–305, 410
Paragraph Styles palette, xxiv, 180, 185–186, 187
Paste As Paths option, 379
Paste As Pixels option, 379
Paste in Front/Back commands, 161, 198
Paste Remembers Layers feature, 159, 332
Pastels effect, 395
pasting
   artwork, 370, 383–384, 385
   frames, 379
   paths, 46, 390
Path Type Effects options, 183
Path type object, 191
Path type tool, 183, 185
Pathfinder commands
   See also Pathfinder palette; specific commands
   basic path construction with, 82–85
   chart, 72–73
   creating objects as basis for, 90–91
   "destructive" nature of, 69, 74
   permanently applying, 82
   purpose of, 69, 74
Pathfinder effects, 300–301
Pathfinder group alert, 301
Pathfinder palette
   combining objects with, 68–69
   commands chart, 72–73

lessons on uses of, 69
restoring Hard/Soft Mix to, 91
setting traps in solid objects with, 30
Pathfinder Trap filter, 100
Pathfinders
 See Pathfinder commands
paths
 adding strokes to, 305
 applying brushes to closed, 133
 automatically creating intermediate, 232
 closing, 85
 combining into new objects, 9
 constructing with Pathfinders, 82–85
 converting compound shapes to, 87
 converting to meshes, 224
 creating, 49, 88
 creating custom guides from, 27
 cutting, 11, 46, 85
 defined, 6
 deleting excess anchor points from, 77
 deleting sections of, 10–11
 dividing overlapping, 88
 joining, 85
 making blends follow, 221–222
 making compound, 49
 offsetting, 91
 outlining, 91
 pasting, 46, 390
 placing text along, 183, 194
 positioning, 88
 reshaping, 10
 rotating part of, 52
 selecting, 12–13
 simplifying, 142
 smoothing points on, 10
 tools for editing, 9–11
pattern brushes, 121, 134–135, 151
patterns
 creating, 76, 214
 creating fabric textures with, 118
 designing complex, 116–117
 filling lettering with, 215
 manual trapping of, 100
 naming, 117
 painting along paths, 121
 repeating, 117
 testing/optimizing, 117
 trapping, 30
Patterson, Tom, 324, 410

"PDF compatibility" option, 24, 383, 385
PDF format
 and AI files, 24
 choosing specific version of, xxiii, 31
 and commercial printers, 32
 creating files in, 385
 and crop areas, 386
 editing files saved in, 386
 flavors of, 262
 Illustrator CS support for, xxiii, 31–32
 and Mac OS X, 19
 meaning of acronym, 31
 presets for, 31–32
 purpose of, 385
 and transparency, 262
Peachpit Press, 411
Pelavin, Danny, 334–335, 410
"Pen and Eyedropper" technique, 308
pen-and-ink drawings, 126–127, 152
Pen tool
 Auto Add/Delete function of, 9–10
 avoiding common mistakes with, 10
 basic cursor feedback for, 8–9
 creating anchor points with, 7
 creating Bézier curves with, 7, 8
 drawing curved path with, 194
 tracing templates with, 165
Pencil tool
 Fidelity/Smoothness options, 12
 refining lines with, 165
 reshaping paths with, 10, 193
 setting options for, 166
 tracing with, 165, 166–167
pencils, 334–335
Pendarvis, Cher Threinen-, 141, 200, 410
performance considerations
 Layers palette, 162
 rasterizing/screen redraw, 117
perspective
 adding to images, 176–177
 changing object's, 296
 creating, with Free Transform tool, 107
 guidelines, 105
Perspective (hot door), 412
Petit, Teri, 221

photographs
 posterizing, 276, 328, 346, 347, 386, 399
 tracing, 130, 251, 308, 346
photorealism. *See also* product illustrations; realism
 with blends, 234–235, 308–310
 with effects, 308–310
 with gradient meshes, 224, 249, 250
 with gradients, 250
Photorealistic Techniques with Photoshop & Illustrator, 387
Photoshop, 388–405
 and Adobe's Creative Suite, xx
 books about, 141, 387
 creating brush strokes in, 140–141
 exporting layers to, 160
 exporting paths to shapes in, 392–393
 Gallery pages, 387, 391, 394–405, 407
 integration of Illustrator with, xx, xxii–xxiii, 384
 lessons on, 388–390, 392–393
 moving artwork from Illustrator to, 384
 pasting frames into, 379
 rasterizing in, 30
 Text Warp feature, 299
 tutorials, 412
Photoshop Studio with Bert Monroy, 387
Photoshop Wow! Book, The, 141
pie chart, 290, 384
Piguet, Yves, 358
pimentos, 355
Pirman, John, 88, 410
Pixel Preview mode, 25, 358, 365, 374, 375
pixelated effect, 397
pixels, 364
pixels per inch, 383
Place command, 82, 112, 194
Placement Options command, 365–366
placesetters, 32
placing
 color, 161
 images, 112
 sketches, 82
 text along paths, 183, 194
PlanTea logo, 198
Plastic Shading option, 297, 321, 322

playing cards, 302
PNG format, xxii, 363
"point map" technique, 220, 235
Point Type objects, 181, 191, 203, 221
Pointillize effect, 346
Polar Grid tool, 12, 344
Polygon tool, 11, 44, 45
portraits, 249
ports, in/out, 182, 184
"Ports illustrated" tip, 182
posterized effect, 276, 328, 346–347, 386, 399
PostScript
   emulation, 33
   language, 33, 34
   printers, 2, 33–34, 258
   "white paper" on, 34
Pounds, David, 399, 411
power-keys. See also finger dances
   importance of mastering, 41, 54
   lessons on, 56–61
   quick reference card, 54
   rules for using, 54–55
ppi, 383
Precision Graphics, 341
Premier (Adobe), 358
"Preparing Art" lesson, 132–133
prepress/production services, 412
   See also service bureaus
Preserve Text Appearance option, 193
Preserve Text Editability option, 193
presets
   compression, 361
   flattener, 259–261
   PDF, 31–32
   Scribble effect, 327
   transparency, 254
pressure-sensitive devices, 126
Preview mode
   interrupting, 25
   toggling between Outline mode and, 158, 167
previewing
   animations, 370
   flattening, 260–261
   layers, 167
   overprints, 260
   prior to printing, 5
primitives, geometric, 11
Print dialog box
   controlling page size/orientation with, 4–5
   new features, xxv, 34
   and Page Setup options, 4–5

   previewing page with, 5
Print presets, 5
printers
   calibrating, 101
   PostScript, 2, 33–34, 258
   preparing PDF files for commercial, 32
   resolution considerations, 383
   separation ICC(M), 28–29
printing
   to file, 383
   gradient mesh objects, 248
   hidden objects, 160, 162
   layers, 158
   new features, xxv, 4–5
   previewing prior to, 5
   profiles, 28–29
   proofing prior to, 34
   troubleshooting, 34, 258
   Web-ready, 34
Private Chef logo, 210
problems. See troubleshooting
process colors
   converting spot colors to, 97
   and printer calibration, 101
   selecting from swatch libraries, 30, 67, 97, 101
procreate (Corel), 412
product illustrations, 78–80, 338–341
   See also photorealism
progressive JPEG, 362
Projecting caps, 75
proofing
   for final printing device, 28–29
   and ICC(M) profiles, 28–29
   on laser printer, 34
   on-screen, 29
   with Overprint Preview, 35
PS3 "white paper", 34
PSD format, 388–390, 391, 392, 393
Pucker & Bloat filter, 77
Pucker tool, 76
pumpkins, 222

Q

"Quality Control" illustration, 242
QuarkXPress, 29, 37, 180, 202
Quartz, 262
"Quick & Easy 3D" lesson, 316–317
Quick Masks, 388
QuicKeys, 55
QuickTime, 412

R

rabbit, 388–390
radial gradients. See also gradients
   creating stylized look with, 239
   defined, 223
   editing, 244
   filling objects with, 109–110, 243
   lessons on, 109–110, 238
   relocating center of, 238
rainbow, 285
Rainbow effect, 183
RAM
   and blends, 220
   and masks/masking paths, 333
   system requirements, 2
raster effects, 293. See also rasterizing
raster images. See also rasterizing
   contrasted with vector, 261
   converting vector art to, 359
   dimming, 158
   distorting, 76
   and Knockout controls, 257
   masking, 390
   and trapping, 30, 100
   and Web applications, 359
Raster/Vector Balance setting, 258, 261–262
Raster/Vector slider, 35
Rasterize and Flatten Transparency command, 30
Rasterize dialog box, 309
rasterizing
   defined, 359
   of drag-and-drop artwork, 384
   and Gaussian Blur effect, 310
   in Photoshop, 30
   with Rasterize and Flatten Transparency, 30
   resolution settings for, 348
   to speed up screen redraw, 117
Ray Dream Studio, 407
rays, 311
Reactor Art + Design, 208
Reader (Adobe), xxiii, 24
realism. See also photorealism
   from geometry/observation, 78–80
   unlocking, with blends, 234–235
Rectangle tool, 44, 78
rectangles, 44, 78, 183
Rectangular Grid tool, 12
Red Grape, The, 372
Reflect tool, 47, 85, 341, 344, 367
reflections, 234–235, 336–337, 355

"Reflective Masks" lesson, 336–337
registration problems, 100
Release to Layers command, 361
Remington, Dorothy, 101, 411
rendering engine, 262
Rendez-vous Café image, 134, 136
Replace Spine command, 222
replacing
    brushes, 143
    fonts, 188–189
    graphic styles, 302
    spine of blends, 221–222
Reset Palette command, 16
Reshape tool, 22
resizing
    appearances, 306
    objects, xxvi, 6
    palettes, 15
    selections, 6
    symbols, 147
    text, 190
resolution
    gradient, 258
    live effects, 261
    mesh, 258
    monitor, 2
    of placed images, 383
    ppi, 383
    printer, 383
    raster effects, 293
    rasterization, 348
resolution templates, 36
resources, 412
restaurant menu
    artwork, 372–373
    template, xxii, 4
Retrospect, 23, 412
Reverse Front to Back command, 222
Reverse Spine command, 222
Revert command, 24
Revolve command, 295
RGB color
    converting to/from CMYK, 29–30, 359
    meaning of acronym, 28
    and monitor calibration, 28
    and print output, 29
    and Web output, 358–359
RGB-to-CMYK conversions, 29–30, 359
rings, 311
Rings option, Flare tool, 311
"Road Lessons" illustrations, 243
rocket ships, 318–319, 403

rolling hills, 244–245
"Rolling Mesh" lesson, 244–245
"Roman Life" illustrations, 105
Romero, Javier, 191, 353, 411
Rotate tool, 44, 344, 350, 351
rotating
    3D objects, 296, 324
    around center point, 52
    parts of meshes, 350
    parts of paths, 52
    rectangles, 44
    symbols, 148
rotation lessons, 52
Rough Pastels effect, 395
Roughen dialog box, 215, 216
Roughen effect, 215
Roughen filter, 77, 110
Round caps, 75
Round joins, 76
Rounded Rectangle tool, 11–12, 78
rows
    adding to meshes, 248
    creating from non-type objects, 183
    defining characteristics of, xxiv
rulers
    hiding/showing, 26
    origin for, 26, 161, 202
    setting measurement units for, 7, 228, 364

S

sailboat, 343
sailor boy, 164
salamander, 282–283
sampling, color, 68, 114, 115
sand effect, 151
Santa, 277
Saturate filter, 74–75
saturation sliders, 98
Save As command, 22, 31
Save as PDF button, 19
Save As Template command, 36
Save for Microsoft Office command, xxii, xxiii
Save for Web command, 358, 360, 361, 362–363, 376
"Save for Web" tip, 361
Save Library command, xxvi
Save Swatch Library command, 67, 68
saving
    appearance attributes, 302
    effect attributes, 292

files, 22–23
images, 22–23, 166
mixed colors, 66
in PDF format, 31–32
resolution settings, 36
slices, 376
swatch libraries, xxvi, 67
transparency settings, 254
warp effects, 313
saw blade, 341
Scalable Vector Graphics format
    See SVG format
scale, self-adjusting, 144
Scale Strokes & Effects preferences, 124
Scale tool, 6
scaling
    artwork, 122
    brushes, 122
    effects, 292
    lesson on, 50–51
    objects, 20, 21, 22, 50–51, 320
"Scaling & Scatter Brushes.ai" file, 124
Scallop tool, 76
ScanFont plug-in, 211
scanning
    artwork, 164–165
    black-and-white images, 168–169
    and blending modes, 161
    grayscale, 161
    sketches for use as templates, 90
scans, tinting, 282–283
scatter brushes, 121, 124, 150, 406
Schneidman, Jared, 95, 236, 409, 411
Scholastic Book Fairs cover, 394
Schwabauer, Mike, 298, 320, 411
Scissors tool, 11, 85, 132
"Scratchboard Art" lesson, 304–305
Screen Blend mode, 352, 355
screen redraw, speeding up, 117
Screener tool, Symbol, 123, 147–148, 149
"Scribble Basics" lesson, 326–327
Scribble effect
    changing settings for, 214, 298
    creating "antiqued" letters with, 216–217
    creating hatches with, 124, 298
    creating holiday card with, xxi
    creating irregular pattern with, 214
    lesson on, 326–327
    purpose of, xxi, 298
    settings/presets for, 327

Scribble Options dialog box, 214,
  298
scripting
  guide, 37
  languages, 36
  new features, xxvi
Scripting Guide, Adobe Illustrator
  CS, 37
Scruncher tool, Symbol, 123
Seabaugh, Max, 411
seascapes, 231
seashells, 128
see-through effect, 284–285
selecting
  all objects, 160
  anchor points, 12–13
  artwork, 162
  color spaces, 29–30
  layers, 156
  with Layers palette, 162
  objects, 160, 181
  paths, 12–13
  stray points, 77
  text/type, 180, 181
  troubleshooting, 159
  vs. targeting, 161
"Selecting type by accident" tip, 180
Selection tools, 12–13
separation ICC(M) printers, 28–29
Separation Setup dialog box, 34
service bureaus
  and color matching, 101
  cost considerations, 34
  and font licenses, 190–191
  preparing images/files for, 33–35
  and RGB-to-CMYK conversions,
    29
"Shades of Blends" lesson, 228
shading
  creating highlights with, 321
  with meshes, 314–315
  surface, 296–297, 322
  vertical line, 228
shadows. See also drop shadows
  creating, 80, 283
  preventing double, 283
  preventing overlapping of, 283
  showing change of light to,
    244–245
  simplifying, 283
  simulating colors for, 248
  using blends for, 227
Shape modes, 71
Shape Options dialog box, 281
"Shape Shifting" lesson, 392–393

shapes. See also objects
  combining simple, 68–69
  compound. See compound shapes
  creating simple, 48–49
  exporting paths to, 392–393
  mapping artwork onto, 297, 319,
    323
Sharif, Robert, 321, 411
Shear tool, 22, 338
Shields, Charles, 411
Shifter tool, Symbol, 148
shoe yév skä design, 411
shortcuts. See keyboard shortcuts
Shostak, Mitch, 411
Show All command, 162
Show Grid command, 27
Show Page Tiling command, 4
Show Tool Tips option, 5
Show Transparency Grid command,
  27
showing/hiding
  bounding box, 20
  edges, 22, 28, 327
  grids, 27–28
  layers, 156, 158, 167
  masks, 333
  objects, 162
  palettes, 16
  rulers, 26
  text threads, 184
  tiling, 4
silhouetted human figures, 88–89,
  153
Silicon Graphics, 405
"Simple Realism" lesson, 78–80
Simplify command, 77, 117, 142, 224
Simulate Colored Paper option, 255
Simulate Paper option, 262
Single-line Composer, 188
Sizer tool, Symbol, 123, 147, 149
sketches
  creating, 82, 168–169
  lending painterly look to, 125
  placing, 82
  preparing for tracing, 267
  scanning for use as templates, 90
Skew effect, 183
"Skin Deep" image, 145, 386
sleeping bag, 237
Slice Select tool, 362, 376
Slice tool, 361, 376
slices
  applying to objects, 360
  creating, 360–361, 376
  deleting, 376

  exporting, 361
  layer-based, 361
  optimizing, 362–363
  purpose of, 360, 376
  saving, 376
  user, 361
sliders
  color saturation, 98
  opacity, 269, 273, 285
  raster/vector, 35
Smart Guides
  and envelopes/warps, 300
  incorporating in workflow, 27
  and large files, 28
  preferences for, 28
  and Scissors tool, 85
Smart Objects, 365
smoke effect, 350, 351–352
Smooth tool, 10, 12, 167
Smoothness option, 12
snap-to arrows, 9
Snap to Grid command, 27
Snap to Pixel option, 375
Snap to Point option, 9, 92–93
snap-to property, for grids/guides, 9,
  27, 177
SnapzPro/ProX, 412
sneaker logo, 102
sneakers, 340
Snoopy, 99, 176
snowman, 53
"Soaring Hearts Futons" logo, 23
Soft Mix Pathfinder, 72, 74, 90–91,
  301
"Software Relay" lesson, 388–390
Sonoran Desert map, 324
"Special Brushes" supplement,
  152–153
special characters, 187
  See also Glyphs palette
Special Modern Design, 103
speed
  blend, 220, 235
  screen redraw, 117
  of swatch creation, 97
Spindler, Steve, 138, 411
spine, blend, 221–222
Spinner tool, Symbol, 123, 148, 149
Spiral tool, 11
Splash brush, 205
Split into Grid command, 183
Spollen, Chris, 403, 411
spot colors, 96–97, 259
Sprayer tool, Symbol, 123, 147
stacking order

for Appearance palette, 265
for layers, 157
for objects within layers, 160–162
for symbols, 148
for text boxes, 191
Stahl, Nancy, 170–173, 275, 411
Stainer tool, Symbol, 123, 147–148, 149
Stair Step effect, 183
Standard Screen mode, 25
Stankiewicz, Steven, 233, 411
Star tool, 11
stars, 150, 319, 343
Statue of Liberty, 225
Stead, Judy, xxi, 326–327, 394–395, 411
Steuer, Sharon
  "Bubbles" image, 274
  contact information, 411
  dog pen-and-ink drawing, 126–128
  flower painting, 268–271
  Gallery page, 149
  house drawing, 266–267
  message from, xvi
  pumpkins, 222
  rolling hills, 244–245
  stars and trees painting, 150–151
  Web site, xvi
"SteuerSharon-Pumpkin Blend.ai" file, 222
Steve Spindler Cartography, 411
stitching, 258
stock car, 338
Stone, Sumner, 206
Strata, 386, 412
Strata3Dplus, 412
stray points, 10, 77
Streamline, 112, 129, 386
"Stretching Type" lesson, 196–197
Stroke icon, 16
Stroke palette, 75
stroke weight, 6
strokes. See also brush strokes
  adding to appearances, 264–265
  adding to paths, 305
  copying, 17
  defined, 64–65
  offsetting, 304–305
  outlining dashed, 76
  setting measurement units for, 7
  swapping attributes for, 65, 85
  using transparency with, 254
Structure Tone brochure, 95
Style Sheets, Cascading, 365

Styler tool, Symbol, 123, 147–148
styles
  character/paragraph, xxiv, 180, 185–186, 187
  end cap, 75
  graph, 17
  graphic. See graphic styles
  group, 279
Styles palette, 292
Stylize commands, 299
stylized images, 239
sublayers
  creating, 269
  deleting, 172
  exporting, 156
  and hierarchical layer structure, 160–161
  importing art into, 172
  naming, 269–270
  organizing, 170
  and print productions, 158
  purpose of, 156
  selecting items on, 162
  troubleshooting, 162
Subtract Pathfinder, 72, 88–89
subtractive colors, 29
subway exit, 347
Sudick, Barbara, 189, 411
sun, 107
surfaces
  mapping artwork onto, 297
  reflections off of, 355
  shading, 296–297, 322
Sutherland, Brenda, 265, 297
SVG 3.0 plug-in, 363
SVG format
  and alpha channels, 363
  benefits of, 364–365
  compressing/decompressing, 364
  exporting, 365
  and JavaScript, 365
  meaning of acronym, 364
  and Save for Web dialog box, 363
  and Symbol artwork, 123
  viewer for, 363, 364
SVG Interactivity palette, 365
SVG Viewer, 364
SVGZ format, 364
Swap Fill/Stroke arrows, 85
swashes, 187, 303, 327
swatch libraries, 30–31, 67, 359, 364
Swatch Options dialog box, 66–67
swatches
  changing attributes of, 66–67
  deleting, 67

naming, 97, 98
sorting by name, xvii
speeding creation of, 97
Web-safe, 359
Swatches palette
  accessing swatch libraries via, 30, 67
  default settings for, 30–31
  saving as custom swatch library, 67
  saving mixed colors in, 66
  and Sort by Name option, xvii
  using global colors in, 68
  viewing color names with, 99
SWF format, 123, 363–364, 373
"Symbol Basics" lesson, 146–148
symbol instances, 123–124, 369, 371
  See also symbols
Symbolism tools, 123–124, 146–149
symbols, 123–124, 146–151
  adding to instance sets, 123
  as alternative to artwork copies, 80, 363, 367
  applying, 147
  assembling artwork from, 367
  blending between, 221
  changing color/transparency of, 147–148
  changing intensity of, 124
  changing stacking order for, 148
  creating, 123, 147
  deleting, 148
  editing, 371
  Gallery pages, 149
  lessons on, 146–148, 150–151
  managing, 142–143
  mapping, 297
  moving, 148
  painting with, 150–151
  resizing, 147
  rotating, 148
  and Scale Strokes & Effects preferences, 124
  separating onto layers, 123
  and Shockwave Flash files, 80
  spraying onto documents, 123
  and SWF files, 363
  updating graphs with, 20
  vs. scatter brushes, 124
Symbols palette, 123
symmetrical designs, 344
system requirements, 2
Szujewska, Laura, 194–195, 411

T

T-shirt logo, 102
tab-delimited text format, 17
tab leaders, xxiv, 182–183
Tabs palette, 182–183
tapered brushes, 143–144
targeting, 161, 264
Tate, Clarke, 99, 411
Taurus, 338
tear-off palettes, 6
technical illustrations, 78–80, 92
Techniques sections, xix
Template layers, 157, 158, 164, 166
templates
    accessing, xxii
    creating documents from, 3–4
    file extension for, 3
    Illustrator's built-in, xxii, 4
    placing, 82
    purpose of, xxii
    saving resolution settings in, 36
    tracing, 82–83, 165
    using graphs as, 19
Templates feature, 358
Templates folder, 3
tents, 237, 316–317
text. *See also* fonts; type
    changing appearance of stroked,
        190
    converting to outlines, 189–191,
        197, 198
    determining where line breaks
        occur in, 188
    distorting, 210, 213190
    formatting, 185–186
    getting professional help with, 189
    hyphenation in, 188
    justifying, 188, 196
    legacy, 186
    placing along path, 183, 194
    preserving editability of, 193
    reflowing, 190
    resizing, 190
    restyling, 190
    selecting, 181
    setting measurement units for, 7
    stacking order for, 191
    using transparency with, 254,
        284–285
    working with threaded, 184–185
    wrapping around objects, 185
text buttons, 265
text engine, 186
Text Label Hints preferences, 28

text variables, 365, 366
Text Wrap Options dialog box, 185
texture maps, 407
Thomas•Bradley Illustration &
    Design, 69, 234, 336–337,
    410, 411
threaded text, 184–185
three-dimensional effects
    See 3D effects; 3D objects
Threinen-Pendarvis, Cher, 141, 200,
    410
TIFF format, 166
tiling, 4
Tim Girvin Strategic Branding &
    Design, 207
Tim Webb Illustration, 411
TIME magazine, 145, 286, 325, 409,
    410
Tinkel, Kathleen, 8, 191, 411
tinting
    lesson on, 282–283
    specifying percentages for, 68
    using fills for, 79
"Tinting a Scan" lesson, 282–283
Tip boxes, xviii
Toast Design, 410
Todd Macadangdang Gallery, 328
tomatoes, 224, 354
Tool Tip option, 5
tool tolerance options, 12
tools. *See also* specific tools
    assigning shortcuts to, 5–6
    tearing off subsets of, 6
Torres, Ivan, 246–248, 348–352, 367,
    411
Toyo, 30, 101
tracing
    artwork, 126, 267
    with auto-tracing program, 112
    lesson on, 166–167
    with Pencil tool, 166–167
    photos, 130, 251, 308, 346
    preparing sketch for, 267
    saving images for, 166
    templates, 165
"Tracing Details" lesson, 166–167
Transform Each command, 19, 20,
    22
Transform Effect dialog box, 307
Transform effects, 292
Transform palette, xxvi, 19, 21
Transform Tools preferences, 28
Transformation Effect, 22
transformations, 19–22
    modifying, 21

    performing multiple, 22
    repeating, 21
    types of, 19
    undoing, 19
transforming
    with isometric formulas, 93
    lettering/type, 212–213, 303
    objects, 19–22, 293–294
    with warps/envelopes, 212–213
transitions
    correcting visible, 258
    softening, 235
    using blends for, 227, 235
transparency, 254–263
    See also opacity
    changing, for symbols, 147–148
    creating cool effects with,
        272–273
    creating naturalistic images with,
        282
    creating posterized effect with,
        276
    cumulative nature of, 257
    defined, 255
    distinguishing from non-
        transparent areas,
        254–255
    export considerations, 262–263
    and file size, 35
    and Flattener Preview palette, 34,
        254, 258
    and flattening, 262–263
    Gallery pages, 275–277, 288–290
    and Hard/Soft Mix Pathfinders,
        301
    and Knockout Group options,
        257–258
    lessons on, 255, 266–274,
        280–287
    and Microsoft Office applications,
        xxii
    and PDF format, 262
    purpose of, 254
    saving settings for, 254
    and Web-safe color, 363
"Transparency 101" lesson, 266–267
Transparency Flattener Preset
    Options dialog box, 259
Transparency Flattener Presets
    dialog box, 254, 259
transparency grid, 27–28, 255
Transparency palette, 255, 257,
    284–285
"Transparent Color" lesson, 268–271
transportation map, 163

Trap filter, 100
trapping
    defined, 100
    of gradients/patterns, 100
    misregistration of CMYK inks, 30
    and Overprint Preview mode, 25
    and raster images, 100
"Trapping issues" tip, 30
traps, previewing, 25
"Travel Ads.ai" file, 37
Traveling Radio Show logo, 210
trees, 150–151
Tremblay, Jean-Claude, 159, 411
Trim Pathfinder, 72
troubleshooting. *See also User Guide*
    with Adobe Online, 35
    changing appearances, 263
    drawing problems, 287
    with Help menu, 35
    join problems, 14
    layers, 162
    masks, 333
    misregistration of inks, 100
    overprinting problems, 169
    Pathfinder effects, 301
    printing problems, 34
    selection of objects, 159
    snapping-to-point, 92
    stitching, 258
TruMatch, 30, 67, 101, 412
tutorials, 412
Tuttle, Jean, 98, 411
Tweak filter, 77
tweening, 379
Twirl tool, 76
Twist filter, 77, 110
type, 180–218. *See also* fonts; text
    adding strokes to, 190
    antiquing, 216–217
    converting to outlines, 189–191,
        197, 198
    default settings for, 181
    distorting, 190, 210, 213
    editing, 217
    experimenting with, 216
    exporting, 193
    filling with scribble pattern,
        214–215
        See also Scribble effect
    Gallery pages, 198–199, 201,
        206–211, 218
    getting professional help with, 189
    "greeked," 180
    lessons on, 194–197, 200, 202–
        205, 212–217

new features, xxiii–xxv, 180
outlining small, 190, 191
selecting by accident, 180
stretching, 196–197
using Appearance palette with,
    191–193
Type & Auto Tracing preferences,
    181, 188
Type engine, 180, 193
Type Object Selection by Path Only
    option, xvii, 180
type objects, 191–193
Type on a Path Options dialog box,
    183, 184
Type tool
    accessing, 180
    and cursor appearance, 185
    making new text object with, 185,
        280
    selecting text with, 181
    toggling between horizontal/
        vertical mode for, 185
    type options accessible through,
        181
typeface, handwritten, 211

U

Ultimate Symbol, 412
Undo command
    and Preferences, 24
    and transformations, 19
    "unlimited undos" for, 23–24
ungrouping objects, 13, 18, 285
"Unified Gradients" lesson, 238
Uniform Resource Locators
    See URLs
United States flag. *See* flags
units, measurement, 7, 15, 228, 364
Units & Display Performance area,
    Preferences, 7, 26
Universal Access preferences, 55
Unlock All command, 161
"Unlocking Realism" lesson,
    234–235
Urban Wildlife Program logo, 86–87
URLs
    assigning to objects, 359–361
    meaning of acronym, 359
User Defined mode, 123
User Guide, xvi
    and Average *vs.* User Defined
        modes, 123
    and Character/Paragraph Styles
        palettes, 186

and choosing appropriate
        rendering intent, 359
    and color management, 28, 29, 30
    and color shifts, 29
    and creation/manipulation of
        type, 180
    and creation of patterns, 76
    and data-driven graphics, 37
    and file format considerations,
        384
    and Illustrator/Photoshop
        techniques, 384
    and legacy files, 32
    and Path Type Effects options,
        183
    and pattern-making basics, 116
    and PDF settings/presets, 32
    and Placement Options
        command, 366
    and setting traps in solid objects,
        30
    and Symbolism tools, 148
    and Tabs palette, 183
    and text wrapping, 185
user slices, 361

V

Valvoline logo, 338
vanishing points, 177
variables
    changing data in, 366
    defining, 366
    importing/exporting, 366
    types of, 365–366
    ways of using, 37
Variables palette, 37, 365–366
"Varied Perspective" lesson, 176–177
vector objects
    applying Gaussian Blur effect to,
        310
    contrasted with raster images, 261
    distorting, 76
    and opacity masks, 287
    rasterizing, 359
"Vector Photos" lesson, 112–114
Vector Studio, 412
VectorBabe, 214
    See also Cohen, Sandee
vectorizing brush strokes, 141
vegetables, 239
veggie cuisine logo, 199
Venus, xx
Vertical Type tool, 181
"Victory Climb" illustrations, 243

View menu, 25, 26
views, 24–26
Virtual Mirror Corporation, 412
visibility variables, 366
Visual Basic, 36

W

Wacom tablet, 126, 130, 139
Wai, Trina, 322, 411
wall mural, 397
Wang, Min, 191, 411
Warner Brothers shield, 102
warp effects
    applying, 299, 312–313
    contrasted with envelope effects, 298–299
    deleting, 313
    editing, 299
    grouping clip art for use with, 312
    Illustrator *vs.* Photoshop, 299
    lesson on, 312–315
    saving as graphic styles, 313
    and Smart Guides, 300
    transforming type with, 212–213
Warp tool, 76. *See also* warp effects
"Warps & Envelopes" lesson, 312–315
wasp, 106–107
Watanabe, Andrew T., 364
water effect, 151, 343
watercolor effect, 268
waves, 231
Web color palette, 30. *See also* Web-safe color
Web graphics, 358–379
    automatically creating/updating, 365–366
    color considerations, 66, 358–359, 363, 374
    export file formats, 362–365
    Gallery pages, 367, 371, 377
    lessons on, 368–370, 372–376, 378–379
    optimizing, 358, 360, 361
    rasterizing artwork for, 359
    tools for working with, 358
Web page layout, 180
Web ready printing, 34
Web safe color, 66, 358–359, 363, 374
Web slices, 361–362. *See also* slices
Web templates, 4, 358
Webb, Tim, 242, 243, 411
"Webward Ho!" lesson, 374–376
wedding certificate, 196–197

Weimer, Alan James, 116, 344–345, 411
Weinstein, Ari M., 196–197, 411
Welcome screen
    accessing templates via, xxii
    preventing launch of, 3
    purpose of, xx–xxi
    starting a session from, 2–3
"West Field Yardbird" image, 407
Western European language fonts, 188
whites, whiteness of, 29
Whyte, Hugh, 240, 372–373, 411
Willcockson, Tom, 406, 411
William Patterson University, 406
window controls, 25
Window menu, 15
windows, bringing file to front in, 26
Windows (Microsoft)
    and color management, 28
    finger dances, 57, 59, 61
    scripting languages, 36
    system requirements, 2
wine bottle, xxi, 297, 323
Winter Olympics mascots, 388–391
wolf, 118
wood grain effect, 284
woodcut effect, 243
Woodstock, 99, 176
Worldstudio Foundation illustration, 88–89
Wow! Actions folder, 36, 330
Wow! CD
    additional lessons on, xvi
    "Art Brush Motions.ai" file, 153
    artwork on, xvi
    brushes on, 120, 304
    "Calligraphic brushes.ai" file, 152
    "Ch02 The Zen of Illustrator" folder, xvi
    "Comet" Gradient tool exercise, 238
    "Fill Rules.pdf" file, 70
    "Henkel-Flared Effect.ai" file, 221
    and isometric formula transformation, 93
    "Open-Type_Guide.pdf" file, 187
    Paste commands exercises, 161
    and Pen tool, 194
    restoring Hard Mix/Soft Mix Pathfinders from, 74
    SandeeCs Soft Mix Chart, 301
    "Scaling & Scatter Brushes.ai" file, 124

"SteuerSharon-Pumpkin Blend.ai" file, 222
Ted Alspach playing card, 302
Wow! Actions folder, 36, 330
Wow! Pathfinder Filter actions, 301
    and Zen Rotation practice, 52
    and Zen Scaling practice, 50–51
Wow! Glossary. See glossary
Wow! Pathfinder Filter actions, 301
wrap objects, 185
wrapping, text, 185
Wrinkle tool, 76
Write Slices option, 361
WYSIWYG font menu, xxv

X

XML
    Grammar guide, 366
    standard, 364, 366
    variables, 37, 366
Xtream Path, 412

Y

Yale University, 410
Yamaha French horn, 251
Yip, Filip, 104, 164, 239, 402, 411
Yves veggie cuisine logo, 199

Z

Zapfino font, 216
Zen
    defined, 40
    of Illustrator, 41
    lessons, 42–61
"Zen Rotation" lesson, 52
"Zen Scaling" lesson, 50–51
zenofthepen.org, 412
Zig Zag filter, 77, 110
"Zimbabwe" artwork, 209
Zimmermann, Neal, 81
Zimmermann Crowe Design, 81
Zion National Park label, 218
zoom percentages, 27
Zoom tool, 165
zooming in/out, 25–26
Zuni Pueblo book title, 216